THE LETTERS OF BEETHOVEN

THE LETTERS
OF
BEETHOVEN

Collected,
Translated and Edited with an Introduction,
Appendixes, Notes and Indexes

by

EMILY ANDERSON

VOLUME II

LONDON
MACMILLAN & CO LTD
NEW YORK · ST MARTIN'S PRESS
1961

MACMILLAN AND COMPANY LIMITED
London Bombay Calcutta Madras Melbourne

THE MACMILLAN COMPANY OF CANADA LIMITED
Toronto

ST MARTIN'S PRESS INC
New York

PRINTED IN GREAT BRITAIN

LIST OF LETTERS

Letters not in the German collected editions are marked *

Letters to which all missing passages have been restored are marked †

VOLUME II

1815–1822

v

1815

1815

1816

1816

1816

1816

1817

1817

1817

1817

1818

1818

1819

1820

1820

1821

1821

xxiv

1822

LIST OF ABBREVIATIONS

AMZ   = *Allgemeine Musikalische Zeitung.* Leipzig.

Breuning   = Gerhard von Breuning, *Aus dem Schwarzspanierhause.* Vienna, 1874.

DKMZ   = *Deutsche Kunst- und Musik-Zeitung.* Vienna.

DM   = *Die Musik.* Berlin and Leipzig.

FRBF   = Theodor von Frimmel, *Beethoven-Forschung.* Vienna, 1911–1928.

FRBH   = Theodor von Frimmel, *Beethoven-Handbuch.* Two volumes. Leipzig, 1926.

FRBJ   = Theodor von Frimmel, *Beethovenjahrbuch.* Two volumes. Leipzig, 1908–1909.

FRBS   = Theodor von Frimmel, *Beethoven-Studien.* Two volumes. Leipzig, 1905–1906.

FRNB   = Theodor von Frimmel, *Neue Beethoveniana.* Vienna, 1890.

GA   = *Beethovens Werke. Kritische Gesamtausgabe.* 25 volumes. Breitkopf & Härtel, Leipzig. 1866–1868, 1888.

Hanslick   = Eduard Hanslick, *Geschichte des Concertwesens in Wien.* Vienna, 1869.

Kalischer   = Alfred C. Kalischer, *Beethovens sämtliche Briefe.* Five volumes.
(Kal.)   Berlin, 1907–1908. Vol. I revised by Kalischer. Berlin, 1909.

KFR   = Kalischer-Frimmel. Volumes II and III of Kalischer's edition of Beethoven's letters, revised and enlarged by T. v. Frimmel. Berlin, 1910–1911.

KHV   = Georg Kinsky. *Das Werk Beethovens. Thematisch-bibliographisches Verzeichnis seiner sämtlichen vollendeten Kompositionen.* Nach dem Tode des Verfassers abgeschlossen und herausgegeben von Hans Halm. Munich, 1955.

           (The works not hitherto given an Opus No. are here numbered and listed as WoO, *i.e.* Werk ohne Opuszahl, 'Work without Opus No.'.)

KK   = Kastner-Kapp, *Ludwig van Beethovens sämtliche Briefe, herausgegeben von Emerich Kastner.* New edition, revised and enlarged by Dr. Julius Kapp. Leipzig, 1923.

Köchel   = *83 Originalbriefe Ludwig van Beethovens an den Erzherzog Rudolph, herausgegeben von Dr. Ludwig, Ritter von Köchel.* Vienna, 1865.

LIST OF ABBREVIATIONS

KST = Emerich Kastner, *Ludwig van Beethovens sämtliche Briefe.* One volume. Leipzig, 1910.

Moscheles = Ignace Moscheles, *The Life of Beethoven.* Two volumes. London, 1841. This work is a translation of the first edition of Schindler's biography of Beethoven (Münster, 1840), edited with footnotes and some additional material.

NBJ = *Neues Beethoven-Jahrbuch,* edited by Adolf Sandberger. Augsburg and Braunschweig.

NFP = *Neue Freie Presse.* Vienna.

NMZ = *Neue Musik-Zeitung.* Stuttgart and Leipzig.

Nohl = Dr. Ludwig Nohl, *Briefe Beethovens.* Volume I. Stuttgart, 1865. *Neue Briefe Beethovens.* Volume II. Stuttgart, 1867.

Nottebohm = Gustav Nottebohm, *Beethoveniana.* Leipzig, 1872. *Zweite Beethoveniana.* Leipzig, 1887.

NV = Gustav Nottebohm, *Ludwig van Beethoven. Thematisches Verzeichnis.* Second edition. Leipzig, 1925.

Peters = L. v. Beethoven. *Seine an den Verlag von Hoffmeister und Kühnel, später C. F. Peters, Leipzig, gerichteten Briefe.* C. F. Peters, Leipzig. No date.

Prelinger [P.] = Fritz Prelinger, *Ludwig van Beethovens sämtliche Briefe und Aufzeichnungen.* Five volumes. Vienna and Leipzig, 1907–1911.

Schiedermair = Ludwig Schiedermair, *Der junge Beethoven.* Leipzig, 1925. New edition. Bonn, 1947.

Schindler = Anton Schindler, *Ludwig van Beethoven.* Fifth edition, with an introduction and notes by Fritz Volbach. Münster, 1927.

Schmidt = Leopold Schmidt, *Beethoven-Briefe.* Berlin, 1909.

Schöne = Dr. Alfred Schöne, *Briefe von Beethoven an Marie Gräfin Erdödy und Magister Brauchle.* Leipzig, 1867.

Schünemann = Georg Schünemann, *Ludwig van Beethovens Konversationshefte.* Three volumes. Berlin, 1941–1943.

Sonneck = O. G. Sonneck, *Beethoven Letters in America.* New York, 1927.

TDR = Alexander Wheelock Thayer, *Ludwig van Beethovens Leben.* Von Hermann Deiters neubearbeitet und von Hugo Riemann ergänzt. Five volumes. Third edition. Leipzig, 1917–1923.
This biography, originally written in English, was translated into German by Deiters. The first three volumes were published by Schneider, Berlin, in 1866, 1872 and 1879. After Thayer's and Deiters's death the fourth and fifth volumes were completed by Riemann and published in 1907 and 1908.

TK = A. W. Thayer, *Life of L. v. Beethoven.* Edited, revised and amended from the original English manuscript by H. E. Krehbiel. Three volumes. New York, 1921.

LIST OF ABBREVIATIONS

Unger   = Dr. Max Unger, *Ludwig van Beethoven und seine Verleger S. A. Steiner und Tobias Haslinger in Wien, Adolf Martin Schlesinger in Berlin*. Berlin and Vienna, 1921.

WRBN   = Franz Wegeler und Ferdinand Ries, *Biographische Notizen über Ludwig van Beethoven*. Coblenz, 1838. With a supplement by F. Wegeler. Coblenz, 1845. Reprint by A. C. Kalischer. Berlin and Leipzig, 1906.

Zekert   = Dr. Otto Zekert, *Apotheker Johann van Beethoven*. Vienna, 1928.

ZMW   = *Zeitschrift für Musikwissenschaft*. Leipzig.

OTHER ABBREVIATIONS

P.P.   = Praemissis Praemittendis, *i.e.* with the necessary introduction, a form of address occasionally used in business letters.

P.T.   = Pleno Titulo, or Praemissis Titulis, a formal type of address similar to P.P.

WoO   = Werke ohne Opuszahl. Cf. *KHV*.

NOTES ON MONEY VALUES

THE following notes have been compiled from information contained in Muret-Saunders's German-English Dictionary, in Professor W. H. Bruford's *Germany in the Eighteenth Century* (Cambridge, 1935), in Professor O. E. Deutsch's *Schubert: A Documentary Biography* (London, 1946) and in the letters of Beethoven, who occasionally quotes the equivalent values of coins and frequently refers to the fluctuating rates of exchange between Austria and some other countries. As in the early nineteenth century there were several standards in common use for the minting of gold and silver coins, the values here given are of necessity only approximate. Furthermore, no allowance has been made for the change in purchasing power of English money since the eighteenth century.

GERMANY AND AUSTRIA

Taking the South German kreuzer as the standard, the following equivalent values of small coins are obtained:

1 kreuzer = four pfennige, about one halfpenny.
[1 heller = about half a farthing.
1 pfennig = less than one heller, a mite.]
1 groschen = about three kreuzer, or 1½d., the value quoted in Sir George Smart's *Journals* during his visit to Vienna in 1825.
1 gulden (60 kreuzer) = about two shillings.
1 reichsthaler (90 kreuzer) = about three shillings.
1 rheinthaler (120 kreuzer) = about four shillings.

The following gold coins were in common use in Germany and Austria:

1 ducat (used all over Europe) = 4½ gulden, about nine shillings.
1 pistole (originally a Spanish coin, used all over Europe) = 7½ gulden, about fifteen shillings.
1 friedrich d'or (used chiefly in Prussia) = 8 gulden, about sixteen shillings.

1 carolin (used chiefly in South Germany) = 9 gulden, about eighteen shillings.

The French louis d'or, the value of which fluctuated considerably, was worth slightly more than two ducats, about twenty shillings.

The Italian zecchino (a Venetian gold coin) was worth slightly more than one ducat, about ten shillings.

During the Napoleonic wars the Austrian State went bankrupt, and by a *Finanz-Patent* promulgated on February 20, 1811 and put into force three weeks later, an emergency currency was introduced. Redemption bonds (*Einlösungsscheine*) were substituted for bank-notes at the rate of one for five. Thus paper money was depreciated to one-fifth of its nominal value and converted into a new State paper currency, called *Wiener Währung* (i.e. Viennese currency, V.C.). Another currency which continued to be used after the introduction of the new paper currency was the old *Konventions-münze* (i.e. Assimilated coinage, A.C.). This currency had been adopted in 1753 by a treaty with Bavaria and was based on the 20-gulden rate, called *Konventionsfuss*. There were 60 kreuzer to the gulden both in the old currency and in the new. But from 1811 onwards 5 gulden V.C. were worth only about 2 gulden A.C. Hence Beethoven's income of 4000 gulden guaranteed by his three patrons in 1809 became in 1811 approximately 1600 gulden. How-ever, the original value of his income was eventually restored, because the quarterly payments were soon made in redemption bonds.

LIST OF ILLUSTRATIONS

VOLUME II

xxxiii

LIST OF ILLUSTRATIONS

LIST OF FACSIMILES OF LETTERS

FACSIMILE OF MUSIC

1815

1815

(520) To Johann Nepomuk Kanka, Prague

[Autograph in the Beethovenhaus, Bonn]

VIENNA, *January* 11, 1815

MY DEAR, MY UNIQUE K[ANKA]!

I received today the communication from Baron Pasqualati in which I note that it is your wish that we should refrain from adopting any new measures. Meanwhile all the necessary written documents relating to this affair have been sent off to Pasqualati. Do be so kind as to inform him of this and ask him to postpone taking any step whatsoever. *A council meeting is to be held here* tomorrow; and the result of this meeting will perhaps be sent off to you and P[asqualati] by tomorrow *evening* [1] — Meanwhile I would like you to read through the fresh statement addressed to the Landrechte which I have sent to Pasqualati,[2] and to *study the supplements very carefully* — You will then notice that you have not given accurate information to Wolf and to some other people — But what is certain is that *in those documents there are enough proofs for whoever wants them.* In the case of a man like Prince Kinsky, whose rectitude and magnanimity were known to all, how could I have thought of *legal witnesses or of having anything in writing?*

With the warmest affection and regard

I remain, in haste, your friend [3]

(521) To Johann Nepomuk Kanka, Prague

[Autograph in the Beethovenhaus, Bonn, H. C. Bodmer collection]

VIENNA, *January* 14, 1815

MY DEAR, MY UNIQUE K[ANKA]!

The long letter which follows was written when we still held the view that we should keep to the 1800 gulden — After

---

[1] This is the substance of the two letters to Kanka which follow this one, Letters 521 and 522.

[2] In the autograph the preceding six words are added at the foot of the page. For Beethoven's statement to the Landrechte at Prague see Appendix I (5).

[3] The autograph has no signature.

Baron Pasqualati's latest communication we again put our heads together, and Dr. Adlersburg advised us not to go beyond the steps you had already taken [1] — But since Dr. Wolf writes that he has made an offer in your name for 1500 gulden a year, please try at any rate to obtain this arrangement for 1500 gulden — With this in view I am sending you the long letter which was written before we received Baron Pasqualati's letter dissuading us from such a step.[2] You may still find in it many arguments to strengthen your case for obtaining at least the 1500 gulden — Besides, the Archduke has written for the second time to the *Oberstburggraf* [3] ; and from the latter's previous reply to the Archduke one can gather that he will certainly put his hand in his pocket and that the 1500 gulden at least can still be obtained —

All good wishes. I am quite unable to write another letter of the alphabet, for even that exhausts me — May your friendship produce a rapid and successful result, for if the affair is going to turn out so badly, I shall have to leave Vienna, because I should not be able to live on that income — For in Vienna things have come to such a pass that the prices of all commodities have soared to untold heights *and must be paid for.* The last two concerts I gave *have cost me* 5108 *gulden.* Had the Empress not given me that *handsome present* [4] — I should have made practically nothing —

In haste, your admirer and friend
BEETHOVEN

(522) *To Johann Nepomuk Kanka, Prague*

[Autograph in the Beethovenhaus, Bonn, H. C. Bodmer collection]

[VIENNA, January 14, 1815] [5]

MY UNIQUE, MY MOST ESTEEMED K[ANKA] !

What am I to think, to say, to feel? — My opinion of W[olf] is that he has not only laid himself open to attack but

---

[1] Beethoven is referring to the 'council meeting' held on January 12th. Cf. Letter 520.   [2] Letter 522, which follows this one.

[3] Cf. Letter 501, p. 473, n. 1.

[4] The Empress contributed 200 ducats, about 1000 gulden.

[5] According to Beethoven's statement in Letter 521 this long letter was written before January 14th, but kept back and enclosed in Letter 521.

also has taken no trouble whatever to cover *his bare spots* — I cannot believe that he attached to his written statement all the proper certificates which belong to it — *The order to the cashier about the scale was given by Prince K[insky] before his agreement to pay me my salary in redemption bonds, as is stated in the certificates — the date of which one need only examine* [1] — *Hence the previous order is not valid.* — *The species facti proves that I was away from Vienna for over six months. As it so happened that I did not require the money, I let things slide. The Prince forgot to cancel his previous order to the cashier, but he did not forget the promise he had given to me, nor the promise he had given about me to Varnhagen (an officer)*, exactly as *Herr von Oliva's* testimony proves. For shortly before his departure from Vienna *and for the next world* the Prince repeated his promise to Herr von Oliva and instructed him to call on him again after his return to Vienna *in order to make the matter right with the cashier* [2]; this, of course, could not be done owing to his unforeseen death [3] — The officer Varnhagen's deposition is accompanied by a letter written from the Russian army, in which he declares his willingness to swear *to this incident on oath* — Herr Oliva's deposition proves that he too is prepared to swear to his statement in a court — As I have sent off the deposition of Colonel Count Bentheim, I cannot state this with absolute certainty; but so far as I remember, *this Count* too declares in *his deposition that in any case he is prepared to swear to the incident in a court of law* — And *I too am willing to swear in a court* that Prince Kinsky told me at Prague 'that *in his opinion it was only fair to arrange for my income to be paid to me in redemption bonds*'. Those were his very words — He himself advanced to me at Prague 60 gold ducats which at that time were supposed to be worth about 600 gulden. Owing to my state of health I could not stay at Prague for long and proceeded to Teplitz — But the Prince's word was *sacred* to me, seeing that I had never heard him say anything which might have induced me to *bring two witnesses with me or to ask him to give me something in writing* — I see from the trend of the whole affair that Dr. Wolf has handled it abominably and that he did not make you sufficiently acquainted with the written documents. — A few words

[1] In the autograph the two clauses from 'as is' to 'examine' are added at the foot of the page.
[2] In the autograph the words from 'in order' to 'cashier' are added at the foot of the page.   [3] On November 3, 1812.

now about the step that I have just taken — A short time ago
the Archduke Rudolph asked me whether the Kinsky affair had
not yet been settled. So he must have heard something about
it. I explained to him that things were not looking well, since
I had heard nothing, nothing whatever. He offered to write a
personal letter, but suggested that I should add a written
statement and also acquaint him with all the necessary documents relating to the K[insky] affair. After convincing himself
of the necessity of doing this, he then wrote to the Oberstburggraf enclosing a letter to him from me. The Oberstburggraf
replied immediately both to the Archduke and to me. In his
letter to me he told me *'that I should lodge an application and all
the proofs with the Landrechte at Prague, whence it would be forwarded
to him, and that he would do his very best to further my cause'*. *To the
Archduke* also he wrote *in the most cordial manner* and even stated
emphatically 'that in regard to this affair *he was perfectly well
acquainted with the intentions of the late Prince Kinsky about me and
that I should lodge an application* and so forth'. Whereupon the
Archduke summoned me at once and *told me that I should have
the written statement drafted and show it to him*. He added that he
thought that an application should be made for an agreement
to pay in redemption bonds, since there were *sufficient proofs,
though not in legal form, of the Prince's intentions, and since no one
could doubt that if the Prince had lived he would have kept his word* —
*If he were the heir today, he would demand no further proofs than those
which have been produced* — Whereupon I then sent *the document*
to Baron Pasqualati, who will be so kind as *to deliver it to the
Landrechte*. It was only after this affair had already been set
going that Dr. Adlersburg received from Dr. Wolf a letter
informing him that *he had made the offer for* 1500 *gulden*. Since
the figure of 1500 gulden has already been reached *and has
been mentioned to the Oberstburggraf*, no doubt it will be possible
to raise it to 1800 gulden — This is no favour, for the late
Prince was one of those who pressed me most of all to refuse
the yearly salary of 600 gold ducats, which I could have had
in Westphalia. At that time he said among other things 'that
indeed I should not eat any Westphalian ham' — A little later
on I also refused another appointment at Naples [1] — I am
legally entitled to demand compensation for the loss I have

---

[1] It has not been possible to trace any particulars of this offer.

sustained. *When my income was paid in bank-notes*, what was I getting? *Not even* 400 *gulden in assimilated coinage!!!* — And that was to be the equivalent of an income of 600 ducats — We have quite sufficient proofs for anyone who wishes to act with integrity — And now what has become of the redemption bonds??!!! Even they are no equivalent of what I have forfeited — In all the papers this affair was being trumpeted forth most pompously whilst I had become almost a beggar. — What the Prince intended is clear; and in my opinion the family is committed to act in accordance with his intention, unless it is prepared to lose caste — Moreover on account of the Prince's death the family income has increased rather than diminished. So there is no valid reason to curtail expenditure —

I received yesterday your friendly communication — But now I am too tired to tell you in this letter what I feel about you — At the same time I am entrusting my affair to your intelligence. Apparently the Oberstburggraf is the protagonist. Do not appear to know anything about what he wrote to the Archduke, for that might not help us. It would be best if no one but you and Baron Pasqualati were to know about it — You have sufficient evidence, if you examine the documents, to show how wrongly Dr. W[olf] set about the affair — and how we *must certainly act, and very differently* — I leave it to your friendly attitude to me to act as you think best — You may expect my warmest thanks; and do forgive me for not being able to write any more today, but I find it exhausting — I would rather undertake the greatest musical task — My heart has already found for you something which will make your heart beat as well; and this you will soon receive [1] — Do not forget me, who am a poor harassed individual; and *act — exert yourself* as much as you possibly can —

With the most cordial regards, your sincere friend

BEETHOVEN

---

[1] So far as is known, Beethoven did not dedicate any composition to Kanka.

(523) To [Baron Joseph von Schweiger ?] [1]

[Autograph in the Beethovenhaus, Bonn]

DEAR FRIEND !   [VIENNA, c. end of January, 1815]

Do whatever you think best, but I fancy that it would be better to write to Count Narischkin [2] than to the Empress.[3] You must keep the original document, however, so that if Narischkin's illness should persist, application could be made to someone else or to the Empress herself. Your Excellency has sent me the very agreeable news that the Empress has been pleased to accept my small offering; and to that extent my greatest wish has been fulfilled [4] — But how highly should I feel myself honoured if I could inform the world of this, and by prefixing her name and so forth enable the world to share this honour. (You will have to express all this more suitably than I can.)

Since the grand symphony in A can be regarded as one of the happiest products of my poor talents (to be expressed very modestly), I would take the liberty of presenting to Her Majesty the pianoforte arrangement of this work [5] together with the polonaise. —

A clear statement that one can certainly *do something* but does not want to receive anything through or from the Russian Empress —

Should Her Majesty desire to hear me play, that would be the highest honour for me. But before doing so I must beg for her indulgence, seeing that for a considerable time I have devoted myself more exclusively to composition (to creative work) [6] —

[1] In his note to this draft of a letter to an unstated recipient (*KFR* no. 437) Frimmel suggests that it was intended for some official of the Imperial Court, such as Baron von Schweiger.

[2] Alexander Lwowitsch, Count Nariskin, Lord Chamberlain of the Empress Elizabeth Alexievna of Russia, had accompanied her to Vienna for the Congress.

[3] Princess Marie Luise Auguste von Baden (1779–1826) had married in 1793 Prince Alexander of Russia (1777–1825), who in 1801 succeeded Paul I as Czar of Russia.

[4] Beethoven dedicated to the Empress Elizabeth his polonaise in C for pianoforte solo, Op. 89, published in March, 1815, by Pietro Mechetti.

[5] The seventh symphony, Op. 92, arranged for two pianofortes by Carl Czerny, was published with this dedication.

[6] At a court function on January 25th, at which the Russian Empress was present, Beethoven accompanied on the pianoforte the famous Viennese singer Franz Wild (1791–1860), who sang his 'Adelaide', Op. 46.

No present, etc —

Do you think it would be better to draft it in the form of a petition to the Empress etc ? ? ? ! ! ! or to put it to Narischkin as a request.

If only I could be so fortunate as to compose for Her Majesty whatever her taste or predilection disposes her to choose. . . .

(524) *To Baron Johann Pasqualati*

[*Autograph in the Nationalbibliothek, Vienna*]

ESTEEMED FRIEND !   [VIENNA, *January*, 1815]

Please be so very kind as to send me by the bearer of this letter, *but not unsealed*, just the formula showing how *the Kinsky receipt* should be written — slightly more than 600 gulden every six months from the month of April until etc.[1] — I will send the receipt immediately to Dr. Kanka at Prague who the last time obtained the money for me very quickly. After receiving this sum I will discharge my debt to you at once. But should it be possible for me to draw the money here before the amount comes from Prague, then I will bring the sum to you in person immediately.

With kindest regards, your admirer and friend

BEETHOVEN

(525) *To Georg Friedrich Treitschke*

[*Autograph not traced*][2]

[VIENNA, *January*, 1815]

I am composing Romulus ! and shall begin to write it down one of these days. I will come to you myself ! at first once — later on several times, so that we may talk over the whole work and have a consultation about it.

With kindest regards, your friend

BEETHOVEN

---

[1] The words from 'slightly' to 'etc.' are added at the foot of the page with a NB. reference.

[2] Taken from *KFR* no. 434 and Aloys Fuchs's transcript in the Benedictine Abbey, Göttweig.

(526) *To Georg Friedrich Treitschke*

[*Autograph not traced*] [1]

DEAR TR[EITSCHKE]!   [VIENNA, *January*, 1815]

I hoped to cut short the affair by sending Herr von Schreyvogel [2] a copy of this letter — but nothing has been done.

You see that this Fuss [3] can attack me in all the papers, if I cannot produce something in writing *against him*, or if you — or the Theatrical Directors do not undertake to come to an agreement with him. [4] On the other hand the question of my contract for the opera has also not yet been settled.

I request you to send me a reply, particularly about Fuss's letter. Before the judgment seat of *art* the question would be easily decided. But in this affair such is not the case, a fact which, although one would gladly think so, can be fully allowed for. [5]

In haste, your friend

BEETHOVEN

[1] Taken from *KFR* no. 435 and Aloys Fuchs's transcript in the Benedictine Abbey, Göttweig.

[2] See Letter 908, p. 774, n. 1.

[3] According to Fuchs's transcript Beethoven here inserted an interrogation mark.

[4] Early in January, 1815, J. E. Fuss had had a notice inserted in the *Allgemeine Musikalische Zeitung* that he had composed for the Theater an der Wien an opera entitled 'Romulus und Remus'. His opera was never performed in Vienna but was produced at Pressburg.

[5] The meaning of this sentence is not clear. Possibly Beethoven was trying to set forth how greatly his and Treitschke's plan would be hampered by the impossibility of arraigning Fuss before the highest tribunal. Moreover, both Jahn and Fuchs may have failed to transcribe this sentence correctly.

(527) *To Sigmund Anton Steiner* [1]

[Autograph not traced] [2]

VIENNA, *February* 1, 1815

MOST HIGHLY BORN LIEUTENANT GENERAL!

I have received your communication addressed to my brother [3] and I am satisfied with its contents. But I must beg you to defray *in addition the costs of the pianoforte arrangements.*[4] First of all, as I have to pay for *everything* in the world and as *everything is dearer for me than for other people*, I should find it difficult to defray the costs. And in any case I do not think that you can complain about the fee of 250 ducats — But I too should not like to take on too much. Therefore you must see to these arrangements yourself. But they must all be checked by me and, wherever necessary, corrected. I trust that you will be satisfied with all this — Furthermore, I fancy you could make *my brother* a present *of the collected pianoforte works of Clementi, Mozart and Haydn.* He needs them for *his little son.* Do this,

---

[1] Sigmund Anton Steiner (1773–1838), whose early life was uneventful, acquired with Rochus Krasnitzky in 1804 Senefelder's lithographic printing works and soon set up as a publisher on his own account. He was joined in 1814 by a young, energetic and musical accountant, Tobias Haslinger, who two years later became his partner. About this time the business became a music publishing firm and started a connexion with Beethoven which persisted for over ten years. All Beethoven's works from Op. 90 to Op. 117 were published by Steiner's firm. Possibly with the intention of poking fun at Napoleon's military rise and fall, Beethoven put his connexion with this firm on a war footing. He himself was the Generalissimo, Steiner the Lieutenant General, Haslinger the Adjutant, Diabelli, who was then employed by the firm as a copyist and a proof-reader, both Diabolus and Provost Marshal. Steiner's bookshop became the Lieutenant General's office or headquarters, inferior work or slackness led to a court martial, etc., all in a very friendly and good-humoured vein, of course. Steiner took over the Bureau des Arts et d'Industrie in 1823. In 1826 he retired and Haslinger became head of the firm, which after his death in 1842 was carried on by his son Karl.

For a full account of Steiner's career and association with Beethoven, see Unger's introduction to his useful book: *Ludwig van Beethoven und seine Verleger* (Berlin, 1921), pp. 5-23.

[2] Taken from *TDR* III, 498-499.

[3] Caspar Carl.

[4] Pianoforte arrangements of the seventh and eighth symphonies, Op. 92 and 93. On April 29, 1815, Beethoven sent Steiner a list of the works which the latter was to regard as his property with the exclusion of England. See Appendix F (6).

my most charming Steiner, and don't be made of stone, however stony your name may be [1] —

All good wishes, my excellent Lieutenant General.

I am ever your most devoted General-in-Chief
                              LUDWIG VAN BEETHOVEN

(528) To Joseph von Varena, Graz

[*Autograph in the Beethovenhaus, Bonn, H. C. Bodmer collection*]

VIENNA, *February* 3, 1815

I was unable, my dear friend, to reply at once to your
esteemed letter and at the same time to thank you again for
your present. I see that you insist on constantly putting me to
shame and making me your debtor — I trust that your health
has improved. I was greatly concerned about you at Baden;
and, as my own circumstances prevented me, I was unable to
show you outwardly as much sympathy as I was feeling and
still feel in my innermost heart for such an excellent person as
yourself — You will soon receive some news about a piano for
your daughter.[2] As I should like to provide you with a very
good one, this cannot be done in a trice. But you will soon
have full particulars and perhaps some satisfaction as well on
this score —

One of my brothers is sick; and since most people in his
condition usually have their fads, he having heard of my
acquaintance with you has asked me to send you this *enclosure*.[3]
Perhaps our *good Ursulines* could help in the matter — Forgive
me for bothering you with this. If without much effort you
could lay your hands on the animals that are described, please
send me the information immediately. I will be responsible
for all the expenses incurred, provided this is going to give him

---

[1] Beethoven is punning on the word Stein which means 'stone'. In the
Beethovenhaus, Bonn, H. C. Bodmer collection, there is a cover with the following
address: Für seine Hochgebohrn Hr: Generalleutnant Steiner von Steinski von
Steiner, etc.

[2] See Letter 536 of March 21st.

[3] Evidently a request from Caspar Carl, who died nine months later. In
his will, dated November 14th, he stated that he kept a carriage, a horse, a goat,
some peacocks and several plants, all of which were henceforth to belong to his
wife. For the full texts of his will and its codicil see *TDR* III, 517-519.

JOHANN NEPOMUK KANKA (1772–1865)
From an engraving by an unknown artist
(*Bildarchiv der Oesterreichischen Nationalbibliothek, Vienna*)

some pleasure. As I have already stated, he is sick and relies on amusements of this kind.

In haste, your friend who sincerely esteems you

LUDWIG VAN BEETHOVEN

(529) *To George Thomson, Edinburgh*

[*MS in the British Museum*] [1]

SIR!   VIENNA, *February* 7, 1815

Many concerns have prevented my answers to your favours, to which I reply only in part. All your songs with the exception of a few are ready to be forwarded, I mean those to which I was to write the accompagnements, for with respect to the 6 canzonettes, which I am to compose, I own that the honorary you offered is totally inadequate. Circumstances here are much altered and taxes have been so much raised after the English fashion that my share for 1814 was near £60. Besides an original good air — and what you also wish — an overture, are perhaps the most difficult undertakings in musical compositions. I therefore beg to state that my honorary for 6 songs or airs must be £35 or seventy Imp. Ducats and for an overture £20 or 50 Imp. Ducats. You will please to assign the payment here as usual, and you may depend that I shall do you justice. No artist of talent and merit will find my pretentions extravagant.

Concerning the overture you will please to indicate in your reply whether you wish to have it composed for an easy or more difficult execution. I expect your immediate answer having several orders to attend, and I shall in a little time write more copiously in reply to your favors already received. I beg you to thank the author for the very ingenious and flattering verses which I obtained by your means. Allow me to subscribe myself Sir your very obed[t] and humble serv[t]

LUDWIG VAN BEETHOVEN

---

[1] Written in English in another hand and signed by Beethoven.

(530) *To Johann Nepomuk Kanka, Prague*

[*Autograph not traced*] [1]

VIENNA, *February* 24, 1815

MY MOST DEARLY BELOVED K[ANKA],

Through Baron Pasqualati I have sent you again and again my thanks for your friendly efforts on my behalf; and now I myself am letting you have in writing a thousand thanks — The Archduke's intervention you must not regard as unduly officious; and it must not have the effect of putting me out of favour with you — You had already done everything when the Archduke began to use his good offices. Had he done this sooner and had we not had the *one-sided* or *many-sided* or *weak-sided* Dr. W[olf], the affair, according to the Oberstburggraf's own assurances given to the Archduke and to myself, might have had an even more favourable result — Hence in my opinion the value of your services to me remains, and ever will remain, the same — The Landrechte are now deducting 60 ducats, which *I alone reported* and about which the late Prince Kinsky never said a word either to the cashier or to anyone else — Whenever the *truth* can injure me they accept it; then why not accept it too *where it might benefit* me? How *unjust*! — Baron Pasqualati will make enquiries from you about several other matters as well — Today I am again too tired, for once more I have had to give poor P[asqualati] a whole lot of instructions. Things like that are much more of an effort to me than the greatest composition. For it is an unfamiliar field which I ought never to till — These affairs are costing me many tears and, I might add, even much sorrow — Well, now it will soon be time to write to the Princess Kinsky — and for the present I must stop. I am delighted when for once I can write to you merely to pour out my heart to you; and this will certainly happen very often, as soon as I have cleared off that tedious business. Once more I ask you to accept my warmest thanks for all you have done for me — and please do

love your admirer and friend

BEETHOVEN

---

[1] Taken from *KFR*, no. 445. Frimmel copied the autograph then in private ownership.

(531) *To the Countess Anna Marie Erdödy*

[*Autograph in the Beethovenhaus, Bonn, H. C. Bodmer collection*]

VIENNA, *February* 29, 1815 [1]

I have read your letter with great pleasure, my beloved Countess, and also what you say about the renewal of your friendship for me. It has long been my wish to see you and your beloved children once again. For although I have suffered a great deal, yet I have not lost my former love for children, the beauties of nature and friendship — The trio and everything else that has not been published are most certainly at your service, my dear Countess — As soon as the trio has been copied you shall have it.[2] It was not without sympathy and interest that I frequently enquired after your state of health. But now I will call on you sometime in person and I shall have the pleasure of being able to participate in everything that concerns you — My brother has written to you. I beg you to make allowances for him, because he is really an unhappy, suffering man [3] —

The prospect of the coming spring will, I trust, have an excellent influence on your health as well, and perhaps surround you with the happiest of life's realities — May all that is good be your portion, dear and beloved Countess. I send my greetings to your dear children whom I embrace in spirit — I hope to see you soon —

Your true friend

LUDWIG VAN BEETHOVEN

[1] The autograph is dated thus. No doubt the letter was written on March 1st.
[2] Probably Op. 97. This trio for pianoforte, violin and cello was first performed by Beethoven, Schuppanzigh and Linke at a charity concert held on April 11, 1814 in the Hotel zum Römischen Kaiser.
[3] Caspar Carl, who died in November, 1815.

(532) To Johann Xaver Brauchle, Jedlersee near Vienna [1]

[Autograph not traced] [2]

MY DEAR B[RAUCHLE],   [VIENNA, March, 1815]

Much as I should like to do so, I shall find it very difficult to come to you today. It was my intention and desire indeed to land today at your place with bag and baggage — At the moment I foresee that it will not be possible to do so today. Wretched, time-wasting affairs, which I still have to deal with this morning, alone can decide what may be undertaken this afternoon — But if it can't be today, then it will certainly be in a few days — It has been difficult for me to shake off several misgivings in regard to this matter; and yet I believe that I really had firmly resolved to go to the Countess — Hence I shall certainly make haste, the more so as at the present moment my spirit can only feel at ease in the presence of the beauties of nature, and so far I have made no arrangements anywhere else to give free play to this irresistible inclination of mine —

A thousand compliments and good wishes to you and the Countess.

Wholly your
BEETHOVEN

(533) To Breitkopf & Härtel, Leipzig

[Autograph in the Beethovenhaus, Bonn, H. C. Bodmer collection]

MY DEAREST SIR!   VIENNA, March 10, 1815

You would be misjudging me if you were to accuse me of ever forgetting you — But since I last wrote to you from Teplitz how much has happened! [3] — and far more evil than good! — However, I would much rather talk to you sometime about all that. If I hesitate about the publication of my numerous more

---

[1] Johann Xaver Brauchle was tutor to the three children of the Countess Erdödy, whose husband Count Peter Erdödy owned an estate at Jedlersee near Vienna. Brauchle was also an amateur musician and composer, as described in the article by Günther Haupt in Der Bär, 1927, pp. 70-99. In 1815 Beethoven wrote a three-part canon on Brauchle and Linke, WoO 167.

[2] Taken from Schöne's transcript in the Stadtbibliothek, Vienna.

[3] Cf. Beethoven's letter of September 17, 1812, Letter 383.

recent works, you must ascribe this hesitation to the *uncertainty* of all things pertaining to human relationships. For compare what used to be *certain* in this respect with *what is still certain now*? Circumstances such as the *need to raise money* drove me to have some dealings with a publisher in Vienna, and of what kind? That you will soon know.[1] And when you do I shall be able, I fancy, to come more easily to some arrangement with you again — Many thanks for your Musik[alische] Z[eitung]. I will soon let you have something for it —

As for the demons of darkness, I realize that even in the brightest light of our time these will never be altogether chased away — One of my acquaintances would like to have Chladni's address.[2] Please let me have it sometime or other — With your latest issues of the Musik[alische] Z[eitung] there was noted, I believe, some *music* as well *which I was to receive*. But I have received nothing. Perhaps it was a *mistake* — or due to the *slackness* of Herr *Traeg*!!![3] —

Well, all good wishes, very good wishes. Your present political conditions do not please me very much either, but — but — but — children before they grow up must have dolls to play with, of course — And that is all there is to be said on the subject —

In haste, your truly most devoted

BEETHOVEN

[1] No doubt a reference to the negotiations begun with S. A. Steiner in February, 1815, for the publication of his works.

[2] Ernst Florens Friedrich Chladni (1756–1827), born at Wittenberg, became a famous authority on acoustics. His outstanding work, *Die Akustik*, was published by Breitkopf & Härtel in 1802. He then lectured on this subject in all the principal towns of Europe. Chladni also invented two unusual musical instruments, the euphon and the clavicylinder.

[3] The original has 'Trägheit des Hr. Traeg', the sort of pun to which Beethoven was addicted.

(534) *To Sir George Smart, London* [1]

[*MS in the Beethovenhaus, Bonn, H. C. Bodmer collection*] [2]

MY DEAR SIR GEORGE,   VIENNA, *March* 16-19, 1815 [3]

I see by the papers that you have brought forth in the theatre Beethoven's battle and that it was received with considerable applause; [4] I was very happy to find that your partiality to Mr. B's compositions is not diminished, and therefore I take the liberty in his name to thank you for the assistance you afforded in the performance of that uncommon piece of music. He has arranged it for the pianoforte, but having offered the original to his R.H. the Prince Regent, he durst not venture to sell that arrangement to any editor, until he knew the Prince's pleasure not only with respect to the dedication, but in general. Having waited so many months without receiving the least acknowledgment, he begged me to apply to you for advice. His idea is to dispose of this arrangement and of several other original compositions to an Editor in London — or perhaps to several united, if they would make a handsome offer — They would besides engage to let him know *the day of the appearance for sale* of the respective pieces, in order that the Editor *here* may not publish one copy before the day to be

---

[1] George Thomas Smart (1776–1867), born in London, belonged to a family of musicians and became an organist, violinist, teacher of singing, conductor and composer. After his many successes as a conductor he was knighted in 1811. In 1813 he was selected as one of the original members of the Philharmonic Society and for over thirty years arranged and directed many of its performances. For more than ten years he organized numerous music festivals and was responsible for the production of several oratorios. For a detailed and entertaining account of Smart's early travels and career see H. B. and C. L. E. Cox, *Leaves from the Journals of Sir George Smart* (London, 1907). This volume also contains particulars of Smart's connexion with Beethoven with a view to the production in England of the latter's compositions and of his meetings with him in Vienna during the autumn of 1825.

[2] This letter from Häring to Smart is written in English and encloses an English letter from Beethoven and signed by him, written in Häring's hand.

Johann Baptist von Häring, a Viennese business man, was an excellent violinist and had a good knowledge of English and conditions in England. He often acted as Beethoven's amanuensis in his correspondence with Thomson, Birchall and Neate. Häring is supposed to have died in 1818. See *FRBH* I, 192.

[3] This letter is quoted in Cox, *op. cit.*, pp. 49–51, with the date April 9, 1815, doubtless the date of receipt.

[4] The Battle symphony was produced at Drury Lane Theatre on February 10, 1815, under the direction of Sir George Smart.

mentioned. At the end of this letter follows the list of such compositions with the price which the author expects. I am persuaded, Sir George, you will exert yourself to benefit this great genius. He talks continually of going to England, but I am afraid that his deafness, seemingly increasing, does not allow him the execution of this favourite idea. You are informed without doubt that his opera : Fidelio, has had the most brilliant success here, but the execution is so difficult that it would not suit any of the English houses.

I submit here his list with the prices — None of the following pieces has ever been published, but no. 2, 4 and 9 — have been performed with the greatest applause —

1.	Serious Quartetto for 2 violins, tenor and bass	— 40 guineas
2.	Battle of Vittoria — Score	70 guineas
3.	„ „ „ arranged for the pianoforte	— 30 guineas
4.	A grand symphony — Score	70 guineas
5.	„ „ „ arranged for the pianoforte	— 30 guineas
6.	A symphony Key F. — Score	40 guineas
7.	„ „ „ „ arranged for the pianoforte	— 20 guineas
8.	Grand Trio for the pianoforte, violin and violoncello	— 40 guineas
9.	Three Overtures for a full orchestra — each	30 guineas
10.	The three arrangements for pianoforte — each	15 guineas
11.	A grand sonata for the pianoforte and violin	— 25 guineas

The above is the produce of four years labour.

Our friend Neate [1] has not yet made his appearance here — nor is it at all known where he is roving about. We — I mean mostly amateurs — are now rehearsing Handel's Messiah — I am to be leader of the 2nd violins; there will be this time 144 violins — first and second altogether, and the singers and remainder in proportion. — I have been so unfortunate as not to receive a single line or answer from England since my stay

---

[1] See Letter 574, p. 535, n. 1. Neate arrived in Vienna early in May.

in Vienna which is near three months; this discourages me very much from writing, for I have despatched immediately after my arrival several letters and have been continuing to send letters, but all in vain. Amongst those to whom I wrote about 2 months ago, is our friend Disi [1] — pray if you meet him, give him and his very respectable family my best regards. I have passed so many happy hours in his house, it would be highly ungrateful for me to forget such an amiable family.

Beethoven happening to call on me just now, he wishes to address a few lines to you, which you find at the bottom of this. My direction is. Monsieur Jean de Häring

No 298 Kohlmarkt

Vienne

Poor B. is very anxious to hear something of the English editors, as he hardly can keep those of this city from him, who tease him for his works.

Give [2] me leave to thank you for the trouble you have taken several times, as I understand, in taking my works under your protection, by which I don't doubt all justice has been done. I hope you will not find it indiscreet if I solicit you to answer Mr. Häring's letter as soon as possible. I should feel myself highly flattered, if you would express your wishes, that I may meet them, in which you will always find me ready as an acknowledgment for the favors you have heaped upon my children —

Yours gratefully

LUDWIG V. BEETHOVEN

And now I shall beg you, my dear Sir George, not to take this long letter amiss, and to believe that I am always, with the greatest regard —

your most humble and obedient servant

JOHN HÄRING

---

[1] No doubt the Belgian harpist and composer François Joseph Dizi (1780–1840), who may have been a friend of Häring's in London.

[2] Beethoven's letter, written in Häring's hand but signed by Beethoven, begins here.

(535) *To Sigmund Anton Steiner*

[*Autograph in the Beethovenhaus, Bonn, H. C. Bodmer collection*]

[VIENNA, *March* 21, 1815] [1]

MOST HIGHLY ESTEEMED LIEUTENANT GENERAL!

If you no longer require the manuscript of the pianoforte sonata, please *lend* it to me, for the Archduke Rudolph had it from me some time ago and now wants to have it again.[2] In any case it seems that my Lieutenant General does not yet feel inclined to take the field with it — Let me add that this m[anuscri]pt will again be at your service at any time — my most excellent L[ieutenant] G[eneral].

Your most devoted

LUDWIG VAN BEETHOVEN

(536) *To Joseph von Varena, Graz*

[*Autograph in the Beethovenhaus, Bonn, H. C. Bodmer collection*]

MY DEAR V[ARENA]! VIENNA, *March* 21, 1815

Being unwell and very busy I found it impossible until yesterday to make the necessary enquiries — Here are my results. You can have from *Schanz* as good a piano as he is able to supply for the price of 400 gulden V.C., including packing. This piano has six octaves — *Seiffert* [3] asks 460 gulden, but would probably let you have one for 400 — There are, however, other excellent makers, I hear, from whom you could purchase a sound and durable instrument for a good deal less than 400 gulden — But one cannot *look for* and *find* one of this type very quickly — I mean, *a good one* — such as you must have by right — Hence I should require more time — Well, let me have an early reply informing me whether you

---

[1] The autograph of the letter bears this date in another hand and also the remark: 'In reply have sent the manuscript to be retained until the end of the week'. In 1815 March 21st fell on a Tuesday.

[2] The E minor pianoforte sonata, Op. 90, published by Steiner in June, 1815. The Archduke's manuscript copy made in 1814 is now in the Nationalbibliothek, Vienna.

[3] This was no doubt Martin Seuffert, not Seiffert, one of the many pianoforte makers in Vienna.

agree to these prices and then in a few weeks you will have a sound and durable piano — As for the payment, well, the Viennese instrument makers insist on being paid here at once in loco [1] before despatching their instruments; for they declare that delay in obtaining payment has frequently caused them inconvenience — That is all I can tell you for the moment, my dear V[arena] — As soon as you let me have your views on this subject, I will take steps to serve you as best I can —

Your sincere and most devoted friend and servant

BEETHOVEN

My best regards to your daughter and to the other members of your family.

(537) *To the Archduke Rudolph*

[Autograph in the Gesellschaft der Musikfreunde, Vienna]

YOUR IMPERIAL HIGHNESS!   [VIENNA, *Spring*, 1815]

Please be so gracious as to have the E minor sonata [2] sent to me. I need it for proof-reading — On Monday I will call on Y.I.H. again in person. The *recent events* [3] necessitate the dispatch as quickly as possible of many works of mine which are being engraved and published. Moreover I am not yet in the best of health — I do most earnestly beg Y.I.H. to be so gracious as to *let me have* a few words about your own state of health. I am still hoping to hear something more reassuring, nay rather, soon the very best news about it.

Your Imperial Highness's

most obedient and most faithful servant

LUDWIG VAN BEETHOVEN

---

[1] On the spot.   [2] Op. 90.
[3] Undoubtedly Napoleon's escape from Elba at the end of February.

(538) *To ?*

[Autograph not traced] [1]

[VIENNA, *Spring*, 1815]

Be so kind, dear W., as to send me a ticket for the concert
which I can give to my brother, the pharmaceutical chemist.[2]

Your most devoted

BEETHOVEN

(539) *To Johann Xaver Brauchle, Jedlersee near Vienna*

[Autograph not traced] [3]

[VIENNA, *Spring*, 1815]

All my affairs are still in such confusion — that as yet I
have not been able to think of doing what I so enjoy, namely,
being with you — Perhaps today or tomorrow, but certainly
the day after tomorrow at latest I shall be with you — The most
wretched, most commonplace and unpoetical scenes surround
me — and make me peevish — And in spite of all the kindnesses of the Countess I shall have to fill to the brim the measure
of my lack of modesty by asking for another kindness, namely,
to have one of her pianofortes in my room just for a few days.
For *Schanz* has sent me such a bad one that he will soon have
to take it back again. And I don't like to send out to you his
instrument which I cannot keep — In haste, all my best wishes
to the dear, kind Countess — I am far from deserving all that;
and my embarrassment becomes all the greater when I wonder
how I am going to make it up to her —

Your friend

BEETHOVEN

[1] Taken from Schlossar, *DM*, 9 (3), 1910, p. 36.
[2] Nikolaus Johann.
[3] Taken from Schöne's transcript in the Stadtbibliothek, Vienna.

(540) *To Johann Nepomuk Kanka, Prague*

[Autograph in the Beethovenhaus, Bonn, H. C. Bodmer collection]

VIENNA, *April* 8, 1815

It is certainly not permissible — to be on such friendly terms as *I thought I was with you*, and then *to live beside one another as such bitter enemies*, without seeing one another!!!!!!!!!![1] Tout à vous, you wrote. Oh, what a windbag you are, said I — No, no, it is too bad — I should be only too glad to thank you nine thousand times for your efforts on my behalf and to rail at you twenty thousand times for having gone off *like that*, and for having come back *like that* — So all is illusion, friendship, kingdom, empire, all is just a mist which a breath of wind can disperse and shape again in a different way!! Perhaps I shall go to Teplitz, but it is not certain. If I did, I might give the natives of Prague an opportunity of hearing something. What do you think, that is, assuming that you still *entertain any opinion* of me? — Since the Lobkowitz affair has been settled too — well, there is now Finis, although a small fi or pfui is the result — No doubt Baron Pasqualati will soon visit you again. He too has had a lot of worry in connexion with my affairs — Yes, indeed, it is easy to say *the right thing*, but it *is difficult to make others do it* — In what way can *I serve you with my art?* Tell me, do you want a musical setting of *the soliloquy* of a refugee king [2] or a song about the perjury of a usurper [3] — or about two friends living in adjacent houses who yet never see one another? [4] — In the hope soon to have some news of you, since you are now so far away from me and it is so much easier for us to keep in close touch than if we lived beside one another, I remain

your ever devoted and respectful friend

LUDWIG VAN BEETHOVEN

---

[1] Evidently Kanka had been in Vienna and had omitted to call on Beethoven.
[2] Possibly Beethoven is alluding to the flight from Paris of Napoleon's eldest brother Joseph, who had been King of Spain.
[3] Possibly an allusion to Napoleon.
[4] I.e. Beethoven and Kanka in Vienna.

(541) *To Karl Amenda, Talsen near Mitau, Courland*

[*Autograph not traced*] [1]

MY DEAR, KIND AMENDA!   VIENNA, *April* 12, 1815

The bearer of this letter, Count Keyserling,[2] who is a friend of yours, has called on me and has thus reminded me of you. He told me that you were leading *a happy life* and that you had *children*. Neither of these happinesses has been my portion. It would take too long to write to you about this. Some other time, if you write to me again, I will tell you more about it — A thousand times I recall you to mind and your patriarchal simplicity. How often have I longed to have people like yourself around me — But for my own good or possibly for that of other people Fate persists in refusing to fulfil my wishes in this respect. I may say that I live almost *entirely alone* in this, the largest, city of Germany,[3] since I must live practically cut off from all the people whom I love or could love — What kind of standing has music in your country? Have you already heard in Courland about my great works? I call them *great* — but compared with the works of the All-highest all human works are small — All good wishes, my dear kind A[menda], and think sometimes

of your friend

LUDWIG VAN BEETHOVEN

If you write to me again, you need put no fuller address than *my name*.[4]

[1] Taken from *KFR* no. 453.

[2] Kalischer in his note to this letter (*KFR* II, 264) suggests that this Count Keyserling was the father of the famous traveller, Alexander Keyserling, born in 1815.

[3] Cf. p. 54, n. 1.

[4] Evidently Beethoven had not yet received a long letter from Amenda, dated March 20, 1815, in which the latter suggested that he should compose the music for an opera 'Bacchus' by Rudolph vom Berge. The autograph of this letter is in the Deutsche Staatsbibliothek, Berlin.

(542) *To Sigmund Anton Steiner*

[*Autograph in the Geigy-Hagenbach collection*]

[VIENNA, *May* 20, 1815]

MOST EXCELLENT AND QUITE AMAZING LIEUTENANT GENERAL!
I still need a few other scores, such as, for instance, those of the symphony in A,[1] the string quartet in F minor [2] and the trio for voices [3] — You can have all these back on Monday together with the other two scores.[4] Some foreigners have turned up here; and I can't refuse to let them see some of my recent compositions. In any case I trust that you are not looking for some pretext on my part where none exists — At about three o'clock this afternoon I will send for the scores I have mentioned above!!! All good wishes, never, never fading and most immortal L[ieutenant] G[eneral],

Your Generalissimo

BEETHOVEN

(543) *To Sigmund Anton Steiner*

[*Autograph in the Beethovenhaus, Bonn, H. C. Bodmer collection*]

[VIENNA, *May* 29, 1815]

I perceive that our chief Diabolus Diabelli [5] of the 1815 kingdom has found several mistakes; but I did not make them. For this purpose I need the *manuscript*.[6] If the L[ieutenant]

---

[1] Op. 92.

[2] Op. 95.

[3] Op. 116. This work, which had been sketched out in 1801–1802, was probably completed shortly before its first performance at Beethoven's concert on February 27, 1814. It was not published by Steiner until February, 1826.

[4] Probably the violin sonata, Op. 96, and one of the overtures listed in Beethoven's statement to Steiner. See Appendix F (6).
In 1815 May 20th, the date of receipt noted on the autograph, fell on a Saturday.

[5] For a note on Antonio Diabelli who was then employed in Steiner's firm, chiefly as proof-reader, see Letter 1091, p. 962, n. 1.

[6] As well as the date of receipt the following remark appears on the autograph in another hand: 'The manuscript of the sonata for pianoforte solo was sent on May 29, 1815'. This was the E minor sonata, Op. 90, which had already been engraved and was published by Steiner in June, 1815.

G[eneral] distrusts me, well then I, the G[eneralissimo], shall cease to have any confidence in him — The devil take you, my worthy L[ieutenant] G[eneral], may God protect you.

The G[ENERALISSIM]O

(544) *To Johann Peter Salomon, London* [1]

[*Autograph in the Beethovenhaus, Bonn, H. C. Bodmer collection*]

VIENNA, *June* 1, 1815

MY HONOURED FELLOW-COUNTRYMAN!

I always hoped for the fulfilment of my desire to speak *to you* sometime in London myself and to hear you, but many obstacles of various kinds have always prevented me from carrying out this wish — And for that very reason, as I am now unable to do this, I trust that you will not refuse my request, which amounts to this, that you would be so kind as to have a word with some London publisher and offer him the following works of mine: ' a grand trio for pianoforte, violin and violoncello (80 ducats), a sonata for pianoforte and one violin (60 ducats), a grand symphony in A major (one of my most excellent works), a smaller symphony in F major — a quartet for two violins, viola and violoncello in F minor — a grand opera in score, 30 ducats — a cantata with choruses and solo voices, 30 ducats — the score of the Schlacht von Vittoria auf Wellingtons Sieg, 80 ducats, and also the pianoforte arrangement of this work (provided that, as people here assure me, it has not already been published)' [2] — Incidentally, I have just added in the case of some works the fees which I consider to be fair for England. But in the case of these works as well as of the

---

[1] Johann Peter Salomon (1745–1815), born at Bonn, was in his early youth a violinist in the Elector's orchestra. He then became Konzertmeister to Prince Henry of Prussia, but soon resigned this appointment. After a short stay in Paris he settled in 1781 in London, where he played a very prominent part in all musical activities. In 1790 he was instrumental in bringing Haydn to London.

The verso of this autograph has in another handwriting the following address: 'Mr. Salomon, most renowned virtuoso in the service of His Royal Highness the Prince Regent'.

[2] Op. 97, 96, 92, 93, 95, 72, 136 and 91. Thanks to Salomon's good offices Birchall bought four of these works for 130 Dutch ducats. These were Op. 91, the pianoforte arrangement of Op. 92, Op. 96 and Op. 97. See *KHV.* 255. In the autograph the title of Op. 91 is misquoted. See p. 512.

others I leave it to you to decide what you consider to be a fair fee.

By the way, I have heard that *Cramer* [1] is also a publisher. But Ries, my former pupil, wrote to me a short time ago that Cramer *had spoken in public against my compositions*, for no other reason, I trust, than from a desire *to promote the art* of music. Hence I have no objection to raise. Should Cramer, however, wish to possess any of these pernicious works of art, I would like to have him as my publisher just as much as any other one — I merely reserve to myself the right to give these same works to my Viennese publisher as well, so that they would really appear in *London* and *Vienna* only and, what is more, at the same time —

Perhaps, too, it would be possible for you to inform me how I could obtain from the Prince Regent at any rate the cost of copying the *Schlachtsymphonie auf Wellingtons Sieg in der Schlacht von Vittoria* which was sent to him.[2] For I have long ago abandoned the idea of obtaining anything more. I have not even been honoured with a reply stating whether I may dedicate this work to the Prince Regent, a work which I am now publishing. I have even heard that the work has already been published in London in a pianoforte arrangement [3] — What bad luck for a composer!!! While the English and German papers are full of the success of this work, which was performed at the Drury Lane Theatre,[4] and the theatre itself has had a few good takings from it, the composer hasn't even a friendly line to show about it, not even a refund of the expense of having the work copied; on the contrary, he has had to forgo all profit. For if it is true that the pianoforte arrangement has been engraved, no German publisher will now take it; nay more,

---

[1] Johann Baptist Cramer (1771–1858), born at Mannheim, became a distinguished pianist who also established a firm of music publishers in 1824. His father settled in London in 1772 and Cramer, who had studied the pianoforte under Clementi, appeared in public in 1781. He wrote an enormous number of works for the pianoforte, all of which, excepting his well-known 84 Studies, are now forgotten. Since 1805 he had been publishing music, working with various partners.   [2] Op. 91. Cf. p. 51 1, n. 2.

[3] This was a false rumour. The pianoforte arrangement of Op. 91 was published by Birchall, but not until January, 1816. It appeared before the Vienna edition which was on the market a month later. Beethoven himself had arranged this work for pianoforte. See *KHV.* 255.

[4] In February, 1815. It was produced on February 10, 1815. Cf. letter 534, p. 502, n. 4.

BEETHOVEN
From the bust by Franz Klein (1812), done from his life mask
(*Beethovenhaus, Bonn*)

it is probable that the pianoforte arrangement will appear pirated by some German publisher from the engraved London edition ; and I shall lose my honour and my fee — Your well-known noble character leads me to hope that you are taking some interest in this matter and are strenuously exerting yourself on my behalf. The bad paper money of our State has once already been depreciated to a fifth of its value. Whereupon I was then treated according to the scale. After a prolonged struggle I have obtained, although at considerable loss, the full value. But now we are so placed that the paper money has been depreciated again far below a fifth of its value ; and I am faced with the prospect of seeing my income being reduced to *nothing* for the second time, and without my being able to hope for any compensation — My only source of income is what I compose. If in this respect I could rely on the sale of my works in England, that would be very advantageous to me — Please count on my most unbounded gratitude.[1] I hope to receive a reply from you soon, very soon.

Your admirer and friend
LUDWIG VAN BEETHOVEN

(545) *To Sigmund Anton Steiner*

[*Autograph in the Deutsche Staatsbibliothek, Berlin*]

[VIENNA, *June* 27, 1815]

If by tomorrow evening *between six and seven o'clock* the *corrected copy of the sonata*[2] which I handed to *Tobias Haslinger*,[3] who is *Adjutant to the L[ieutenant] G[eneral]*, *together with another copy in which there are no more mistakes* (so that it is evident *that the mistakes* have been corrected in the *copperplates*), that is to say, the versions corrected (by me) and the faultless copies are not in my hands, we have decided to adopt the following measures : For the time being the L[ieutenant] G[eneral] will be suspended, his Adjutant T[obias] H[aslinger] locked cross-wise ; — our Chief Provost Marshal Diabolus Diabelli[4] will

---

1 The original has 'unbegrenzteste Dankbarkeit'.
2 The E minor pianoforte sonata, Op. 90.
3 See Letter 547, p. 517, n. 1.
4 See Letter 1091, p. 962, n. 1.

be authorized to carry out these punishments — Only the most punctual execution of the order issued above can save the offenders from the punishment already deserved and recognized as just.

The G[ENERALISSIM]O
(in thunder and lightning)

(546) *To [Prince Paul Esterházy ?]* [1]

[MS not traced] [2]

YOUR EXCELLENCY!   [VIENNA, *June*, 1815.]
    After my work Wellingtons Sieg in der Schlacht bei Vittoria had been produced here in Vienna with the greatest success, several of my esteemed patrons and, in particular, the late Prince von Lichnowsky and also his consort, who is still living, believed that it was bound to be well received, particularly in England, because it not only celebrates the Duke of Wellington, one of her greatest military commanders, but also commemorates an event which is so gloriously renowned in the history of England and has been such a splendid contribution to the liberation of Europe. They advised me, therefore, to send it to H.R.Highness the Prince Regent; and the Princess was of the opinion that this could best be arranged through Your Excellency's kind intervention. So Your Excellency was also kind enough to despatch it to H.R.Highness in person. It was delivered to the Prince Regent with a written dedication and with an enquiry whether H.R.Highness would graciously permit this dedication to appear when the work would be printed and given to the public? — I am now taking the liberty of acquainting Your Excellency with the outcome of this step.
    After waiting for a long time, but in vain, for some news from London about this matter and when several rumours about

---

[1] Frimmel in his note to *KFR*, no. 455 maintains that this draft of a letter may have been intended for Viscount Castlereagh or, more probably, for Prince Paul Esterházy who in October, 1815, was appointed Austrian Envoy to London.
    [2] Taken from *KFR*, no. 455. The draft was dictated and signed by Beethoven. The Beethovenhaus, Bonn, has a French version of this letter.

it, which were detrimental to me, had already been circulated here both verbally and in writing, and probably by my enemies, I learnt in the end both from letters which English people residing in Vienna had received from their country and also from the public newspapers and subsequently from letters written to me by my pupil Ries, who is living in England, that H.R.Highness the Prince Regent had given my work to the musical directors of the Drury Lane Theatre in London to have it produced there. The performance took place on February 10th under the direction of the brothers Smart and was repeated on the 13th of that month. At both performances all the movements had to be repeated and were received each time with thunderous applause.

Meanwhile I was being frequently approached from several quarters with offers to publish the Schlacht von Vittoria at last, and on the most favourable terms. But I was still convinced that I must wait for the reply of H.R.Highness conveying his permission for the dedication. In vain did I wait! — By that time the report of the performances which had been given in London and of the extraordinarily good reception of the work had been circulated here by German newspapers; and a communication from London, dated February 14th, which has been reprinted in the *Morgenblatt*, even remarks that the old English families prided themselves on the circumstance that the Schlacht von Vittoria which had been composed in Vienna had been produced and dedicated to the Prince Regent at a time when Austria was still an ally of France! — All the papers were full of the praises and the extraordinary applause which this work had won in England. Yet no one thought of me, its composer; nor did I receive the least mark of gratitude or acknowledgment of indebtedness; nay more, not even a syllable came to me from London in reply! —

Having heard of these incidents and believing that I could no longer hope for a reply, I considered that I owed it to my countrymen not to keep back the work from them any longer. I accepted the pressing invitations to publish it; and on that account I gave it to a publisher.

But how startled I was when I learnt recently from the letter of an Englishman to one of his countrymen in Vienna the repeated confirmation of the extraordinarily good reception of my work in London, with the additional remark, that a pianoforte arrangement of it had appeared in that city! — So as compensation for my having done those Englishmen the honour of sending them my Schlacht von Vittoria and of dedicating it to their Prince Regent, of affording the London public the enjoyment of a work of art calculated to interest it in so many respects, and of being the cause why, thanks to this work, the largest theatre in London had twice, by packed houses, brought the Directors enormous profits, I have not only not received a syllable of thanks but am even obliged, since a pianoforte arrangement of my work has appeared in London, to return the fee for it to the German publisher and to bear without compensation the heavy expense of having the copy made which was sent to London. And, moreover, when it is published I shall have the mortification of having to suppress, because I have not received his permission, the dedication to the Prince Regent which thanks to the London newspapers is now generally known — Nay more, I have already been placed in the distressing position of having to reply merely with a shrug of the shoulders to every enquiry about my Schlacht bei Vittoria which was sent to London, since all I can produce are Press notices and the reports in foreign letters which have been shown to me — Had I dedicated my work to one of the allied monarchs at the Congress, I should certainly have been speedily and honourably rewarded.[1]

I herewith return my most dutiful thanks to Your Excellency for your gracious intervention in this matter and regret that Your Excellency's magnanimous exertions and your favourable disposition in regard to myself have been frustrated by the lack of consideration on the part of those who ought to have felt themselves honoured. Yet I venture to appeal a second time to Your Excellency's favour in this matter so that through the carelessness with which this affair is being handled in London I may not have to suffer loss of honour, property and financial gain.

I have the honour to remain with the deepest respect
Your Excellency's most humble servant
LOUIS VAN BEETHOVEN

---

[1] This sentence is added at the foot of the page.

(547) *To Tobias Haslinger* [1]

[*Autograph in the Deutsche Staatsbibliothek, Berlin*] [2]

MOST EXCELLENT FELLOW!   [VIENNA, *June*, 1815]

Please be *so kind* [3] as to send me *what Rochlitz has written about what B[eethoven] has written.* [4] We shall send it back to you at once by the flying, driving, riding or walking post —

Yours most exclusively

B[EETHOVE]N

(548) *To Nikolaus Zmeskall von Domanovecz*

[*Autograph in the Nationalbibliothek, Vienna*]

[VIENNA, *July* 5, 1815]

Would it not be possible to see you today, dear Z[meskall], and, if so, where? — Indeed I have wanted to visit you several times, but in spite of my best intentions it has been impossible for me to do so. I know, moreover, that you are at home only at certain hours, of which, however, I have now no record —

[1] Tobias Haslinger (1787–1842), born at Zell am See near Salzburg, first received some musical training at Linz. He came to Vienna in 1810, was employed in various bookshops and had a few of his own compositions published. He joined S. A. Steiner in 1814 and became his partner in 1816. To the end Haslinger was a staunch friend to Beethoven, gently tolerating the latter's explosions of rage and threats and, more frequently, his ridiculing of Haslinger's Salzburg dialect. In 1826 Haslinger succeeded Steiner as manager of the famous firm in the Paternostergasse; and he himself was succeeded by his son Karl Haslinger. For a full account of Haslinger's career see Unger's introduction to his work, *Ludwig van Beethoven und seine Verleger, Steiner, Haslinger, Schlesinger* (Berlin, 1921), pp. 5-23.

[2] Now on deposit in Tübingen University Library.

[3] The original has 'Sejd von *der Gütte*'. The last word should be spelt 'Güte'; but Beethoven is making fun of Haslinger's pronunciation.

[4] Beethoven is referring to Professor Amadeus Wendt's flattering articles on his compositions and, in particular, 'Fidelio', which had been appearing since the end of May in the Leipzig *Allgemeine Musikalische Zeitung*, edited by Johann Friedrich Rochlitz. In one of these articles Beethoven was described as the 'Shakespeare of Music'.

There is just something I want to ask you; and I am waiting to hear from you when I can do so?

Your
BEETHOVEN

(549) *To the Countess Anna Marie Erdödy, Jedlersee near Vienna*

[*Autograph in the Koch collection*]

[DÖBLING, *shortly after July* 20, 1815] [1]

MY DEAR AND BELOVED COUNTESS!

You are again bestowing gifts upon me and so soon too; and that is not right. For you thereby rob me entirely of the merit of having rendered you a small service —

It is uncertain whether I can go to you tomorrow, however much I should like to do so. But certainly I shall visit you in a few days' time, even if it has to be in the afternoon. My situation at the moment is very difficult. I shall tell you more about this when I see you. Greet and press to your heart in my name all your children who are so dear to me — Give the Magister [2] a gentle box on the ear, and the chief steward [3] a solemn nod. To the violoncello [4] the task has been allotted of betaking himself to the left bank of the Danube and continuing to play until everything on the right bank has been drawn across to the other side. In this way your population will soon increase. Let me add that I shall confidently take the road across the Danube as I did before. *Courage*, provided it *be justified*, enables one to triumph everywhere —

I kiss your hands many times. Remember with pleasure your friend

BEETHOVEN

[1] July 20, 1815, is the date of the poetical invitation, to which this letter seems to refer. See p. 519, n. 1.
[2] J. X. Brauchle, the family tutor.
[3] His name was Sperl. See p. 519, n. 1.
[4] Joseph Linke, who after the disbanding of the Razumovsky quartet in December, 1815, went to live with the Countess's family.

So don't send a carriage. I would rather *dare*! than take a
carriage! [1]
The music I have promised will be sent from town. [2]

(550) *To Johann Xaver Brauchle, Jedlersee near Vienna*

[*Autograph in the American Academy of Arts and Letters, New York*] [3]

[VIENNA, *Summer*, 1815]

I am not well, dear B[rauchle], but as soon as I feel better
I will visit you — Peevish about many things, more sensitive
than all other mortals, and tormented by my poor hearing I
often feel only *pain* in the society of others — I hope that the
health of our dear Countess is improving — Do have a Kugel-
hupf [4] *baked* in the form of a violoncello for our cellist, [5] so that
he can practise on it, even though not with his fingers, yet
with his stomach and his mug — As soon as I can do so, I will
come to you for a few days —

I will bring the two cello sonatas [6] —

All good wishes — I kiss and embrace all three children
in thought —

The chief stewardship is likewise one of my chief concerns [7] —

---

[1] Beethoven is punning on the word 'wagen' which can mean 'carriage'
or 'to dare'. He is probably referring to this poetical invitation, the autograph
of which is in the Deutsche Staatsbibliothek, Berlin.

> From Jedlersee I've been sent to you, Sir,
> Who are next to God the greatest composer.
> Our gracious Countess Erdödy
> Invites you to take punch, you see,
> And any other country fare.
> The two-horsed carriage waiting there
> Will drive us both to her estate;
> Till half past one for you I'll wait.

July 20, 1815.   SPERL
                                                   Chief Steward

[2] This sentence is added on the verso beside the address.
[3] At present on deposit in the Library of Congress, Manuscripts Division.
[4] The correct spelling is 'Guglhupf'. It is a famous Austrian yeast cake.
[5] Joseph Linke.
[6] No doubt the two cello sonatas, Op. 102, which were published by Simrock
at Bonn in March, 1817, with a dedication to the Countess Erdödy.
[7] In the original Beethoven is indulging in a pun on 'Oberamt' and 'oben'.

All good wishes, dear B[rauchle]. My very best greetings to the C[oun]tess and my wishes for her welfare.

Your

BEETHOVEN

(551) *To the Archduke Rudolph*

[*Autograph in the Gesellschaft der Musikfreunde, Vienna*]

YOUR IMPERIAL HIGHNESS!   [VIENNA, *Summer*, 1815]
I hope to be forgiven if I ask Y.I.H. for the favour of kindly arranging to send me the two sonatas with cello obbligato [1] which I have had copied for Y.I.H. I need them just for a few days; and then I will immediately return them to Y.I.H. —

Your Imperial Highness's
most obedient servant
L. V. BEETHOVEN

(552) *To the Countess Anna Marie Erdödy, Jedlersee near Vienna*

[*Autograph in the Beethovenhaus, Bonn, H. C. Bodmer collection*]

[VIENNA, *Summer*, 1815]
Forgive me, dear Countess, for having kept your music for such a long while. I only wanted to have a copy of it, but the copyist kept me waiting a long time for this work — I hope I shall soon see you again and for longer than I did yesterday. I press your dear children to my heart in thought and I beg you to say something on my behalf to the others who would like to have news of me — I am heartily delighted to hear of your steady recovery, and also of your increasingly happy circumstances (which you, dear C[ountess], so greatly deserve); though indeed I trust that you will never count me among those who hope to gain something from your change of fortune. The most heartfelt and warmest wishes go to you from your friend

BEETHOVEN

[1] Op. 102.

(553) *To Johann Baptist Rupprecht*

[*Autograph in Harvard College Library, Locker–Warburg–Grimson Album*]

MY DEAR R[UPPRECHT]!   [VIENNA, *Summer*, 1815]

A very long time ago I jotted down two melodies for
your 'Merkenstein'. — But both these compositions were buried
under a pile of other papers. The day before yesterday I found
the one which I am enclosing.[1] The other one is *for two voices*
and in my opinion is a better work.[2] But I have not yet been
able to find it — Since, however, in spite of *my great untidiness*
nothing in my house is ever lost *as a rule*, I will let you have the
other setting too, as soon as I find it — You would afford me a
great pleasure if you were to send me sometime six of your
poems which have not yet been published, so that I might
set them to music. How or in what way you dispose of them
afterwards would be entirely your concern — As I am not
very well, I am postponing my visit to you, but only for the time
being —

With sincere regards, your most devoted
LUDWIG VAN BEETHOVEN

(554) *To the Countess Anna Marie Erdödy, Jedlersee near Vienna*

[*Autograph not traced*][3]

[VIENNA, *Summer*, 1815]

I have heard, my dear Countess, that there is a druggist's
here, to which letters to you can be sent; for I thought that

---

[1] According to Beethoven's own note this first setting of 'Merkenstein' as a
song with pianoforte accompaniment in E♭ (WoO 144) was written down on
December 22, 1814. It was published late in 1816 as a music supplement to the
almanac *Selam*, edited by I. F. Castelli and printed by Anton Strauss. Cf. Letter
506, p. 477, n. 3.

[2] This second setting for vocal duet with pianoforte accompaniment in
F major (Op. 100) was composed early in 1815. It was dedicated by Rupprecht
to Count Joseph Karl Maria von Dietrichstein (1763–1825) and published by
Steiner in September, 1816.

[3] Taken from Jahn's transcript in the Stadtbibliothek, Vienna.

you might not have been able to read what I wrote to you about the trio [1] — I see that the violin and cello parts have already been copied. I am sending them to you herewith. You may use them as long as you like, until I give them to be engraved [2] — Your dear daughter M[imi]'s letter has given me much pleasure.[3] I hope soon to see her and her dear mother and all the members of her family. And this I shall arrange to do as soon as ever I can — All good wishes, dear Countess, from

your true friend

BEETHOVEN

Brauchle must visit me as soon as he sets foot in town. I am always available in the morning until about 12 o'clock.

(555) *To Johann Xaver Brauchle, Jedlersee near Vienna*

[Autograph not traced] [4]

DEAR BRAUCHLE!   [VIENNA, *Summer*, 1815]

Hardly had I reached home when I found my brother [5] plaintively asking about the horses — Please do me the kindness to go to Lang-Enzersdorf [6] about the horses. Just take horses at Jedlersee *at my expense*. I shall be extremely delighted to refund you — His illness (my brother's, I mean) makes him rather restless. Do let us help where we can. At any rate I must *act thus and not otherwise*! — I expect to have from you an early fulfilment of my request and a friendly reply about this — Spare no expense. I will gladly meet it. It is not worth while to let anyone suffer for the sake of a few wretched gulden —

In haste, your true friend

BEETHOVEN

All my best greetings to the dear Countess.

---

[1] Op. 97. Beethoven is probably referring to his illegible handwriting.
[2] Op. 97 was published by S. A. Steiner in September, 1816.
[3] The Countess Erdödy's eldest daughter Mimi, who later entered a convent
[4] Taken from Schöne's transcript in the Stadtbibliothek, Vienna.
[5] Caspar Carl who died in November, 1815.
[6] Lang-Enzersdorf was then a village not far from Jedlersee.

(556) *To Johann Xaver Brauchle, Jedlersee near Vienna*

[*Autograph not traced*] [1]

Most Excellent Magister, [DÖBLING, *Summer*, 1815]
Send your servant early on Tuesday morning to my rooms in town where what I promised for the Countess, to whom and to all those belonging to her I send my heartfelt greetings, is lying ready for her — Presumably I shall see you soon.

Your
BEETHOVEN

This note was written three days ago.[2]

(557) *To Joseph von Varena, Graz*

[*Autograph in the possession of the Harvard Musical Association*]

VIENNA, *July* 23, [1815]
You will certainly receive it, my dear V[arena], in twelve days at latest.[3] It was impossible to get it off to you before. Besides, in all matters pertaining to arrangements, the carrying out of commissions and so forth I am an extremely awkward fellow — The cost is 400 gulden including packing; anyone else would have had to pay 600 gulden — *Schuster* [4] will put down the 400 gulden here immediately. If you want to add 50 gulden more for embellishments, write to me at once. — The instrument has been made by *Schanz* — I too possess one of his —

In haste, your
BEETHOVEN

My kind regards to your family.

---

[1] Taken from Jahn's transcript in the Stadtbibliothek, Vienna.
[2] According to Jahn this remark is written in pencil beside the address on the verso.
[3] I.e. the pianoforte which Beethoven had been asked to choose for Varena's daughter. Cf. Letter 536.
[4] Evidently a banking house in Vienna or, possibly, Johann, Ritter von Schuster, who was employed in the Austrian National Bank.

(558) *To the Archduke Rudolph*

[*Autograph in the Gesellschaft der Musikfreunde, Vienna*]

YOUR IMPERIAL HIGHNESS!   VIENNA, *July* 23, 1815

When you were in town a few days ago, this chorus again occurred to me.[1] I hurried home to write it down. But I delayed over it longer than I first thought that I should, and thus to my very great grief I missed Y.I.H. — The bad habit I formed in childhood of feeling obliged to write down my first ideas immediately, apart from the fact that they certainly have often come to nothing, let me down on this occasion also —So I am sending Y.I.H. my own indictment and my apology and hope to receive your gracious pardon — I shall probably be able to betake myself soon to Y.I.H. in order to enquire about your health which is so precious to all of us —

Your Imperial Highness's

faithful and most obedient

LUDWIG VAN BEETHOVEN

(559) *To Georg Friedrich Treitschke, Vienna*

[*Autograph in the Koch collection*]

DÖBLING, *September* 24, [1815]

DEAR AND BELOVED FRIEND!

It was not possible for me to see you this week. I have been very busy, and I have just come out here today in order still to enjoy something of the beauties of the season which is gradually departing, and to ramble through woods which have already lost half their leaves — I would have begun your Romulus long ago, but the Directors refuse to grant me for a work of this kind anything more than the *takings for one night*.

---

[1] According to *KHV.* 322 this was Beethoven's setting of Goethe's poems 'Meeresstille' and 'Glückliche Fahrt' for four voices with orchestral accompaniment. The work was first performed on December 25, 1815, at a charity concert in the Grosser Redoutensaal. It was dedicated to Goethe and published in score by Steiner in February, 1822 as Op. 112.

And although I have so willingly offered, and still offer, many sacrifices to my art, yet by accepting such a condition I should lose far too much — For instance, I am paid 200 gold ducats for an oratorio, 'Christus am Ölberge' [1], which takes up only half an evening or, rather, normally lasts only one hour and nine minutes.[2] — Well, supposing that I were to produce a work of that kind at a concert in Vienna or anywhere else, what additional profit might I not make? — And indeed I am convinced that any town in Germany or anywhere else would pay me or any other composer in gold at any rate —

I have asked the Theatrical Directors to pay me for Romulus 200 gold ducats and the takings for one night — Now, dear Treitschke, see what you can do to persuade them to offer me different and more honourable conditions than that of the takings for only one night.   If I were to proceed to work out for you *what kind of fees* I receive for my other compositions, I assure you that you would not consider the conditions I have just stated and laid down for one opera, to be exaggerated — I beg you, therefore, to have a very friendly talk with the Theatrical Directors.   They cannot expect me to be a loser. On the conditions I have made I am willing to compose the opera at once and to have it staged by February or March at latest — You have four days until Thursday when I shall call on you to get your reply.[3]   There is nothing I should like better than to be able to compose without demanding any fee.   But indeed a German or, I should say, an Austrian artist will hardly ever reach that eminence — *London* alone can fatten a man so thoroughly that in Germany or, rather, in Vienna he can afterwards put up with the leanest fare —

Wholly yours.

I shall come for your reply on Thursday.

In haste, your friend

BEETHOVEN

---

[1] Op. 85.

[2] In a note to this letter in his catalogue of the Koch collection, no. 90, Kinsky points out that Müller-Reuter's *Lexikon der deutschen Konzertliteratur* (supplement to Vol. I, p. 79) gives thirty-six minutes as the approximate duration of the performance.

[3] A note on the fourth page of the autograph, probably in Treitschke's hand, says: 'Letter received September 26th and answered verbally on September 28th'. In 1815 September 28th fell on a Thursday.

(560) *To Georg Friedrich Treitschke, Vienna*

[*Autograph in a private collection*] [1]

[DÖBLING, *shortly after September* 24, 1815]

DEAR, MOST ADMIRABLE, MOST POETICAL POET!

On Thursday at latest I shall be with you, and then I will give you a verbal explanation of everything [2] —

I am not well —

In haste, your

BEETHOVEN

(561) *To Sigmund Anton Steiner, Vienna*

[*Autograph in the Beethovenhaus, Bonn, H. C. Bodmer collection*]

[DÖBLING, *September*, 1815]

MY MOST EXCELLENT LIEUTENANT GENERAL!

It has pleased Heaven to let the Schlacht [3] arrive safely in London. But Heaven has taken time over it. I have just received a communication from the business correspondent [4] in London stating that he has only now received this work. He adds a particular request that arrangements be made for the work not to appear *in Vienna* for three or four months — So although this may not please you, I beg you to postpone your publication for that period. On this occasion, too, I have at last been convinced that the rumour that the Schlacht had been engraved in London was all a lie — a fact which again must be gratifying to you, as much as it is to me. — Do what you can. No doubt some other occasion will present itself when I can show my goodwill to you *in preference to all the others* — My brother will discuss this with you —

The begging G[ENERALISSIM]O

---

[1] This short letter, which is addressed on the verso, is in pencil. As Aloys Fuchs suggests on his transcript, now in the Stadtbibliothek, Vienna, it was probably written in bed.

[2] Cf. preceding Letter 559, p. 525, n. 3.

[3] Op. 91.

[4] Probably Christopher Lonsdale, who was Birchall's business representative.

(562) *To Nikolaus Zmeskall von Domanovecz*

[*Autograph in the Nationalbibliothek, Vienna*]

[VIENNA, *October* 16, 1815]

This is just to inform you that I am *here* and not *there* [1] and that I too desire to hear from you whether you are *there* or *here* — I should like to speak to you for a few moments, when I know that you are alone at home — Enjoy life, but not voluptuously — Proprietor, Governor, Pasha of various rotten fortresses ! ! ! ! ! —

In haste, your friend

BEETHOVEN

(563) *To the Countess Anna Marie Erdödy,* *Schloss Paukowitz, Croatia* [2]

[*Autograph in the Beethovenhaus, Bonn, H. C. Bodmer collection*]

MY DEAR BELOVED COUNTESS !   VIENNA, *October* 19, 1815

I see that my anxiety about you in connexion with your journey must have been reflected in your intermittent sufferings during your travels. But — you really seem to be able to achieve your object. Hence I console myself with this thought and am now trying to console you. We finite beings, who are the embodiment of an infinite spirit, are born to suffer both pain and joy ; and one might almost say that the best of us obtain *joy through suffering* — Well, I hope soon to have news of you again. Your children must really be a great comfort to you. Their sincere affection and their endeavour to secure in every way the welfare of their dear mother must surely be an ample reward for her sufferings — Then there is the honourable Magister, her most loyal shield-bearer [3] — then there are a whole collection of other rascals, including the periwigged

---

[1] Beethoven means that he is in Vienna and not at Döbling, where he had spent most of the summer and the early autumn.
[2] The Countess Erdödy and her family had left Vienna for good and were then living on her estate in Croatia.
[3] J. X. Brauchle.

violoncello,[1] and sober justice in his *high office* [2] — in truth, a retinue that many a king would long to possess. — No news from me — that is to say, *nothing from nothing* — May God grant you greater strength to enable you to reach your *Temple of Isis*, where the purified fire may swallow up all your troubles and you may awake like a new phoenix [3] —

In haste your faithful friend

BEETHOVEN

(564) *To Nikolaus Zmeskall von Domanovecz, Vienna*

[*Autograph in the Nationalbibliothek, Vienna*]

[BADEN, *October* 24, 1815]

Well- and also ill-born (as we all are) [4] —

We are at Baden today and are bringing to that admirable naturalist Ribini [5] a collection of fallen leaves — Tomorrow we shall descend on you, i.e. *visit* you [6] and so forth.

Your most cordial

L. V. BEETHOVEN

(565) *To Nikolaus Zmeskall von Domanovecz*

[*Autograph in the Nationalbibliothek, Vienna*]

DEAR Z[MESKALL]!   [VIENNA, *October* 28, 1815]

You will have thought it very disobliging of me yesterday not to wait until you were dressed. But I had to go to a house where I was expected; and I was still with you when it was already a quarter of an hour later than I was expected to arrive there. From your place to that house it was at least a

---

[1] Joseph Linke.   [2] Sperl.

[3] Possibly this is a reference to Mozart's ' Zauberflöte '.

[4] This sentence is added in pencil at the top of the page. The rest of the note is written in ink.

[5] Johann Peter Ribini (1760–1820), born at Pressburg, became a Court Secretary and an eminent scientist. In a note to *KFR*, no. 484, p. 296, the suggestion is put forward that Beethoven had met him at the Birkenstocks.

[6] Here Beethoven is playing on the verbs 'heimsuchen' and 'besuchen', which both mean 'to visit', but with a slight difference.

BEETHOVEN
From the engraving by Blasius Höfel after the drawing by Louis Letronne (1814)
(*Historisches Museum der Stadt Wien*)

quarter of an hour's walk, so that I was being awaited for a whole half hour. Hence contrary to my desire to stay with you a little longer I had to rush off in a great hurry so as not to arrive there even later.

Yours
L. v. BEETHOVEN

(566) *To Robert Birchall, London* [1]

[*Autograph in the British Museum*] [2]

SIR!   VIENNA, *October* 28, 1815

I inform you that the pianoforte arrangement of the Schlacht und Siegessymphonie on Wellington's victory was sent off to London several days ago and, what is more, to the House of Thomas Coutts in London,[3] where you can fetch it — Please make all haste to engrave it and *to inform me of the day* when you intend to publish it so that I may notify the Viennese publisher in good time [4] — Such great haste is not necessary with the three works which will follow, which you will receive very soon and *in the case of which I shall take the liberty of fixing the day of publication myself.*

Herr Salomon will be kind enough to explain to you more fully why greater haste is necessary with the Schlacht und Siegessymphonie —

While expecting a very early reply about fixing *the day of publication* of the work you will have now received,

I remain your obedient servant
LUDWIG VAN BEETHOVEN

[1] Robert Birchall was a well-known music publisher and promoter of concerts in London from 1784 until his death in 1819. For details of his connexions with other publishing firms see the article on Robert Birchall in Grove's *Dictionary of Music*, 5th edition.

[2] The letter is addressed in another hand to Mr. Birchall, music seller, 133 New Bond Street, London.

[3] The preceding five words are in another hand.

[4] The pianoforte arrangement of Op. 91 was published by Birchall in January, 1816. It appeared in Vienna a month later.

(567) *To Sigmund Anton Steiner*

[*Autograph in the Deutsche Staatsbibliothek, Berlin*]

DEAR STEINER!   [VIENNA, *October* 30, 1815]

There is a Polish Countess here who is quite infatuated with my compositions, far more than they deserve. She would like to be able to play the pianoforte arrangement of the symphony in A exactly as I think it should be played; and since she will be in Vienna only today and tomorrow, she would like to play it at my rooms —

I earnestly request you, therefore, to lend it to me today or tomorrow just for a few hours, even if the copy has been made by the Diabolus Diabelli.[1] I give you my word of honour that no use will be made of it to your detriment.[2]

Your most devoted

L. v. BEETHOVEN

(568) *To Nikolaus Zmeskall von Domanovecz*

[*Autograph in the Nationalbibliothek, Vienna*]

DEAR Z[MESKALL],   [VIENNA, *October* 31, 1815]

It is impossible for me to come to you today, for I am invited to dinner and shall not be able to leave that house before five o'clock — So please order the tailor for three o'clock tomorrow when I shall condescend, for ought I care and if it really has to be, to drop into the Z[meskall]ian D[omanovecz]ian coffee house — Should you be prevented, however, from meeting me tomorrow, then let me know this in good time — If you *neither* write nor cancel this arrangement, then *I shall come.*

In haste, your friend

BEETHOVEN

---

[1] Diabelli had made an arrangement for pianoforte solo of the seventh symphony, Op. 92. This arrangement was published by Steiner in 1816.

[2] On the verso of the autograph near the address there is a remark in another hand that 'the pianoforte arrangement of the symphony in A has been lent'.

(569) *To Nikolaus Zmeskall von Domanovecz*

[*Autograph in the Nationalbibliothek, Vienna*]

[VIENNA, *October* 31, 1815]
I shall be with you definitely, my dear Z[meskall], at ten
o'clock tomorrow morning.   I am only very sorry that you
are being put to so much trouble on my account —

In haste, your
BEETHOVEN

(570) *To Antonia Brentano, Frankfurt am Main* [1]

[*Autograph in the Beethovenhaus, Bonn*]

MOST BELOVED FRIEND!   [VIENNA, *early November*, 1815]
Having heard that you are in touch with Geymüller I am
therefore enclosing the testimonial — Indeed the receipts are
rightly described as such [2] — I am sorry that in spite of all
your generosity to me you have to experience this as well —
Truly our situation has again become very distressing owing to
these wretched financial arrangements, the end of which is not
yet in sight — There is another matter which I must tell you
about.   It's about a pipe-bowl!   A pipe-bowl? — Among the
individuals (the number of which is infinite) who are now
suffering, there is also my brother, who on account of his poor
health has had to retire on a pension.[3]   His position at the

---

[1] Antonia Josepha Brentano (1780–1869) was a daughter of the famous art
collector in Vienna, Hofrat Johann Melchior von Birkenstock (cf. Letter 316,
p. 328, n. 2).   She married in 1798 Franz Brentano, a Frankfurt business man and
half-brother of the poet Clemens Brentano and Bettina von Arnim.   Beethoven
dedicated to Antonia Brentano his pianoforte variations on a waltz by Diabelli,
Op. 120.

[2] Beethoven is playing on the word 'Schein' which can mean 'appearance'
as well as 'receipt'.

[3] Caspar Carl, who was in very poor health, had been retired from his bank
on November 2nd.   He died on November 15th.
In the Beethovenhaus, Bonn, there is an official document, dated October 23,
1815, refusing leave of absence to Caspar Carl and ordering him to return to work
on November 2nd.   On this document Beethoven pencilled the following comment: 'This miserable product of financial officialdom was the cause of my

moment is very difficult. I am doing all I can to help him, but it is not enough. — He possesses a pipe-bowl which he believes he could dispose of most advantageously at Frankfurt. In his weak state of health it is difficult to refuse him anything. So on that account I am taking the liberty of asking you to let him send you this pipe-bowl. So many people are constantly calling at your house that perhaps you could manage to sell it — My brother thinks that you might possibly get ten louis d'or for it — I leave that to you to decide — He needs a lot of money, he has to keep a carriage and horse in order to be able to live (for his life is very precious to him, though indeed I would gladly relinquish mine!!) All good wishes, my beloved friend. My heartfelt greetings to Franz [1]; and I wish him the happiest and most joyful life. My greetings also to your dear children.[2]

Your true admirer and friend

BEETHOVEN

(571) *To the Archduke Rudolph*

[Autograph in the Gesellschaft der Musikfreunde, Vienna]

YOUR IMPERIAL HIGHNESS!   [VIENNA, *November* 16, 1815]

Ever since yesterday afternoon I have been lying down exhausted by great exertions necessitated by the very sudden death of my unfortunate brother. It was impossible for me to send you word yesterday that I could not come; and therefore I beg you not to treat this omission ungraciously. But I feel sure that I shall be able to wait upon Y.I.H. tomorrow.

Your Imperial Highness's
most loyal and most obedient servant

LUDWIG VAN BEETHOVEN

brother's death. For he was really so ill that he could not discharge the duties of his office without hastening his death — A nice memorial provided by those vulgar superior officials.'

[1] Franz Brentano, Antonia's husband.

[2] The Brentanos had been in Vienna for three years, from 1809 to 1811. No doubt Beethoven had met them frequently.

(572) *To Ferdinand Ries, London* [1]

[*Autograph in the Beethovenhaus, Bonn, H. C. Bodmer collection*]

DEAR R[IES], VIENNA, *Wednesday, November 22*, 1815

I hasten to inform you that I sent today to the post the pianoforte arrangement of the symphony in A addressed to the House of Thomas Coutts & Co.[2] As the Court is not here, hardly any, or very few, couriers are leaving; and in any case the post is the safest way — The symphony ought to appear about March and I will fix the day. On this occasion things have dragged on too long for me to fix a shorter time-limit. More time can be spent on the trio and the violin sonata, both of which will also be in London in a few weeks [3] — I do earnestly request you, dear Ries, to interest yourself in these matters and to ensure also that I shall receive the money. The expense of dispatching all these works has been great and I need this money — I have lost 600 gulden a year from my salary — In the bank-note period that meant nothing — but then the redemption bonds were introduced, and so I forfeited these 600 gulden and had to face hardship for several years as well as the complete loss of my salary. Now we have reached a point when the redemption bonds are worth less than the bank-notes used to be. I am paying 1000 gulden in rent. That will give you some idea of the misery which paper money is causing — My poor unfortunate brother has just died. He had a bad wife. I may as well tell you that for some years he had suffered from consumption; and in order to make life easier for him, I must have given him 10,000 gulden in Viennese currency. To an Englishman that is nothing, I know, but it is a large sum for a poor German or, I should say, a poor Austrian. During his last years the poor fellow had changed greatly; and I may say that I mourn his loss with all my heart

---

[1] After travelling for several years Ferdinand Ries settled in London in 1813. During the eleven years he spent in England he did much to promote the performance and the publication of Beethoven's compositions; and for this purpose he frequently corresponded with his former master.

[2] The pianoforte arrangement of Op. 92 was published by Birchall in 1817 as Op. 98.

[3] Op. 97 and Op. 96 were published by Birchall in 1816.

and that I now rejoice at being able to feel sure that so far as his comfort was concerned I have nothing to reproach myself with — Tell H[err] B[irchall] to refund to H[err] Salomon and to you the postage which your letters to me and mine to England are costing. He can deduct the amount from the sum which he is to pay me. I desire that those who are active in my interest should suffer as little loss as possible —

Wellingtons Sieg in der Schlacht bei Vittoria (this is also the title of the pianoforte arrangement)[1] must have reached Thomas Coutts and Co. a long time ago. Herr Birchall need not pay the fee until he has received all the works — But do hurry, do see that I am informed of the *day* on which H[err] B[irchall] is going to publish the pianoforte arrangement[2] — All that I can add today is my most ardent plea that you should further my interests; and I am at your service for anything you may require — My heartfelt wishes for your welfare, dear R[ies].

Your friend
BEETHOVEN

(573) *To Robert Birchall, London*

[*MS not traced*][3]

VIENNA, *November 22, 1815*

I am sending you herewith the pianoforte arrangement of the symphony in A.[4] The pianoforte arrangement of the symphony entitled Wellingtons Sieg in der Schlacht von Vittoria[5] was despatched four weeks ago through the chargé d'affaires Herr Neumann[6] to the House of Thomas Coutts and Co. in London. Therefore it must have reached you a long time ago.

Furthermore, you will receive in a fortnight the trio and the sonata.[7] Whereupon you will kindly pay to Thomas

---

[1] The remark in brackets is added at the foot of the page.
[2] Ries noted on the autograph of this letter that he sent a reply on December 18th.
[3] Taken from *KFR*, no. 492.   [4] Op. 92.   [5] Op. 91.
[6] Philipp von Neumann, who was Counsellor at the Austrian Embassy in London. Cf. Letter 227.
[7] Op. 97 and 96.

Coutts and Co. the sum of 130 gold ducats. Please make haste with the publication of these musical compositions and inform me immediately of the day of publication of Wellington's symphony so that I may take the necessary steps here in accordance with your arrangement.

With kindest regards I remain your most devoted

LUDWIG VAN BEETHOVEN

(574) *To Charles Neate* [1]

[MS not traced] [2]

MY DEAR MR. NEATE,   VIENNA, *December,* 1815

I have received a letter from Mr. Ries, as amanuensis to Salomon (who has had the misfortune to break his right shoulder in a fall from his horse),[3] and he tells me, on the 29th of September, that the three overtures which you took from me for the Philharmonic Society four months ago, had not then reached London.[4] This being the second remembrancer which Mr. Salomon sends me on the subject, I thought I had better let you know. Should you not have sent them off, I should like to revise the overture in *C major,* as it may be somewhat incorrect. With regard to any written agreement you may like to have about these things for England, that is very much at your service at a moment's notice. I would not have them suppose that I could ever act otherwise than as a *man of honour.* There are dispositions so fickle that they think *one way* today and *another way* tomorrow, and fancy others as ready to

---

[1] Charles Neate (1784–1877), born in London, was trained by William Sharp and John Field, and became a pianist, cellist and composer. He helped to found the Philharmonic Society in 1813. In May, 1815, he came to Vienna where he remained until about February 7, 1816, and saw a good deal of Beethoven. On returning to England Neate corresponded with Beethoven, and in 1824 invited him to London to conduct a concert of his own compositions including the ninth symphony. For an excellent account of Beethoven's relations with Neate see *FRBH* I, 446-448.

[2] Taken from Moscheles, II, pp. 227-228. The letter was written in English.

[3] Salomon had died on November 28th.

[4] Op. 113, 117 and 115. Op. 115 in C major, entitled 'Zur Namensfeier', was first performed at a charity concert in the Grosser Redoutensaal on December 25, 1815. This work was published by Steiner in April, 1825, with a dedication to Prince Anton Radziwill.

change their mind; and with such tempers one cannot be positive and mistrustful enough. So fare you well, my dear Mr. Neate.

Yours truly,

LUDWIG VAN BEETHOVEN

(575) *To Sigmund Anton Steiner*

[Autograph in the Royal College of Music]

DEAR STEINER! [VIENNA, *December,* 1815]

I need the score of the opera Fidelio for a few days in order *to revise a quartet arrangement with it.*[1] I shall then return it to you at once — Please let me have also the *score of the pianoforte trio together with the two written-out parts of the violin and violoncello,*[2] and the *score of the violin sonata in G major* [3] — I need both works just for one evening and can return them to you at once early on the following morning —

Never doubt my sincerity and my honesty. Thus our connexion will never be severed, I hope, although my poor unfortunate brother is no longer alive —

Your friend

BEETHOVEN

(576) *To Sigmund Anton Steiner*

[Autograph in the Deutsche Staatsbibliothek, Berlin]

MY DEAR STEINER, [VIENNA, *December,* 1815]

As soon as you send me the opera, which I require (I have told you why),[4] you may have the parts of the symphony [5] at

---

[1] In the summer of 1814 Beethoven had sent to Artaria & Co. a copy of the score of 'Fidelio' with his permission to publish pianoforte, quartet and wind-instrument arrangements of this opera. A pianoforte arrangement was published in August, 1814; but nothing is known of a quartet arrangement.

[2] Op. 97.

[3] Op. 96.

[4] See preceding Letter no. 575.

[5] The seventh symphony, Op. 92, which Steiner published in November, 1816.

any time — I am doing this not *in accordance with the terms of our contract* — but out of kindness — *I never attempt to reply to insults* —

Your most devoted

LUDWIG VAN BEETHOVEN

For everything else, such as, *how* or why I have come by it, I am willing at any moment to be answerable.

(577) *To Sigmund Anton Steiner*

[*Autograph in the Deutsche Staatsbibliothek, Berlin*]

[VIENNA, *December*, 1815]

Here, my dear St[einer], I am letting you have the parts of the symphony in A.[1]   I was the first to suggest to Diabelli [2] that you should engrave *the symphony from these parts*.   Consequently those statements about it which you are hurling at me are completely wide of the mark — Once more I request you to send me the opera so that I may correct Artaria's quartet arrangement from it.[3]   *Surely you will not wish to give expression to any feelings of jealousy about this* and keep it back *on that account*? For that would do you little honour —

I have always been willing to oblige you, but *my character does not allow me to be distrustful*.   According to our contract *I may give to England as well all the works which you possess*;   and I can prove to you that in this respect I have not nearly made use of *my privilege* and that had I remained sole owner of my works the English would have paid me very differently from you.   Yet despite all this I have adhered, and do loyally adhere, to what is laid down in our contract —

And now I inform you that in a few days a very solemn court martial is going to be held, with the result that the whole regiment, beginning with the L[ieutenant] G[eneral], is to be completely disbanded and also declared to have forfeited all its future honours, privileges and the like.

For the last time the G[ENERALISSIM]O

---

[1] Op. 92.   [2] See Letter 1091, p. 962, n. 1.   [3] Cf. Letter 575.

(578) *To Sigmund Anton Steiner*

[Autograph not traced] [1]

[VIENNA, *December*, 1815]

The L[ieutenant Genera]l is requested to send his Diabolus [2] so that I may give him a piece of my mind about the
Schlacht which has been translated into the purest Turkish [3] — A
good deal will have to be altered —

The G[ENERALISSIM]O

(579) *To Johann Xaver Brauchle, Jedlersee near Vienna*

[Autograph not traced] [4]

[VIENNA, 1815]

I am not coming today, my dear fellow — but I will
certainly do so tomorrow evening or during the following
morning at latest — It would be wrong if you were to measure
my fondness for the Countess and all of you solely by the fre-
quency of my visits to you — There are reasons for the behaviour of certain people which are not always easily explained
and which are nevertheless based upon some unavoidable
necessity — I should be very glad if the dear Countess were to
send me a bottle of Spa water. I don't like to give up taking
it for so long —

Let me add that I remain your debtor and friend

BEETHOVEN

(580) *To Baron Johann Pasqualati*

[Autograph not traced] [5]

HONOURED FRIEND !   [VIENNA, 1815]

I must return the money you kindly advanced to me, but
I should like to hand it to you *in person,* because I have some-

---

[1] Taken from Unger, no. 10, which was transcribed from the autograph.
[2] Antonio Diabelli. See Letter 1091.
[3] For particulars of this arrangement of Op. 91 for Turkish military music
see *KHV.* 254-255.
[4] Taken from Jahn's transcript in the Stadtbibliothek, Vienna.
[5] Taken from Aloys Fuchs's transcript in the Benedictine Abbey, Göttweig.

thing else to discuss with you. Any hour this afternoon would be convenient to us, and tomorrow morning too, if it suits you. But please do not fix too early an hour, for the condition of my health does not permit me to go out very early. Further, please be so kind as to let me know whether I am to call at your rooms in the Kohlmarkt or go to your house.

Ever your admirer and your grateful

L. v. BEETHOVEN

(581) *To Pietro Mechetti* [1]

[*Autograph in the Library of Congress*]

SIR !   [VIENNA, 1815]

I see that Herr Schuppanzigh [2] has been the cause of some misunderstanding. I had instructed him to tell you that something else had occurred which prevented me, to my regret, from negotiating with you this time, as I wanted to, about the works in question.[3] — During the next few days I myself will tell you why; and I know that you will then forgive me — I am only sorry that H[err] S[chuppanzigh] did not inform you about this sooner, as I requested him to do. — Meanwhile I remain, with my best regards, your [4]

(582) *To* [*the Countess Anna Marie Erdödy ?*]

[*Autograph in the Beethovenhaus, Bonn, H. C. Bodmer collection*] [5]

[VIENNA, 1815]

I told you today, dear C[ountess], that *for my own sake* I would have come, but what I really wanted to say was that I would have come for your sake and mine — Even if you don't

---

[1] Pietro Mechetti (1775–1850), born at Lucca, had succeeded his uncle Carlo Mechetti in 1811 as an art dealer and music publisher. See *FRBH* I, 399.
[2] See Letter 1168, p. 1027, n. 2.
[3] In March, 1815, Mechetti published Beethoven's C major polonaise for pianoforte solo, Op. 89, and in June of the same year he included Beethoven's song 'Des Kriegers Abschied' (WoO 143) in a collection of six poems by Reissig set to music by various composers.   [4] The signature has been cut off.
[5] This note is written in pencil. It was probably addressed to the Countess Erdödy.

see me, I would like you to believe this of me, namely, that *without any other reasons and considerations and without any other human admixture* [1] I really do like to be with you and your children who are dear to me —

BTHVN

(583) *To Sigmund Anton Steiner*

[*Autograph in the Stadtbibliothek, Vienna*]

[VIENNA, 1815]

Most highly born, most amazing and most wonderful

L ————————————————

————————————————————

———————————————— L ! [2]

We beg you to change for us 24 gold ducats into bank-notes according to yesterday's exchange quotation and to let us have them this evening or tomorrow evening; whereupon we shall immediately hand over and deliver the 24 ducats — It would be very pleasant and agreeable for us if your deserving Adjutant would bring me the bank-notes, because there is something I really must discuss with him. As a Christian he should forget all his resentment. We recognize his merits and do not fail to recognize what he does not merit. In short and to be brief, we want to see him. — This evening would suit us best. — We remain, most amazing L[ieutenant Genera]l, your

most devoted

G[ENERALISSIM]O

(584) *To Joseph Lind* [3]

[*Autograph in the possession of Dr. Hans Schwarz-Glossy*]

DEAR LIND, [VIENNA, 1815]

Do stop sending messages to me so often, as if I were *a defaulter* — If I could pay you, I would not hesitate to do so. —

---

[1] The phrase used in the original is 'menschliche Beimischung'. Perhaps Beethoven means 'ulterior motives'.

[2] Lieutenant General.

[3] Joseph Lind (1773–1837), born at Mainz, was one of the best tailors in Vienna. See *FRBH* I, 363-364.

I have always paid you without your having to remind me; and I will do the same on this occasion also. As soon as I can, I will discharge my debt to you without having to be reminded —

Your devoted servant

L. v. BEETHOVEN

(585) *To the Archduke Rudolph*

[Autograph in the Gesellschaft der Musikfreunde, Vienna]

YOUR IMPERIAL HIGHNESS!   [VIENNA, 1815]
You must have almost thought that my illness was feigned. But I assure you that it was not. I have always to be home early in the evening; and on the first occasion when Your Imperial Highness was so gracious as to send a message to me, I arrived home immediately afterwards. But seeing that since that time I seemed to be better, during the evening of the day before yesterday I made the first attempt to remain out of doors a little longer — Unless Your Imperial Highness countermands your suggestion, I shall have the honour of paying my respects to you at five o'clock this evening. I shall bring the new sonata, but only for today. For, as it is being engraved at once, it is really not worth the trouble to have it copied.[1] —

Your Imperial Highness's

most obedient and faithful servant

L. v. BEETHOVEN

(586) *To Baron Franz Alexander von Neffzer* [2]

[Autograph in the Beethovenhaus, Bonn]

DEAR BARON!   [VIENNA, 1815]
You promised to let me have a reply about the carriage. I do most earnestly beg you for an answer — If you can't let

---

[1] This letter is not dated. Hence it is difficult to determine to what sonata Beethoven is referring.
[2] Little is known about Baron Franz Alexander von Neffzer (*c.* 1780–1864) who, according to Frimmel (see *KFR*, no. 471, note), had an estate near Grätz in Silesia where Prince Lichnowsky owned considerable property. In 1816 Neffzer was appointed an Imperial and Royal Chamberlain. See *FRBH* I, 461.

me have it today, then do send it to me tomorrow to Pasqualati's house on the Mölkerbastei.   My servant will be there and
he will forward it at once to Baden — As a rule my servant
has to be at home from early morning until noon and from
three o'clock in the afternoon until seven — Should he not be
there, then let the bearer leave your reply with the caretaker —
Perhaps too you will find something else in the meantime.
Forgive my importunity.   Not one of all my other friends is
here; and I am quite at sea and absolutely helpless in such
matters —

I am off to Baden tomorrow, but shall return to town on
Saturday and will then call on you at once —

Your most devoted
BEETHOVEN

(587) *To [Tobias Haslinger ?]* [1]

[Autograph in the Gesellschaft der Musikfreunde, Vienna]

[VIENNA, 1815]

Please *cross out immediately* the tempo according to the metronome marking entered in the work delivered to you today.
Some tests I have just made have failed; the fault probably
lies with my metro[nome] —

(588) *To [Herr Frech ?]* [2]

[Autograph in the Stadtbibliothek, Vienna]

[VIENNA, 1815]

Perhaps it would be possible, my most esteemed friend,
for you to give my servant an order for two fathom cords of
hard wood, to be delivered tomorrow morning — In haste and
asking you to forgive me,

your
BEETHOVEN

---

[1] The name of this recipient is entered on the file which contains this pencilled
note.   It is not signed.
[2] The recipient of this pencilled note may have been this tradesman who is
mentioned in Letter 176.

(589) *To Sigmund Anton Steiner*

[Autograph in the Stadtbibliothek, Vienna]

[VIENNA, 1815]

MOST HONOURED L[IEUTENAN]T G[ENERA]L!
I still need your final advice about the agreement which
I mentioned to you. Meanwhile I cannot go out today; and
yet we should like to see the question settled. Would it not
be possible for my esteemed Primus of the G[enera]l Staff[1]
to invade my premises today, *or perhaps tomorrow morning,* so
that I could discuss the matter with him? I beg him most
earnestly to do this. In return for this favour, as often as the
L[ieutenan]t G[enera]l is in need, I shall make a note.[2]

Your
CONTRA UT[3]

NB. But the discussion would have to last a short half
hour.

The Adjutant's disgraceful behaviour has been *registered,*
(but not in the organ register, for, if that were done, what a
horrid sound would then be heard![4]

(590) *To Sigmund Anton Steiner*

[Autograph in the Stadtbibliothek, Vienna]

[VIENNA, 1815]

Hoping soon to be able to see the L[ieutenan]t G[enera]l
wholly *redeemed,* we shall thus await him as formerly with open
arms. And we are sending herewith a detachment of our body-

---

[1] I.e. Steiner himself.
[2] One of Beethoven's favourite puns, i.e. 'Not' which means 'need', and
'Note' which means 'note'.
[3] Bass C.
[4] In the autograph there is an opening bracket before 'but'. There is no
closing bracket, however, which should have been put after 'heard'.

guard, 25 of the *most honest fellows* [1] who in the business of war are the *most important* props of the state — We thus remain and we look forward to seeing our L[ieutenan]t G[enera]l soon with cheerful looks — The little lobe of the Adjutant's left ear should be pulled fairly hard —

THE G[ENERALISSIM]O

(591) *To Tobias Haslinger* [2]

[Autograph in the Gesellschaft der Musikfreunde, Vienna]

DEAR CARO OGGETTO AMABILE! [3]   [VIENNA, 1815]

See to it that the overture [4] is sent back to my rooms, since it has already been disposed of and since things *might happen* in the way they have already *happened* — By the way, my best compliments to His Seyfriedelity [5]

from your amicus

BEETHOVEN

(592) *To the Archduke Rudolph*

[Autograph in the Gesellschaft der Musikfreunde, Vienna]

YOUR IMPERIAL HIGHNESS!   [VIENNA, 1815]

Please be so gracious as to have the trio in B^b [6] with the parts and also both parts of the violin sonata in G [7] sent to me. As I cannot find at once my scores of these works among so many other scores, I am having them quickly copied for me — I trust that this horrible weather will have no bad effect on Y.I.H.'s health. But it always upsets me a little — In three

---

[1] I.e. 25 ducats. Evidently Beethoven had borrowed some money from Steiner which he was gradually repaying.

[2] The address in Beethoven's hand on the verso of this note is: 'To the extraordinarily highly born Herr Tobias Haslinger, Patrician'.

[3] Dear amiable object.

[4] Possibly Op. 115. But Steiner did not publish this overture until April, 1825.

[5] Beethoven is referring to Ignaz Xaver von Seyfried. Cf. Letter 302, p. 317, n. 3.

[6] Op. 97.

[7] Op. 96.

CHARLES NEATE (1784–1877)
From a photograph taken in 1860
(*Miss Helen G. Nussey*)

HANS GEORG NÄGELI (1773–1836)
From an engraving by an unknown artist (*c.* 1825)
(*Graphische Sammlung der Zentralbibliothek, Zürich*)

or, at most, four days I shall have the honour of returning
both works to their appropriate quarter —
Your Imperial Highness's
most obedient
LUDWIG VAN BEETHOVEN

Are the musical pauses still continuing?

(593) *To* ? [1]

[*Autograph not traced*] [2]

DEAR KIND FRIEDRICH! [VIENNA, 1815]
I am truly in despair that I have not yet been able to dine
with you again — I shall probably be able to come tomorrow
towards evening. But my servant will let you know this more
definitely tomorrow — I have just begun a very urgent task
today, or I should have been to see our kind Countess — I am
so sorry that I am unable to contribute to the recovery of her
health as much as my heart desires — But the Countess must
take courage and then she will certainly overcome her illness to
a great extent at least —
In haste, your friend
BEETHOVEN

(594) *To Herr Riedel* [3]

[*Autograph not traced*] [4]

HERR RIEDEL, organ-builder. [VIENNA, 1815]
Be so kind as to come to me so that I may have a talk with
you. For I cannot use the instrument you have installed.
Your most devoted
BEETHOVEN

---

[1] According to Frimmel (*KFR*, no. 494, note) the autograph bears no address.
The recipient was probably somebody connected with the Countess Erdödy's
household, possibly Sperl (cf. Letter 549).
[2] Taken from *KFR*, no. 494.
[3] Not identified.
[4] Taken from Chantavoine, *Le Ménestrel* 94 (1932), 356.

(594a) *To Ferdinand Ries, London*

[*Autograph in the possession of Helmut Mahler*] [1]

[VIENNA, 1815]

Nos. 1. 2. 3.
Grand symphonies composed by L. van Beethoven
arranged by Mr. Masy

Nos. 4. 5. 6.
Grand symphonies performed at the Philarmonic Society
composed by L. v. Beethoven, arranged for 2 violins, 2 Tenors,
1 Flute, 2 Violoncellos or Violoncello and basso by W. Watts
London.
printed for the Editor by L. Lavenat. his Music Ware house
26 New Bond Street [2]

Both works to be despatched by the first opportunity to
Mr. Philipp Pericoli in Paris.
Cours de Fontaines no. 7 [3]
who will forward them to Vienna.

MY DEAR RIES —
I would like you to ask for these works at the *publisher's for
me*. He will probably act with consideration and I shall be
enabled to afford a great pleasure in this way to one *of my most
valued and dearest friends in Vienna* — No doubt you will understand this; and you yourself must certainly know that for my
part I am willing to serve you most devotedly on all occasions
that may arise —

Wholly your
LUDWIG VAN BEETHOVEN

---

[1] The letter to F. Ries, which is not dated, is in Beethoven's hand, but the
particulars of the works quoted in English are in another hand. No attempt has
been made to correct the spelling.

[2] For particulars of these arrangements by G. Masi and W. Watts see the article
on *Contemporary English Editions of Beethoven* by P. Hirsch and C. B. Oldman, published in *The Music Review*, Vol. XIV, No. 1, February, 1953. Lewis Lavenu had
removed his firm in 1811 to 28 New Bond Street.

[3] Probably Lavenu's agent or banker in Paris.

1816

1810

(595) *To Frau Anna Milder-Hauptmann, Berlin*

[*Autograph in the Deutsche Staatsbibliothek, Berlin*] [1]

VIENNA, *January* 6, 1816

MY PRECIOUS, MY ONE AND ONLY MILDER, MY DEAR FRIEND!
After a very long time you are at last receiving a letter
from me. How I should like to be able to contribute in person
to the enthusiasm of the Berliners which your performance in
Fidelio has aroused.[2] A thousand thanks from me that you
have remained so loyal to my Fidelio — If you would ask
Baron de la Motte Fouqué [3] on my behalf to think out a
subject for a grand opera which would also be suitable for *you*,
then you would win great honour for me and for Germany's
theatre — Moreover I should like to set it to music solely for
the *Berlin theatre*, for I shall never contrive to come to an
arrangement with these niggardly Directors in Vienna for a new
opera — Let me have a reply soon, very soon, very quickly, as
quickly as possible, extremely quickly — to say whether such
a thing can be done — Herr Kapellmeister W[eber] [4] has
praised you to the skies to me, and he is right. That composer
can count himself fortunate whose fate it is to serve your Muses,
your genius, your splendid qualities and excellent talents —
and that I certainly do — Whatever may befall, anyone near
you can only call himself a *man in line*. I alone am rightly

---

[1] Not available. Taken from *KFR*, no. 503.

[2] Performances of 'Fidelio' had been given at the Berlin Court Opera on
October 11, 1815, with Frau Josephine Schultze, *née* von Kilitzky, Schuppanzigh's sister-in-law, singing the title part, and with far greater success on October
14th and 17th with Frau Milder-Hauptmann in that part.

[3] Baron Friedrich de la Motte Fouqué (1777–1843), an eminent poet of the
German Romantic movement, wrote libretti in close collaboration with the composers of his day. He adapted his charming tale 'Undine' for E. T. A. Hoffmann
and provided the texts for various less successful operas and oratorios.

[4] Bernhard Anselm Weber (1766–1821), born at Mannheim, was a pupil
of Abt Vogler and Holzbauer. He first studied law and theology but soon
devoted himself to music, working and travelling with Vogler. In 1792 he
settled in Berlin where he eventually became Kapellmeister at the Court Opera.
He was a prolific but mediocre composer of operas and various types of vocal
music.

entitled to the respectful name of *Captain* [1]; and only quite silently do I call myself

your true friend and admirer

BEETHOVEN

(My poor unfortunate brother has died [2] — that is the reason for my long delay in writing.)

As soon as you have replied to this letter, I will write to Baron de la Motte Fouqué as well. I feel sure that your influence in B[erlin] will easily enable me to compose a grand opera for the Berlin theatre, and especially with an eye to yourself, and under acceptable conditions — *But do reply soon* so that I may fit in this task with the other works I am composing.

(Away with all other false Captains) [4]

(596) *To Ferdinand Ries, London*

[Autograph in the possession of Julius Wegeler]

MY DEAR RIES,   VIENNA, *January* 20, 1816

I see from your letter of January 18th [5] that you have safely received both compositions [6] — As no couriers are travelling, *the post* is no doubt the safest way, but it is very expensive.

---

[1] Beethoven is playing on the words 'Nebenmann' (man in line) and 'Hauptmann'(captain).

[2] Caspar Carl had died in November, 1815.

[3] In *KHV.* this canon is listed as WoO 169.

[4] Anna Milder married in 1810 Peter Hauptmann, a wealthy jeweller, but continued to sing in public. The marriage was an unhappy one and was dissolved in 1816.

[5] Beethoven's mistake for December 18th, the date of Ries's letter from London. Cf. Letter 572, p. 534, n. 2.

[6] The pianoforte arrangements of Op. 91 and 92.

I will send you shortly an account of what I have paid here for *copying* and *postage*; it is a very small sum for an Englishman, but a comparatively large one for a *poor Austrian musical drudge*! Please see that Mr. B[irchall] refunds me this amount, for *by English standards* he has got these compositions very cheaply. — Neate, who has been wanting to leave Vienna every other moment but has always stayed on, is taking the overtures with him.[1] I have constantly reminded him of all your admonitions about these and of those of our late friend S[alomon] —

The symphony is being dedicated to *the Empress of Russia.* — But the *pianoforte arrangement of the symphony in A* must not appear before the *month of June*, for the *Viennese publisher cannot* bring it out before then. — My dear kind R[ies], please inform Mr. B[irchall] of this immediately.[2] —

The violin sonata, which will be sent off to you by the next post, can also *be published* in London *in the month of May* [3] — But the trio should appear later (this too you will receive by the next post); I myself will fix the time for this in due course [4] —

And now accept my heartfelt thanks, dear R[ies], for all your kindnesses, and particularly also in respect of the proof-reading — May Heaven bless you and enable you to make ever greater progress; and in this I take the warmest interest — Please give my regards to *your wife.*[5]

Ever your sincere friend

LUDWIG VAN BEETHOVEN

[1] Neate left Vienna early in February. He took with him the overtures Op. 113, 115 and 117. See Letter 605.

[2] Carl Czerny had made an arrangement of Op. 92 for two pianos, which was dedicated to the Empress of Russia. It was published by Birchall in 1817 as Op. 98. Beethoven was responsible for this mistake, for he sent the wrong opus no. to Birchall in October. See Letter 662, p. 603.

[3] Op. 96 was published by Birchall in 1816.

[4] Op. 97 was published by Birchall in 1816.

[5] Ries had married in 1814 Harriet Mangeon, a beautiful and accomplished Englishwoman.

(597) *To Nikolaus Zmeskall von Domanovecz*

[*Autograph in the Nationalbibliothek, Vienna*]

[VIENNA, *January* 21, 1816]

Yes! and include me too, even if it's at night —

In haste,

BEETHOVEN

(598) *To Cajetan Giannatasio del Rio* [1]

[*Autograph not traced*] [2]

[VIENNA, *end of January*, 1816]

Not until yesterday when I was at home did I read your letter properly. I am ready to give Karl to you at any time. But I think that I ought not to do this until after the examination on Monday — and yet I might do it earlier, that is to say, as soon as you consider it advisable. In any case it will certainly be best to remove him later on from Vienna and send him to Mölk or somewhere else. There he will neither see nor hear anything more of his beastly mother; and where everything about him is strange he will have fewer people to lean upon and will be able solely by his own efforts to win for himself love and respect.

In haste, your

BEETHOVEN

[1] Cajetan Giannatasio del Rio, of Spanish extraction, had opened a boarding school in the centre of Vienna in 1798. The school was removed early in 1816 to a building in the Landstrasse outside the city. Beethoven's nephew Karl was educated at this boarding school from February, 1816, until January, 1818. Giannatasio del Rio had two daughters, Fanny, born in 1790, and Anna (Nanni), born in 1792, who married Leopold von Schmerling, a lawyer, in January, 1819. Fanny, who never married, kept a full and rather sentimental diary from 1812 onwards, chiefly about Beethoven's visits to the school, his difficulties in connexion with his nephew, his sufferings and his outbursts of temper. Extracts from this diary were published in 1875 by Ludwig Nohl in a book entitled *Eine stille Liebe zu Beethoven*. See also *FRBH* II, 69-74 and *TDR* IV, Appendix 2.

[2] Taken from *TDR* III, 539. Thayer transcribed the autograph of this letter then in the possession of Witt & Co., London. Of the thirty-two extant letters from Beethoven to Giannatasio del Rio sixteen are now in the Royal College of Music, London.

(599) *To Charles Neate*

[*Autograph in the Royal Society of Musicians of Great Britain*] [1]

[VIENNA, *January*, 1816]

Mon chere Compatriote et ami
aujourd'hui il n'est pas possible, de voir ches moi, mai
j'espère d'avoir le Plaisir demain de vous voir a midi
aimes votre vrai ami
BEETHOV[EN]

Volti subito [2]
je m'avis, que vou deves donner une academie avant votre
depart d'ici a cause de votre honneur, si vous m'aves besoin
dans ce cas, je vous sui tout à fait a vos services.[3]

(600) *To Tobias Haslinger* [4]

[*Autograph in the Deutsche Staatsbibliothek, Berlin*] [5]

[VIENNA, *January*, 1816]
The horn part and the score will follow too [6] — Most
excellent fellow, we are amazingly attached to you. Observe

---

[1] This Society also possesses the copy of the portrait of Beethoven engraved by
Blasius Höfel after Letronne's pencil drawing (published by Artaria in 1814),
which the composer gave to Charles Neate in January, 1816, with the following
autograph inscription :
Meinem Freunde Neate
von dem Seinigen
L. v. Bthvn

[2] P.T.O. The postscript is on the third page of the autograph, which is addressed :
Pour Monsieur de Neate

[3] Neate did not give another concert before his departure from Vienna early
in February. See Letter 607.

[4] This note is addressed on the verso in Beethoven's hand : 'To the Honourable Herr Tobias Peter Philipp Hasslinger'.

[5] Now on deposit in Tübingen University Library.

[6] According to *KHV*. 261 this note refers to the proof-reading of the seventh
symphony, Op. 92, published by Steiner in November, 1816.

the laws and frequently sing my canon about silence.[1]
Per resurrectionem etc [2] —

All good wishes, your friend

BEETHOVEN

(601) *To [Sigmund Anton Steiner ?]*

[Autograph in the Stadtbibliothek, Vienna]

[VIENNA, *January*, 1816]
The publishers must send the written-out parts of the rattles.[3]

(602) *To [Sigmund Anton Steiner ?]*

[Autograph in the Stadtbibliothek, Vienna]

[VIENNA, *January*, 1816]
I am now sending you all the wind-instrument parts and shall certainly let you have the stringed instrument parts today.[4]
The

(603) *To Cajetan Giannatasio del Rio*

[Autograph in the Royal College of Music][5]

SIR !   [VIENNA, *February* 1, 1816]
It affords me much pleasure to inform you that at last I am bringing you tomorrow the precious pledge that has been

[1] A reference to Beethoven's canon 'Lerne schweigen', one of two written in Charles Neate's album shortly before his departure from Vienna. Beethoven's entry is dated January 24, 1816. In *KHV.* these canons are listed WoO 168.

[2] Quoted from 'Deus qui per resurrectionem filii tui Domini nostri Jesu Christi . . .' at the end of the 'Regina Coeli' Easter hymn.

[3] This pencilled note probably refers to the Schlachtsymphonie, Op. 91, published by Steiner in February, 1816.

[4] This note, which is neither dated nor addressed, probably refers to the proof-reading of Op. 91, published by Steiner.

[5] Cf. p. 552, n. 2.

entrusted to me.¹ — And now I beg you once more in no
circumstances to allow his mother to influence him. How or
when she is to see him, all this I will arrange with you tomorrow
in greater detail. — But you yourself must have some sort of
watch kept on your servant, for *she has already bribed my servant,*
though for another purpose! — I shall give you fuller particulars about this when we meet, though indeed I would much
prefer to say nothing about it — But in the interest of your
future citizen of the world I must give you this information,
much as I regret having to do so. —

    With best regards,
        your most faithful friend and servant
                       BEETHOVEN

I am greatly looking forward to going to you, and I remain
your
                  CARL VAN BEETHOVEN ²

(604) *To Robert Birchall, London*

                  [*Autograph not traced*] ³

Vous receues ci-joint.   VIENNA, *February* 3, 1816
  Le Grand Trios p. P[ianoforte], V[ioline] et V[ioloncelle],⁴
sonata pour P[ianoforte] et Violin ⁵ — qui form le reste de ce
qu'il vous à plu à me comettre. Je vous prie de vouloir payer
le some de 130 Ducats d' Holland comme le poste lettre à Mr.
Th. Cutts et Co. de votre Ville et de me croire avec toute
l'estime et considération.
        Votre très humble Serviteur
            LOUIS VAN BEETHOVEN

¹ Karl entered this boarding school on February 2, 1816.
² In the autograph this sentence is added by Beethoven's nephew, then
aged nine.
³ Taken from *KFR*, no. 512.
⁴ Op. 97.
⁵ Op. 96.

(605) *To [the Philharmonic Society, London]* [1]

[Autograph not traced] [2]

VIENNA, *February* 5, 1816

H[err] Neate took from me in July 1816 [3] three overtures on behalf of the Philharmonic Society in London and arranged that there I should be sent for those works a fee of 75 guineas, in return for which I gave him an undertaking to have them engraved *nowhere else* either in parts or in score.[4] But I have retained the right to have *those works* performed wherever I like, and also to publish them in pianoforte arrangements, not, however, until H[err] Neate has informed me in writing that they have been performed in London. — Moreover H[err] Neate has assured me that he will kindly undertake to obtain for me from the Philharmonic Society permission to publish after an interval of one or two years those three overtures both *in score and in parts*, since I can do this only with the Society's permission — Finally, I send my best compliments to the P[hilharmonic] S[ociety].

LUDWIG VAN BEETHOVEN

(606) *To Charles Neate*

[Autograph in the Beethovenhaus, Bonn, H. C. Bodmer collection]

[VIENNA, *shortly before February* 6, 1816]

Mon cher ami je vou prie de ne parler pas de ces oeuvres, que je vou donnerai pour vous et pour l'Angleterre, les raisons pour cela, je vous dirai sincèrement en bouche. Votre vrai ami

BEETHOVEN

---

[1] The Philharmonic Society in London was founded in 1813 as a concert-promoting institution. Through Ries, Salomon, Smart and Neate, Beethoven was brought into association with the Philharmonic Society who arranged for the performance of some of his works, encouraged him to write his ninth symphony, invited him to London in 1824 and sent him when dying a gift of £100 in recognition of his services to music. Moreover there are sketches for a tenth symphony which Beethoven was hoping to compose for the Philharmonic Society. See J. M. Levien, *Beethoven and the Royal Philharmonic Society* (London, 1927). See also *FRBH* II, 18-19 and Grove's *Dictionary of Music*, 5th edition.

[2] From a facsimile in Sonneck, p. 88. The autograph, which bears no address, was then in private ownership in America. [3] A mistake, of course, for 1815.

[4] These were Op. 113, 115 and 117. The words 'or in score' are added at the foot of the page. The Philharmonic Society did not accept Beethoven's offer.

J'espère de vous voir bientôt, quant a moi, je viendrai le plus possible chez vous.

(606a) *To Charles Neate* [1]

[Autograph in the possession of Miss E. M. H. Croker]

[Vienna, shortly before February 6, 1816] [2]

Mon chere Voyageur,

Quand ce depend de moi, vous pouves demain surement partir d'ici, mais j'espère pourtant, que vous restès encore quelques jours a cause de vos amis et particulierment a cause de moi.

Votre sincère
Beethoven

le quatuor est copiè, et
la Partition du Concert
pour le Violon vous ne refuserès
come sovenir de moi. [3]

(607) *To Antonia Brentano, Frankfurt am Main*

[Autograph not traced] [4]

My beloved Friend!   Vienna, *February* 6, 1816

I am taking the opportunity afforded me by Herr Neate, who is not only an amiable person but also an excellent English

---

[1] This undated letter, which is written on an oblong 8vo sheet, is addressed on the verso in Beethoven's hand as follows: ' Pour Mr. de Naete '.

[2] Neate, who had been in Vienna since May, 1815, and had seen a good deal of Beethoven at Baden during that summer, left for England about February 7, 1816. See Letter 607.

[3] In the course of a conversation with A. W. Thayer 45 years later Neate, speaking from memory, stated that before he left Vienna Beethoven entrusted to him manuscript copies of his violin concerto, Op. 61, with an arrangement for pianoforte solo composed by Beethoven, the two sonatas for cello and pianoforte with a dedication to Neate, Op. 102, the score of the seventh symphony, Op. 92, the score of 'Fidelio' and the F minor string quartet, Op. 95. See *TDR* III, 543. Neate's manuscript copy of Op. 61 is now in the British Museum. See *KHV.* 148. English publishers were found for Op. 61, 92 and 95. In his postscript to this short letter Beethoven is referring to Op. 95 and Op. 61.

[4] Taken from *KFR*, no. 514. Kalischer transcribed the autograph which was then in the Stadtbibliothek, Frankfurt am Main.

artist, to remind you and your kind 'husband Franz as well of my existence. At the same time I am sending you a copper engraving on which my face is stamped.¹ Several people maintain that in this picture they can also discern my soul quite clearly; but I offer no opinion on that point — In the meantime I have fought a battle for the purpose of wresting a poor, unhappy child from the clutches of his unworthy mother, and I have won the day ² — Te Deum laudamus — He is the source of many cares, but *cares which are sweet to me*. I wish you and Franz the deepest joys on earth, those which gladden our souls. I kiss and embrace all your dear children in thought and should like them to know this. But to you I send my best greetings and merely add that I gladly recall to mind the hours which I have spent in the company of both of you, hours which to me are the most unforgettable —

With true and sincere regards,

your admirer and friend

LUDWIG VAN BEETHOVEN

(I know that you will be glad to welcome Herr Neate as a friend of mine.)

(608) *To Nikolaus Zmeskall von Domanovecz*

[*Autograph in a private collection*]

MY DEAR Z[MESKALL]!   [VIENNA], *Friday, February* 9, 1816

I am horrified at discovering only today that I have not yet replied to the offer made to me to compose an oratorio for the Gesellschaft der Musikfreunde of the Austrian Imperial State.³ My brother's death two months ago, the guardianship of my nephew which devolved on me in consequence, and very

---

¹ Almost certainly the copper engraving made in 1814 by Blasius Höfel after the drawing by Louis Letronne. See Frimmel, *Beethoven Studien*, I, 51-59.

² Beethoven was determined to remove Karl from the influence of his mother.

³ For particulars of the recently formed 'Gesellschaft der Musikfreunde in dem österreichischen Kaiserstaate' (Society of the Friends of Music in the Austrian Imperial State) see Letter 949, p. 816, n. 1. This Society had offered to commission Beethoven to compose an oratorio. The offer was renewed in 1818 and J. K. Bernard undertook to write the text 'Der Sieg des Kreuzes' which Beethoven, however, could not bring himself to set to music. Hence the Society's commission was never carried out.

many other troubles and events of various kinds are the reason why you are receiving this letter so late — Meanwhile Herr von Seyfried has already begun to write his poem for the oratorio and I too will soon set it to music.[1] I need hardly tell you that I feel greatly honoured by this commission. That is clearly understood. And, what is more, I shall endeavour, so far as my poor capabilities permit, to carry out the task as worthily as possible — In regard to the *artistic means* of the performance, I shall give due consideration to these, of course ; but I hope that I shall not be forbidden to deviate from *the forms which have been introduced until now into this type of composition* — I trust that I have expressed myself intelligibly on this subject. — Since the Society insists on knowing what fee I am asking, I should like to hear whether it would consider a minimum fee of 400 gold ducats to be suitable for such a work [2] — I again ask the society most humbly to forgive my delay in replying. Meanwhile I assume that you too, dear Z[meskall], have doubtless already informed the society verbally that I am willing to compose this work ; and this to some extent sets my mind at rest.

My dear Z[meskall], I remain, with kindest regards,

your devoted friend

BEETHOVEN

(609) *To Ferdinand Ries, London*

[*MS in the Beethovenhaus, Bonn, H. C. Bodmer collection*] [3]

DEAREST FRIEND ! VIENNA, *February* 10, 1816

No doubt you will have received my communication of the   .[4] This letter is merely to inform you that on February 3rd I did send to Mr. Birchall through the House of Thomas Coutts and Co. the grand trio and the sonata,[5] for

---

[1] Possibly Seyfried had been suggested as the writer of the text.

[2] In 1819 Beethoven received from the Society the sum of 400 ducats ; and although he did not compose the oratorio, he was never asked to return the fee. In 1826 he was made an honorary member of the Society.

[3] Written and addressed in another hand and signed by Beethoven.

[4] In the MS this empty space is not filled in. But Beethoven is probably referring to Letter 596 of January 20th.

[5] Op. 97 and 96. Cf. Letter 604, p. 555, n. 4 and 5.

which he must pay to the latter the agreed sum of 130 Dutch ducats. But he must also defray the expenses of copying and postage, particularly as the money was given to the letter post solely on his account, so that he should be served quickly. You will find the itemized statement at the end of this letter [1] — I earnestly beg you to exert your influence most powerfully so as to ensure that Mr. Birchall shall pay to Messrs. Coutts and Co. the amount of these expenses, the equivalent of ten Dutch ducats. For the loss of this sum has eaten up a large portion of my whole fee — I believe that I shall soon find an opportunity of obliging Mr. Birchall in some other way.

I look forward to receiving a reply from you very soon and I remain, with the most friendly regards,

your devoted friend
LUDWIG VAN BEETHOVEN

(610) *To Carl Czerny* [2]

[Autograph in the Beethovenhaus, Bonn, H. C. Bodmer collection]

DEAR Z.,[3]   [VIENNA, *February* 12, 1816]

I can't see you today, but I shall come to you myself tomorrow in order to have a word with you — I burst out with that remark yesterday and I was very sorry after I had done so. But you must forgive a composer who would rather have heard his work performed exactly as it was written, however beautifully you played it in other respects [4] —

[1] There is a list of copying and postal expenses at the end of the original letter.

[2] Carl Czerny (1791–1857), of Slav origin but born in Vienna, was a son of the Viennese pianoforte teacher Wenzel Czerny. He took lessons from Beethoven from 1801 to 1803 and in 1820 was considered to be one of the foremost pianists of the day. In 1806 he was the soloist in Beethoven's first pianoforte concerto at a concert in the Augarten and thereafter he constantly performed his master's works. Czerny gave pianoforte lessons to Beethoven's nephew during the years 1816–1818 when the latter was at Giannatasio del Rio's boarding school. Czerny, who was not only a very popular teacher but also a most prolific composer for the piano, made arrangements of several works by Beethoven, assisted him in various ways and remained loyal to him to the end. See *FRBH* I, 102-104.

[3] Beethoven's spelling of Czerny was occasionally 'Zerni'. And the address on the verso of the autograph is: 'For Herr von Zerni, celebrated virtuoso'.

[4] The incident occurred on February 11, 1816, at the first of two farewell concerts given by Schuppanzigh after the dispersal of the famous Razumovsky quartet. Czerny took the pianoforte part in the quintet for pianoforte, oboe, clarinet, horn and bassoon, Op. 16.

CARL CZERNY (1791–1857)
From a lithograph by Joseph Lanzedelly
(*Gesellschaft der Musikfreunde, Vienna*)

I shall make this up to you, however, with the violoncello sonata and in a way that all shall *hear about*.[1] Rest assured that as an artist I cherish the greatest goodwill for you and that I shall always endeavour to prove this to you —

Your true friend
BEETHOVEN

(611) *To Cajetan Giannatasio del Rio*

[Autograph not traced] [2]

[VIENNA, before February 20, 1816]

This, my dear friend, is the substance of the *interview* I had with Herr von Schmerling [3] *the day before yesterday*: under no pretext whatsoever may Karl be fetched from the boarding school without his guardian's permission; *and the mother is never to visit him there* — If she desires to see him, she must apply to the guardian who will make the necessary arrangement. *In any case he is to remain entirely under the headmaster's supervision.*[4]

The Landrechte are going to draft for me a statement to this effect [5] — For the time being you may use the above information as a reliable guide for your treatment of that woman. I shall have to trouble you at about noon today by calling on you with my friend Bernard.[6] For we are going to draft the statement at your house at once; and also what you wish must be entered in it. S[chmerling] too wants your letter to be attached to the statement. Last night that *Queen of Night* [7] was at the Artists' Ball until three a.m. exposing not

---

[1] Op. 69, which Czerny according to his own statement (see Nohl I, no. 129, n. 2) performed with Linke during the following week.

[2] Taken from *KFR*, no. 517. Frimmel transcribed the autograph then in the possession of Giannatasio del Rio's granddaughter, Frau Anna Pessiak-Schmerling.

[3] Probably Leopold von Schmerling, a lawyer, who married in February, 1819, Giannatasio del Rio's second daughter Anna; or, less probably, his brother Joseph, who held an appointment in the Court of Appeal.

[4] According to *KFR* this sentence is added at the foot of the second page.

[5] The decision of the Landrechte in Beethoven's favour was dated February 20, 1816. This letter was written a few days before.

[6] For a note on J. K. Bernard see Letter 947, p. 812, n. 1.

[7] Karl's mother. Beethoven is referring to Mozart's 'Zauberflöte', which was one of his favourite operas.

only her mental but also *her bodily nakedness* — it was whispered that she — was willing to hire herself — for 20 gulden! Oh horrible! And to such hands are we to entrust our precious treasure even for one moment? No, certainly not.

With all my heart I embrace you as my friend and do so at the same time as the father of Karl.[1]

Your

LUDWIG VAN BEETHOVEN

(612) *To Cajetan Giannatasio del Rio*

[*Autograph in the Beethovenhaus, Bonn, H. C. Bodmer collection*]

HONOURED FRIEND! [VIENNA, *February* 21, 1816] [2]

The Queen of Night [3] paid us a surprise visit yesterday and, what is more, uttered a dreadful imprecation upon you. Her usual sauciness and impertinence to me was displayed on this occasion also; it startled me for a moment and almost made me believe that what she stated was perhaps the truth. But when I came home later in the day, I received the following decision by order of the Landrechte. It has proved to be exactly *what I desire*. I am informing you of the essential points which concern her, although you may perhaps *receive a copy of it* this very evening —

'An order of the Landrechte which has been handed to me, declares that in regard to the visits of the mother of my nephew or to his being taken away from the house, nothing whatever must be done save what I myself have arranged, agreed to and permitted; and that at all times the arrangement and the decision about this shall rest entirely with me — Therefore the boy's mother has only to apply to me when she desires to see him; whereupon at my discretion I shall decide whether and when and how a meeting can take place.'

---

[1] See Letter 654, p. 597, n. 2. Beethoven frequently described himself as Karl's father.

[2] On the top of the first page of this undated autograph there is a pencilled remark in another hand: 'To Giannatasio del Rio, February, 1817'. But on internal evidence, i.e. the decision of the Landrechte dated February 20, and the reference to the carnival in the second half of the letter, the above date has been assigned.

[3] Karl's mother.

The enclosed 'suitable' little book was given to Karl yesterday in secret by his mother *who forbade him to tell me anything about it* — You will understand, therefore, that we must return it to her, and you will realize also that we must be on our guard — If it *suits you,* I will fetch my *little fellow at about one o'clock today for lunch,* so that he too may see something of the *carnival,* which no doubt is being celebrated at your boarding school and especially by *his schoolmates* (as he tells me) — With all my heart I embrace you as that man to whom I shall gladly be indebted for all the good and great deeds which my Karl is likely to perform —

In haste but with kind regards, your friend

BEETHOVEN

(*Please* let me know whether I may *fetch Karl* and take him out to *lunch.*)

(613) *To Cajetan Giannatasio del Rio*

[*Autograph in the Royal College of Music*]

[VIENNA, *February* 22, 1816]

I must apologize to you, my dear friend, about Karl's returning to school at a late hour.[1] We had to wait for someone who happened to turn up very late; and so *we* too were detained. But I shall never again commit this breach of your regulations — In regard to Karl's mother I have now decided to comply fully with your desire that *she should not see him at all at your school.* This arrangement is much more suitable and safer for our dear Karl. For experience has convinced me that every visit of his mother leaves a bitter memory in his heart, and that so far from gaining anything he is only the loser. — I will now arrange for her to be able to see him at my home; and the result of this arrangement will certainly be that relations with her will be completely broken off much sooner. — You will receive the Landrechte's written statement this afternoon and, what is more, the original document, for I

[1] Probably after the carnival. See preceding letter.

am having only one copy made for me.[1] — *Since our opinions of Karl's mother coincide completely*, we two can arrange *by ourselves* the details of his education. —

In haste.   Your friend, who embraces you warmly,

BEETHOVEN

(614) *To Cajetan Giannatasio del Rio*

[*Autograph in the Royal College of Music*]

[VIENNA, *late February*, 1816]

I am sending you, Sir, the cloak and another schoolbook belonging to my Karl. Will you please also let me have the list of the clothes and other things he took with him, so that I may have it copied out for myself. It is incumbent on me as his guardian to look after his property wherever it may be — About half past twelve tomorrow morning I shall fetch Karl, as already arranged, in order to take him to a little concert. He will dine with me afterwards and then I shall bring him back to you. — As to his mother, I request *you, on the pretext that he is busy*, not to let her see him at all for a few days. No one can know or judge this better than I can. All the plans I have thought out for the welfare of the child would thus be upset to a certain extent. I myself will arrange with you how *his mother* is to see Karl *in future*. In any case I no longer wish them to meet in the way they did yesterday — I assume full responsibility for this; and, so far as I am concerned, the Landrechte have given me full power and authority ruthlessly to remove everything that militates *against* the welfare of the child. If the Landrechte had been able to regard her as the lawful mother, they would certainly not have excluded her from the *guardianship* of her child. — However much she may gossip, the fact remains that nothing underhand has been done against her; as is well known, in full council there was only one voice on the matter. — I should like to be free of all anxiety about this; for, as it is, the burden is heavy. I gathered from my interview with Adlersburg yesterday that we may have to wait a long time before we can even find out definitely what

---

[1] I.e. the decision of the Landrechte in Beethoven's favour, which was dated February 20, 1816. See preceding letter.

property belongs to the *child*. — In addition to these cares am I again to be oppressed by the worries which I believed that *your boarding school had completely dispelled, so far as I was concerned?* — All good wishes. I shall have the pleasure of seeing you today.

With kind regards, your most devoted

LUDWIG VAN BEETHOVEN

(615) *To Ferdinand Ries, London*

[*Autograph in the Beethovenhaus, Bonn*]

MY DEAR RIESS!   VIENNA, *February* 28, 1816

A very long time ago I wrote to inform you that the trio and the sonata too had been despatched.[1] In my last letter I asked you, as I had still so many expenses to meet, to see to it that Herr B[irchall] should refund me this expenditure, which amounts to ten gold ducats at least.[2] In any case he got the pianoforte arrangements for practically nothing; and only the fact that at that time we did not think that the Viennese publisher would take so long to publish the Schlacht which has not yet appeared, was the reason why we gave it to Herr B[irchall] for such a small fee — So I hope, my dear R[ies], that you will bestir yourself a little so that I may soon receive the 140 ducats here in Vienna. In my previous letter I have already told you *where* to send the money —

Neate went off at the beginning of this month and is bringing you the overtures as well as some other compositions [3] — I have not been well for a considerable time. My brother's death has affected my spirits and my nerves —

I am greatly distressed at the death of Salomon, for he was a noble-minded man whom I well remember since my childhood [4] —

You have become the executor of a will and at the same time I have become the *guardian* of the child of my poor

---

[1] Op. 97 and 96. Beethoven is probably referring to Letter 596 of January 20th.   [2] Cf. Letter 609, p. 560, n. 1.

[3] The overtures were Op. 113, 115 and 117. But Neate also took manuscript copies of Op. 72, 92, 95, 102, 112 and 136. See Letter 664, pp. 605 and 606.

[4] Salomon, who was a native of Bonn, had died in England on November 28, 1815.

deceased brother. You will hardly have had as much vexation as I have had on account of this death. At the same time I am experiencing the sweet consolation of having rescued a poor innocent child from the clutches of an unworthy mother —

All good wishes, dear R[ies]. If ever I can render you any service in Vienna, look upon me wholly as your

true friend

BEETHOVEN

(616) *To Cajetan Giannatasio del Rio*

[Autograph not traced] [1]

[VIENNA, *February*, 1816]

However gladly I would spare you a wearisome task, which for me too is unnecessary and thankless, yet it is not possible for me to relieve you of it — When I was obliged to search yesterday for several documents, I found the packet about Karl which had been sent to me — I can't sort these papers quickly. So you would do me a great favour if you would ask someone in your house to calculate for me the full amount of Karl's expenses at your boarding school. But I must be able to have it fetched at your house tomorrow — I hope that you have not misunderstood me. For when the conversation turned yesterday on magnanimity, the allusion could not possibly have been to you — It was intended solely for the Queen of Night, who never ceases to let out all the sails of her vindictiveness against me. And only for that reason do I require the necessary documents, and much more on account of other people than on her account (for never, never should I have to give her an explanation of my actions). A stamped form is not necessary and you need only quote the total sum for each quarter without listing the items. I am inclined to think that most of the bills have been found. Hence it is only necessary to attach them *to your statement.*[2] With kind regards,

L. v. BEETHOVEN

---

[1] Taken from *KFR*, no. 601.

[2] In all the *Gesamtausgaben* there is mention at this point of an illegible final sentence or clause or words.

(617) *To Tobias Haslinger*

[Autograph in the Stadtbibliothek, Vienna] [1]

[VIENNA, *February*, 1816]

All the written-out parts, instruments, cannon, mortar-guns and so forth, *of the Schlacht* [2] are to be delivered by tomorrow on pain of severe punishment —

THE G[ENERALISSIM]O

(618) *To the Archduke Rudolph*

[Autograph in the Gesellschaft der Musikfreunde, Vienna]

YOUR IMPERIAL HIGHNESS! [VIENNA, *February*, 1816]

My condition once again deteriorated so that I was able to take a few walks only in the daytime. Meanwhile it has now improved again and I may have the good fortune of being able to wait upon Y.I.H. once more at least three times a week. Let me add that the cares we have to face in these terrible times, which exceed all that we have hitherto experienced, are heavy and are intensified by the fact that since November of last year I have been father to a poor orphan. All this is a hindrance to my complete recovery — I wish Y.I.H. all the good and beautiful things that one can conceive; and I beg you not to be ungracious nor to misjudge Your Imperial Highness's most obedient servant

LUDWIG VAN BEETHOVEN

[1] Written in pencil with an address to the Adjutant on the verso.
[2] Op. 91.

(619) *To Franz Brentano, Frankfurt am Main* [1]

[*Autograph in the Beethovenhaus, Bonn*]

VIENNA, *March* 4, 1816

I am introducing to you, my dear friend, the chief connoisseur of wines in Europe, Herr Neberich.[2] Even in the aesthetic arrangement of the succession of the various products of the vineyard he is a thorough master and merits all the acclaim he receives. I feel sure that he will do you honour at the Supreme Council of Frankfurt. He ought to act as high priest at every sacrifice which is offered to Bacchus ; and there is no man who can produce a better 'Evoe! Evoe!' — I trust that now and then you like to think of me, of your friend

L. v. BEETHOVEN

NB. The music could not be obtained today. [3]

(620) *To Heinrich Schmidt, Brünn* [4]

[*MS not traced*] [5]

SIR !   VIENNA, *March* 11, 1816

It has afforded me much pleasure to send you the Schlachtsymphonie with the engraved parts and the score. As soon as you have made use of it, kindly return it to me — Since it will perhaps be performed here, I could not let you have the parts copied out. As the title of the Schlachtsymphonie is quite

[1] Franz Dominik Maria Joseph Brentano (1765–1844), born at Frankfurt, was the second son by the first marriage of his father, Peter Brentano, whose large import business he inherited and extended. In 1798 he married Antonia von Birkenstock, a daughter of the famous art collector in Vienna. During the three years the Brentanos spent in Vienna, 1809–1811, they formed a close friendship with Beethoven, to whom indeed they later rendered financial assistance. Franz Brentano was a half-brother of Clemens, the poet, and of Bettina, the writer, who married in 1811 the poet Achim von Arnim.

[2] Evidently a wine merchant who in 1820 was asked to deliver a letter from Beethoven to E. T. A. Hoffmann. See Letter 1014.

[3] This NB. is written on the verso of the letter.

[4] The recipient was Director of the Theatre at Brünn (Brno). In 1805 he had been Director of the theatre at Schloss Eisenstadt and formed a friendship with Haydn.

[5] Taken from *TDR* III, 550-551.

wrongly printed, I am informing you of the exact wording and how it should appear, that is to say : '*A grand instrumental composition for full orchestra, composed on the subject of Wellington's victory in the battle of Vittoria. Part I. Battle. Part II. Victory symphony.*' [1] As for the opera, you may have it, of course, but for 125 gulden at least, I repeat, one hundred and twenty-five gulden, that is to say, 25 gulden more than before. For thanks to our delightful currency in the superlatively desirable paper condition of our paper money the copyist receives for his work exactly as much again as he did at the time when the opera was offered to you for 100 gulden — If this meets with your approval, let me know and then you can have the opera in a fortnight — My compliments to your wife and also to Kapellmeister Strauss [2] — Perhaps I shall visit Brünn sometime when circumstances are different. I wish you all success there and I remain your most devoted

LUDWIG VAN BEETHOVEN

NB. Please reply at once about the opera so that you may receive it in time.

(621) *To Tobias Haslinger*

[*Autograph in the Stadtbibliothek, Vienna*]

[VIENNA, *March*, 1816]

We are awaiting the highly born and worthy Adjutant who is to bring us three copies of the Schlacht,[3] that is to say, one for the common man [4] and *two, intended for illustrissimi, with vignettes, but not of copperplate* — This is to inform you that, first of all, you will be well received and then sent off again to the L[ieutenant Genera]l with honourable commissions —

THE G[ENERALISSIM]O

---

[1] For the title of the engraved score of Op. 91, which so annoyed Beethoven, see *KHV.* 254.

[2] Not identified. Perhaps the name was wrongly transcribed.

[3] Beethoven is referring to his own pianoforte arrangement of his Schlacht-symphonie, Op. 91, published by Steiner in February, 1816, at the same time as the score of this work. The English edition of this pianoforte arrangement, printed by Birchall, appeared in January, 1816, i.e. a month earlier. For a full discussion of all these points see *KHV.* 252-255.

[4] In the original the words from 'for' to 'man' are in Viennese dialect.

(622) *To Carl Czerny*

[*Autograph in the Beethovenhaus, Bonn, H. C. Bodmer collection*]

DEAR CZ[ERNY]!   [VIENNA, *Spring*, 1816]

Kindly let me know what time you get home *in the evening on the day* when you give Karl a lesson.[1] From what I hear, you sometimes give him more than *an hour*; and for this kindness I cannot thank you sufficiently. Meanwhile some fresh difficulties have again arisen about sending for Karl. So it is necessary for me to know whether *you come home* at half past six or at seven; and please let me have a reply about this. But, of course, you must not alter in the very least any arrangement that may suit you — It would be best if you were to go out there again, as soon as you can. Well, that is all for the time being. We shall discuss this, of course, in greater detail.

Your true friend
BEETHOVEN

NB. In case my letter does not find you at home, I will send for a reply this afternoon.[2]

(623) *To Anton Halm* [3]

[*Autograph not traced*] [4]

VIENNA, *April* 1, 1816

I am delighted, my dear H[err] v[on] Halm, to accept your dedication to me of your sonata in C minor and to agree to this dedication being engraved as well —

Your most devoted
LUDWIG VAN BEETHOVEN

---

[1] Carl Czerny began to give pianoforte lessons to Beethoven's nephew soon after the latter was placed at Giannatasio del Rio's boarding school, and he continued to do so for about two years.

[2] This NB. is written on the verso to the left of the address.

[3] Anton Halm (1789–1872), born in Styria, became a pianist, a composer and a highly esteemed teacher. From 1811 to 1815 he lived and worked at Graz and then settled in Vienna for the remainder of his life. He was an enthusiastic admirer of the pianoforte works of Beethoven to whom he dedicated his own C minor pianoforte sonata, Op. 15. For a full account of Anton Halm and his friendship with Beethoven see *FRBH* I, 192-196.

[4] Taken from the version given in *FRBH* I, 193. Frimmel copied the autograph which he saw in an exhibition at Baden.

(624) *To Ferdinand Ries, London*

[Autograph in the Beethovenhaus, Bonn, H. C. Bodmer collection]

MY DEAR RIESE! [1]   VIENNA, *April* 3, 1816.

Mr. B[irchall] will probably have received by now the trio and the sonata.[2] In my previous letters I demanded an additional sum of ten ducats for the copying and the postage. No doubt you will succeed too in obtaining these ten ducats for me — I am always rather worried lest you should have to pay a good deal for postage on my account. I should very much like you to be so kind as to charge to me all my letters to you, for I shall then compensate you by payments from the House of Fries [3] in Vienna to the House of Coutts in London — If the publisher B[irchall] raises no objections (but if he does, I request him to notify me at once by post), then the pianoforte and violin [4] sonata is *to appear in Vienna on June* 15*th and the trio on July* 15*th*. As for the pianoforte arrangement of the symphony I will let Herr B[irchall] [5] know *when that is to appear* — Neate must surely be in London by now. I gave him several of my compositions to take back and he promised me to make the best use of them in my interest. Give him my compliments — The Archduke Rudolph plays your works too, my dear Ries, and among these I find 'Il Sogno' [6] particularly delightful — All good wishes, my dear R[ies], and my kindest regards to your dear wife and also to all those beautiful Englishwomen to whom my greetings may give pleasure —

Your true friend
BEETHOVEN

[1] The German word 'Riese' means 'giant'. Evidently Beethoven is poking fun at his former pupil.

[2] Op. 97 and 96.

[3] See Letter 765, p. 672, n. 3.

[4] The words 'and violin' are added at the foot of the page.

[5] In the autograph Beethoven uses in all three instances the letter V. But he is undoubtedly referring to Birchall. Possibly the V stands for Verleger [publisher].

[6] It has not been possible to identify this work, the title of which means 'the dream'.

(625) *To Nikolaus Zmeskall von Domanovecz*

[*Autograph in the Nationalbibliothek, Vienna*]

[VIENNA, *April* 7, 1816]

The undersigned asks most politely for the book by *Weissenbach*,[1] because it does not belong to him and he is therefore exceedingly embarrassed.

In haste, your

BEETHOVEN

(626) *To Sigmund Anton Steiner* [2]

[*Autograph in the Beethovenhaus, Bonn, H. C. Bodmer collection*]

[VIENNA, *April*, 1816]

The Lieutenant General is receiving herewith the promised composition for voice with pianoforte accompaniment.[3] But it can only be delivered in exchange for 50 gold ducats which the L[ieutenant Genera]l must pay into the G[eneralissim]o's war chest at once. Although the war chest still owes the L[ieutenant Genera]l a sum of 1300 gulden, yet the war chest has to insist that the 50 ducats be deposited forthwith and without deduction —

In regard to the aforesaid sum which is still owing, we will soon make a point of satisfying the L[ieutenant Genera]l in this respect and of letting many other benefit monies flow into his treasure house, chiefly on account of his services to the state. — The Diabolus in the person of the Grand Provost Marshal [4] is the bearer of this communication, with the most cordial greeting from the G[eneralissim]o —

[1] Probably Weissenbach's very popular book, *Meine Reise zum Kongress*, published in 1816, which everyone was then reading. Evidently somebody had lent a copy to Beethoven, who had lent it in turn to Zmeskall.

[2] The address in Beethoven's hand on the verso of the autograph is 'Für den General Leutnant Steinender'.

[3] The song cycle 'An die ferne Geliebte', a setting with pianoforte accompaniment of six poems by Alois Jeitteles (1794–1858), a physician and poet living at Brünn (Brno). It was dedicated to Prince Franz Joseph von Lobkowitz and was published as Op. 98 by Steiner in October, 1816.

[4] Beethoven is referring to Antonio Diabelli, who was then employed in Steiner's publishing firm and to whom the title of 'Grossprofoss' had been given.

(627) *To Tobias Haslinger*

[*Autograph in the Beethovenhaus, Bonn, H. C. Bodmer collection*]

[VIENNA, *April*, 1816]

MOST EXCELLENT AND HIGHLY BORN LITTLE ADJUTANT
AND ADJUVANT,

We earnestly request you to let us have the copy for the Princess Kinsky very soon, since in any case it will take some time to reach Prague by the mail-coach [1] —

We are amazingly attached to you —

THE G[ENERALISSIM]O

(628) *To Sigmund Anton Steiner* [2]

[*Autograph in the Stadtbibliothek, Vienna*]

[VIENNA, *Spring*, 1816]

MOST EXCELLENT L[IEUTENANT] G[ENERAL],

Well then, I will fix on Tuesday provisionally. The two holidays would be inconvenient for you [3] — In any case I shall let you have a reply — I don't understand your reference to eating meat — Please explain it —

Your

bass F [4]

---

[1] No doubt Beethoven was asking for a copy of his second setting of Tiedge's poem 'An die Hoffnung', Op. 94, published by Steiner in April, 1816. It was dedicated to the Princess Karoline Kinsky. The note was first published in the *Beethoven-Jahrbuch*, 1953/54, p. 34.

[2] Beside the address to Steiner on the verso there is this musical notation:

[3] Probably either Easter or Whitsuntide.

[4] A form of signature occasionally used by Beethoven when writing to Steiner's firm.

(629) *To Tobias Haslinger*

[*Autograph in the Beethovenhaus, Bonn, H. C. Bodmer collection*]

[VIENNA, *Spring*, 1816]

As we understand that our esteemed Adjutant has something to report to us, we instruct him to betake himself at about three o'clock to the G[eneralissim]o's rooms in the Seilerstätte, on the third floor ¹ —

(630) *To Johann Nepomuk Kanka, Prague*

[*Autograph in the possession of Julius Wegeler*]

VIENNA, *May* 1, [1816]

On May 1st!!!!! when Beethoven had to write for a 600 gulden *warrant and again a warrant and nothing but a warrant.*²

MY MOST ESTEEMED K[ANKA]!

If I don't write very much or even not at all, I know that you interpret my behaviour exactly as it should be understood. Truth is to be found in a good character even without written evidence; and that is the way things must remain between the two of us —

Already on the last occasion I received my pension from Kinsky three or, at least, two months late; and this time too I have not received this *miserable sum when it was due*, for I ought to have been able to draw it at Prague on April 1st. Baron Pasqualati has written to the House of Ballabene at Prague asking them to cash this half-yearly sum of 600 gulden. But two letters have not yet brought any reply from those *business hounds*, I mean, business men. What the reason was the last time and what the reason is now why I am not receiving *at the proper time even this curtailed and unfairly reduced income* I really do not know. Hence I request you to prove to me once

---

¹ Beethoven was then living in rooms on the third floor of the Lambertisches Haus (a house belonging to Count Peregrin Lamberti) in Seilerstätte 1055-1056. The house no longer exists. The note was first published in the *Beethoven-Jahrbuch*, 1953/54, p. 33.

² Here Beethoven is punning on the word 'Schein' which among many meanings signifies 'warrant' and 'illusion'.

more your friendly readiness to help by explaining to me as soon as possible the reason for this *iniquitous* treatment and by doing your utmost to ensure that I shall receive this pittance at any rate — Owing to our present circumstances I am losing on all sides and my income is barely sufficient for three months, let alone for twelve months. That is how things are now in this monarchical anarchical Austria ! ! ! ! ! ! ! !

I have just handed in to the post a dedication to the Princess Kinsky ; ¹ and I shall send another letter applying in the most respectful manner for the money to which I am by right entitled — The reason why I have not yet sent you the promised sonatas is because they are to be published soon ; ² and any engraved work is better than a manuscript — I will think about a present for Wolf as soon as possible — Meanwhile my circumstances are such that I have become both richer and poorer, *for I have to support my brother's child entirely* — I embrace you with all my heart and am ever, with

> my sincere regards, your
>
> LUDWIG VAN BEETHOVEN

(631) *To Johann Nepomuk Kanka, Prague*

[*Autograph not traced*] ³

[VIENNA, *May* 2, 1816]

MY DEAREST AND MOST BELOVED FRIEND !

My letter of yesterday is already being followed by a second one today, May 2nd. After one month and six days Pasqualati informed me today that the House of Ballabene was *too grand* to deal with such a matter. Hence I have to invoke the help of *your smallness* (for indeed it never worries me to have to be so small as to serve others) ⁴ —

My rent amounts to 550 gulden and is paid out of the sum I have mentioned —

---

¹ The dedication of Op. 94.

² Probably the two cello and pianoforte sonatas, Op. 102, composed in 1815 but not published until March, 1817, by Simrock at Bonn.

³ Taken from Nohl I, pp. 355-356. Nohl copied the autograph still in the possession of Kanka who was then (1865) 94 years old.

⁴ Nohl quotes on p. 356 the text of the document, dated May 2, 1816, authorizing Kanka to draw 600 gulden V.C. from the House of Ballabene at Prague.

As soon as my latest engraved pianoforte works have been published, you will receive copies of them and also of the Schlacht and so forth — I crave your forgiveness, I beg you to forgive me, my noble friend. I will think out some other means of pressing on with this affair in the most suitable way.

In haste, your friend and admirer

L. v. BEETHOVEN

(632) *To Ferdinand Ries, London*

[Autograph in the Beethovenhaus, Bonn, H. C. Bodmer collection]

MY DEAR RIES!   VIENNA, *May* 8, 1816

This is a rather belated reply to your letter. But I have been ill and have had a great deal to do. So it was not possible to send an answer any sooner — Well, let me deal first with the most necessary matter — Of the ten gold ducats I have not yet received one farthing; and now I am beginning to think that Englishmen too are generous only in England. Such is the case, for instance, with the *Prince Regent* from whom I have not even received the cost of copying *my Schlacht which I sent him*, nay more, not even a written or verbal acknowledgment — And here *Fries* [1] *deducted* six gulden A.C. from the amount I received from Birchall, and, in addition, for postage 15 gulden A.C. Tell that to B[irchall]. And see to it that you yourself receive the draft for the ten ducats, or we shall have the same experience as we had the first time — What you *tell me about Neate's undertaking would be a desirable proposition for me.* I need the money. My income amounts to 3,400 gulden in paper money. I pay 1,100 for rent, and my servant and his wife cost me about 900 gulden. So you can work out how much is left. Moreover I have to support my little nephew entirely. Until now he has been at a boarding school. That costs up to 1,100 gulden and, even so, it is not a good school. Hence I shall have to start a proper household where I can have him to live with me — In order to be able merely to exist in Vienna, one must earn a great deal! Yet the end is never in sight, because — because — because — well, you know all about that — In regard to the dedication I will write to you some other

[1] See Letter 765, p. 672, n. 3.

TOBIAS HASLINGER (1787–1842)
From an engraving by Joseph Kriehuber (1842)
(*Historisches Museum der Stadt Wien*)

time — As well as a concert I should also welcome a few commissions from the Philharmonic Society — By the way, my dear pupil Ries ought to sit down and dedicate *some sound composition* to me, whereupon *the master would reply and pay him back in the same coin — How am I to send you my portrait?* I hope soon to have news *from Neate also; do hustle him a bit.* Rest assured, however, of my real interest in your good fortune. *Do urge Neate to bestir himself and to write — My best greetings to your wife.* Unfortunately I have no wife. I have found *only one* [1] whom no doubt I shall *never possess. Yet I am not* on that account a *woman-hater.*

Your true friend

BEETHOVEN

(633) *To the Countess Anna Marie Erdödy, Padua* [2]

[*Autograph in the possession of Dr. A. Rosenthal*]

MY DEAR AND BELOVED FRIEND! VIENNA, *May* 13, 1816
Perhaps you believe, and quite rightly, that I have completely *forgotten all about you.* But indeed that is only what appears to be the case. My brother's death caused me great sorrow ; and then it necessitated *great efforts* to save my nephew, who is very dear to me, from the influence of his depraved mother. I succeeded in doing this. But so far I have not yet been able to make a *better arrangement* for him than to place him at a boarding school, which means that he is separated from me ; and what is a boarding school compared with the immediate sympathetic care of a father for his child? For I now regard myself as his father ; and I keep on wondering how I can have this treasure, who is very precious to me, nearer to me, so as to be able to influence him more directly and to his greater advantage — But how difficult is that for me! — Moreover, for the last six weeks I have been in very poor health, so

---

[1] This is a literal translation of the original German. Beethoven obviously means that he had found only one woman whom he would like to marry.

[2] The address on the verso of the autograph is 'Padua, in Italy'. According to Schöne, p. 7, the Countess, her family and her household after living for a time on her estate, Schloss Paukowitz in Croatia, spent a year at Padua and then settled at Munich. Schöne does not specify the year, but from the address on this letter, which is dated, it must have been 1816.

much so that frequently I have thought of my death. I do not dread it. Yet I should be dying too soon so far as my poor Karl is concerned — I gather from your last few lines to me that you, my dear friend, are still suffering a great deal. Man cannot avoid suffering; and *in this respect his strength must stand the test*, that is to say, he must *endure without complaining and feel his worthlessness* and *then again* achieve *his perfection*, that perfection which the Almighty will then bestow upon him — Well, Linke will by this time be with you.[1] May he *afford you pleasure by means of his gut strings* — Brauchle, no doubt, will not refrain from *using everything* and, as usual, you will make use of him day and night [2] — As for that bird Sperl,[3] I hear that you are not satisfied with him, but why I do not know. I hear, however, that you are looking for another steward. I beg you not to be hasty and to acquaint me with your *views and intentions* in this matter. Perhaps I can give you *some helpful information*; but perhaps you are not quite fair to *Sperl in his cage?* — I embrace your children and I am expressing this in a trio.[4] No doubt your children are progressing every day towards perfection — Let me know quite soon, very soon, how you are faring on that little *foggy spot of the earth* where you are now.[5] Certainly, even if I do not always mention or express this to you at once, I take the greatest interest in *your joys* and *sorrows*. How long do you intend to stay at Padua and where are you going to live in future? — There is going to be an alteration in the dedication of the *violoncello sonatas*, which, however, will not alter either *you* or *me* [6] —

Dear precious Countess, in haste I remain your friend

BEETHOVEN

---

[1] Linke, the cellist, was then living with the Countess and her family.

[2] Beethoven, as usual, is punning, this time on the various meanings of the verb 'brauchen'.

[3] Sperl was the Countess's steward. The German 'Sperl' or 'Sperling' means 'sparrow'.

[4] Beethoven was then composing another trio in F minor for pianoforte, violin and cello. See Nottebohm, *Zweite Beethoveniana* (Leipzig, 1887), p. 345.

[5] I.e. Padua.

[6] See *KHV.* 284. Beethoven thought of dedicating Op. 102 to Charles Neate. But Artaria's edition of these sonatas, published in 1819, included the dedication to the Countess.

(634) *To the Countess Anna Marie Erdödy, Padua*

[*Autograph not traced*] [1]

DEAR AND BELOVED FRIEND!   VIENNA, *May* 15, 1816

I had already written the enclosed letter [2] when I met Linke today and heard about your grievous blow, the sudden loss of your dear son [3] — What comfort can I give you? Nothing hurts more than the rapid and unforeseen departure of those who are near and dear to us. Thus I too cannot forget the death of my poor brother. The only consolation is — that one can believe that those who have suddenly departed suffer less — But I feel the deepest sympathy for you in your irreparable loss — Perhaps I have not yet told you that I too have not been feeling at all well for a considerable time. That is another reason for my long silence. Then, in addition, there are the cares connected with my Karl whom I often intended to attach to your dear son — I am overcome with grief on your account and also on my own, for I loved your son — Heaven watches over you and will not want to increase the great sorrows with which you are already afflicted, particularly as your state of health may possibly become still more enfeebled. But bear in mind that your son might have had to go into battle and like millions of others there meet his death. And remember that you still are the *mother* of two dear and promising children — I trust that I shall soon have news of you. I weep with you here. And now let me ask you not to lend an ear to all the gossip about why I was not writing to you. And pay no attention to Linke who is devoted to you, I admit, but who is *very fond of gossiping* — Besides I firmly believe, dear Countess, that you and I need no go-between.

In haste, with kind regards, your friend

BEETHOVEN

[1] Taken from Jahn's transcript in the Stadtbibliothek, Vienna.

[2] I.e. the preceding letter no. 633. Both letters were probably sent off together.

[3] The Countess's son Fritzl, who had died suddenly, not in Croatia, as stated in *TDR* III, 552, but evidently at Padua.

(635) To Charles Neate, London

[Autograph in the Heineman Foundation collection, Cambridge, Mass.]

MON TRES CHER AMI!   VIENNA, May 15, 1816

L'amitiè de vous envers moi me pardonnerà touts le fauts contre la langue Françaises, mais la hâte ou j'ecris la lettre, ce peu d'exercice et dans ce moment même sans dictionnaire Francais tout ce la m'attire surement encore moins de critique qu'en ordinairement —

Avanthier on me portait un extrait d'une gazette anglaise nomèe Morning Cronigle, ou je lisois avec grand plaisir, qu'on la sociétè philarmonique à donne ma sinfonie en A, le 23ᵐᵉ Mars c'est une grande satisfaction pour moi. Mais je souhais bien d'avoir de vous même des nouvelles, que vous ferès avec tous les compositions, que j'ai vous donnès, vou m'aves promis ici, de donner un concert pour moi, mais ne prenes mal, si je mefis un peu, quond je pense que le prince regent d'angleterre ne me dignoit pas ni d'une reponse ni d'une autre reconnoissance pour la Bataile, que j'ai envoye a son Altesse, et lequelle on a donnèe si souvent a Londre, et seulement les gazettes annoncoient le reussir de cet oeuvre et rien d'autre chose — come j'ai deja ecrit une lettre anglaise a vous mon tres cher ami, je trouve bien de finir, je vous ai ici depeignèe ma situation fatal ici, pour attend tout ce de votre Amitiè, mais helas pas une lettre de vous — Ries ma ecrit, mais vous connoisses bien dans ces entretiens entre lui et moi, ce que je vous ne trouve pas necessaire d'expliquer —

J'espère donc cher ami bientôt une lettre de vous, ou j'espere de trouver de nouvelles de Votre sante et aussi de ce, que vous aves fait à Londres pour moi — adieu donc,

quant à moi je suis

e je serai toujour votre vrai ami

BEETHOVEN

(636) *To Charles Neate, London*

[*MS in the Beethovenhaus, Bonn, H. C. Bodmer collection*] [1]

MY DEAR NEATE!   VIENNA, *May* 18, 1816

By a letter of Mr. Ries I am acquainted with your happy arrival at London. I am very well pleased with it, but still better I should be pleased if I had learned it by yourself.

Concerning our business, I know well enough, that for the performance of the greater works, as: the Symphony, the Cantata, the Chorus and the Opera you want the help of the Philharmonic Society, and I hope your endeavour to my advantage will be successful.

Mr. Ries gave me notice of your intention to give a concert to my benefit. For this triumph of my art at London I would be indebted to you alone; but an influence still wholesomer on my almost indigent life would be to have the profit proceeding from this enterprise. You know that in some regard I am now father to the lovely lad you saw with me; hardly I can live alone three months upon my annual salary of 3400 florins in paper, and now the additional burden of maintaining a poor orphan — you conceive how welcome lawful means to improve my circumstances must be to me. As for the Quatuor in F minor, you may sell it without delay to a publisher, and signify me the day of its publication as I should wish it to appear here on the very day.[2] The same you be pleased to do with the two Sonatas Op. 102 for pianoforte and violoncello [3]; yet with these last it needs no haste.

I leave entirely to your judgment to appoint my reward for both the works, to wit, the Quatuor and the Sonatas.[4] The more the better.

Be so kind to write me immediately for two reasons: 1st

---

[1] Written in English in another hand and signed by Beethoven.

[2] Op. 95, published by Steiner in September, 1816. In C. B. Oldman's opinion the London edition of this work may have been published by Clementi & Co. a little earlier.

[3] The following sentence has been added in another hand: 'These were dedicated by the author to Mr. Neate'. Beethoven, who intended to dedicate these two cello sonatas, first published by Simrock in March, 1817, to the Countess Erdödy, dedicated a manuscript copy of them to Charles Neate in January, 1816. See *KHV*. 283.   [4] Op. 95 and 102.

that I may not be obliged to shrink up my shoulders when they ask me, if I got letters from you, and 2dly, that I may know how you do, and if I am in favour with you. Answer me in English if you have to give me happy news (for example those of giving a concert to my benefit), in French if they are bad ones.

Perhaps you find some lover of music to whom the Trio, and the Sonate with the violin,[1] Mr. Ries had sold to Mr. Birchall, or the Symphony arranged for the harpsichord might be dedicated,[2] and from whom there might be expected a present.

In expectation of your speedy answer, my dear friend and countryman, I am wholly yours

LUDWIG VAN BEETHOVEN

Je vous pries de remettre l'incluse à Monsieur Ferdinand Ries chèz Mr. B. A. Goldschmidt.

(637) *To Sigmund Anton Steiner*

[Autograph in the Stadtbibliothek, Vienna]

[VIENNA, May, 1816]

Since no other course is practicable, in the devil's name the L[ieutenan]t G[enera]l must betake himself tomorrow to Herr von Rupprecht — If this is not done, we shall regard the omission as a declaration that this property which we disposed of has now returned to our possession and that we can make use of it as we like [3] —

THE G[ENERALISSIM]O
(in thunder and lightning)

---

[1] Op. 97 and 96. Both these works were published by Birchall.

[2] Probably the pianoforte arrangement of the seventh symphony, Op. 92, also published by Birchall.

[3] Possibly a reference to the 25 Scottish songs, Op. 108, which Beethoven set to music for George Thomson and which J. B. Rupprecht was to translate. The English edition appeared in June, 1818. The German edition was published in July, 1822, by A. M. Schlesinger, Berlin, with a dedication to Prince Anton Heinrich Radziwill.

(638) *To the Archduke Rudolph*

[*Autograph not traced*] [1]

[VIENNA, *May*, 1816]

I took the rooms thinking that Y.I.Highness would refund me to a small extent. Otherwise I would not have taken them —

(639) *To Ferdinand Ries, London*

[*Autograph in the Beethovenhaus, Bonn*]

MY DEAR R[IES]!   VIENNA, *June* 11, 1816

I am sorry that you must again disburse some postage money on my behalf. As much as I like to help and serve everybody, so much does it distress me to have to trouble other people with my affairs — So far not one of the ten ducats has put in an appearance. And thus the conclusion to be drawn is that in England as in our country there are windbags and people who do not keep their word — When saying this I am not making you responsible for anything that has happened — In any case I must beg you to apply once more to Herr Birchall for the ten ducats and to see that you yourself get them. I assure you on my honour that I have defrayed expenses amounting to 21 gulden A.C.; and that sum does not include the copyist's bill and several postage fees in bank-notes. The money was not even remitted to me in ducats, although you yourself wrote to me that it was to be remitted to me in Dutch ducats — So in England too there are some conscientious people who think nothing of breaking their word ? ! ! — As for the trio, the *Viennese publisher* has suggested to me that *this work should appear in London on the last day of August.*[2] Please therefore be so kind as to speak to Herr B[irchall] about it — H[err] B[irchall] can make preparations for the pianoforte arrangements of the symphony in A, for as soon as the Viennese

---

[1] Taken from Nottebohm, *Zweite Beethoveniana* (Leipzig, 1887), p. 346. This draft of a letter, or portion of a letter, is written in a sketch-book for 1815 and 1816.

[2] Op. 97, published by Steiner in September, 1816.

publisher names the day, I will inform you or B[irchall] immediately [1] —

As I have not had a syllable from Neate either since his arrival in L[ondon], please ask him now to let you have a reply to my question whether he has already disposed of the F minor quartet,[2] because I should like to publish it immediately in Vienna as well, and also to let me know what I am to expect in connexion with the cello sonatas? [3] I am almost ashamed to mention all the other works which I gave him, ashamed, that is, of myself for having again given in to him so trustfully, so completely and without making any conditions save those which friendly considerations would devise for my own advantage — Someone gave me to read the translation of a notice in the *Morning Cronigle* about the performance of the symphony.[4] No doubt to this work and to all the others which Neate took away with him exactly the same thing will happen as happened to the Schlacht; and presumably in this case too all that I shall gain, as in the case of the Schlacht, will be to read about the performances in the newspapers — The pianoforte arrangement of the symphony in A was copied quickly; and after carefully checking it I made the person who arranged it alter a few passages which I will let you know about. All my best greetings to your wife. In haste, your sincere friend

BEETHOVEN

NB.[5] Have you dedicated your E♭ concerto to the Archduke Rudolph? And why did you not write to him yourself about it? —

(640) *To the Archduke Rudolph, Baden*

[Autograph in the Gesellschaft der Musikfreunde, Vienna]

YOUR IMPERIAL HIGHNESS!   VIENNA, *July* 11, 1816

In view of your gracious favours to me I am surely justified in hoping that you will not attach *any ulterior motive* to the dedi-

---

[1] The pianoforte arrangement of Op. 92.
[2] Op. 95.   [3] Op. 102.
[4] Here the remark 'probably in A' has been added in another hand. Op. 92.
[5] Written on the left side of the second page.

cation I am enclosing, a dedication which I have rather mischievously ventured to make (but only so as to give you a surprise). The work was composed for Y.I.H. or, rather, owes its existence to you; and is the world (the world of music, I mean) not to know about it? ¹ — I shall soon have the pleasure of being able to wait upon Y.I.H. at Baden. Until now the condition of my chest has not allowed me to do so, notwithstanding all the efforts of my doctor, who on that account did not want me to leave Vienna. All the same, I am better. I hope to hear only good and heartening news about the condition of your health which is causing us anxiety —

Your Imperial Highness's

loyal and most obedient

LUDWIG VAN BEETHOVEN

(641) *To Sigmund Anton Steiner, Vienna*

[*Autograph in Stifts- och Landsbiblioteket, Linköping*]

DEAR LIEUTENANT G[ENERA]L !   BADEN, *July* 16, 1816

No doubt you have now received the other verses.² The tempo has been marked in pencil. Please do not forget it — In regard to B[aron] J[ohann] P.³ I noticed, as was to be expected, that things were not being done without a fair amount of cheating, nothing to be set going until August 3rd and so forth. Well, may God not punish him — But one must be on one's guard — Cavatevi ⁴ —

At the moment I have not got the specification beside me in order to see when the bills of exchange will fall due. Meanwhile so as to be ready for all emergencies, just enter in your book that you have received them from me for safe keeping until it is time to dispose of them, or if I go into town; and

---

¹ The sonata for violin and pianoforte, Op. 96, was published by Steiner in July, 1816.
² According to *KHV.* 278, Beethoven is referring to his second setting of Rupprecht's poem 'Merkenstein'. It was published by Steiner in September, 1816, as Op. 100.
³ Baron Johann Pasqualati.
⁴ In the opinion of Professor E. R. Vincent Beethoven has conflated his Latin and Italian to produce a word meaning 'be on your guard'. The Latin 'caveo' which has this meaning has been given an Italian verbal imperative inflection.

the same arrangement applies to the interest — 'He did not think that *you would be* so cunning', that is what he writes. Meanwhile I have achieved my object; and, at an rate, it was better than *to tell him the exact truth* —

You see that I place entire confidence in you. All I ask of you is to act as a friend and to see that this sum which is my sole capital (and small at that) shall bring me in as much interest as possible *and also as safely as possible.* At the moment I am in an embarrassing situation on account of my nephew, who at the same time is dearer to me than everything else. But things will right themselves. Let me add that you will always find me behaving to you not only as a man of honour but also as a true friend —

With all my heart I embrace you —

Your friend

L. v. BEETHOVEN

The best G[eneralissim]o to those who are good —
— very devil ——————————————————— bad.

(642) *To Gottfried Christoph Härtel, Leipzig*

[*Autograph in the Beethovenhaus, Bonn, H. C. Bodmer collection*]

MY DEAR HERR VON HÄRTEL!   VIENNA, *July* 19, 1816

You have sent me several times a most friendly invitation to offer you once again some of my compositions. Without recalling our former connexions I must remind you that it has always given me very great pleasure to deal with you. But I greatly fear that in view of the prices which my compositions now fetch, you will want to cut down my fees to an unduly low figure. Nevertheless I will make the attempt. But at any rate you cannot expect me to be a loser. For instance, I remember that you refused to give me 100 gulden A.C. for a grand pianoforte trio.[1] And yet I get 50 or even 60 gold ducats for that kind of composition.

Boasting is foreign to my character. So all I can do is to

---

[1] See Letter 304 of April 12, 1811, in which Beethoven offered Breitkopf & Härtel the trio which Steiner published in September, 1816, as Op. 97.

offer you the following works: a new sonata for pianoforte solo,[1] variations with an introduction and a beginning for pianoforte, violin and violoncello on a well-known theme by Müller.[2] These belong to my early works, but they are not poor stuff. Eighteen Scottish songs which you can easily have translated at Leipzig.[3] They are all for voice and pianoforte with violin and violoncello accompaniment. A grand scena for bass voice with several choruses (German text).[4] A march with chorus and full orchestra.[5] I offer you all these works for a fee of 130 gold ducats. I cannot let you have any of them separately, because, if I did, I should be a loser — But please let me have a reply at once, so that I may know what steps to take accordingly — It so happens that I am never in very good health and owing to many other set-backs can only now go into the country [6] — My unhappy brother died on November 15, 1815. The care of his child has devolved entirely on me, for unfortunately he is *morally without a mother* as well — We will not say anything about our other world affairs or, rather, our national affairs. *Eurus* [7] will be always and ever with us, producing a stagnant swamp!!!

In haste, your most devoted

L. v. BEETHOVEN

[1] The pianoforte sonata in A, dedicated to the Baroness Ertmann, was published by Steiner in February, 1817, as Op. 101.

[2] Variations in G major for pianoforte, violin and cello on a song 'Ich bin der Schneider Kakadu' in Wenzel Müller's light opera 'Die Schwestern von Prag'. These variations were published by Steiner in May, 1824, as Op. 121a.

[3] These 18 Scottish songs were gradually added to and became 25 songs, which were published by Thomson in June, 1818, and by A. M. Schlesinger, Berlin, in July, 1822, as Op. 108.

[4] Probably the score of Beethoven's setting of G F. Treitschke's text 'Es ist vollbracht', the pianoforte arrangement of which had been published by Steiner in July, 1815. In *KHV*. this composition is listed as WoO 97.

[5] Probably no. 6 of Op. 113, Beethoven's incidental music for Kotzebue's 'Die Ruinen von Athen'. This march and chorus were rewritten for 'Die Weihe des Hauses' produced at the opening of the new theatre in the Josephstadt on October 3, 1822. The work was first published in October, 1822, by Steiner in a pianoforte arrangement as Op. 114. The score was not published until April, 1826, again by Steiner.

[6] According to Letter 641 Beethoven was either in the country or had only gone there for a few days to make arrangements for his stay.

[7] I.e. the east wind, the pernicious effect of which is constantly referred to by classical writers, notably Homer.

(643) *To Robert Birchall, London*

[*MS in the Beethovenhaus, Bonn, H. C. Bodmer collection*] [1]

MONSIEUR,   VIENNA, *July* 22, 1816

J'ai reçue la Declaration de propriété de mes Oeuvres ulterierement cédé à Vous pour y adjoindre ma signature. Je suis tout à fait disposés à seconder vos voeux sitôt, que cette affaire sera entièrement en ordre en égard de la petite somme de 10 ducats d'or la quelle me vient encore pour le frais de la copiature, de poste de lettre etc. comme j'avois l'honneur de vous expliquer dans une note détaillée sur ces objects.[2] Je vous invite donc Monsieur de bien vouloir me remettre ces petit object, pour me mettre dans l'Etat de pouvoir vous envoyer le Document Susdit. Agrées Monsieur l'assurance de l'estime la plus parfait avec laquelle j'ai l'honneur de me dire

LOUIS VAN BEETHOVEN

(644) *To Cajetan Giannatasio del Rio*

[*Autograph not traced*] [3]

DEAR FRIEND !   [VIENNA, *July* 28, 1816]

Several circumstances induce me to have Karl to live with me. So, as I have this in view, allow me to send you the amount for the coming quarter, at the end of which Karl will leave your boarding school — Do not attribute this move to any unfavourable criticism of yourself or your respected boarding school, but ascribe it to many other urgent factors connected with the welfare of Karl. It is an experiment; and as soon as I have begun it I will ask you to assist me with your

---

[1] Written in another hand and signed by Beethoven.

[2] An itemed statement of expenses incurred for copying and postage, amounting to £5, is quoted in Nohl, no. 141, *KFR*, no. 542 and *P.*, no. 444, but is not in the autograph. Perhaps it was written on a separate sheet which has since disappeared. On the other hand the autograph of Beethoven's letter to Ferdinand Ries of February 10, 1816 (Letter 609) has a list of copying and postal expenses amounting to ten Dutch ducats, approximately £5.

[3] Taken from *TDR* III, 561. Thayer transcribed the autograph, which was then in London.

advice, in fact, to allow Karl to visit your boarding school occasionally. We shall always be grateful to you ; and indeed we shall never forget your attention and the excellent care of your worthy wife, such care as can only be compared to that of the very best of mothers — I would send you at least four times the amount I am now sending you, if only my situation would allow it. Meanwhile if my circumstances improve in the future, I will seize every opportunity of honouring and recalling in some definite way the remembrance of your having laid the foundations of the physical and moral well-being of my Karl — In regard to the Queen of Night the present arrangements are to stand ; and even if K[arl] should be operated on at your school,[1] in which case he will be laid up for a few days and therefore more sensitive and irritable than usual, she is to be admitted even less often, seeing that so far as K[arl] is concerned, all those impressions might easily be renewed ; and that we cannot allow. How much we can count on her improvement, you will see from the disgusting scrawl which I am enclosing ; the only reason why I am sending it to you is that you may see how right I am to hold fast to the attitude I have adopted towards her once and for all. Meanwhile I have replied to her this time not like a Sarastro [2] but like a Sultan — Should Karl's operation take place at your school, although I would gladly spare you this trouble, please do let me have details of all the disturbing arrangements and extra expenses which it will cause in your house. With the deepest gratitude I will repay you all. And now all good wishes. My warmest greetings to your dear children and your excellent wife, to whose further care I even now entrust my Karl. I am leaving Vienna tomorrow morning, but I shall come in frequently from Baden.[3]

With kindest regards, I remain ever yours

L. v. BEETHOVEN

[1] According to Beethoven's diary Karl underwent his operation for hernia at his boarding school on September 18th.

[2] Beethoven is pursuing his comparison of his situation to that of the characters in Mozart's 'Zauberflöte'. He often referred to Karl's mother as the 'Queen of Night'.

[3] At Baden Beethoven stayed in Count Ossolinsky's house, Allandgasse 9. The house still exists as Schloss Braiten, Braitnerstrasse 26.

(645) *To Nikolaus Zmeskall von Domanovecz, Vienna*

[Autograph in the Nationalbibliothek, Vienna]

[BADEN, *Summer,* 1816]

The next time I shall write about something else — Don't be angry — Be so kind as to let me have the number of your house, so that I can write to you direct — Now don't be angry and do reply at once — Beethoven is at C[ount] Ossolinsky's house in the Allandgasse.[1]

(Herr von Czerny is politely requested to deliver this letter to Herr von Zmeskall, as I don't know the latter's number)[2]

(646) *To Dr. Johann Bihler, Vienna* [3]

[Autograph in the collection of the late Stefan Zweig]

DEAR BIHLER!   [BADEN, *Summer,* 1816] [4]

This is just to inform you that at present I am at Baden and in excellent health — thanks not to the company here, but most certainly to the really lovely natural surroundings [5] —

---

[1] I.e. at Baden. See Letter 644, p. 589, n. 3.

[2] This bracketed sentence is written on the verso of the note which is addressed in Beethoven's hand. The note has no signature.

[3] Dr. Johann Bihler (or Biehler), a physician by profession, was tutor to the son of Baron Johann Baptist von Puthon, a wealthy business man and banker. Later he became tutor to the family of the Archduke Karl.

[4] This letter, which is generally dated 1817, was probably written in 1816, when Beethoven had settled at Baden.

[5] The autograph is not signed.

(647) *To Peter Joseph Simrock* [1]

[*Autograph in the Beethovenhaus, Bonn, H. C. Bodmer collection*]

[VIENNA, *Summer*, 1816]

MY VERY FINE OVERCOAT OF YOUR WORTHY PAPA! [2]

I am here and — not there, where I was [3] — Should you want to see me again, you will find me at home this morning at about eleven (11) o'clock —

I am expecting you and I remain your most devoted

L. v. BEETHOVEN

(648) *To Nikolaus Zmeskall von Domanovecz, Vienna*

[*Autograph in the Beethovenhaus, Bonn, H. C. Bodmer collection*] [4]

BADEN, *August* 18, 1816

DEAR AND BELOVED Z[MESKALL]!

Since there is not much time to write to you about several matters, I am just asking you to be so kind as to let me know how you set about engaging a new servant. Do you send a message to the police? or what do you do? — My present servant thrust himself upon me. Although I had reason to be dissatisfied with the other one, yet, if this one had not forced me to take him, I should have waited until I had found a really excellent one — But please give up the idea that no servant can ever put up with me. I myself have given notice to all, or most, of them, with the exception of the one who left me to go to the C[ountess] Erdödy; and he had been seven years in my service — If you took on the one whom *I myself* recently *got rid of,* (please note that I dismissed him), then I think that, seeing that I discharged him in a manner for which

---

[1] Peter Joseph Simrock (1792–1868), the second son of the Bonn music publisher Nikolaus Simrock, first established his own publishing firm at Cologne in 1812. But after his father's death in 1832 he took over the firm at Bonn. He was succeeded by his youngest son, Friedrich August, born at Bonn in 1837, who in 1870 moved the business to Berlin.

[2] Beethoven is here playing on the words 'Überrock' (overcoat) and 'Simrock'.

[3] Beethoven means that he has come into Vienna from Baden where he is staying. Young Simrock was staying in the Landstrasse, no. 40.

[4] Letters 647 and 648 were first published in the *Beethoven-Jahrbuch*, 1953/54, pp. 51 and 62.

he should be grateful to me, he may be willing to help us to engage another one ; or perhaps we should go to the police — whatever you think — I should like to have one who is a bit of a tailor, or even a tailor by trade, married and, if possible, without children — For the time being I would engage him alone, but later on perhaps his wife as well — Monthly, 4 gulden boot money and 40 gulden — and livery.

If his wife were to join him, we should, of course, make a different financial arrangement — And please let me know exactly how much you now pay a servant with a wife? Or perhaps a housekeeper only? These are all matters which I, a poor Austrian musical drudge, must know. — Please forgive me, first of all, for worrying you with this business and, secondly, for asking you to reply at once. I could get rid of this one by the 25th ; and I am in a position to recover the 50 gulden which I very foolishly advanced to him — In haste, your

L. v. BEETHOVEN

(649) *To [Sigmund Anton Steiner]* [1]

[Autograph in the Stadtbibliothek, Vienna]

[VIENNA, *August,* 1816]

There are still some mistakes — to be corrected — in the q[uartet].[2] When are you going to send the list of the mistakes in the score, the parts and the quartet parts — You are asleep — I see that in order to liven things up I shall have to appear in thunder and lightning —

The G[ENERALISSIM]O

(650) *To Nikolaus Zmeskall von Domanovecz, Vienna*

[Autograph in the Nationalbibliothek, Vienna]

DEAR Z[MESKALL] !   [BADEN, *September* 3, 1816]

I have a servant who makes his way into other people's rooms with counterfeit keys. So it is an urgent matter. I ought

---

[1] The autograph bears no address. But in view of the signature this note was obviously intended for Steiner's firm.
[2] Op. 95.

BEETHOVEN
From a copy of the oil portrait by W. J. Mähler (1815)
(*Gesellschaft der Musikfreunde, Vienna*)

to have another servant by the 25th of this month. Indeed, if it were possible to get one now, I would chuck out my present one immediately — I will try to see you this afternoon after three o'clock or about four — In haste,

your friend

BEETHOVEN

(651) *To Sigmund Anton Steiner, Vienna*

[*Autograph in the Beethovenhaus, Bonn, H. C. Bodmer collection*]

MOST EXCELLENT GENERAL, BADEN, *September* 4, [1816]

The following letters are for *Schlemmer* [1] and Häring. *The latter lives quite close to you in the Kohlmarkt, at the Schwäbisches Haus.* Please deliver them at once, in the greatest haste, prestissimo, as speedily as possible; and sell these *sows* [2] immediately.

Volti subito [3]

You are to hand over to the Adjutant everything pertaining to the violoncello. I should like to have it clearly entered in the trio — Please report to me as soon as the trio is ready, so that I may send the Archduke a copy of it [4] — You must hurry, therefore, presto prestissimo; and spur on the Adjutant — If anyone sends me a letter, please forward it here citissime.[5] Everyone is making haste so that the public exchequers may be filled and the General Staff be suitably entertained! — Schlemmer lives in the Kohlmarkt at the little Brandauisches Haus. It is important too that this scoundrel should receive his communication immediately — Volti subito.[6] I hear that the song about 'Merkenstein' is to appear during the skating season,[7] i.e. Veni, Vidi, Vinci!!! [8] The Adjutant is still under suspicion in connexion with the score of the quartet.[9] Hence I recommend the most thorough investigation. *I have had a*

---

[1] See Letter 973, p. 844, n. 4. [2] Ink blots.

[3] P.T.O., here at the foot of page 1.

[4] Op. 97, published in September, 1816, was dedicated to the Archduke Rudolph. [5] With all speed. [6] This P.T.O. is at the foot of page 3.

[7] The song 'Merkenstein', Op. 100, was announced by Steiner on September 21, 1816. On account of its references to summer Beethoven is urging Steiner to publish it before the onset of winter. See *KHV*. 277-278.

[8] Beethoven's version of Julius Caesar's famous saying: 'Veni, vidi, vici'.

[9] Op. 95, published by Steiner in September, 1816.

look at it here, and it cannot be corrected without the score [1] — With all my heart I embrace the L[ieutenant] G[eneral] and wish him the penis of a stallion.

In haste, the G[ENERALISSIM]O

(652) *To Sigmund Anton Steiner, Vienna*

[*Autograph in the Beethovenhaus, Bonn, H. C. Bodmer collection*] [2]

[BADEN, *September* 4, 1816]

So as to avoid all errors you must know that in all those works of mine where in the violoncello part the treble clef is used, the notes should be played an octave lower, i.e. this passage

must sound as follows:

But if 'in 8va' is written over it, as here,

then it should sound like this:

If 'loco' is written,

---

[1] Beethoven probably means 'without his own manuscript'.
[2] The sheet with these directions was probably enclosed in the preceding letter (Letter 651). See *KHV*. 272-273.

then the notes are in the same position as in the treble clef,
namely :

(653) *To Nikolaus Zmeskall von Domanovecz, Vienna*

[*Autograph in the Nationalbibliothek, Vienna*]

DEAR Z[MESKALL]!   BADEN, *September* 5, 1816
    I don't know whether you found a note which I recently
left on your threshold.[1] I had too little time to be able to
see you — So I must repeat my request to you about a new
servant, since on account of his behaviour I cannot keep this
one — He was engaged on April 25th. Thus on September
25th he will have been with me for five months. He was paid
50 gulden in advance. His boot money is calculated from the
third month (in my service) and from that month at 40 gulden
a year ; likewise his livery should be calculated from the third
month. Although from the very first I never intended to keep
him and would gladly have had my 50 gulden back, yet I
continued to postpone making any change. At the same time
if I could find another servant, I would let this one go on the
25th of this month and would pay him 20 gulden as boot
money in my service and five gulden a month for livery, both
items calculated from the third month onwards and amounting
to a total of 35 gulden ; so I really ought to get back 15 gulden,
though no doubt I shall have to write them off. Meanwhile,
however, I should be recovering to a certain extent my 50
gulden — If you find someone suitable, he can earn here at
Baden 2 gulden a day ; and if he can cook a bit, he can use my
wood in the kitchen to cook on (I have a kitchen, although no
cooking is done for me) ; if he cannot cook, then, of course,
I would add a few kreuzers to his wages. — In Vienna, as soon
as I return to town for good, he will have 40 gulden a month,
and the remainder, livery, boot money and so forth calculated
from the third month in my service, just as I have done with

---

[1] Probably Letter 650.

the other servants — If he is something of a tailor, that would be very useful — There, I have again put forward my request. Please let me have a reply by the 10th of this month at latest, so that on the 12th I may give my servant 14 days' notice as usual. — Otherwise I must again keep him until next month ; yet every moment I would gladly be rid of him — You must know by now what sort of person *more or less I should like my new servant to be, that is to say, good, orderly behaviour, suitable references, married and without any murderous tendencies,* so that my life may be safe. For although the world is full of rascals of all kinds I should like to live a little longer —

Well, I shall expect your report on the servant question by the 10th of this month at latest — Don't be annoyed. I will soon send you my treatise on the four violoncello strings, worked out very systematically ; the first chapter is about *guts* in general — the second chapter deals with *gut strings* — and so forth.

I need not warn you any more to take care not to be wounded near certain fortresses. *Why, everywhere there is profound peace! ! ! ! !* All good wishes, most excellent little Zmeskall — I am ever un povero musico [1] and

your friend
BEETHOVEN

(NB. It may well be that I shall keep the servant for a few months only, since on account of my Karl I really must have a housekeeper —) [2]

(654) *To Johann Nepomuk Kanka, Prague*

[*Autograph in the Beethovenhaus, Bonn, H. C. Bodmer collection*]

MY DEAREST K[ANKA] !   BADEN, *September* 6, 1816
I am sending you herewith the receipt you asked for. Please be so kind as to arrange for me to receive the money at once and certainly before October 1st, and, what is more, without any deduction, such as has hitherto always been made. Further, I most earnestly beg you *not to send a draft for this money*

---

[1] A poor musician.   [2] This NB. is written at the foot of page 5.

to Baron P[asqualati] (when we meet, you shall hear the reason !!); but for the moment let this request remain between ourselves. Send the draft to me or, if necessary, to somebody else, but certainly not to Baron P[asqualati] — In future the best arrangement would be to pay me my share here, since, after all, *the rent for the great Kinsky house is paid in Vienna* —

Now for some of my present thoughts — The trio in question will soon be engraved and published ; and this is always preferable to copied music.[1] So you will receive it in engraved form together with several *other naughty children* of mine. Meanwhile please look only at their fine qualities and forgive these poor innocents any incidental human frailties —

By the way, I am full of cares, for I am now the real and true father [2] of my deceased brother's child ; and in this connexion I too could well have produced the second part of the Zauberflöte,[3] seeing that I also have a Queen of Night to deal with [4] —

Well, I kiss you and press you to my heart ; and I trust that soon again I shall be so successful that you will feel rather grateful to my Muse. My dear and beloved Kanka, I am your warm-hearted friend who greatly esteems you.

BEETHOVEN

(655) *To Sigmund Anton Steiner, Vienna*

[Autograph in the Stadtbibliothek, Vienna]

BADEN, *September 6,* [1816]

The General Staff is advised to despatch at once by tomorrow's post the enclosed open letter to Dr. Kanka at Prague,[5] concerning which, however, the greatest secrecy about the entire contents and especially about Baron P[asqualati] is

[1] Op. 97.

[2] The original has 'wirklicher leiblicher Vater' which, translated literally, should be 'the real bodily (or natural or factual) father'.

[3] Beethoven is referring either to Goethe's fragmentary sequel to 'Die Zauberflöte', published in 1802, or to Peter von Winter's opera 'Das Labirint', a sequel to Mozart's opera, which was produced in Vienna in 1798.

[4] Karl's mother, Johanna van Beethoven.

[5] The words 'to Dr. Kanka at Prague' are added at the foot of the first page of the autograph, on the third page of which Haslinger noted the year 1816. The letter referred to is, of course, the preceding one, Letter 654.

enjoined (good practice for persons of such lofty rank). It should be accompanied by the receipt which is already with the L[ieutenant] G[enera]l in Vienna ; and a cover should be wrapped round both documents. How are you getting on with the trio? ¹ Please let me have it soon. As I am staying on here for a while, do inform me when it is ready, so that I may have it sent to the Archduke from Vienna — Has Baron Pasqualati left for Milan yet? Please let us have a responsio — We are expecting some information soon from the General Staff — We present our compliments and in return are prepared to receive yours — The

G[ENERALISSIM]O

Please send citissime ² to me at Baden any letters which may arrive.

(656) *To Franz Christian Kirchhoffer, Vienna* ³

[Autograph in the Beethovenhaus, Bonn, H. C. Bodmer collection]

SIR !   BADEN, *September* 9, 1816
  You are receiving herewith from me the written communication intended for London. I have also signed it — Two experiences of dealing with Englishmen have intimidated me, although indeed Herr B[irchall] has been maligned. — Please be so kind as to give him my best regards. I will write to him myself in a few days *about the titles* of the various works.

I remain, Sir, your most devoted

LUDWIG VAN BEETHOVEN

  (Should you receive any other messages from L[ondon] for me, please write direct to me here, stating that your letter should be delivered at C[ount] Ossolinsky's house.) ⁴

¹ Op. 97.
² With all speed.
³ Little is known about Franz Christian Kirchhoffer, who in 1824 was an accountant in the firm of Offenheimer & Herz, where Franz Oliva was employed. See *FRBH* I, 263. This letter was first published in the *Beethoven-Jahrbuch*, 1953/54, p. 40.
⁴ This bracketed sentence is written on the verso with the date. Beethoven was living in a large house and park owned by the Polish Count Joseph Max Ossolinsky. Cf. Letter 644, p. 589, n. 3.

(657) *To Karl van Beethoven* [1]

[*Autograph in the Romain Rolland collection*]

[VIENNA, *shortly before September* 18, 1816]

MY DEAR K[ARL],

According to Herr v. Smetana's [2] prescription it is necessary for you to bathe a few times more before the operation.[3] Today the weather is favourable and just now it is still the right time. I shall wait for you at the Stubentor — Of course you must first ask H[err] v[on] G[iannatasio] for permission — Put on a pair of underpants or take them with you, so that you may put them on immediately after you have bathed, should the weather again become cool — *Has the tailor not yet called?* When he does, he is to measure you for linen underpants as well, for you need these. If Frau von G[iannatasio] knows where he lives, my servant too could ask him to go to you —

Well, all good wishes — I am — even on your account

your trouser button

L. V. BEETHOVEN

(658) *To Cajetan Giannatasio del Rio*

[*Autograph in the Royal College of Music*]

[VIENNA], *Sunday, September* 22, 1816

There are certain emotions which it is impossible to describe. Thus, when I received from you the news that Karl had got

---

[1] Karl van Beethoven (1806–1858), the only child of Beethoven's brother Caspar Carl and Johanna Reiss, was born on September 4, 1806. After his father's death in November, 1815, he became the ward of his uncle, the composer. The legal dispute between his mother and his uncle can be followed in the ensuing letters. In 1820 Beethoven finally succeeded in securing the entire responsibility for the education and upbringing of his nephew, an arrangement which was fraught with disaster for both parties. After an attempt at suicide in July, 1826, Karl was allowed to join the army. He obtained his officer's commission in 1832, married in the same year Karoline Naske, by whom he had five children, and then settled in the country near Vienna. For an excellent account of Karl van Beethoven see *FRBH* I, 452–461. His relations with his uncle have been made the subject of an interesting psychoanalytic study by E. and R. Sterba, *Beethoven and his Nephew* (New York, 1954, and in an English edition, 1957).

[2] Dr. Karl von Smetana (1774–1827) was a well-known surgeon in Vienna.

[3] Karl underwent his operation on Wednesday, September 18th.

over his operation successfully, my feeling of gratitude especially I found difficult to express — So you will spare me the effort of uttering or barely stammering out such words. — I know that you would have no objection to raise to the tribute which my feelings would gladly pay you — So I shall be silent — You will understand that I long to hear how my beloved K[arl] is now progressing. When informing me, please do not forget to send me your full address, so that I may write to you direct — Since you left me I have written several times to Bernard,[1] asking him to enquire at your house, but have received no reply. I am beginning to think that you must look upon me as a rather thoughtless barbarian, for H[err] B[ernard] has probably called on you just as seldom as he has written to me — It is out of the question, nay, absolutely impossible for me to have any fears about your excellent wife's attentions to Karl. But you will fully understand that it pains me not to be able to share the sufferings of my K[arl] and that I desire to hear *something at least* about his condition, and that too, very often. Well, now that I have given up such a heartless, unsympathetic friend as H[err] B[ernard], I must appeal to your friendship and kindness in this matter — I hope to have a few lines from you soon. Meanwhile please convey my best regards and a thousand thanks to your dear wife —

In haste, your
LUDWIG VAN BEETHOVEN

Please give Smetana my best respects and regards [2] —

(659) *To Antonia Brentano, Frankfurt am Main*

[Autograph in the Beethovenhaus, Bonn]

MY DEAR FRIEND,   [VIENNA, *September* 29, 1816] [3]

All my difficult circumstances which, admittedly, are soon going to improve, have prevented me from hesitating to accept the cheque which you and F[ranz] have sent me — I received it apparently from some stranger. He, however, did not go to

---

[1] For a full note on Joseph Karl Bernard see Letter 947, p. 812, n. 1.
[2] This postscript is added on the right side of the first page of the autograph.
[3] A note pinned to the autograph of this letter bears this date.

very much trouble over the matter, for as he did not find me at home when he first called, he came again a week later and delivered the cheque without asking to enter my room. Then when I went to Pacher's [1] the day before yesterday, they had received no notice and, according to their statement, knew nothing of the person who had signed the cheque — Hence I thought it necessary to inform you at once ; and I await your decisions in the matter — I would have returned the cheque to you, but, as you know, I understand nothing about business of this kind and therefore might easily make some mistake —

In haste, your devoted

BEETHOVEN

(660) *To Antonia Brentano, Frankfurt am Main*

[*Autograph in the Beethovenhaus, Bonn*]

MY BELOVED FRIEND ! VIENNA, *September* 29, 1816

I am introducing to you the son of Herr Simrock at Bonn.[2] I have made his acquaintance here. He can and will tell you a good deal about my present situation and, what is more, something too about Austria, your native land — I hear that you are in good health and that F[ranz], to whom I send very many greetings, has been made a senator and instead of becoming older is becoming younger and younger. May I ask F[ranz] very politely to be so kind as to assist Herr Simrock in the event of his having to make payments to me here and to arrange for drafts to be forwarded to me in the least expensive way —

I hear too that F[ranz] is now one of the pinnacles or, I should say, one of the pillars of that ancient town of Frankfurt ; and indeed we send him our heartfelt congratulations — Doubtless you have heard how I have become a father and how burdened I am with a father's very real cares — My poor nephew has been suffering from hernia, for which he recently underwent an operation and, I am glad to say, very successfully — Otherwise I have no important news to send you from

---

[1] Johann Martin Pacher, who became in 1820 one of the Directors of the Austrian National Bank, was a partner in the business firm of Pacher & Co.

[2] Peter Joseph Simrock, the second son of Nikolaus Simrock, the music publisher at Bonn, had been on a visit to Vienna in September. Cf. letter 647, p. 591, n. 1.

Vienna, apart from the fact that our government shows more and more that it will have to be *governed* and that we are convinced that we have not by any means experienced the *worst* — My heartfelt greetings to all your family; and I should like you to remember me for a moment with pleasure —

In haste, your friend

BEETHOVEN

(661) *To Franz Gerhard Wegeler, Coblenz* [1]

[*Autograph in the possession of Julius Wegeler*]

VIENNA, *September* 29, 1816

I am taking the opportunity of sending this note by Herr Simrock to remind *you of me* [2] — I hope that you received my copperplate engraving [3] and also the Bohemian glass.[4] When I take another trip to Bohemia you will again receive some present of that kind. — All good wishes. You are a husband and a father. So am I, but without a wife — My greetings to all your family and to our friends.

Your friend

L. V. BEETHOVEN

(662) *To Robert Birchall, London*

[*MS not traced*] [5]

MY DEAR SIR, VIENNA, *October* 1, 1816

I have duly received the £5 and thought previously you would not increase the number of Englishmen neglecting their word and honor, as I had the misfortune of meeting with two

---

[1] Franz Gerhard Wegeler, who had married Eleonore von Breuning in 1802, had been living at Koblenz since 1807 as a successful practitioner and Professor of Medicine.

[2] The autograph of this note which Beethoven gave to Peter Joseph Simrock to deliver has the following address on the cover: 'To friend Wegeler'.

[3] The engraving done in 1814 by Blasius Höfel after a pencilled sketch by Louis Letronne. It was published by Artaria. See illustration facing page 528.

[4] This drinking goblet is still in the possession of the Wegeler family and is illustrated on p. 55 of Stephan Ley's book, *Beethoven als Freund der Familie Wegeler-von Breuning* (Bonn, 1927).

[5] Taken from *KFR*, no. 558. The letter was written in English.

of this sort. In reply to the other topics of your favor, I have no objection to write variations according to your plan, and I hope you will not find £30 too much, the accompaniment will be a flute or violin or a violoncello; you'll either decide it when you send me the approbation of the price, or you'll leave it to me. I expect to receive the songs or poetry — the sooner the better, and you'll favor me also with the probable number of works of Variations you are inclined to receive of me. The sonata in G with the accompan^t. of a violin is dedicated to His Imperial Highness Archduke Rudolph of Austria — it is Op. 96. The Trio in B♭ is dedicated to the same and is Op. 97.[1] The Piano arrangement of the symphony in A is dedicated to the Empress of the Russians — meaning the wife of the Emp^r. Alexander — Op. 98.[2]

Concerning the expenses of copying and packing it is not possible to fix them beforehand, they are at any rate not considerable, and you'll please to consider that you have to deal with a man of honor, who will not charge one sixpence more than he is charged for himself. Messrs. Fries and Co.[3] will account with Messrs. Coutts and Co. — The postage may be lessened as I have been told. I offer you of my works the following new ones. A Grand Sonata for the pianoforte alone £40.[4] A Trio for the piano with accomp^t. of violin and violoncello for £50.[5] It is possible that somebody will offer you other works of mine to purchase, for ex. the score of the Grand Symphony in A. — With regard to the arrangement of this symphony for the Piano I beg you not to forget that you are not to publish it until I have appointed the day of its publication here in Vienna. This cannot be otherwise without making myself guilty of a dishonorable act — but the Sonata with the violin and the Trio in B flat may be published without any delay.

With all the new works, which you will have of me or which

---

[1] Op. 96 and 97 were published by Birchall in 1816.

[2] If the transcription of the original letter is correct, Beethoven himself made the slip of affixing the wrong opus number to the pianoforte arrangement of Op. 92.

[3] See Letter 765, p. 672, n. 3.

[4] Beethoven was then finishing his pianoforte sonata, Op. 101. See *KHV.* 279.

[5] Sketches for a pianoforte trio in F minor are extant. See Letter 633, p. 578, n. 4.

I offer you, it rests with you to name the day of their publication at your own choice; I entreat you to honor me as soon as possible with an answer having many orders for compositions and that they may not be delayed.

My adress or direction is

Monsieur Louis van Beethoven
No. 1055 and 1056 Seilerstätte,
3d. Stock, Vienna.

You may send your letter, if you please, direct to your most humble servant

LUDWIG VAN BEETHOVEN

(663) *To Cajetan Giannatasio del Rio*

[Autograph in the Royal College of Music]

[VIENNA, *early October,* 1816] [1]

Provided you have no objection, please send Karl immediately with the bearer of this note — As I was in a hurry, I forgot to mention that I have entered in my large book of debts all the affection and kindness which Frau v[on] G[iannatasio] bestowed upon my Karl during his illness, and that I will soon show that I still bear it in mind. —

Perhaps I shall see you today with Karl. In haste,

your devoted friend

L. V. BEETHOVEN

(664) *To Sir George Smart, London*

[MS not traced] [2]

DEAR SIR GEORGE, [VIENNA, *c. October* 11, 1816] [3]

Mr. Häring told me often that you directed and kindly arranged that my compositions were performed with vigour

---

[1] See Nohl, *op. cit.* p. 111, where Fanny gives the substance of the above letter, stating that Beethoven wrote it a few days after his visit with P. J. Simrock to her family on September 28th.

[2] Taken from *Leaves from the Journals of Sir George Smart,* by H. B. and C. L. E. Cox (London, 1907), pp. 52-54. The letter was written in English.

[3] In *op. cit.* the date of receipt of the above letter is given as October 25, 1816. Hence it was probably sent from Vienna a fortnight earlier.

and success. This induces me to hope that you will also take some trouble with the artist and assist him in a perplexity quite as unexpected as it is unmerited. I gave to Mr. Neate in great confidence in his honour and his views the following works. His intention was, as he said, to hand them all to the Philharmonic Society in my name, which Society would in lieu of any Honorarium or gift arrange a benefit concert for me. He mentioned this plan whenever he came here, adding that the execution would be the easier as he would come again into the direction of that Society on his return. However I heard nothing more of him or my works for many months. With astonishment I read in the papers an account taken from the *Morning Chronical* mentioning with enthusiasm the effect which one of my new symphonies had produced, and I suppose it was that in A,[1] but I heard nothing from Mr. Neate. At last after many applications he wrote me a letter, which I am sorry to say, throws his character in my eyes in a very bad light. He pretends to be in love with a young lady to distraction — he is to be refused if he continues to follow his profession, etc.[2] Before he ends, he very dryly says, that having given my three overtures to the above Society, they have spoilt all to such a point, that he lost all courage to undertake something for me. He on account of that young lady is prevented from playing my Sonatas in public, etc. I own that the three overtures do not belong to my best and great works, they being all occasional pieces composed for the theatre. The one in C did not displease when performed on the 4th of October last year in the presence of Mr. N[eate].[3] The one in E flat was composed for the opening of the theatre in Pesth in Hungary and pleased.[4] The 3rd in G is the overture of a little afterpiece, of course the style could not be great — it was often performed here and always with applause.[5] It is calculated not to begin a concert, but to be performed in the middle. Mr. Neate had in his possession

---

[1] Op. 92.

[2] For an elucidation of this episode the present editor is greatly indebted to Mr. A. R. Neate who, though not related to the family of Charles Neate, succeeded in tracing his present living descendants. The latter have kindly sent me the photograph (see illustration facing page 545) and some documents referring to Neate's marriage in October, 1816 to Catherine Mary Cazenove (1787–1861) of the Protestant branch of the famous de Cazenove family, some of whose members emigrated to England after the revocation of the Edict of Nantes. See Letters 683 and 1144.

[3] Op. 115.   [4] Op. 117.   [5] Op. 113.

other more essential works, he chose those three and it is very unfortunate that on account of them according to his judgment my musical name is all at once sunk to nothing. He paid twenty-five guineas for each of these overtures as his property according to a formal writing I gave him, but for all the other manuscript works which I gave him he returned nothing at all, not even a complimentary letter of acknowledgment or thanks. These works are:

Score of a Symphony in A. First movement in A, second in A minor, third in F, fourth in A.[1]

Score of a great Cantata, consisting of a Chorus in A No. 1, No. 2, Rec. in B with Chorus in F. No 3, Rec. in B and air with chorus.

No. 5, Rec. in A and Quartett in A, No. 6. Chorus in C.[2]

Score of a Grand Opera: Fidelio.

Do. of a great Chorus in D. Words of Goethe: Tiefe Stille.[3]

Do. of a Quartett in F minor for 2 Viol. ten. and Bass.[4]

Do. of a Sonata in C Piano and Violoncello.[5]

Do. do. do. do.[6]

NB. The Quartett is written for a small circle of connoisseurs and is never to be performed in public. Should you wish for some Quartetts for public performance I would compose them to this purpose occasionally. I mention here that I should like to receive regular orders from England for great compositions. All the above compositions were delivered to Mr. Neate in confidence and with the power to dispose of them for my sole benefit in London. I still am the right owner of them. The 5 guineas, which he has paid for copying them, and for which I thought he would think himself sufficiently repaid by performing them at his leisure, may be restituted to him on delivering the works to you.

I therefore take the liberty to empower you herewith to receive of Mr. Neate the above cited 7 works and I hope to his honour he will have no objection of delivering them into your hands. My view is that you should first select some of them, and arrange a concert for my benefit. After that you are welcome to give one or two nights for yourself — I hope it

[1] Op. 92. [2] Op. 136. [3] Op. 112. [4] Op. 95.
[5] Op. 102, no. 1. [6] Op. 102, no. 2, which is in D major, not C.

will be with success. Finally you'll please to offer these works of which some at least will easily enough find purchasers, for sale, I leave it entirely to the high sense of honour and love for the art, which Mr. Häring repeatedly assured me none possessed more than yourself. At least I am thoroughly persuaded that the two Englishmen, who have treated me very ill — very meanly — are very rare exceptions of the general character of your great nation. These two are the Prince Regent and Mr. Neate — enough of them!

All I beg you is to favour me with an answer as soon as possible. The season in your great city is soon coming, and I should wish to know my fate, and am very anxious to publish most of the above works here, which I will not do before your answer. Mr. N[eate] wished I should dedicate the two sonatas to him and I promised it — if he does not desist himself, let it be so. I hope my signature is sufficient to effectuate the delivery of the music to you as is my will and wish. Should anything be wanting, I am ready to perform it.[1]

Signed

LUDWIG VAN BEETHOVEN

My direction is : M. Louis van Beethoven
Sailerstätte 3 Stock
No. 1055 and 1056 à Vienne.

(665) *To Sigmund Anton Steiner*

[*Autograph in the possession of Dr. Max Thorek*]

[VIENNA, *c. October* 22, 1816]

MOST EXCELLENT L[IEUTENANT GENERA]L [GENERA]L [GENERA]L [GENERA]L —

Please send me the last proofs of the song cycle 'An die Entfernte'.[2] It is about time. By rights the most shocking

---

[1] A fragment of this letter is in the possession of J. E. Kite. It consists of the previous two sentences and the remainder of the letter, but Beethoven's signature is in his own hand.

[2] I.e. the song cycle 'An die ferne Geliebte', Op. 98, dedicated to Prince Lobkowitz and published by Steiner in October, 1816. In the autograph of this work, which is in the Beethovenhaus, Bonn, the title is 'An die entfernte Geliebte'.

607

blunders ought to be corrected in pencil in the copies which
have already appeared!!!! I request you, I mean to say that
I command you, to send me at about eleven o'clock tomorrow
morning the corrected copy I sent you from Baden as well as
one which has been corrected from it. I would now like to
send a copy soon to Prince Lobkowitz.[1] For, of course, I
cannot make use for that purpose of a single copy sent to me
from *Barbary* — Nobody asks how I am ; and yet I have been
in bed for the last eight days [2] —

The G[ENERALISSIM]o (in bed) [3]

(666) *To Tobias Haslinger*

[*Autograph in the Milwaukee Public Library, Dr. and Mrs. L. F. Frank collection*]

SIR — Adjuvans,　　　　　　　　　　　[VIENNA, *October*, 1816]
　　　I have seen nothing of the red-faced subaltern.[4] Probably
he did not wait at the house of the cashier Herr Damm, from
whom he should have brought me back a communication.[5]
So please send *him* again to the cashier about this, for some
money is due to me there. It is understood that the red-faced
fellow is to come to me straight from the Herr K. Damm.
I am sorry to have to trouble the L[ieutenan]t G[enera]l's
office, but I cannot use my own people for messages of this
kind. — So please send the red-faced fellow to the cashier Herr
Damm and thence to me. Please do not show Hebenstreit's [6]
letter about a German equivalent for pianoforte, but return it

---

[1] Prince Franz Joseph von Lobkowitz to whom the work was dedicated. He
died, however, on December 15, 1816, before receiving a copy of the work.

[2] Beethoven had contracted a violent chill and had been in bed since October
14th. See Letter 669.

[3] The address on the verso of the autograph is 'An den Generalleutnant
Gottlieb und Gottdank von Steiner'.

[4] Probably one of Steiner's employees.

[5] *KHV*. 350 quotes a copy of Beethoven's Diabelli variations, Op. 120,
dedicated in his handwriting to Herr von Damm, July, 1823. This copy is in the
Beethovenhaus, Bonn, H. C. Bodmer collection.

[6] Wilhelm Hebenstreit (1774–1854), born at Eisleben, settled in Vienna
about 1811 and from 1816 to 1818 edited the *Wiener Zeitung*. He was also a
writer of a journalistic vein and interested himself in various contemporary movements, such as the abolition of foreign musical terms in favour of their German
equivalents.

SIR GEORGE SMART (1776–1867)
From the oil portrait by William Bradley (1829)
(*National Portrait Gallery, London*)

to me; since I am neither empty-headed nor unscholarly,[1]
I have now got into the habit of taking his advice —
Have a good time, Herr A[DJUTAN]T,
2 — nd little R[A]SC[A]L.

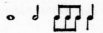

(667) *To Karl van Beethoven*

[*Autograph not traced*] [2]

[VIENNA, *October*, 1816]

To my nephew Karl! So far as I can see, there is still
a certain amount of poison in your system. Hence I do entreat
you to note down your mental and bodily requirements. The
weather is becoming colder. Do you need another blanket
or possibly your eiderdown? — Since I requested him to do
so, Herr von Smetana will have been to see you. The truss-
maker has called once already, but to no purpose. He has
promised me to call again, to bring you another truss and to
take away the old one to have it washed. He has already been
paid for everything —
All good wishes. May God enlighten your heart and soul.

Your uncle and friend
BEETHOVEN

(668) *To Carl Czerny*

[*Autograph in the Gesellschaft der Musikfreunde, Vienna*]

DEAR Z,[3]   [VIENNA, *October*, 1816]
If you can do so today, I request you to come to me at
about one o'clock, so that Karl may not fall behind too
much [4] —
Your most devoted
LUDWIG VAN BEETHOVEN

---

[1] Beethoven is playing on the words 'geleert' (empty) and 'ungelehrt' (un-
learned).   [2] Taken from *KFR*, no. 549.
[3] For an explanation of Beethoven's form of address see Letter 610, p. 560, n. 3.
[4] Carl Czerny had begun to give pianoforte lessons to Beethoven's nephew.

He went out yesterday for the first time. So he must not yet undertake too much all at once.

(669) To Nikolaus Zmeskall von Domanovecz

[*Autograph in the Nationalbibliothek, Vienna*]

DEAR Z[MESKALL] !   [VIENNA, *November* 3, 1816]
Your refusal to recommend the servants I have engaged I also cannot recommend — Please let me have at once through Herr Schlemmer [1] the papers, testimonials and so forth which you have about them — I have reason to entertain strong suspicions that they have committed a theft — Since the 14th of last month [2] I have been continually ill and have had to stay [3] in bed and in my room — All my plans for my nephew [4] have collapsed on account of those wretched people —

Ever yours
L. v. BEETHOVEN

(670) To Cajetan Giannatasio del Rio

[*Autograph in the Royal College of Music*]

DEAR FRIEND !   [VIENNA, *early November*, 1816] [5]
My household is almost exactly like a shipwreck or tends to resemble one. In short, a soi-disant expert in such matters has cheated me over these people. And, moreover, my health does not seem to be improving so very rapidly. So in these circumstances to engage a tutor, about whose qualifications and character I know nothing, and to leave the education of my Karl to mere chance, that I can never do, however great may be the manifold sacrifices that I may again have to make. Hence I request you, my dear G[iannatasio], to keep Karl for

---

[1] See Letter 973, p. 844, n. 4.
[2] In the autograph the words 'of last month' are added at the foot of the page.
[3] Followed by 'zum Theil' (partly), deleted.
[4] I.e. to remove Karl from his boarding school and have him taught at home.
[5] According to Nohl, *op. cit.*, p. 114, this letter was written during the first week of November, 1816.

another quarter. To your proposal that Karl should devote himself to music I will accede to this extent, that two or even three times a week he shall leave your school at about six o'clock in the evening and stay with me until the following morning, when he can be with you again at about eight o'clock. A daily arrangement would probably be too tiring for K[arl] and, since it would always have to be at the same time, too irksome and too great a tie for me also — During the present quarter we shall discuss more fully what arrangement would be most appropriate for K[arl] and, at the same time, would suit me financially; for in view of the present living conditions which are becoming ever worse and worse, I must regretfully allude to that aspect of the question. If your house at the end of the garden had been suitable from the point of view of my health, everything could have been easily arranged — In regard to what I owe you for the present quarter, I must ask you to come to me so that I may discharge my debt in person. For God has bestowed on the bearer of this letter a certain stupidity which no one could well begrudge him, if only it did not affect other people as well. — As to the other expenses entailed by Karl's illness or connected therewith, please be patient for a few days longer, because at the moment I have heavy disbursements to make in all directions. —

As to Smetana I should like to know also what I should do for him in return for the operation he has successfully performed, i.e. how he should be rewarded. If I were rich or, at any rate, not in the position in which we all (apart from the Austrian profiteers) are whom Fate has chained to this country, I would not raise such a matter. In any case, I only want a rough estimate of the amount. — All good wishes. With all my heart I embrace you and shall always regard you as a friend of myself and of my Karl —

With kindest regards from your

L. v. BEETHOVEN

(671) *To the Archduke Rudolph*

[*Autograph in the Gesellschaft der Musikfreunde, Vienna*]

YOUR IMPERIAL HIGHNESS!   [VIENNA, *c. November* 12, 1816]

I heard yesterday, and this report was confirmed by Count Troyer when I met him, that Y.I.H. had returned to Vienna — I am sending herewith the dedication of the trio to Y.I.H.[1] It is mentioned on this work; but indeed all the works on which your name is not mentioned and which are of any value whatsoever, are intended for Y.I.H. But you must not think that I have any design in this action. Since our great lords, however, are in the habit of suspecting self-interest in any action of this kind, I am going to let this prejudice *appear* to be justified on this occasion. For I must now beg Y.I.H. to do me a favour, the well founded reasons for which you will surely understand and which I hope you will most graciously grant — At the beginning of last month, i.e. October, I began to feel ill at Baden; and from October 15th until about eight days ago I was confined to my room and to bed. I had a rather dangerous feverish cold and I am still not allowed to be out of doors for very long. That too is the reason why I did not write to Y.I.H. when you were at Kremsir — May all the rich blessings which Heaven can shower on this earth be your portion. Such is the wish of Your Imperial Highness's

most obedient servant

LUDWIG VAN BEETHOVEN

(672) *To Cajetan Giannatasio del Rio*

[*Autograph in the Royal College of Music*]

DEAR FRIEND!   [VIENNA, *November* 14, 1816]

I should like to have Karl for tomorrow, for it is the anniversary of his father's death and we want to visit his

---

[1] Op. 97, which had been engraved and published by Steiner in September, 1816.

grave.[1] I shall come and fetch him perhaps at about twelve or one o'clock — I should like to know what has been the result of my treatment of Karl after your recent complaints — Meanwhile I have been very much touched at finding him so sensitive about his honour. While we were still at your house I dropped some hints about his tendency to be lazy. We walked along together more seriously than usual. Timidly he pressed my hand but found no response. At table he ate practically nothing and said that he felt very sad; but I failed to find out from him the cause of his sadness. Finally, during our walk he explained *that he was feeling very sad because he had not been able to work as hard as usual.* I then did my share and was even more friendly than before. This certainly shows his feeling of delicacy; and it is precisely traits of this kind that lead me to entertain hopes of his developing a fine character — If I don't come tomorrow, please send me just a few lines about the outcome of my meeting with K[arl]. —

I am again asking you to send me your account for incidental expenses during the last quarter. I felt certain that you had misunderstood my letter; and perhaps that was not the first time that this has happened — I entrust my dear orphan to your care and send you all my best remembrances — as always —

Your friend
BEETHOVEN

(673) *To Karl van Beethoven*

[*Autograph not traced*] [2]

[VIENNA, *late November*, 1816]

MY DEAR KARL OF MY HEART!

I can't see you today, not yet, because I have a great deal to do! And, moreover, I am not completely recovered. But do not be anxious about anything. Indeed I too mourn for your father, but the best way for us both to honour his memory is for you to pursue your studies with the greatest zeal and to endeavour to become an upright and excellent fellow, and for

---

[1] Karl's father had died on November 15, 1815.
[2] Taken from Aloys Fuchs's transcript in Tübingen University Library.

me to take his place and to be in every way a father to you;
and you see that I am making every effort to be all this to you.
Your faithful and loving uncle

L. v. BEETHOVEN

I will see you tomorrow for certain. All sorts of kind
messages to the whole G[iannatasio] family.

(674) *To Sigmund Anton Steiner*

[*Autograph in the Deutsche Staatsbibliothek, Berlin*]

[VIENNA, *November,* 1816]

I am sending you herewith — (as a present) — a little
field piece which should be put into the armoury at once.[1]
As for that worthy Diabolus,[2] he ought to be retained on
account of his skill in other pursuits; what should be altered
anywhere can be remedied as it was the last time with the
symphony in F [3] — As for a new sonata for pianoforte solo, well
then, as soon as 60 fully armed men present themselves, it can
be produced immediately.[4] My mind is running too on some
variations that would be suitable for a special festive occasion
and which could appear at once if only 40 fully armed men
would present themselves — For in regard to the State debt
of 1300 gulden, this cannot be attended to at the moment.
And in any case the 1300 gulden would look their best if they
were expressed as follows o o o o —
I am amazingly deferential to the L[ieutenan]t G[enera]l's
office.

L. v. BEETHOVEN

[1] Beethoven's song 'Der Mann von Wort', a setting of a poem by Friedrich
August Kleinschmid (1749–*c.* 1838) for treble voice with pianoforte accompaniment,
was published by Steiner in November, 1816, as Op. 99.

[2] I.e. Diabelli, who was employed in Steiner's firm, chiefly as proof-reader.

[3] Op. 93. Beethoven is referring to the corrections.

[4] Op. 101. The autograph, now in the Koch collection, bears the date
'November 1816' in Beethoven's hand. By the '60 fully armed men' Beethoven
means 60 gold ducats.

(675) *To Sigmund Anton Steiner*

[*Autograph in the Deutsche Staatsbibliothek, Berlin*]

[VIENNA, *November*, 1816]

The business connected with *this symphony* [1] is very distasteful to me. There, you see how disastrous it all is! —
Neither the engraved parts nor the score are faultless. In the copies which are already completed the mistakes will have to be corrected with Indian ink; and Schlemmer [2] can be brought in for that purpose. In any case, a list of *all the mistakes* without exception will have to be printed and dispatched. The most unskilled copyist would have copied the score exactly as it has now been engraved; so far, such a defective, imperfect version of a work composed by me has never — appeared in this fashion in engraved form — That is what comes of refusing to read the proofs, of not giving me the work to check beforehand — nor reminding me to do so.[3] These very same copies, which I am now sending you, should be returned to me as soon as possible with the copy which has been corrected from them, so that I may see whether they are accurate or not — Thus obstinacy provides its own punishment and the innocent too must suffer in consequence — So far as I am concerned I do not want to hear anything more about that mutilated, crippled symphony —
Faugh, the devil ÷ ÷ ÷ [4]!
Hence on you I can really fasten the accusation that you treat the public with no respect and blacken a composer's reputation without any twinges of conscience!!! Volti subito.[5]
The excuses you may advance when you announce the list of errata are that I was, and still am, in poor health and that the public was clamouring for this work and so forth —
May God protect you —
May the devil take you — [6]

---

[1] Op. 92.
[2] See Letter 973, p. 844, n. 4.
[3] The words from 'nor' to 'so' are added at the foot of the page.
[4] An indication that the ejaculation is to be repeated.
[5] P.T.O., at the foot of page 3 of the autograph.
[6] The autograph has no signature.

(676) *To Sigmund Anton Steiner*

[*Autograph not traced*] [1]

[VIENNA, *November*, 1816]

I am only now returning the copied score.[2] I have not looked at it; and presumably it is not without mistakes. My opinion is: if arrangements have to be made, they should be done immediately after the present proofs, which should be returned to me when completed, and then the offprints which will follow, from which the transcriptions too can be completed.[3] Please inform me where I can obtain pure grey blotting sand; my supply has run out and my asini [4] around me can't procure anything of the kind.

Your

L. v. BEETHOVEN

Gerade Pause

(677) *To Sigmund Anton Steiner*

[*Autograph in the Deutsche Staatsbibliothek, Berlin*]

[VIENNA, *November*, 1816]

My special request is that the list of errata be drawn up both in the separate parts and in the score.[5] I shall then compare it with the separate parts and the score. Whereupon it must be sent out with great speed into all corners of the earth. It is a pity that this must be so, but that is all that we can do. Moreover in the literary world similar cases of this have often occurred —

---

[1] Taken from Aloys Fuchs's transcript in Tübingen University Library.

[2] Of either the seventh or eighth symphony, Op. 92 or Op. 93.

[3] The original sentence is obscure. Either Beethoven omitted a clause or the transcript is faulty.

[4] I.e. asses.

[5] The list of errata in Steiner's edition of Op. 92. See *KHV.* 261.

But let us have no more stubbornness and obstinacy, or else the disease will become worse and worse — Instead of these pieces of five I need pieces of 20. Just now to save my honour I have to give on behalf of my poor little Karl 370 gulden to the surgeon who has cured him of hernia.[1] *The bills of exchange of my capital of* 100,000 *kreuzers I needed just for a few days, but not out of distrust*!!! — On Saturday I shall no doubt have to change 100 gulden A.C. again — Thus everywhere one woe treads upon another. May the Lord not forsake me —

Your etc. G[ENERALISSIM]O

(678) *To Baron Johann Pasqualati*

[*Autograph not traced*] [2]

[VIENNA, *November*, 1816]

DEAR AND ESTEEMED FRIEND!

If this note does not catch you at home, I do earnestly request you to be so kind as to give to, or to leave behind for, Rampel the copyist [3] *the F minor quartet composed by me*,[4] so that he may copy it — for what purpose, I will tell you *when I see you*.

In haste, your most cordial

BEETHOVEN

(679) *To Nikolaus Zmeskall von Domanovecz*

[*Autograph in the Nationalbibliothek, Vienna*]

MY DEAR YOUNG HOFRAT! [5]   [VIENNA, *December* 5, 1816]

Please return to me the three copies of my Schlacht von Vittoria. Don't bother about B[aron] K[rufft]. It will be some time, I hope, before we are let down into that vault.[6]

---

[1] Karl's operation had been performed on September 18th.

[2] Taken from *KFR*, no. 557 and from a transcript in the Stadtbibliothek, Vienna.

[3] For a note on Rampel see Letter 1335.

[4] Op. 95.

[5] Zmeskall had just been given the honorary title of Hofrat.

[6] Beethoven is playing on the words Krufft (cf. Letter 349, p. 358, n. 3) and 'Gruft' which means 'crypt' or 'vault'.

Let me know where one can find the best barometers and about how much one would cost.

I shall see you soon.

Ever your friend

BEETHOVEN

(680) *To Robert Birchall, London*

[*MS in the Gemeentemuseum, The Hague*] [1]

DEAR SIR   VIENNA, *December* 14, 1816
I give you my word of honor that I have signed and delivered the receipt to the House of Fries and Co.[2] some day last August, who as they say have transmitted it to Messrs. Coutts and Co. where you'll have the goodness to apply. Some error might have taken place that instead of Messrs. C. sending it to you, they have been directed to keep it till fetched. Excuse this irregularity, but it is not my fault, nor had I ever the idea of withholding it from the circumstance of the £5 not being included. Should the receipt not come forth at Messrs. C. I am ready to sign any other, and you shall then have it directly with return of post —

If you find Variations — in my style — too dear at £30, I will abate for the sake of your friendship one third — and you have the offer of such Variations, as fixed in our former letters for £20 each air —

Please to publish the symphony in A immediately — as well as the sonata — and the Trio — they being ready here.[3] The grand opera Fidelio is my work. The arrangement for the Pianoforte has been published here under my care, but the score of the opera itself is not yet published.[4] I have given a Copy of the Score to Mr. Neate under the seal of friendship and whom I shall direct to treat for my account in case an offer should present — I anxiously hope your health is improving. Give me leave to subscribe myself Dear Sir your very obedient h[umble] serv[an]t

LUDWIG VAN BEETHOVEN

---

[1] Written in English in another hand and signed by Beethoven.
[2] See Letter 765, p. 672, n. 3.   [3] Op. 92, 96 and 97.
[4] The first edition of the pianoforte arrangement of 'Fidelio' made by Ignaz Moscheles under Beethoven's supervision had been published by Artaria in August, 1814. The score of the opera was first published in Paris in 1826.

(681) *To Nikolaus Zmeskall von Domanovecz*

[*Autograph in the Nationalbibliothek, Vienna*]

[VIENNA, *December* 16, 1816]

Well, dear Z[meskall], you are now receiving my friendly dedication.[1] I want it to be a precious memento of our friendship which has persisted here for so long; and I should like you to treat it as a proof of my esteem and not to regard it as the end of what is now a long drawn out thread (for you are one of the earliest friends I made in Vienna).

All good wishes. Keep away from rotten fortresses, for an attack from them is more deadly than one from well preserved ones.

Ever your friend

BEETHOVEN

(NB. If you have a moment to spare, please let me know the approximate cost at present of a livery, without a cloak, but with hat and boot money.) Wonderful changes have taken place in my establishment. The husband, thank God, has gone to the devil; but the wife, it seems, is all the more determined to settle down in my home.

(682) *To Nikolaus Zmeskall von Domanovecz*

[*Autograph not traced*][2]

[VIENNA, *after December* 16, 1816]

MOST EXCELLENT FRAU VON SENESCHAL![3]

The following passage[4] in the first violin part of the quartet in the first Allegro:[5]

---

[1] Of Op. 95.

[2] Taken from *KFR*, no. 614 and Frimmel, *Neue Beethoveniana* (Vienna, 1890), pp. 105-106. Frimmel transcribed the autograph then in private ownership.

[3] Zmeskall was unmarried. The pronunciation of this Hungarian name is Smeschkal, which Beethoven occasionally altered to Seneschal, thus poking fun at Zmeskall's aristocratic connexions.

[4] In *KFR*, no. 614 the word given is 'Note' (note). But in Frimmel's earlier version in *op. cit.* the word given is 'Stelle' (passage).

[5] The 36th bar of the first movement of the F minor quartet, Op. 95, dedicated to Zmeskall.

Instead of the four notes marked with an X there should be only three, that is to say, triplets, such as:

Frau von Seneschal, I am charming and all.[1]

(683) *To Charles Neate, London*

[*MS in the Beethovenhaus, Bonn, H. C. Bodmer collection*][2]

MY DEAR SIR,   VIENNA, *December* 18, 1816
     Both letters to Mr. Beethoven and to me arrived. I shall first answer his as he has made out some memorandums and would have written himself, if he was not prevented by a rheumatic feverish cold. He says: 'What can I answer to your warm-felt excuses? Past ills must be forgotten and I wish you heartily joy that you have safely reached the long wished-for port of love.[3] Not having heard of you I could not delay any longer the publication of the symphony in A which appeared here some few weeks ago [4] — It certainly may last some weeks longer before a copy of this publication appears in London, but unless it is soon performed at the Phil[harmonic] and something is done for me afterwards by way of benefit, I don't see in what manner I may reap some good. The loss of your interest last season with the Phil[harmonic], when all my works in your hands were unpublished, has done me great harm—but it could not be helped,—and at this moment I know not what to say. Your intentions are good and it is to be hoped that my little fame may yet help — With respect to the two sonatas, Op. 102, for pianoforte and violoncello, I wish to see them sold very soon, as I have several offers for them in Germany, which depend entirely upon me to accept; but I should not wish, by publishing them here, to lose all and every

---

     [1] The original, which is not signed, has one of Beethoven's humorous concoctions 'scharmanteskall'.
     [2] This letter was written in English and signed for Beethoven by Häring.
     [3] Cf. Letter 664, p. 605, n. 2. Neate was married on October 2, 1816.
     [4] Op. 92.

advantage with them in England. I am satisfied with the 10 guineas offered for the dedication of the Trio,[1] and I beg you to hand the title immediately to Mr. Birchall, who is anxiously waiting for it; you'll please to use my name with him — I should be flattered to write some new works for the Philhar-[monic]—I mean Symphonies, an Oratorio, or Cantatas etc.— Mr. Birchall wrote as if he wished to purchase my Fidelio. Please to treat with him unless you have some plan with it for my benefit concert, which in general I leave to you and Sir George Smart, who will have the goodness to deliver this to you. The score of the Opera Fidelio is not published in Germany or anywhere else. Try what can be done with Mr. B[irchall] or as you think best. I was very sorry to hear that the three Overtures were not liked in London.[2] I by no means reckon them amongst my best works (which however I may boldly say of the Symphony in A), but still they were not disliked here and in Pest, where people are not easily satisfied. Was there no fault in the execution? Was there no party spirit?

And now I shall close with the best wishes for your welfare, and that you enjoy all possible felicity in your new situation of life —

Your true friend
LOUIS VAN BEETHOVEN

(684) *To Sir George Smart, London*

[*MS in the Fitzwilliam Museum, Cambridge*] [3]

MY DEAR SIR, VIENNA, *December* 18, 1816

You honor me with so many encomiums and compliments that I ought to blush, tho' I confess they are highly flattering to me, and I thank you most heartily for the part you take in my affairs. They have rather gone a little back through the strange situation in which our lost — but happily recovered — friend, Mr. Neate, found himself entangled. Your kind letter

---

[1] Op. 97.
[2] Op. 113, 115 and 117.
[3] Written in English by Häring and signed by Beethoven.

of 31 Octr explained a great deal and to some satisfaction and I take the liberty to enclose an answer to Mr. Neate, of whom I also received a letter, with my entreaties to assist him in all his undertakings in my behalf.

You say that the Cantata might serve your purpose for the Oratorios, and I ask you if you find 50 £ too much to give for it? I have had no benefit for it whatever until now, but I still should not wish to ask of you a price by which you might be a loser. Therefore we shall name 40 £ and if your success should be great then I hope you will have no objection of adding the 10 £ to make the sum as mentioned. The *Copyright* would be *yours*, and I should only make the condition of my publishing it *here* at a period which *you will be pleased* to appoint and not before.

I have communicated to Mr. Häring your kind intentions, and he joins with me in the expression of the highest regard which he always entertained for you —

Mr. Neate may keep the different works, except the Cantata if you accept it and I hope he will have it in his power with your assistance to do something for me, which from my illness and from the state of the Austrian finances would be very welcome. —Give me leave to subscribe myself with the greatest esteem and cordiality —

LUDWIG VAN BEETHOVEN

(685) *To [Count Moritz Dietrichstein ?]*

[Autograph not traced] ¹

[VIENNA, probably December 25, 1816]

I advise you — not to let Herr Felsenburg [2] play. Yesterday I took to be nervousness what today I maintain to be lack of skill — I have composed the cadenza — but, mark my words, he will come to grief before he reaches the cadenza [3] — It would be better to perform two symphonies — — I myself

---

[1] Taken from an article by Schlossar in *DM*, ix. 13 (Berlin, April 1, 1910), p. 37.

[2] Probably Stainer von Felsburg, a Court Secretary and amateur pianist, who liked to perform Beethoven's works. Hanslick, p. 214, calls him a dilettante.

[3] Beethoven is here playing on the German verb 'fallen' and the Italian verb 'cadere', both of which mean 'to fall'.

have told Herr Felsenburg that I do not advise him to play tomorrow — If he does, it will be an awful mess.

NB. As soon as he knows the concerto better, he may then play it.[1]

(686) *To Johann Nepomuk Kanka, Prague*

[*Autograph in the National and University Library, Prague*]

VIENNA, *December* 28, 1816

MY VERY DEAR AND ESTEEMED FRIEND!

By tomorrow's mail coach there will be sent to you a symphony of mine in score, the notorious Schlachtsymphonie in score, a trio and a violin sonata and a few vocal compositions [2] — I know that *in my case* you are always aware that I am grateful to you for everything you do for me, and thus too for the remittance of my half-yearly income which was recently sent to me with such speed.

But now I am again appearing before you with a request, indeed one might rather describe it as an imposition, and even better, perhaps, as a commission — The town of Retz which consists of about 500 houses is going to appoint you curator of a certain Johann Lamatsch at Prague.[3] For Heaven's sake do not refuse a charge which is a legal one and calculated to be appreciated by the public. For if you lend a hand, my poor nephew will at last come into possession of a small property. Of course, the question will have to be threshed out later on in Vienna by our Magistrat which deals with such matters,[4] seeing that the mother too will probably derive some benefit from the arrangement. Just think how much time is still going to be wasted on this question. My poor unfortunate brother died before seeing the outcome of it all. For the judicial authorities are under particular caution from His Majesty,

---

[1] According to Schlossar this postscript is written at the side of the page. The letter is not signed.

[2] Op. 92, 91, 97 and 96. It is uncertain which vocal works were sent.

[3] Beethoven's sister-in-law Johanna was related to the family of Lamatsch at Prague. She was the granddaughter of Paul Lamatsch, a former burgomaster, who had died in 1813. This Johann Lamatsch was probably a cousin of hers.

[4] The Magistrat of Vienna was the City Corporation or Urban Council.

so that the predecessor of the present official receiver of the town of Retz wanted to let my brother have 5000 gulden instead of 500 gulden. The present official receiver took only 30 days and almost as many nights merely to extricate this affair from the confusion in which it had been previously left.[1] Yes, those are the honourable men with whom we now have to deal. Oh, how kind are our Christian monarchs — The present official receiver, however, is an honest, energetic fellow at heart (for, if he did not choose to be so, he could behave in exactly the same way as his predecessor). Meanwhile the Lamatsch at Prague whom I mentioned above (and who is a business man) has not yet declared his adherence.[2] (NB. He has been thinking about it for the last four or five years.)

Bajer, the official receiver at Retz, will send you, therefore, your certificate of appointment as curator together with a duplicate copy, which has been drafted by the Retz Magistrat —I am only too well aware how petty and insignificant such matters must seem to a man of your intellectual abilities. Should you consider the task quite unsuitable for yourself, please find someone to undertake it and help to further it as much as possible — But certainly from every point of view you yourself would carry out the task most successfully. Perhaps just a few words with that person at P[rague] would clinch the whole affair —

My nephew, who is dear to me, is at one of the best boarding schools in Vienna.[3] He shows great talent. But his education is entirely at my expense ; and perhaps if the Retz business were definitely settled I might be able to spend a few more hundred gulden a year on the teaching of my dear orphan — I embrace you as one of my dearest friends.

Your
BEETHOVEN

---

[1] In the autograph this sentence is added at the foot of page 3. The remark is ironical.
[2] See Letter 771, p. 676.
[3] I.e. at Giannatasio del Rio's boarding school.

(687) *To Tobias Haslinger*

[*Autograph in the Beethovenhaus, Bonn, H. C. Bodmer collection*]

[VIENNA, *c. December* 29, 1816]

Our worthy Adjutant is requested, first of all, to send me today by an orderly the two receipts for the letters recently despatched. Should the letters not have been delivered, however, we ask that they be returned to me at once —

As for the parcel to Dr. Kanka, the arrangement still stands that it is to be handed today to the mail coach for Prague in exchange for a receipt — The following two parcels also are being sent to Prague today. Further, by today's mail coach the pianoforte arrangement of the symphony in A, the pianoforte arrangement of the Battle of Vittoria, the songs 'An die Hoffnung' and 'An die ferne Geliebte' are also to be despatched to Dr. Reger at the enclosed address [1] — Again, by today's mail coach also the scores of the symphony in A, and of the Battle of Vittoria, the trio in B♭, the violin sonata in G major and the songs 'An die Hoffnung' and 'An die ferne Geliebte' are to be sent to Herr von Gloschek [2] — A really careful despatch of these documents will redound to the credit of the Adjutant when the question of his promotion arises. As for the L[ieutenan]t G[enera]l, an order will be issued tomorrow about increasing the penalty.

(688) *To the Archduke Rudolph*

[*Autograph in the Gesellschaft der Musikfreunde, Vienna*]

YOUR IMPERIAL HIGHNESS!   VIENNA, *December* 31, 1816

Ever since the concert for the citizens [3] I have again had to remain in my room; and it will probably be some time before I shall be able to cease worrying about the state of my health — The year is coming to an end. My warmest wishes

---

[1] Pianoforte arrangements of Op. 92 and 91, and the songs Op. 94 and 98.

[2] The scores of Op. 92 and 91, and Op. 97, 96, 94 and 98.

[3] This concert was given in aid of the St. Marx poorhouse in the Grosser Redoutensaal on December 26th. Beethoven conducted his symphony in A major, Op. 92. Before 1785 St. Marx had been connected with the Bürgerspital in the city of Vienna. This explains Beethoven's allusion.

for the welfare of Y.I.H. begin with the New Year. With me, it is true, these wishes neither begin nor end. For every day I cherish these same wishes for Y.I.H. If I may add another wish for myself, then I should like Y.I.H. to allow me to grow and thrive in your grace and favour. The master will constantly strive not to be unworthy of the favour of his illustrious master and pupil —

Your Imperial Highness's

most obedient servant

LUDWIG VAN BEETHOVEN

(689) *To Franz Christian Kirchhoffer*

[*Autograph in the Beethovenhaus, Bonn, H. C. Bodmer collection*]

SIR!   [VIENNA, *December*, 1816]

Some time ago I gave Herr Simrock from Bonn a document signed by me belonging to Herr Birchall in London.[1] Herr S[imrock] assured me that he would deliver this document to you; and I asked you to forward this communication to Herr Fries & Co.,[2] who would kindly transmit it to H[err] B[irchall] in London. — But a few days ago I received a letter from H[err] B[irchall] from which it is clear that he has not yet received this written communication. So if you have not yet delivered it to Fries, please return it to me. But if you have sent it to London in some other way, please let me know —

I am, Sir, your most devoted servant,

L. V. BEETHOVEN

(690) *To Sigmund Anton Steiner*

[*Autograph in a private collection*][3]

[VIENNA, *December*, 1816]

The penalty is to be increased, and, what is more, by a sugar-basin with a small key and so forth, as is proper — You

---

[1] Probably Beethoven, then at Baden, gave this document in September to Peter Joseph Simrock to deliver to Kirchhoffer.   [2] See Letter 765, p. 672, n. 3.

[3] The verso of the autograph has this address: 'To the L[ieutenan]t G[enera]l's office (and also for the Adjutant)'.

may copy the engraved editions of the following quintets, which were written by a fellow who knows how to compose — [1]
The devil take you —
God protect you.

The G[ENERALISSIM]O

(691) *To Sigmund Anton Steiner*

[Autograph in the Stadtbibliothek, Vienna]

[VIENNA, *December,* 1816]

It was agreed that in all the finished copies of the quartet [2] and other works the mistakes were to be corrected. Nevertheless the Adjutant has been shameless enough to sell them without these corrections. But I will make a point of requiting and punishing him for that today. The lists, I see, are only being made a subject for ridicule. But here too I will do what my honour demands, and will certainly not yield an inch — Meanwhile send me the song 'Ein Schüsserl u. a Reinderl',[3] for I need it — Please note that if by tomorrow I have not been convinced of the Adjutant's greater zeal in my service, he will be threatened with a second ignominious loss of rank, although in accordance with our well-known magnanimity we would rather have promoted him. — NB. The song 'Ein Schüsserl u. a Reinderl' is to be found in the catalogue as a separate composition or with variations.[4]

The G[ENERALISSIM]O

---

[1] It has not been possible to identify these quintets.
[2] Op. 95.
[3] See *KHV.* 289, where it is pointed out that the 'air autrichien', which is no. 3 of Op. 105, is a formerly popular Austrian folksong: 'A Schüsserl und a Reinderl'.
[4] In *KHV.* 289 reference is also made to Johann Wanhal's 'Sechs leichte Vorspiele und sechs Variationen über a Schüsserl', published by Steiner.

(692) *To Frau Nanette Streicher* [1]

[*Autograph not traced*] [2]

[VIENNA, *December*, 1816]

I sent you word yesterday that you could keep N's [3] letter as long as you liked — I hope that you are feeling better. The weather is such that no delicate person can go out. So I don't go out and very likely you don't either — By the way, I hope that you don't misunderstand me. I have neither rights nor claims — I trust that you will soon be in better health; and then we shall surely meet.

Ever your friend

BEETHOVEN

(693) *To Cajetan Giannatasio del Rio* [4]

[*Autograph in the Royal College of Music*]

[VIENNA, *December*, 1816]

Forgive me, dear friend, but this sum has been lying here for you for at least twelve days or even longer. I have been very busy and am only just recovering from my illness; but

---

[1] Nanette Streicher (1769–1833) was a daughter of the famous pianoforte manufacturer Johann Andreas Stein of Augsburg. As a child she was an *enfant prodige* on the pianoforte, and Mozart in a letter to his father from Augsburg, dated October 23, 1777, while ridiculing her mannerisms in his lively way, admitted that she was very talented and might become a great pianist. After her father's death in 1792 Nanette and her younger brother Matthäus Andreas carried on his business. But in 1794 she married Johann Andreas Streicher and she and her husband and her brother immediately moved to Vienna where they established their firm in the Landstrasse. Their house became a centre for musical parties, given on Sunday mornings, which were frequented by the leading musicians in Vienna. As will be seen from his numerous letters to Nanette, she and her husband proved to be staunch and loyal friends to Beethoven, assisting him particularly in his domestic difficulties.

[2] Taken from *KFR*, no. 584. Very few original letters from Beethoven to Nanette Streicher have been traced. But Nohl obtained for his 1865 and 1867 collections copies of these letters made by Nanette's son, who still possessed the originals. The above note, however, is not in Nohl's edition, but was copied by Otto Jahn and deposited in the Berlin Library.

[3] Kalischer, who first found Otto Jahn's copy, suggests Neate. See note to *KFR*, no. 584.

[4] The autograph is not addressed. But it is in the file of letters from Beethoven to Giannatasio del Rio, now in the Royal College of Music.

indeed the word recovery cannot yet be used to describe my condition —

With kindest regards, but in haste, yours, as always,

L. v. BEETHOVEN

(694) *To Tobias Haslinger* [1]

[Autograph in the Stadtbibliothek, Vienna]

[VIENNA, *December*, 1816]

Please send me a copy of the score of the symphony in A; and do so today.[2] But send me a fine copy, for, as usual, I have to send two to Count Fries.[3] If possible, let me have the copy not later than three o'clock.

(695) *To Tobias Haslinger*

[Autograph not traced] [4]

[VIENNA, *December*, 1816]

MOST EXCELLENT AND MOST HIGHLY BORN ADJUTANT OF THE L[IEUTENAN]T G[ENERA]L —

Please come to me tomorrow morning about the proofs of the symphony.[5] By that time I shall have finished correcting them; and I have something to say about a few points in them. Let me tell you that there are still quite enough blunders —

I shall expect you for certain, for I can't come to you.

The G[ENERALISSIM]O

---

[1] The verso of this autograph has the following address in Beethoven's hand : 'To the Adjutant, even if he is being punished'.

[2] The seventh symphony, Op. 92, dedicated to Count Moritz von Fries.

[3] See Letter 765, p. 672, n. 3.

[4] Taken from Unger, no. 17, which is a transcript of the autograph.

[5] Either the seventh symphony, Op. 92, or the eighth, Op. 93.

(696) *To Carl Czerny*

[*Autograph in the Gesellschaft der Musikfreunde, Vienna*]

[VIENNA, 1816]

MY DEAR AND MOST EXCELLENT CZ[ERNY],

An unforeseen impediment prevented me from fetching you. But I will certainly be with you today at three o'clock; and we shall then go to the boarding school at once.

Your true friend

BEETHOVEN

(697) *To Nikolaus Zmeskall von Domanovecz*

[*Autograph in the Nationalbibliothek, Vienna*]

[VIENNA, 1816]

I myself am coming to you, my dear Z[meskall]. If this has not happened for some time, please ascribe it to illness, to my guardianship and to all kinds of miserable affairs [1] — I had resolved to *refute* your last letter in a surprising manner — I shall see you tomorrow or the day after.

B.

(698) *To Frau Giannatasio del Rio* [2]

[*Autograph in the Royal College of Music*]

[VIENNA, 1816]

Frau von Giannatasio is most politely requested to have a few pairs of good linen underpants made for Karl. I fully entrust to her my Karl and I rely entirely on her motherly care for him. —

L. V. BEETHOVEN

---

[1] The word used by Beethoven is 'Miserabilitäten'.

[2] Frau Katharina Giannatasio del Rio, née Quenzer, was the wife of the head-master of Karl's boarding school and the mother of Fanny and Anna, who were both musical. She died in 1825.

(699) *To Tobias Haslinger*

[*Autograph in the Stadtbibliothek, Vienna*]

[VIENNA, 1816]

I am sending you herewith the proofs of the parts.¹ You will easily sort out what belongs together. And again I recommend you to be scrupulously conscientious in everything we arranged about this — We are still waiting to hear today that the punishments for the Adjutant consisting of the works ordered yesterday have been carried out. Their execution was to be reported to the G[eneralissim]o.

THE G[ENERALISSIM]O

(700) *To Baron Ludwig von Türkheim* ²

[*Autograph not traced*] ³

[VIENNA, 1816]

I went several times yesterday to your house, my dear T[ürkheim], with my brother, who really must see you about a certain matter. As I have been told that you will be at the Bohemian Chancellery at about one o'clock today, I will go there again with my worthy brother, who is a *civil pharmaceutical chemist* at Linz ; ⁴ this time not in order *not* to find you there, but to find you *at that place* — Do not forget our old friendship ; and if you can do something for my brother without *overthrowing the Austrian Monarchy*, I hope to find you willing — All good wishes, dear Baron, and see that we *find you today.*

¹ Of the seventh and, possibly, eighth symphonies, Op. 92 and 93, published by Steiner in November, 1816, and at Easter, 1817, respectively. See *KHV.* 261 and 263-264.

² Baron Ludwig von Türkheim (1777–1846), a Viennese physician who had an appointment in the Bohemian Chancellery. See *FRBH* II, 341-343.

³ Taken from *FRBH* II, 342-343. Frimmel transcribed the autograph then in private ownership.

⁴ Beethoven's youngest brother, Nikolaus Johann, had acquired in 1808 a chemist's shop at Linz which he sold in December, 1816, having made a small fortune as a war profiteer. He then ran a chemist's shop at Urfahr near Linz, but seems to have spent most of his time in Vienna. In 1819 he purchased a large estate at Gneixendorf near Krems.

Remember that I too am a *Freiherr*,[1] even though I may not bear the title!!!!
With cordial regards, your friend and servant

LUDWIG VAN BEETHOVEN

(701) *To Sigmund Anton Steiner*

[*Autograph in the Stadtbibliothek, Vienna*]

DEAR STEINER! [VIENNA, 1816]

I request you to have the next proofs sent to me in uncut galleys — Moreover complaints are being made about the L[ieutenant Genera]l, about his Adjutant and also about the Provost Marshal [2] — No doubt a court martial will have to deal with them —

(702) *To the Archduke Rudolph*

[*Autograph in the Gesellschaft der Musikfreunde, Vienna*]

YOUR IMPERIAL HIGHNESS! [VIENNA, 1816]

Unfortunately I am again compelled to remain indoors for a few days. But I have reason to hope that a complete recovery may be granted sooner than I think and that therefore I shall not be deprived of the privilege of being allowed to wait upon Y.I.H. —

Your Imperial Highness's
most obedient servant

LUDWIG VAN BEETHOVEN

[1] Beethoven is playing on the two meanings of 'Freiherr', i.e. 'baron' and 'freeman'. [2] Diabelli.

(703) *To Joseph Anton Ignaz, Edler von Baumeister*

[*Autograph in the Gesellschaft der Musikfreunde, Vienna*]

[VIENNA, 1816]

P.P.

Please lend me for a short time the Scottish songs ¹ which I gave to His Imperial Highness, for two copies, including my own manuscript, have been lost, and the songs will have to be copied again for dispatch —

Your most devoted servant

LUDWIG VAN BEETHOVEN

(704) *To Carl Czerny*

[*Autograph in the Gesellschaft der Musikfreunde, Vienna*]

MY DEAR Z! ²   [VIENNA, 1816]

Be so kind as to give this to your parents for the recent midday meal. I simply can't accept that without paying for it — Besides, I shall certainly not order your lessons without paying for them; even the ones you have already given must be included in the reckoning and will be paid for. But please be patient for the time being, for I cannot yet *demand* anything from the widow ³ and I have had, and still have, great expenses to meet — But it is only *borrowed* from you for the time being — The little fellow is going to you today and I too will turn up later —

Your friend

BEETHOVEN

---

¹ Op. 108. For full particulars of these 25 Scottish songs with pianoforte, violin and cello accompaniment, which were first published by Thomson in August, 1818, see *KHV*. 300-310. For an exhaustive discussion of Haydn's and Beethoven's contributions to Thomson's Collections of National Song see C. Hopkinson and C. B. Oldman, *Thomson's Collections of National Song* (Edinburgh, 1940).

² For Beethoven's odd spelling of Czerny see Letter 610, p. 560, n. 3.

³ His sister-in-law Johanna, the mother of Karl.

(705) *To Sigmund Anton Steiner* [1]

[*Autograph in the Stadtbibliothek, Vienna*]

[VIENNA, 1816]

The L[ieutenant Genera]l is requested to change these 100 gulden, kreuzer and groschen into paper today and, *what is more, without debiting the transaction,* as befits such a heavily armed soldier in accordance with his rank — At the same time, in respect of the new 4000 gulden in pieces of twenty, which are to flow into the exchequer, he is reminded to think before and after and behind as well, and to inform us of the result of this operation; and for these fresh services the *highest rank* will be conferred upon him — With an indescribable descriptiveness I append

my signature which is that of the

G[ENERALISSIM]O

(706) *To Sigmund Anton Steiner*

[*Autograph in the Stadtbibliothek, Vienna*]

[VIENNA, 1816]

We request you not to forget the application we made to-day, since we cannot go out and really do need the money for tomorrow morning — As for the Adjutant, he should be put in carcere at once and told to prepare himself for tomorrow's court sitting at half past three in the afternoon. He is charged with great crimes against the state. Among other things he has even failed to observe the rule enjoined upon him to be silent about important affairs of state —

Given without giving anything on the etc., etc.

THE G[ENERALISSIM]O

---

[1] The address on the verso in Beethoven's hand is: 'Für den G——t hoch u. wohlgebohrn Hr. v. Steinaki Steiner von Steinen'.

(707) *To Sigmund Anton Steiner* ¹

[Autograph in the Stadtbibliothek, Vienna]

[VIENNA, 1816]

The L[ieutenan]t G[enera]l's office is authorized to send me immediately 100 gulden V.C. by the bearer of this note ; whereupon I shall buy the stamped paper at once and hand in the receipts — As for our mines,² nothing can be done for the time being. But should the L[ieutenan]t G[enera]l's office desire to open his mines,³ this can only be done by means of a supplicandum, for no more tenders are being put forward —

The G[ENERALISSIM]O

(708) *To Sigmund Anton Steiner*

[Autograph in the Stadtbibliothek, Vienna]

MOST EXCELLENT FELLOWS !   [VIENNA, 1816]

If only you could procure for me for a few days the works of the poets Klopstock ⁴ and Gleim,⁵ but in good copies of most recent editions ⁶ ? ! ! Then you would, I mean to say, you will, I mean to say, you *should* kindly lend them to me for a few days — With the most outstretched arms I embrace you all.

Yours

BEET ⁷

NB. *Little Tobias, pluck out a few of your quills.
I will put in an appearance on Saturday.*⁸

---

¹ The address on the verso in Beethoven's hand includes the Adjutant Haslinger.

² I.e. Beethoven's work of composing.

³ I.e. Steiner's exchequer.

⁴ Notwithstanding his great admiration for Klopstock's poetry Beethoven, so far as is known, did not set any of his poems to music.

⁵ In 1792, while he was still at Bonn, Beethoven had set to music a poem by J. W. L. Gleim entitled 'Selbstgespräch'. It was not published until 1888 as a supplement to Breitkopf & Härtel's *Gesamtausgabe*. In *KHV*. it is listed as WoO 114.

⁶ The German original has 'nach guten neuesten Originalausgaben', which is almost a contradiction in terms. Beethoven may have meant 'good copies of the most recent editions based on the original text'.

⁷ Part of the signature has been torn off.

⁸ Both these postscripts are written on the verso.

(709) *To the Archduke Rudolph*

[*Autograph in the Gesellschaft der Musikfreunde, Vienna*]

YOUR IMPERIAL HIGHNESS!   [VIENNA, 1816]

I am again obliged to stay in my bedroom. However unpleasant it may be for me to have to forgo the privilege of visiting Y.I.H., yet I must patiently resign myself to this privation. Meanwhile I shall not be obliged to claim Y.I.H.'s most gracious indulgence for too long a period, for I hope to be able to wait upon Y.I.H. very soon. And I wish Y.I.H. really excellent and perfect health.

Your Imperial Highness's
faithful and most obedient servant
LUDWIG VAN BEETHOVEN

(710) *To the Archduke Rudolph*

[*Autograph in the Gesellschaft der Musikfreunde, Vienna*]

YOUR IMPERIAL HIGHNESS!   [VIENNA, 1816]

In a few days I shall have the honour of being able to wait upon you again. I crave your indulgence for having stayed away for so long. Notwithstanding my healthy appearance, I have all this time been really ill and suffering from a nervous breakdown. However, during the last few days I have felt better, which means that soon I shall no longer bewail my loss in not enjoying the benefit of Y.I.H.'s presence and shall be able to show you how fervently I desire to merit your favour —

Your Imperial Highness's
most faithful and most obedient servant
LUDWIG VAN BEETHOVEN

(711) *To Sigmund Anton Steiner*

[*Autograph in the Stadtbibliothek, Vienna*]

[VIENNA, 1816]

The little Paternostergasse [1] must acknowledge the receipt and likewise inform me when the proof-sheets are going to arrive. For, if not, it will only have itself to thank for all the misery which boiling like molten sealing-wax will drip down on evil-doers —

B.

(712) *To the Archduke Rudolph*

[*Autograph in the Gesellschaft der Musikfreunde, Vienna*]

YOUR IMPERIAL HIGHNESS!   [VIENNA, 1816]

My warmest thanks to Y.I.H. for your gracious condescension in enquiring about my health — If my condition had not been so precarious, I would certainly have waited upon Y.I.H. long ago. But my state of health, instead of improving, has become worse; and I am very much afraid lest even at Y.I.H.'s residence something might happen to me. The effects of such a heavy feverish cold are extremely slow to disappear and they demand a very careful regimen — Yesterday I felt very poorly, but today I am better. The doctor assures me that thanks to this favourable weather my condition ought soon to show a marked improvement; and since I already feel so very much better today, I hope that next week, at any rate, I shall again be able to wait upon Y.I.H. — My condition is all the more painful to me as I am unable to prove to Y.I.H. my most ardent devotion to your service —

Your Imperial Highness's
loyal and most obedient servant
LUDWIG VAN BEETHOVEN

---

[1] In 1805 Steiner, who had acquired Senefelder's lithographic printing works, moved his firm from the Singerstrasse into a narrow street off the Graben, called the Paternostergasse. Cf. Letter 527, p. 495, n. 1.

(713) *To Carl Czerny*

[*Autograph in the Gesellschaft der Musikfreunde, Vienna*]

[VIENNA, 1816]

Kindly remind the musical circle to write down again for me the necessary particulars about the exchange market.[1] I will thank them for this both *in writing* and in person — I will try to send you another message about this tomorrow morning —

Your friend
BEETHOVEN

(714) *To the Archduke Rudolph*

[*Autograph in the Gesellschaft der Musikfreunde, Vienna*]

YOUR IMPERIAL HIGHNESS! [VIENNA, 1816]

I earnestly crave your forgiveness for not informing Y.I.H. that I was not coming. I was unable to do so. When I see you I shall explain the reason. Since Saturday my condition has again become worse; and it will certainly be some days before I can wait upon Y.I.H. once more, for I must be very careful about going out of doors. I am doubly grieved, not only for my own sake but also because I am unable to show my zeal in your service —

Your Imperial Highness's
most obedient servant
LUDWIG VAN BEETHOVEN

(715) *To Nikolaus Zmeskall von Domanovecz*

[*Autograph not traced*][2]

[VIENNA, 1816]

With all my heart I thank you, my dear Z[meskall], for the discussions you have allowed me to have with you. In

---

[1] The German word is 'Börse'. Possibly Beethoven was thinking of selling a bank share, as he did several years later. The note is written in pencil.

[2] Taken from *KFR*, no. 577. The autograph was originally in private ownership.

regard to the fortresses, I fancy that I have already given you
to understand that I do not want to spend any time in marshy
districts. In any case it is more difficult for me than for anyone else to set up a household, because I am ignorant, quite
ignorant about all such matters. And no doubt I shall always
be liable to make mistakes. — Well, in regard to your latest
letter, what am I to say? From my earliest childhood I have
always liked to recall and bear in mind whatever is good in
other people. Then, of course, there came a time when
especially in an effeminate century a youth might be forgiven
if he was perhaps rather intolerant. Now, however, we have
renewed our strength as a nation; and in any case I have
recently endeavoured to acquire the tendency not to condemn
the whole man for some individual shortcomings, but to be
just and to bear in mind what is good in him. Although this
tendency has recoiled on me and has even taken the form of
actions directed against me, yet I have not only befriended the
whole human race, but also have always regarded more
especially some individuals as my friends and have called them
so. In this sense, therefore, I call you my friend also. Even
though in many respects we both act and think quite differently, yet we have agreed on many points. — Well then —
now I shall cease from chattering — But I trust that you will
very often put my friendly affection to the test!

As always   your friend
                                              BEETHOVEN

(716) *To Vincenz Hauschka* [1]

[*Autograph in the State Archives, Třeboň*]

[VIENNA, 1816]
I am sending you, my dear H[auschka], eight basses, four
violas, six second violins and six first violins as well as two wind-
instrument parts; I can't let you have a score, because the

---

[1] Vincenz Hauschka (1766–1840), born at Mies in Bohemia, came to Vienna
in 1792 and obtained an appointment as financial adviser to the Department of
Public Works. He was an excellent amateur cellist and a competent composer.
He was a founder member of the Gesellschaft der Musikfreunde in Vienna and
arranged its first concert in 1815. Hauschka and Beethoven were on very friendly
terms. See *FRBH* I, 201-2.

only one I possess is my own and it is written in too small a hand for anyone but myself to read. But it is a good thing to have a score at hand. You will find one at Steiner's in the little Paternostergasse —
I am again unwell, but I will certainly have a word with you soon.

Your friend
BEETHOVEN

NB. I have several other written-out parts which, if necessary, you may fetch at my home.[1]

(717) *To Sigmund Anton Steiner & Co.*

[*Autograph not traced*] [2]

TO THE TWO TOBIASES [3]   [VIENNA, 1816]
    Whenever I see no proofs, I refuse to believe in their existence — Make a note of that.

BEETHOVEN

(718) *To Frau Giannatasio del Rio*

[*Autograph not traced*] [4]

[VIENNA, 1816]

The highly born and very well born Frau v[on] G[iannatasio] etc., is most politely requested to let me know very soon, so that I need not keep in my head so many pairs of trousers, stockings, shoes, pants, etc., I repeat, to let the undersigned know how many ells of cashmere my upstanding and worthy nephew requires for a pair of black trousers; and in the interest of the Castalian fount [5] I ask her to reply without my

---

[1] The letter and signature cover three pages of the autograph. The NB. is added on the fourth page.
[2] Taken from Unger, no. 37. Unger transcribed the autograph then in the Doblhoff collection of the Wissenschaftlicher Klub, Vienna.
[3] No doubt Steiner and Haslinger.
[4] Taken from Nohl I, no. 132. First published in *Der Grenzbote*, 1857, p. 2.
[5] I.e. the fountain of the Muses. Beethoven is alluding to his musical inspiration.

having to remind her again.   As to the Lady Abbess,[1] a vote
is to be taken this evening about the question which concerns
Karl, namely, whether he is to remain with you.

Your well and ill born

L. v. BEETHOVEN

(719) *To Cajetan Giannatasio del Rio*

[*Autograph not traced*] [2]

[VIENNA, 1816]

I have heard, my dear friend, that you have something
to deliver to me.   Unfortunately I heard this only yesterday
evening and too late, or I would have gone to you at once.   So
please send it over to me, for surely it can't be anything but a
letter to me from the Q[ueen] of N[ight] [3] — Although you
have granted me permission to fetch Karl on two occasions,
yet I do request you to let me fetch him at about eleven o'clock
tomorrow, for I want to take him to an interesting musical
recital.   Moreover I intend to make him play at my home
tomorrow, because he has not done so for a long time — In
any case please give him much more to do today than usual
so that he may make up, so to speak, for this holiday —

With all my heart I embrace you and remain your

LUDWIG VAN BEETHOVEN

(720) *To Cajetan Giannatasio del Rio*

[*Autograph not traced*] [4]

[VIENNA, 1816]

I beg you, my dear G[iannatasio], to send Karl to me
immediately with the bearer of this letter.   If you don't, I

---

[1] I.e. Fanny, the eldest daughter of Giannatasio del Rio.   See Nohl, *op. cit.*
pp. 115-116, where Fanny in her diary gives expression to her strong objection
to being called an Abbess, which in her opinion was merely a euphemism for the
word 'housewife'.

[2] Taken from Nohl I, no. 133.   [3] Karl's mother.

[4] Taken from Nohl I, no. 138.

shall not be able to see him for the whole day, and this would not be a good thing for him, since it is necessary that I too should influence him. And now that we are on this subject, please give him also a few lines for me about his behaviour so that I may take up with him at once any points where an improvement is desirable — I am going into the country today and I shall probably not return until late in the evening. As I am loth to disturb your arrangements in the very least, please see that Karl takes with him some night attire so that if it is perhaps too late to bring him back to you I could keep him with me tonight and take him to you very early tomorrow morning. —

In haste as always, yours
BEETHOVEN

(721) *To Joseph von Varena, Graz*

[Autograph in the Deutsche Staatsbibliothek, Berlin]

[VIENNA, 1816]

NB.[1] I see that with my help you have again performed a good deed. May God reward you for this, noble sympathizer — Why are both of us not rich? Just keep the music — Your frank and honourable character is a guarantee to me for its best *preservation and use*!!!

(722) *To the Countess Anna Marie Erdödy*

[Autograph not traced] [2]

DEAR, DEAR, DEAR, DEAR COUNTESS,   [VIENNA, 1816]
    I am taking baths and am not stopping them until tomorrow. Hence I was unable to see you and all your dear ones today — I trust that you are enjoying better health. It is no consolation for more noble-minded people to tell them that others are suffering too. Yet no doubt comparisons must

---

[1] In the autograph (now on deposit in Tübingen University Library) the NB. is written slightly above the first line. This unsigned note, addressed on the verso, must be a postscript to a letter to Varena which has disappeared.
[2] Taken from Jahn's transcript in the Stadtbibliothek, Vienna.

always be drawn ; and, if one does, one will certainly find that we all *suffer, that we all err, though each in a different way* — Accept the better edition of the quartet [1] and give the bad one to the violoncello [2] with a gentle handshake. As soon as I am with you again I shall make a point of driving him into a tight corner for a bit — All good wishes, hug and kiss your dear children on my behalf, although it just occurs to me that I may no longer kiss your daughters, for they are now too grown up. Well, I don't know what to suggest. Act, dear Countess, as your own wise judgment dictates.

Your true friend and admirer

BEETHOVEN

(723) *To Sigmund Anton Steiner*

[Autograph not traced] [3]

[VIENNA, 1869]

A copy of the score of the symphony in A is requested with all speed.[4] —

The G[ENERALISSIM]O ! — ! !

(724) *To [Dr. Joseph Reger ?]* [5]

[Autograph in the Beethovenhaus, Bonn, H. C. Bodmer collection]

MY DEAR R[EGER] !   [VIENNA, 1816]

Please be so kind as to answer the following questions, using this same sheet, since for many reasons it is necessary for me to know how our affairs stand. Bernard [6] is not well and I too am not yet quite recovered. At the same time I should like to know how much more I could do in addition to what I am already doing for K[arl]. For in my present circumstances

---

[1] Possibly Op. 95.   [2] Linke.
[3] Taken from Unger, no. 42. According to Unger who transcribed the autograph this note was written in pencil.
[4] Possibly a reference to Beethoven's proof-reading of his seventh symphony, Op. 92, published by Steiner in November, 1816.
[5] The autograph does not bear the name of the addressee, and Beethoven just calls him R. But on internal evidence the recipient was very probably Dr. Joseph Reger, who was then in Vienna. Cf. Letter 441, p. 430, n. 1.
[6] For a note on J. K. Bernard see Letter 947, p. 812, n. 1.

643

it would be extremely difficult for me to do anything more, unless I had some additional help on the lines set forth below.

Question : Why could we not draw the house rent ? [1]
Answer :
Question : Will this also be impossible in future ?
Answer :
Question : What information have you about Retz ? [2]
Answer :
Question : What is the name of the official receiver at Retz ? I have forgotten it [3] —
Answer :
Question : I want to send a courier about this matter. What should I write to him ?
Answer :

I earnestly request you not to give any more verbal messages to the servant.   First of all, he is incapable of delivering them properly; and, secondly, I don't like to entrust my private affairs to people of that stamp. —
Don't be annoyed. Perhaps I shall ask you to take charge of and promote our affair as much as possible. Rest assured not only of my esteem but also of my most genuine gratitude. —
As always

Your friend
BEETHOVEN

(725) *To Baron Johann Pasqualati*

[*Autograph in the Beethovenhaus, Bonn, H. C. Bodmer collection*]

DEAR AND ESTEEMED FRIEND,   [VIENNA, 1816]
    Although there is a court function today, yet I have a great favour to ask of you ; and that is, that you will be so kind as to visit *me*, because for some days now I have not been well. *But do come today*, if you can manage to do so, for my request concerns discussions with Dr. Adlersburg about my nephew's affairs, and in these discussions it is extremely necessary that

---

[1] Probably the rent of the house at Retz which belonged to Caspar Carl and had been bequeathed to his son.
[2] A small town between Vienna and Prague.
[3] See Letter 771, p. 676, where his name is given as Bayer. But cf. Letter 686, p. 624.

I myself should have something to say. But I cannot and must not go out — So please be so kind as to let me know *when* you can manage to see me *today*?!!!???

Your
BEETHOVEN

(726) *To Cajetan Giannatasio del Rio*

[*Autograph in the Beethovenhaus, Bonn, H. C. Bodmer collection*]

[VIENNA, 1816]

P.P.

The idle talk of that wicked woman [1] has upset me so much that I cannot reply to everything today. You will receive full information about everything tomorrow. But in no circumstances whatever must you allow her to see Karl; and keep to the arrangement that she is to see him only once a month; and now that she has seen him this month, she may see him again next month, but not any sooner —

In haste, yours
BEETHOVEN

(727) *To Frau Johanna van Beethoven* [2]

[*Autograph in the Stadtbibliothek, Vienna*]

[VIENNA, 1816]

In future when you are here in Vienna, please be so kind as always to add your place of residence to the receipt. If you are not here, you must send a life and residence certificate from your local priest. I will refund the six kreuzer for the stamped form — Moreover you should send a messenger every quarter to Steiner's where on producing the receipt you will receive the

---

[1] Karl's mother.
[2] Beethoven's sister-in-law Johanna, née Reiss (*c.* 1784–1868), was the daughter of a well-to-do house decorator. She married Caspar Carl van Beethoven in 1806. Full particulars of her immoral character and generally unsatisfactory behaviour, as seen by Beethoven, are given in the latter's long memorandum to the Court of Appeal when he was striving to exclude her from the guardianship of her son. See Appendix C (15). She outlived Beethoven and her own son by many years and died in neglect.

money. There must be no mention in your receipt about *surrendering* the pension, for how could I surrender something *that is by no means my property*? You have only to write a receipt for the amount of the sum you have received. Nothing else is required — According to what my brother tells me he would advance the 1000 gulden A.C. if a guarantor could be found, however much or not you would have [to guarantee or receive?]. Hence you yourself must enquire from him about this — [1]

BEETHOVEN

(728) *To the Archduke Rudolph*

[Autograph in the Gesellschaft der Musikfreunde, Vienna]

YOUR IMPERIAL HIGHNESS! [VIENNA, 1816]

I had not been well for a few days before Your Highness sent me your message; and then I was just going out for dinner, since I have no one to keep house for me. That was the only walk I took. But on that very day when Y.I.H. sent the message I became worse and a heavy feverish cold set in. So unfortunately I have to stay indoors for a few days. It was not possible for me to inform Y.I.H. of this until today — Moreover my previous indisposition which I have mentioned above was the reason why during Y.I.H.'s illness I did not enquire in person after your health. — I hope soon to be well enough to hasten to Y.I.H. and to tell you that I am and shall ever be Your Imperial Highness's

most faithful and most obedient servant

LUDWIG VAN BEETHOVEN

(729) *To the Archduke Rudolph*

[Autograph in the Gesellschaft der Musikfreunde, Vienna]

YOUR IMPERIAL HIGHNESS! [VIENNA, 1816]

An attack of colic to which I suddenly succumbed yesterday evening prevents me from waiting upon you today notwithstanding my desire and my best intention to do so.

---

[1] Two lines have been obliterated at the end of the autograph, which is addressed on the verso.

Although my condition has improved, I must remain in my room today and tomorrow. But I hope to be able to enjoy on the day after tomorrow at latest the happiness of seeing Y.I.H. and of receiving a share of your favour. If this message is rather late in reaching you, I trust that Y.I.H. will kindly ascribe the delay to hampering circumstances —

Your Imperial Highness's

faithful and most obedient servant

LUDWIG VAN BEETHOVEN

(730) *To Baron Joseph von Schweiger*

[*Autograph in the Gesellschaft der Musikfreunde, Vienna*]

[VIENNA, 1816]

MOST EXCELLENT, MOST CHARMING AND PRIME CHAMPION OF GYMNASTICS IN EUROPE!

The bearer of this letter is a poor devil (like many other people!!!)

You can help him by enquiring of our gracious lord whether he would perhaps like to buy one of his very small but elegant and well-made pianos? — Furthermore, please introduce him to one of the chamberlains or adjutants of the Archduke Karl, in case H.I.H. might perhaps buy one of these instruments for his consort? [1] — In short, we are asking for an introduction for this poor devil from the prime champion of gymnastics to the chamberlain or adjutant in residence.

Likewise your poor devil

L. v. BEETHOVEN

(731) *To Joseph Czerny* [2]

[*Autograph in the Gesellschaft der Musikfreunde, Vienna*]

DEAR CZERNY! [VIENNA, 1816]

Would it be possible for you perhaps to help in some way this person, whom I am sending to you and who is a tuner and

---

[1] The Archduke Karl had married on September 17, 1815 the Princess Henriette von Nassau. See Letter 456, p. 441, n. 4.

[2] The autograph is addressed on the verso in Beethoven's hand to J. von Czerny. Joseph Czerny (1785–1842), who was not a relative of Carl Czerny,

647

manufacturer of pianofortes at Baden, to sell his instruments which are quite elegant after their fashion and yet soundly made —

In haste, your friend and servant

L. v. BEETHOVEN

(732) *To Sigmund Anton Steiner*

[*Autograph in the Stadtbibliothek, Vienna*]

[VIENNA, 1816]

The L[ieutenan]t G[enera]l's office must arrange for all the parts to be returned to me today. The bearer of this note will *fetch them this evening.* On the day after tomorrow I will send back all the parts together with the score ; and then the proof-correcting will be finished — I insist that in future nothing shall be *pasted on* my works, or else I will give expression not to the *forbearance* commended in the M[usik] Z[eitung] [1] but to my just *annoyance* [2] *with asses' ears* —

Yours and so forth ——

was a pianist, composer and teacher of the pianoforte. He succeeded Carl Czerny as the music teacher of Beethoven's nephew. He also joined the music publishing firm of Cappi & Co.

[1] In his note to this letter Unger quotes a reference in this Leipzig paper dated October 11, 1815, which may have some bearing on this passage. See Unger, no. 16, note, and *TDR* III, 624.

[2] Here Beethoven is playing on the words 'Langmut' (forbearance) and 'Unmut' (annoyance).

1817

(733) *To Nikolaus Zmeskall von Domanovecz*

[*Autograph in the Nationalbibliothek, Vienna*]

[VIENNA, *January* 6, 1817]

Let me know today, dear Z[meskall], at what time to-morrow I can have a word with you. I should much prefer the afternoon — I expect you to send a favourable reply to

your friend

BEETHOVEN

(734) *To Hofrat Karl Peters* [1]

[*Autograph in the Beethovenhaus, Bonn, H. C. Bodmer collection*]

SIR!   VIENNA, *January* 8, 1817 [2]

I heard only yesterday from Herr von Bernard,[3] whom I happened to meet, that you are now in Vienna. I am sending you, therefore, these two copies which unfortunately were finished just when people had begun to talk about the death of our dear late Prince Lobkowitz.[4] Please be so kind as to deliver them together with this letter to His Excellency the eldest Prince Lobkowitz.[5] This very day I was about to request the treasurer to be responsible for taking them to Bohemia, for I really thought that none of you were in town. If I may be permitted to say something about my humble self, then I can tell you that I shall soon be in reasonably good health again; and I trust that such is also the case with you — I dare not ask you to come to me, for I should have to *tell you why*; and that I cannot presume to do at the moment, any

---

[1] Karl Peters was tutor to the children of Prince Lobkowitz. In April, 1820, he was appointed co-guardian with Beethoven of the latter's nephew. See *FRBH* II, 15-16.

[2] The autograph bears the date January 8, 1816, which should be 1817. Prince Lobkowitz died on December 15, 1816.

[3] For a note on J. K. Bernard see Letter 947, p. 812, n. 1.

[4] Copies of the song cycle 'An die ferne Geliebte', dedicated to Prince Franz Joseph von Lobkowitz and published by Steiner in October, 1816. Beethoven had received his copies only in December and after the Prince's death.

[5] See the following Letter 734a.

more than I can expect you to tell me why you *don't come* or *will not come* — Please write on the letter the address of the Prince, for I don't know his Christian name — Kindly keep this third copy for your wife —

All good wishes.

Your friend and servant

L. v. BEETHOVEN

(734a) *To Prince Ferdinand von Lobkowitz* [1]

[Autograph in the Stadtarchiv, Braunschweig] [2]

YOUR EXCELLENCY !   VIENNA, *January* 8, 1817 [3]

I take the liberty of sending you this dedication which was intended for your late highly esteemed father but unfortunately, owing to circumstances which prevented it, was never seen by him.[4]   I hope that you will accept it from me as a small thank-offering which I desired to make to your late highly esteemed father — Let me add a request that you should count me among those who are convinced that you will wholly fulfil all the glorious promises and expectations which your exalted station affords you the opportunity of fulfilling, by performing good and useful deeds for very many people.

Your Excellency's

most devoted

LUDWIG VAN BEETHOVEN

[1] The autograph bears no address, but the letter was certainly intended for Prince Ferdinand von Lobkowitz (1797–1868). He was the eldest son of Prince Franz Joseph von Lobkowitz, who died on December 16, 1816. Cf. the preceding Letter 734.

[2] This letter was first published by Dr. Willi Wöhler in an article in *Salve Hospes*, Braunschweig, September, 1958, pp. 70-72.

[3] As in Letter 734, this autograph bears the date January 8, 1816, which should be 1817.

[4] The song cycle 'An die ferne Geliebte', Op. 98.

(735) *To Tobias Haslinger* [1]

[Autograph in the Stadtbibliothek, Vienna

[VIENNA, *shortly after January* 9, 1817]

Whether he is *guilty* or *innocent*, the Adjutant is requested
to send me the proofs of the symphony in F [2] and of the sonata
in A,[3] for I am now staying indoors and thus can more easily
get on with this work. In particular, there are people who
worry me about the sonata, which is technically difficult to
perform.[4] What can be done about technical difficulties such

as ? We hope that both the *rude and
the courteous Adjutant will improve to some extent,* so that he may
be promoted at last.

L. v. BTHV.

(736) *To George Thomson, Edinburgh*

[Autograph not traced] [5]

MON CHER AMI !   [VIENNA, *January* 18, 1817]

Tous les chansons, que vous m'avez prie au moi de 8
Juillet 1816 de composer pour vous, étaient dejà finis a la Fin
du mois Septembre,[6] mais comme je me fus proposé moi même
de les porter chez Mess. Friess,[7] la chose se prolongeait, surtout
que j'avais une grande Maladie, et dans ce moment, je ne me
trouve pas encore tout à fait sain, c'est aussi la cause pourquoi
je les envoie a Messr. les Fries — Quant à chansons de divers
Nations, vous n'avez que prendre des paroles en prose, mais
non pas en vers, enfin si vous prendrès *des paroles en Prose* vous
y reussirès parfaitement —

---

[1] The address on the verso in Beethoven's hand is : 'To the Adjutant, the
second sc[oundre]l of the Empire'.   [2] Op. 93.   [3] Op. 101.
[4] This remark gives the approximate date of this undated letter. For on
January 9, 1817, the *Allgemeine Musikalische Zeitung* of Vienna published an article
in which reference was made to Beethoven's symphony in A, Op. 92, which 'is
difficult to perform'.
[5] Taken from *TDR* IV, p. 12, where it is stated that the letter was written
by Beethoven.
[6] I.e. 25 Scottish songs, Op. 108, and 12 Scottish songs, WoO 156. See *KHV*.
624-628.   [7] See Letter 765, p. 672, n. 3.

Quant a vos autres propositions, j'aurai l'honneur de vous
repondre le plus prochain, je vous presenterai mes idees de ce
project, et j'espère, que vous les applaudires, et alors j'expedirai
tout ce, que vous demandez de moi, ainsi vite qu'exactement —
J'ai l'honneur d'être mon très cher Thomson, votre ami
et Serviteur

L. v. BEETHOVEN

(737) *To Sigmund Anton Steiner*

[Autograph in the Beethovenhaus, Bonn, H. C. Bodmer collection]

VIENNA, January 23, 1817

After a personal examination of the case and after hearing
the opinion of our council we are resolved and hereby resolve
that from henceforth on all our works, on which the title is
German, instead of pianoforte *Hammerklavier* shall be used.[1]
Hence our most excellent L[ieutenan]t G[enera]l and his
Adjutant and also all others whom it may concern, are to
comply with these orders immediately and see that they are
carried out.

Instead of Pianoforte
Hammerklavier —
This is to be clearly understood once and for all —
issued etc., etc.,

by the G[ENERALISSIM]O
on January 23, 1817

(738) *To Frau Nanette Streicher*

[Autograph not traced] [2]

MY DEAR FRAU STREICHER!   VIENNA, *January* 27, 1817
You surprise me, and thanks to my swiftly working
imagination I am immediately transported to Bremen.[3]   At

---

[1] Beethoven's order was carried out only in the titles of the pianoforte sonatas,
Op. 101, 106 and 109.   [2] Taken from Nohl II, no. 155.
[3] Beethoven is referring to Wilhelm Christian Müller of Bremen and his
talented daughter Elise. See Letter 1035. Writing in her diary on January 31,
1817, Fanny Giannatasio del Rio mentions a present which Beethoven had
received from a young admirer living at Bremen. Cf. Nohl, *op. cit.* p. 136.

the same time it is rather too far for me to betake myself thither at the moment, for I lack Oberon's horn [1] — Besides I am in the Landstrasse today and can pay you the visit which I planned a long time ago, the more so as I have something to discuss with you — About three o'clock this afternoon I shall tell you in person how greatly I am

your friend and servant

L. v. BEETHOVEN

(In haste)

(739) *To Tobias Haslinger*

[Autograph in the Stadtbibliothek, Vienna]

VIENNA, January 30, 1817

LITTLE ADJUTANT, MOST EXCELLENT LITTLE FELLOW!

Do make enquiries again about that small house and let me know the result — Also I do beg you to obtain for me the *essay on education*. I am particularly anxious to be able to defend my views on this subject against those of other people and to correct them still more carefully. As for the little Adjutant, I now believe that I have almost struck the right path in his education —

Your CONTRA FA.

(740) *To Nikolaus Zmeskall von Domanovecz*

[Autograph in the Nationalbibliothek, Vienna]

DEAR Z[MESKALL]! [VIENNA, *January* 30, 1817]

By desiring to associate me with a Schuppanzigh [2] and the like you have defaced my pure and honest work. You are not my debtor, but I am yours; and now you have made me your debtor even more. I cannot tell you in writing how much this present pains me; but with my usual frankness I must add that I cannot give you a friendly look *for this*. Although you are only a performer in your art, yet you have

---

[1] Paul Wranitzky's opera 'Oberon, König der Elfen' had been produced at the Theater auf der Wieden in 1789. Both this opera and Weber's 'Oberon' were based on the story by Wieland.

[2] For a note on Schuppanzigh see Letter 1168, p. 1027, n. 2.

655

frequently used your imagination; and I am inclined to think that your imagination sometimes prompts you to indulge in unnecessary whims. At any rate I have gained that impression from your letter in reply to my dedication [1] —

In spite of all that is good in me and my appreciation of all that is good in you, yet I am angry, angry, angry —

Your debtor once more, who, however, will certainly have his revenge,

L. v. BEETHOVEN

(741) *To Nikolaus Zmeskall von Domanovecz*

[*Autograph in the Nationalbibliothek, Vienna*]

[VIENNA, *January* 31, 1817]

DEAR Z[MESKALL] VON D[OMANOVEC]z and so on and so on and so on, together with grapes from Burgundy. —

I am sending you herewith the trio together with the cello part belonging to it.[2] Please keep it — Moreover I should very much like you to send me your servant the day after tomorrow in the morning and, let me add, — about eleven o'clock or half past, if possible. I shall certainly be at home until twelve. —

Kindly instruct him too to let me know if he finds someone for my service. I myself have already looked around in other quarters for such a person. For indeed these people are quite impossible. In fact they might land me sometime in a very embarrassing situation. They are both tarred with the same brush; and it is only compassion, which they by no means deserve and, strictly speaking, do not need, that has made me have patience with them for so long —

All good wishes, lord and despotic ruler over all the mountains of Ofen and Burgundy.

Your

L. v. [BEETHOVEN] [3]

---

[1] Of the F minor quartet, Op. 95. Cf. Letter 681.
[2] Probably the B♭ pianoforte trio, Op. 97, published by Steiner in September, 1816.
[3] The surname of the signature has been torn off the autograph.

(742) *To Tobias Haslinger*

[*Autograph in the Beethovenhaus, Bonn, H. C. Bodmer collection*]

[VIENNA, *January*, 1817]

Quite by chance I have hit on the following dedication :

'Sonata
for the Pianoforte
or — — Hämmer-Klavier
composed and
dedicated to
the Baroness Dorothea Ertmann,
née Graumann,
by L. v. Beethoven'

This is for the new sonata.[1] But should the title be already engraved, then I have the following two proposals to make, that is to say, either I shall pay *for the new title*, i.e. *it will be engraved at my expense*, or this title will be reserved *for another new sonata which I shall compose*.[2] *And indeed to bring another sonata into the world, all that is necessary is that the L[ieutenan]t G[enera]l's or, better still, pleno titulo, the L[ieutenan]t G[enera]l's and First State Councillor's mines should be opened — The title must first be shown to a linguist.*

Hämmer-Klavier is certainly German and in any case it was also a German invention.[3] Honour to whom honour is due — How is it that I have received no reports of the executions which have doubtless taken place ? —
Ever your best amicus ad amicum de amico.

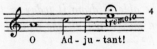

O   Ad - ju - tant!

Please observe the strictest silence about the dedication, for I want it to be a surprise [5] —

---

[1] The A major pianoforte sonata, Op. 101, published by Steiner in February, 1817.

[2] Probably a reference to the Hammerklavier sonata, Op. 106, which Beethoven began to compose during the following autumn.

[3] This is not so. It was invented in 1711 by an Italian, Bartolomeo Cristofori (1655–1731) of Florence. See Letter 746, p. 660.

[4] This musical quip is listed in *KHV.* as WoO 205ᵉ.

[5] This sentence is added at the left side of the fourth page.

(743) *To Franz Salzmann* [1]

[Autograph in the Beethovenhaus, Bonn, H. C. Bodmer collection]

ESTEEMED FRIEND! [VIENNA, *January*, 1817]

Gladly though I would have called on you, yet it was impossible for me to do so, partly because I was so very busy and partly because I did not know your address. And I was not even allowed to pay you a New Year courtesy visit. I wanted to call on you with my nephew, but an unfortunate incident prevented this, and now he is rather ill — But I need your help again, for I can't do very much more in the world than write down somehow or other a few notes. As in all business matters I am a bit of a dunce, forgive me for having to trouble you again. But please be so kind as to name the *months and to quote their amounts.* Then *at the very hour which you fix to receive me, I myself will come to see you at your office, when you will kindly give me your address*; *and as soon as my nephew is recovered we will visit you sometime.* In any case I must *apologize to your wife.* For I remember that *I made a most dreadfully rude remark to her, though not deliberately, of course.* But I must make things right with her and I expect that I shall have to make amends and do penance —

With cordial regards,

your friend and servant

BEETHOVEN

Postscript. In regard to that most desirable dividend, please arrange for me to be able to draw it today or tomorrow. For people like me always need money and all the notes I write do not extricate me from my needs!! [2] —

---

[1] Franz Salzmann (1787–1865), who was Secretary General of the Austrian National Bank from 1843 to 1858, had been appointed chief accountant of this bank in 1817. See *FRBH* II, 98-99.

[2] Beethoven's favourite pun on 'Noten' and 'Nöten.'

(744) *To Sigmund Anton Steiner*

[*Autograph in the possession of Mrs. Oscar Johnson*]

[VIENNA, *January*, 1817]

DEAR L[IEUTENANT] G[ENERAL]!

It seems to me that there are still a few small mistakes in the sonata.[1] Please therefore send me my manuscript for a few hours so that I may check them. You may have the m[anuscript] back at once if you are anxious to have it — My thanks for your copies.

Wholly your G[ENERALISSIM]O

LVBTHVN

(745) *To* [*Tobias Haslinger*]

[*Autograph in the Beethovenhaus, Bonn, H. C. Bodmer collection*]

[VIENNA, *January*, 1817]

Sonate must be printed in German letters [2] — Musée musical should be given first in German, for example, Musikalisches Museum, and underneath this, Musée musical, or printed in German only, Sonate des Museums für Klaviermusik, etc.[3]

(746) *To Tobias Haslinger*

[*Autograph not traced*] [4]

[VIENNA, *January*, 1817]

You must send me at once the proofs which have still to be corrected [5] — As for Page 15 in the last movement, it would be well to add the alphabet letters at bars 18, 19, 20

---

[1] Possibly the pianoforte sonata, Op. 101, published by Steiner in February, 1817.

[2] The A major pianoforte sonata, Op. 101, formed the first number of the 'Museum für Klavier-Musik' and appeared as such in the title of the original edition of February, 1817. See *KHV*. 280.

[3] The autograph is not signed.

[4] Taken from Nottebohm, *Zweite Beethoveniana* (Leipzig, 1887), p. 344.

[5] I.e. the proofs of Op. 101.

and 21 [1] — That should be entrusted to the worthy Adjutant —
In regard to the title, a linguist should be consulted as to
whether Hammer or Hämmer-Klavier or, possibly, Hämmer-
flügel should be inserted [2] — But be sure to let me see the title
for my approval —

L. v. BEETHOVEN

(747) To Tobias Haslinger

[Autograph in the Beethovenhaus, Bonn, H. C. Bodmer collection]

MOST EXCELLENT A[DJUTAN]T,   [VIENNA, January, 1817]
    Second S[coundrel] of the Empire,
    The guilty and the innocent are commanded to see to
the proof-reading with all speed and to return the proofs to
me —
    In the last movement in the passage where low E appears
in the four chords,[3] I should like the letters to be added,
namely :

E   E   E   E   E
A   Fis Gis A   h
E   E   E   E   E

Furthermore, the words which have been added in certain
places must be noted and inserted — The innocent and the
guilty, the rude and the courteous second S[coundre]l of the
Empire etc., etc., etc., cannot be promoted.[4]

(748) To Tobias Haslinger

[Autograph in the Beethovenhaus, Bonn, H. C. Bodmer collection]

[VIENNA, January, 1817]

    The worthy A[djutant] must still see that the few mis-
takes are corrected in the last movement where low E

---

[1] See page 15 of the original edition.

[2] Beethoven wrote on the autograph of this sonata : 'Neue Sonate für Ham —
1816 im Monat November'.

[3] The passage occurs in the A major pianoforte sonata, Op. 101, in the second
half of the last movement at bars 195 to 199, where Beethoven used low E for
the first time.

[4] The autograph is not signed.

occurs.[1] Meanwhile I should like *the letter to be put under the first note, as I have indicated* — Tastenflügel is a good expression but can only be regarded as a *general* term for Federflügel, Klavier (or Clavichord) etc.

Hence I think I can decide on *Tasten- und Hammerflügel*, that is to say, by uniting in this way both these expressions. However, I will consult today an empty-headed man, I mean to say, a scholar, on this point [2] —

L. v. BEETHOVEN

(749) *To Sigmund Anton Steiner*

[Autograph in the possession of the Historical Society of Pennsylvania]

[VIENNA, *January*, 1817]
MOST EXCELLENT AND WORTHY L[IEUTENAN]T G[ENERA]L !

The penance is herewith completed and, moreover, to our satisfaction. This pleasant news is for the information of our dear and trustworthy L[ieutenan]t G[enera]l.— As for the title of the new sonata, all you need do is to transfer to it the title which the Wiener Musikzeitung gave to the symphony in A, i.e. 'the sonata in A which is difficult to perform'.[3] No doubt my excellent L[ieutenan]t G[enera]l will be taken aback, for he will think that 'difficult' is a relative term, e.g. what seems difficult to one person will seem easy to another, and that therefore the term has no precise meaning whatever. But the L[ieutenan]t G[enera]l must know that this term *has a very precise meaning, for what is difficult* is *also beautiful, good, great* and so forth. Hence everyone will realize that this is *the most lavish* praise that can be bestowed, since what is *difficult makes one sweat.*—Since the Adjutant by recently indulging in tittle-tattle has again disclosed his treacherous and seditious opinions, his *right ear* must be *sharply* seized and pulled today — and this must be done immediately. We reserve to ourselves all further punishments to be carried out in our presence and in that of our most excellent L[ieutenan]t G[enera]l —

[1] In the last movement of Op. 101. See preceding Letter, no. 747.
[2] Beethoven is punning on the words 'geleert' (emptied) and 'gelehrt' (learned).
[3] The symphony is Op. 92, the sonata Op. 101. For the remark quoted by Beethoven see Letter 735, p. 653, n. 4.

We wish our dear L[ieutenan]t G[enera]l all that is good, and especially a better Adjutant.

LVBTHVN

(750) *To Sigmund Anton Steiner*

[Autograph in the Deutsche Staatsbibliothek, Berlin]

[VIENNA, *January*, 1817]

I am sending herewith to my most excellent L[ieutenan]t G[enera]l the corrected pianoforte arrangement. Czerny's corrections should be accepted [1] —

In any case the worthy L[ieutenan]t G[enera]l should again have a look at the many criminal mistakes in the Adjutant's pianoforte arrangement.[2] Consequently the same treatment as yesterday's is to be applied today to the other ear of the A[djutant].[3] And even if it should be proved that he is *perfectly innocent, yet the treatment must be given,* so that fear and dread of committing any crimes in future may be instilled into him. Meanwhile a report must be sent about yesterday's and today's treatment.

I embrace my most excellent L[ieutenan]t G[enera]l and send him the pianoforte arrangement of the symphony in F which is difficult to perform.[4]

Your etc., etc., etc.

(751) *To Sigmund Anton Steiner*

[Autograph in the Beethovenhaus, Bonn, H. C. Bodmer collection]

[VIENNA, *January*, 1817]

MOST EXCELLENT L[IEUTENAN]T G[ENERA]L!

Please send me some *vocal duets, trios and quartets from various operas and also some arrangements of them as violin quartets or quintets; and please include the songs 'Merkenstein', 'Der Mann*

---

[1] Carl Czerny had arranged the eighth symphony, Op. 93, for two pianos.
[2] Haslinger had arranged the eighth symphony, Op. 93, for pianoforte duet.
[3] See preceding Letter, no. 749.
[4] For this Press comment which evidently amused Beethoven see Letter 735, p. 653, n. 4.

von Wort', 'An die Hoffnung' and 'An die ferne Geliebte'.[1] Please let me have the whole lot by this afternoon at latest, for I have found an opportunity of dispatching them. The L[ieutenan]t G[enera]l must butter up the G[eneralissim]o who in turn must butter up other people. Had it not been for the vast mines of the L[ieutenan]t G[enera]l and the brain-pan of the G[eneralissim]o we should have been ruined long ago — In my capacity as guardian I am obliged to make presents of this kind so that the carriage wheels may be oiled to take me to my destination — I have had a letter from the Countess Erdödy. All sorts of things are happening in that quarter too. Brauchle, the Magister, is in an advanced state of pregnancy, which means that I must send him a midwife immediately [2] — I should very much like to have a report about the two executions.[3] The third one I will carry out myself as soon as I can go out again —

But I am etc., etc., etc., etc.

I hope that the L[ieutenan]t G[enera]l's mines are in a most flourishing condition.[4]

L. v. BTHVN

When am I likely to have the proofs of the sonata and the other sprouting bulbs? [5]

(752) *To Sigmund Anton Steiner*

[*Autograph in the Stadtbibliothek, Vienna*]

[VIENNA, *January*, 1817]

MOST DEAR EMBARRASS — MENTS !!! [6]

Most politely do I request you to have the songs listed in some kind of catalogue in which only the first three bars of each are quoted, but this must be done prestissimo; and

---

[1] Op. 100, 99, 94 and 98.
[2] Brauchle was also a composer.   [3] Cf. Letters 749 and 750.
[4] Beethoven is referring to the financial situation of Steiner's firm.
[5] This sentence is added on the right side of the third page of the autograph. As well as the pianoforte sonata, Op. 101, Steiner was publishing the eighth symphony, Op. 93, and several minor compositions.
[6] Beethoven is punning on the words 'Verleger' (publisher) and 'Verlegenheit' (embarrassment).

then I will immediately decide about the order — It is clear that an English publisher is a commodity which is damaged just as much by lying too long as a German one, or such a reminder would not be necessary.[1] I have retained the papers belonging to the songs, since they must be despatched with them later on — I remain most respectfully and with amazingly respectful sentiments

your

L. v.[2]

(753) *To Nikolaus Zmeskall von Domanovecz*

[*Autograph in the Nationalbibliothek, Vienna*]

[VIENNA, *February* 4, 1817]

I shall be with you, my dear despot, at twelve o'clock precisely. Thanks, thanks, many thanks.

Gratias agimus tibi domine.[3]

Your

L. v. BEETHOVEN

(754) *To Frau Nanette Streicher*

[*Autograph not traced*][4]

MY DEAR FRAU STR[EICHER]!   VIENNA, *February* 7, 1817

I ask you a thousand times to forgive me about yesterday. We had a meeting on the question of my nephew, a meeting which had already been fixed on the previous day; and on such occasions I am really always in danger of losing my head. And that's what did happen yesterday. I only hope that you may not have felt offended and that you will give me the pleasure of a visit some other time. Yesterday afternoon I was taken up with the same question and again at ten o'clock today. Hence I will call on you at about twelve or half past. If you are prevented from seeing me, well, I will call some

---

[1] Another pun on 'Verleger' (publisher) and 'verlegen', the past participle of 'verliegen' (to be spoilt by lying too long in store).

[2] The remainder of the signature has been cut off.

[3] We render thanks to thee, O Lord.

[4] Taken from Nohl II, no. 160 and *TDR* IV, 484.

other time — Once more I beg you to ascribe what happened yesterday to all the bewildering circumstances into which the care for my dear nephew has plunged me.

In haste, your friend

BEETHOVEN

(755) *To Frau Nanette Streicher*

[*Autograph not traced*] ¹

VIENNA, *February* 13, 1817

MY DEAR AND PRECIOUS FRAU STREICHER!

I dare not go out today. But I shall turn up at your home at ten o'clock tomorrow. Do ensure that the caretaker on the first floor shall give us some idea of the upper rooms. Then if I find them suitable for me, I will take them at once — Owing to several impediments yesterday I was not able to see you — Make sure, therefore, that we shall be granted a day's postponement.

In haste, your friend

BEETHOVEN

(756) *To Nikolaus Zmeskall von Domanovecz*

[*Autograph in the Nationalbibliothek, Vienna*]

DEAR Z[MESKALL],   [VIENNA, *February* 13, 1817]

This is a very interesting book, but I cannot spare it for long.² The person who wrote it has sent it to me. And in the meantime I have promised it to other lovers of reading as well — Please let me have your servant again tomorrow. He will doubtless tell you how, at what time and to what extent his coming today has produced a good effect.

¹ Taken from *TDR* IV, 484.
² In his note to this letter (see *KFR*, no. 649) Kalischer suggests that the book in question was Dr. Aloys Weissenbach's popular work, *Meine Reise zum Kongress*, published in Vienna during the previous year. Cf. Letter 505, p. 476, n. 4.

(757) *To George Thomson, Edinburgh*

[*Autograph in the National Library of Scotland*]

Mon cher Ami!   Vienna *February* 15, 1817 [1]

J'espère que vous aviez reçû a cette heure les derniers 12 chansons, quant à celles des divers Nations etrangers, elles etoient deja composeès, lorsque votre Lettre arriva.— vous m'avez autrefois parlè d'une chanson danois et d'une Sicilienne, que je ne savois alors trouver malgrè tous mes efforts, à present j'ai reussi à en avoir et les voila au lieu des deux ecossaises. Come vous aurès remarquè, j'ai traitè l'une en trio, l'autre en quatuor. Celle en F-dur $\frac{2}{4}$ est un chanson a la Sainte Vierge *des Navigateurs Siciliene en Navigeant;* l'autre est une danoise originelle. J'ose esperer que vue l'affinité de la *langue anglaise* avec la *danoise* elle ne vous sera pas desagreable. quant *aux overtures* je suis prêt a vous servir, seulement je dois vous prier de m'envoyer les *Comencemens de chaque melodie de ces 19 airs,* il suffit seulement quelques Mesures où Battutes de chaque Melodie, alors je ferai mon possible pour vous contenter.— Est ce que vous demandès, *qu'elles sont à peù près aussi faciles de traiter pour le Clavecin come les Chansons ecrits de ja pour vous j'usqu'ici*? avec ces 19 airs je ferai 6 overtures characteristiques avec accompagnement des deux Violons, Viola et Violoncelle, ou seulement con un Violon et Violoncelle selon votre goût — Pour la 7[tiéme] overture que vous souhaites permettre à la Collection des chansons ecoissaises il me faut savoir si elle doit être aussi tirèe des chansons ecoissaises mêmes et de quelles? Vous avez sans doute remarquè, que dans toutes votres *Comissions le plaisir de vous rendre mes services l'emportait* sur *mon interêt* ayant traité les accompagnements en quatuor trio et duo *au même prix come les simples aussi les longues Chansons come les courts.* La Collection des chansons des divers Nations m'a aussi donnè beaucoup de peine. le moindre prix pour les 7 ouvertures en question est 124 ducats en espèce. ajant à present quelque moment a moi, je pourrais vous les

---

[1] The date is at the foot of the third page of the autograph, on which Thomson wrote the following comment: 'Beethoven asks 124 ducats to compose 7 overtures for Piano Forte, etc., and speaks of composing for English verses long ago sent to him etc., etc.'.

fournir *dans bien peu de tems* pourvû, que les cōmencemens du chaque *Theme me perviennent bien tôt* — Plus tard il vous conviendra attendre d'avantage. le copiateur ne couterà d'orenavant que bien peu de choses; *cette fois-ci il etait trop occupè,* et *il ètoit pressé par* moi a vous servir de suite. je tiens encore de votres *Poesies anglaises bien interessantes,* je les examinerai de nouveau pour vous faire au moins un proposition, il serait bien dōmage de les oublier tout à fait. je vous prie de m'envoyer un Exemplaire de la Collection des chansons ecoissaise aussitôt qu'elles quitteront la presse et de prendre bien garde *dans l'ordre cōme elles se suivent de modifier autant que possible le differents charactères pour eviter une monotonie degoutante.*— Peut-etre que j'aurai l'anne Future le bonheure de voir en l'angletère; dans çe cas-la, je ne manquerais pas de vous faire une visite a Edimbourg pour vous temoigner en personne le sentiments d'estime, avec les quelles je suis

votre très-humble serviteur

LOUIS VAN BEETHOVEN

(758) *To Franz Brentano, Frankfurt am Main*

[*Autograph not traced*] [1]

MY ESTEEMED FRIEND!   VIENNA, *February* 15, 1817

Some time ago I sent you several musical works in order to recall myself to your friendly remembrance. All the members of the Brentano family have ever been dear to me; and you especially, my esteemed friend, I shall always remember with sincere regard. I myself would like you to believe that frequently I have prayed to Heaven for long preservation of your life so that for many years you may be usefully active for your family as its esteemed head. You will always find me imbued with sentiments of that kind ——

As for me, my health has been undermined for a considerable time. *The condition of our country* has been partly responsible for this; and so far no improvement is to be expected, nay rather, every day there is a further deterioration — Herr

---

[1] Taken from *KFR,* no. 651. Kalischer transcribed this autograph letter, then in private ownership.

Kessler has sent me through you a work which shows that he is talented.[1] I have not yet been able to write to him, but I shall do so soon and in detail — I very greatly miss your company and that of your wife and your dear children. For where can I find anything like it here in our Vienna? Hence I hardly go to see anyone, for I have never been able to get on with people unless there is some exchange of ideas — Well, all my very best wishes. I hope that all possible good and beautiful things may come to you during your lifetime to crown your merits. May you now and then call me to mind; and may you not think me unworthy of your remembrance —

With sincere regard and devotion,

your friend

L. v. BEETHOVEN

All my best greetings to my beloved friend Toni[2] and to your dear children.

(759) *To Peter Joseph Simrock, Bonn*

[*Autograph in the Beethovenhaus, Bonn, H. C. Bodmer collection*]

VIENNA, *February* 15, 1817

Very soon, my dear little Simrock, I will send you everything you asked for; and I shall also be able to give you particulars about the publication —

The opus no. is 101 [3] —

I never received your letter of October 23rd. That is another of the excellent arrangements for which we have to thank the age we live in. It has happened to me that four or five letters were sent to me from a place abroad, whence the receipts were forwarded to me immediately so as to assure me that the letters had been despatched. But I received — *not a single one of them* — Since October 15th I have been very ill with a feverish cold, from the *effects of which* I am still suffer-

[1] For a note on Kessler see Letter 769.

[2] Franz Brentano's wife Antonia.

[3] As the A major pianoforte sonata, published by Steiner, was about to appear, this work was given the opus number 101; and the two cello and pianoforte sonatas, published by Simrock in March, 1817, appeared as Op. 102.

ing; and I shall probably not recover until the end of spring or even the summer. — As soon as you can, do send me your views on the publication of my collected works, beginning with my compositions for the pianoforte. It would be a profitable undertaking, since so many inaccurate editions of my works are prancing about in the world. —

I wish your parents, and particularly your father, all that is beautiful and good. Your father no doubt will clearly remember how I questioned him about many a note on the horn; and he will surely perceive that the former pupil is now giving his master some hard nuts to crack — All good wishes to you, my dear little Simrock, and when you are publishing may you never be embarrassed.[1]

In haste, your friend

L. v. BEETHOVEN

(760) *To Nikolaus Zmeskall von Domanovecz*

[*Autograph in the Nationalbibliothek, Vienna*]

DEAR Z[MESKALL],   [VIENNA, *February* 20, 1817]

The servant has been given 27 gulden and a pair of trousers. I don't think that he can ask for anything more. But I will come to you tomorrow afternoon, or perhaps even today, and we can then discuss the matter —

In haste, yours,

L. v. BEETHOVEN

(761) *To Nikolaus Zmeskall von Domanovecz*

[*Autograph in the Nationalbibliothek, Vienna*]

DEAR Z[MESKALL],   [VIENNA, *February* 21, 1817]

It is merely a question of one single point affecting the servant. Then I myself will go at once to the police; and *instead of being presented with a bouquet* Master *Strauss* [2] will be

[1] One of Beethoven's favourite puns, i.e. on 'Verleger' (publisher) and 'verlegen' (embarrassed).

[2] Evidently the name of Beethoven's servant. 'Strauss' also means 'bouquet'.

locked up for 24 hours. So I request you to let me know when I can see you at your place for a moment today. I should much prefer to come in the afternoon. But if you can't manage to see me then, do let me know at what other time I can see you. Further, it would be well if you could have the former *servant questioned about his lodging.* Don't say anything yet about the police, until we have had a talk —

In haste, your [1]

(762) *To Nikolaus Zmeskall von Domanovecz*

[Autograph in the Nationalbibliothek, Vienna]

[VIENNA, *February* 22, 1817]

Just let me know whether the person in question has turned up. *Even if she has not done so*, I may perhaps not go to the police until *tomorrow*, for at the moment I am engaged on urgent work. Just send me a few words about this.

In haste, your

BEETHOVEN

(763) *To Tobias Haslinger*

[Autograph in the Deutsche Staatsbibliothek, Berlin]

[VIENNA, *February*, 1817]

The Adjutant's innocence and nothing else!

We request you kindly to send us two copies of the score of the symphony in A [2] —

Further, we should like to know when we could have a copy of the sonata for the Baroness von Ertmann? [3] For she may perhaps leave here the day after tomorrow at latest —

No. 3, that is to say, the enclosed note is from a musical friend in Silesia, who, however, is not exactly rich and for whom I have already had some of my scores copied.[4] He would like to have these works of Mozart for his library. But

---

[1] The signature has been torn off the autograph.   [2] Op. 92.
[3] Op. 101.   [4] Probably Count von Oppersdorff. Cf. p. 187, n. 3.

as my servant has the heavenly privilege of being one of the chief asses of the Imperial State (which is saying a good deal), I can't use him for that purpose. Please, therefore, be so good as to send to Herr Traeg (the G[eneralissim]o of course can have no dealings with a hawker) and *ask him to write down how much each work will cost*? And send me his estimate together with my two scores in A [1] and the reply to my question about the Baroness Ertmann this very day and as soon as possible (presto prestissimo) — mark well, *in double quick charge towards the end* —

Let me add that I advise you to behave as well as possible — so that there may be no further obstacle likely to impair my good health —

L. v. BHVN

(764) *To the Baroness Dorothea Ertmann*

[*Autograph in a private collection*]

MY DEAR VIENNA, *February 23*, 1817 [2]
AND BELOVED DOROTHEA
CAECILIA!

You must have often misjudged me, for I must have seemed unpleasant to you. A good deal should be put down to my circumstances, particularly in former times when my Muse was less appreciated than now. You know the explanations given by the unbidden apostles who made shift with means very different from the Holy Gospel.[3] Well, I did not want to be reckoned among their number. Please accept now what was often intended for you and what may be to you a proof of my devotion both to your artistic aspirations and to your person [4] — That I could not hear you play at Cz[erny]'s [5] recently was due to an indisposition which at last seems to be yielding to my healthy constitution — I hope to hear from

[1] Op. 92.
[2] Actually Beethoven dated this letter 1816. But on internal evidence, namely, the publication of the pianoforte sonata, Op. 101, dedicated to the Baroness, the year must be 1817.
[3] Possibly a reference to Acts, chap. 8, verses 9-24.
[4] Evidently Beethoven was sending her an engraved copy of Op. 101.
[5] Carl Czerny gave musical parties on Sundays.

you soon how the Muses are faring at St. Pölten [1] and whether you cherish any regard for your friend and admirer

L. v. BEETHOVEN

My best compliments to your beloved *husband and consort*.[2]

(765) *To Count Moritz von Fries* [3]

[*Autograph not traced*] [4]

[VIENNA], *Tuesday, February* 25, 1817

HIGHLY BORN AND WORTHY COUNT!

Tomorrow morning I shall have the honour to send you the last songs for Mr. Thomson in Scotland. Please be so kind as to arrange for them to be forwarded to their destination immediately, because this time he is in a great hurry. And so that there may be no possibility of any other uncertainties arising, please issue in general all the other instructions about the complete settlement of this business.

I remain, highly born Count, with the best regards and highest esteem,

your most devoted servant

L. v. BEETHOVEN

(766) *To Sigmund Anton Steiner*

[*Autograph in the Beethovenhaus, Bonn, H. C. Bodmer collection*]

[VIENNA, *February*, 1817]

FOR THE L[IEUTENAN]T G[ENERA]L'S OFFICE!

I have received no reports whatever. Yet I constantly hear of acts of treason and of plots; and indeed I myself have

---

[1] The regiment of the Baroness's husband, who was an army colonel, was then stationed at St. Pölten.

[2] In the autograph this sentence is added on the left side of the page.

[3] Count Moritz von Fries (1777–1826), a partner in the firm of merchants and bankers, Fries & Co., was a director of the Austrian National Bank, a famous art collector and patron of artists and musicians. Beethoven dedicated to him his violin and pianoforte sonatas, Op. 23 and 24, his string quintet, Op. 29 and his seventh symphony, Op. 92. For a full account of the Fries family see *FRBH* I, 154-156.

[4] From a photograph in the Beethovenarchiv, Bonn, of a facsimile of the autograph.

been detecting them. These and similar circumstances as well as several other factors might well lead to a complete disbanding of the L[ieutenan]t G[enera]l's office?!! [1]

At the moment the Widows' Society who are performing the symphony in A require a copy of the score.[2] They will return it after they have used it. The L[ieutenan]t G[enera]l's office must deliver most humbly another copy of the same work to Salieri, the Court Kapellmeister, who is all-powerful at Court and a patriarch of his good intentions for German vocal music and German singers, and at the same time is to thank him with all due respect for his *fortunate physiocratic invention*, inasmuch as he has found the suitable pitch and voice to sing the part of God [3] —

Your
CONTRA UT[4]

(767) *To Cajetan Giannatasio del Rio*

[*Autograph in the Royal College of Music*]

[VIENNA, *February*, 1817] [5]

At any rate it is the first time that I have had to be reminded of what is for me a pleasant duty. But very pressing business connected not only with my art but also with several other less important matters made me completely forget your account. I assure you, however, that never again will it be necessary to remind me — I have already arranged for *my* servant to bring Karl home in the evening. Meanwhile I thank you for your kindness yesterday *in arranging for your servant to fetch him*. As I knew nothing whatever about this beforehand, it might well have happened that Karl would have had to remain at Czerny's. —

---

[1] I.e. Steiner's publishing firm.

[2] This concert was given twice, on March 30 and 31, 1817. Beethoven's symphony in A, Op. 92, and his oratorio 'Christus am Ölberge' were performed.

[3] Salieri was vice-president of the Society of Widows and Orphans of Viennese musicians. In 1787 he had composed a sacred cantata, 'Le Jugement Dernier', in which God was given a part to sing. The cantata was produced in Paris in March, 1788.   [4] Bass C.

[5] This approximate date has been derived from Nohl, *op. cit.* p. 137, where Fanny says that Beethoven, when writing this letter, must have been in one of his 'misanthropic moods'.

Karl's boots are too tight and he has already complained about them several times. Indeed they are so uncomfortable that he has hardly been able to walk and has taken ages to pull on his boots. To wear such boots ruins one's feet. So I request you not let him put on these boots until they have been stretched —

In regard to his hours for practising the pianoforte I beg you always to ensure that he puts in the time; for otherwise his teacher will not be able to help him. Yesterday Karl was not able to play at all. Indeed I myself have had this experience several times when I counted on being able to go through some music with him and had to go off without having achieved my purpose. — 'La musica merita d' esser studiata'.[1] Moreover, the few hours which he is allowed at present for his musical studies are really not sufficient. Hence it is all the more necessary for me to insist that he puts in the time — It is not at all unusual for such matters to be attended to at a boarding school. One of my closest friends also has a boy at a boarding school; and this boy is intended for the musical profession. At his boarding school he is given every possible encouragement. Indeed I was very much surprised to find the boy practising there quite alone in a distant room where he neither was disturbed himself nor could disturb others! — Please allow me to fetch Karl tomorrow about half past ten, for I have to go through some music with him and am also taking him to some musical performances —

With all kindest regards,
your friend
L. v. BEETHOVEN

[1] Music deserves to be studied. See p. 814.

(768) *To Tobias Haslinger*

[*MS not traced*] [1]

[VIENNA, *February*, 1817]

MOST EXCELLENT MEMBER OF THE COMPANY OF PRINTERS
AND ENGRAVERS!

Be so excessively kind and have a hundred offprints made
from this little plate — I will compensate you twofold and
threefold for *all this engraving and printing* —
All good wishes.

Yours
BEETHOVEN [2]

(769) *To Ferdinand Kessler, Frankfurt am Main* [3]

[*Autograph not traced*] [4]

[VIENNA, *March*, 1817]

Your symphony shows much talent, but what feeling agi-
tates your breast, and whither it will lead you, that the Muses
who never age will best be able to tell you. . . .

(770) *To Ferdinand Kessler, Frankfurt am Main*

[*Autograph not traced*] [5]

[VIENNA, *March*, 1817]

He is sorry that Kessler has not sent his translation [6] of
the *Fidelio*, which he wishes to have played before him, but

---

[1] Taken from Seyfried, *op. cit.* Appendix, p. 35.

[2] According to Seyfried the address on the verso in Beethoven's handwriting
runs as follows: 'For the highly born Herr Haslinger, associate extraordinary
attached to the Courts of the Graben and the little Paternostergasse'.

[3] Ferdinand Kessler (1793–1856) was a violinist, composer and teacher of
music living at Frankfurt am Main. Out of admiration for Beethoven's compositions he later undertook the proof-correcting of the 'Missa Solemnis' and the
ninth symphony.

[4] Taken from sale catalogue of Messrs. Sotheby & Co., July 17, 1883, no. 20,
where the letter is described as autograph and dated 1817.

[5] Taken from sale catalogue of Messrs. Puttick and Simpson, December, 1848,
no. 47, where the letter is described as autograph and dated 1817. Letter 769
and the above extract may be portions of one letter.

[6] Probably 'arrangement', such as a 'pianoforte arrangement'.

does not doubt that it is well executed. He speaks in glowing terms in praise of the art; and compliments Kessler on his attainments, advising him to follow his own genius and promising him advice, etc.

(771) *To Johann Nepomuk Kanka, Prague*

[Autograph in the Beethovenhaus, Bonn, H. C. Bodmer collection]

[VIENNA, *end of March*, 1817]

MY DEAR, BELOVED AND AFFECTIONATE K[ANKA]!

I have this moment received good news from the official receiver Bayer at R[etz], news which you yourself gave him about J[ohann] L[amatsch].[1] As to the remaining matters, you will be fully satisfied. —

I take the liberty of again asking you to obtain my money from the household of Prince Kinsky; and I enclose in this letter the necessary receipt for it. Perhaps some other way may yet be found which will enable me to obtain the money in future without my having to bother you; but it is too late now to think of one — On October 15th I succumbed to an inflammatory fever, from the after effects of which I am still suffering, and my art also. But I have reason to hope that my condition will gradually improve and that soon again I shall be able to *display my wealth*, at any rate *in my little empire of harmony*. For indeed in every other respect I am *poor* — owing to the times? To poverty of spirit and to what else????? — All good wishes — I must add that *everything around* and near us compels us to be *absolutely silent*. But this must not be the case in the bond of friendship and kinship of souls which we have established. And loudly I proclaim myself as always your friend who esteems you and loves you.

L. V. BEETHOVEN

[1] Cf. Letter 686, p. 624.

(772) *To Johann Nepomuk Kanka, Prague*

[*Autograph in the Stadtbibliothek, Vienna*] [1]

[VIENNA, *end of March*, 1817]

Question?

How will it be with my *life certificate* if I leave Vienna and, possibly, Austria? Will a life certificate signed *in non-Austrian territory* be valid? —

NB. Please let me have an account of all the expenses to which the letters have put you.[2] —

(773) *To Johann Baptist Rupprecht*

[*Autograph in the New York Public Library, Rubin Goldmark collection*]

[VIENNA, *March*, 1817]

Since you have agreed to translate the Scottish songs [3] for me, my dear Rupprecht, I cannot refrain from yielding to my [most urgent] desires and begging you very earnestly to apply your masterly pen to this product — Rest assured that I shall [use] all ways and means to prove my gratitude to you for doing so —

Soon I shall express to you in person the great regard I cherish for you.

Your most devoted

LUDWIG VAN BEETHOVEN

(774) *To Nikolaus Zmeskall von Domanovecz*

[*Autograph in the Nationalbibliothek, Vienna*]

DEAR Z[MESKALL]! [VIENNA, *March*, 1817]

I am introducing to you the bearer of this note, young Bocklet, who is a very able violinist.[4] If you can be of use to

---

[1] This additional note was originally attached to the preceding Letter no. 771. See Koch Catalogue no. 92, pp. 103-104.

[2] This postscript is written on the verso of the note.

[3] The preceding three words are added at the foot of the page. Probably a reference to Op. 108. Cf. Letter 776.

[4] Carl Maria von Bocklet (1801–1881), born at Prague, was a very promising violinist. He first visited Vienna in 1817 and stayed for six

him with the help of your acquaintances, please assist him, the more so as he has been very warmly recommended to me from Prague [1] —

Ever your true friend

BEETHOVEN

(775) *To Sigmund Anton Steiner*

[Autograph in the Beethovenhaus, Bonn, H. C. Bodmer collection]

[VIENNA, *March*, 1817]

The L[ieutenan]t G[enera]l's office must assist in every way this young artist Bocklet from Prague.[2] He, the bearer of this note, is a virtuoso on the violin. We hope that attention will be given to our communication, the more so as with the most violent affection we describe ourselves as your

G[ENERALISSIM]O

(776) *To Johann Baptist Rupprecht*

[Autograph in the Beethovenhaus, Bonn, H. C. Bodmer collection]

MOST ESTEEMED RUPPRECHT!   VIENNA, *April* 1, 1817

I earnestly request you to proceed with and finish the translation of the Scottish songs.[3] I have given them to the publisher Herr Steiner who himself will get in touch with you with a view to discusssing any further points connected with this task. It would be a pity if only a few little sparks of your poetical talent should have whetted our desire and if we should not have you to thank for the whole work — Wherever you would like to have alterations in the music I am quite willing to make them. In order to avoid monotony, I have

weeks. He gave a concert in the Kleiner Redoutensaal on April 8th. Later he abandoned the violin for the pianoforte.
    [1] According to Nohl I, no. 175, note, Bocklet had brought a letter of introduction from a Dr. Berger at Prague.
    [2] Cf. preceding Letter no. 774.
    [3] Probably Op. 108. See Beethoven's letter to Adolf Martin Schlesinger of April 30, 1820, Letter 1021. See also *KHV*. 310.

chosen, as you will see, an absolutely different order in the succession of the songs.

With very special and sincere regards,

your admirer

L. v. BEETHOVEN

(777) *To Cajetan Giannatasio del Rio*

[*Autograph in the Royal College of Music*]

[VIENNA, *early April*, 1817]

I request you, my esteemed friend, to have enquiries made for me in the houses in your neighbourhood whether there is an apartment of a few rooms with a kitchen to let from St. George's Day to Michaelmas. This must be done, however, by tomorrow, so that if there are none to be had in your district I may look around for another one.[1] —

Your friend and servant

L. v. BEETHOVEN

NB. Much as I should like to avail myself of your kind offers to let me live in your garden house, yet owing to various circumstances I cannot do so. —

My best greetings to your family.

(778) *To Charles Neate, London*

[*MS not traced*][2]

MY DEAR NEATE!   VIENNA, *April* 19, 1817

As long ago as October 15th I contracted a serious illness, from the after effects of which I am still suffering; and I am not yet restored to health. You know that I am obliged to live entirely on the profits from my compositions. Since the

---

[1] At the end of April, 1817, Beethoven moved into rooms on the second floor of a house in the Landstrasse, no. 268, near Giannatasio del Rio's boarding school. See *TDR* III, 541-542 and IV, 23, n. 3, and IV, 26, where extracts confirming this fact are quoted from Fanny's diary. The house, now Landstrasse, Hauptstrasse 26, still stands.   [2] Taken from *KFR*, no. 658.

onset of my illness I have been able to compose only extremely little and therefore have been able to earn only extremely little. So it would have been all the more welcome to me if you had done something for me — But I presume that the result of all that — is *nothing*.

You even wrote to *Häring complaining about me*; and my honourable treatment of you hardly deserves that — All the same, I must justify my conduct in this matter; and I should like you to know that the opera Fidelio was written several years ago, but that the book and the text left much to be desired. The book had to be entirely revised, which meant that several musical numbers had to be lengthened, others shortened, and others again had to be new, additional compositions. Thus, for instance, the overture is quite new and so are several other numbers. But it is quite possible that in London perhaps the opera is in its *first* version. If so, then it was stolen, a thing which in the theatre it is practically impossible to prevent. — As for the symphony in A, since you sent me absolutely no reply which would satisfy me, well then, I had to publish it.[1] But I would gladly have waited for three years if you had written to say that the Philharmonic Society would take it — but from all quarters I heard nothing — nothing. Well now, in regard to the *piano sonatas* with *violoncello* I am giving you *a month's time* for them; and if by then I have received no reply from you, I will publish them in *Germany*.[2] As I have heard from you just as little about these works as about the other compositions, I have given them to a German publisher who earnestly begged me for them. *But I have insisted on having it in writing (Häring has read this written statement) that he will not publish the sonatas until you have sold them in London.* I thought that you might be able to dispose of those two sonatas for 70 or 80 gold ducats at least. The English publisher can fix the day on which *they are to appear* in London. Then *on the same day* they will appear *in Germany* as well. In this way Birchall bought and got from me too the grand trio and the pianoforte sonata with violin.[3] I beg you therefore to do me this last kindness, i.e. *to let me have a reply*

[1] Op. 92, published by Steiner in November, 1816.

[2] Op. 102 was published by Simrock at Bonn in March, 1817. It was not published in England.

[3] Op. 97 and 96 were published by Birchall in 1816.

about the sonatas as quickly as possible. Frau von Jenney [1] swears about *all you have done for me*, and so do I, that is to say, I swear that *you have done nothing* for me and that you will do nothing and again *nothing* for me, summa summarum, *nothing! nothing! nothing!!!*

I assure you of my most absolute regard and I hope at least *for a last favour in the form of an early reply —*

Your most devoted servant and friend

L. v. BEETHOVEN

(779) *To Frau Nanette Streicher*

[*Autograph not traced*] [2]

[VIENNA, *April*, 1817]

All this while I have not been very well and hence could see very little of you ; and as I am worried by so many things and am in such confusion I need country air. Karl was to have gone to you today and would have been with you by this time ; but now my brother has turned up from Linz and the whole day will be spent with him and we shan't be able to see you and thank you. Meanwhile I must be back here again in a few days, when I shall see you and hope to have definite news of your recovery. Of course we expect you to visit us.

In haste, your

BEETHOVEN

(780) *To Frau Nanette Streicher, Vienna*

[*Autograph not traced*] [3]

[HEILIGENSTADT, *May* 16, 1817]

All that I can tell you today, my dear Frau von Streicher, is that I am here. *How* I am *here* and *where* I am *here*, that I

---

[1] O. E. Deutsch in his *Schubert, a Documentary Biography* (London, 1946), p. 61, suggests that this Frau von Jenny was a pianist, one of two sisters, Therese and Susanna von Jenny, who in 1820 were members of the Gesellschaft der Musikfreunde in Vienna.

[2] Taken from *TDR* IV, 485.

[3] Taken from *TDR* IV, 485.

will soon describe to you.¹ — Please have the enclosed sent to
the washerwoman who was recommended to me, for it belongs
to the washing which has to be mended. All my best greetings
to your family.

In haste, your friend and servant

L. v. BEETHOVEN

(781) *To Frau Nanette Streicher, Vienna*

[Autograph not traced] ²

DEAR FRIEND!   HEILIGENSTADT, *May* 16, [1817]
    I am making use of your permission to send you the
laundry so that you may kindly attend to this. I shall soon
see you; and I am as always your friend and servant

BEETHOVEN

All my best greetings to your family.

(782) *To Georg Friedrich Treitschke*

[Autograph in the Beethovenhaus, Bonn, H. C. Bodmer collection]

[VIENNA], *June* 9, 1817

    Herr von Treitschke's imaginings and aspirations are in-
formed that they should give the manuscript immediately to
the non-commissioned officer of the L[ieutenan]t G[enera]l's
office, so that the engraved portion which is pitted with mistakes can be engraved again directly,³ as it will have to be,
and indeed the more so as, if this is not done, the imaginings
and aspirations will receive the most horrible cuts and thrusts ⁴
— Handed in at the most unfatherly firm of all publishers in
the little Paternostergasse —

---

¹ No doubt Beethoven means the sort of house he is living in at Heiligenstadt.
² Taken from *TDR* IV, 486, and *KFR*, no. 660.
³ This clause is full of puns, on the verb 'stechen' in its various meanings,
as is also the last sentence of this unsigned note, where there is a play on the
meaning of 'Pater noster'.
⁴ Beethoven is referring to his setting of Treitschke's poem 'Ruf vom Berge',
published in June, 1817, as a musical supplement to the original edition of the
latter's poems, Vienna, 1817. In *KHV*. 617-618 this song is listed as WoO 147. In
Nohl, *op. cit.* pp. 122-124, Treitschke's poem is quoted in its entirety.

(783) *To the Countess Anna Marie Erdödy*, [*Munich*] [1]

[*Autograph in the Beethovenhaus, Bonn, H. C. Bodmer collection*]

HEILIGENSTADT, *June* 19, 1817

MY BELOVED SUFFERING FRIEND,

MY DEAREST COUNTESS!

Of late I have been tossed about far too much and over-whelmed with far too many cares. Then after feeling constantly unwell since October 6, 1816 I developed on October 15th a violent feverish cold, so that I had to stay in bed for a very long time; and only after several months was I allowed to go out even for a short while. *Until now* the after effects of this illness *could not be dispelled.* I changed my doctors, because my own doctor, a wily Italian,[2] had powerful secondary motives where I was concerned and lacked both honesty and intelligence. That was in April, 1817. Well, from April 15th until May 4th I had to take six powders daily and six bowls of tea. That treatment lasted until May 4th. After that I had to take another kind of powder, also six times daily; and I had to rub myself three times a day with a volatile ointment. Then I had to come here where I am taking baths. Since yesterday I have been taking another medicine, namely, a tincture, of which I have to swallow 12 spoonfuls daily [3] — Every day I hope to see the end of this distressing condition. Although my health has improved a little, yet it will be a long time apparently before I am completely cured. You can imagine how all this must affect the rest of my existence. My hearing has become worse; and, as I have never been able to look after myself and my needs, I am even less able to do so now; and my cares have been increased still further by the responsibility for my brother's child. — Here I have not yet found even decent lodgings. As it is difficult for me to look after myself, I have recourse now to this person and now to that; and everywhere I am abominably treated and am the prey of detestable people — Thousands of times I have thought of you, dear and beloved friend, and I do so

---

[1] According to Schöne, p. 7, the Countess was then at Munich.
[2] Doubtless Dr. Johann Malfatti.
[3] The words from 'of' to 'daily' are added at the foot of the page.

now; but my own misery has made me feel depressed. — Sperl has delivered Linke's letter to me. He is with Schwab.[1] I wrote to him recently to enquire how much the journey to you would probably cost, but I have received no reply — As my nephew has *holidays from the last days of August* until the *end of October*, I *could* come to you *then*, *if* I have perhaps *recovered my health*. Of course, we should have to have the necessary rooms to enable us to pursue our studies and lead a comfortable existence. But if only I could spend some time with old friends who, notwithstanding the various intrigues of devilish people, have remained loyal to *me*, *as I to them*, perhaps good health and cheerfulness would again be my portion. — Linke need only write to tell me how I could undertake the journey most economically — For unfortunately my expenses are very great and owing to my illness, since I can compose very little, my earnings are meagre; and the small capital, for the possession of which I have to thank my deceased brother, I dare not touch. For since my income is always diminishing and has almost vanished, I must hold on to this sum. — I am writing to you very frankly, my dearest Countess, but precisely on that account you will not misunderstand me. Nevertheless I need nothing and would certainly accept nothing from you. The question merely is to work out the most economical way of visiting *you*. Everybody without exception is now in *the same* position and has to consider *such things*. So my friend must not be surprised at my referring to this. — I hope that your health is in a more reassuring state than it was when I heard about it some time ago. May Heaven preserve for her dear children that *most admirable mother*. Indeed if only on that account, I mean, for the sake of your family, you would deserve to have the greatest measure of good health — All good wishes, most excellent and most beloved Countess. Let me have news from you soon —

Your true friend
BEETHOVEN

---

[1] Not identified. In *FRBH* I, 459, Frimmel mentions a Viennese music teacher called Schwab.

(784) *To Nikolaus Zmeskall von Domanovecz, Vienna*

[Autograph in the Nationalbibliothek, Vienna]

DEAR KIND ZMESKALL, NUSSDORF, *July* 7, [1817] [1]
As you have now undertaken to have the letters copied, I am enclosing a sheet of paper for the copy of that one letter. From this you will surely gather what I have found to be necessary. Häring's handwriting would easily be recognized; and that I should not like. And moreover I have found it necessary to add this copy. Meanwhile please arrange for the letter to Ries to be sent off on Wednesday [2] at the latest, but be sure to obtain a receipt for it. That is the safest method for such a long distance. You will find Ries's address in his letter. Perhaps I shall see you tomorrow, as I have to go into town —

In haste, your grateful friend

BEETHOVEN

(785) *To Frau Nanette Streicher, Vienna*

[Autograph not traced] [3]

MY BELOVED FRIEND! NUSSDORF, *July* 7, [1817]
Your letter has reached me here; and, what is more, it confirms the reported news of your serious fall. I hope that you will soon recover; warm and tepid baths heal all wounds — The bad weather we had the day before yesterday, when I was in town, prevented me from going to see you. I hurried back here yesterday morning but did not find my servant at home; and he had even taken away with him the key of my lodging. It was very cool and I had come out of town with nothing on me but a thin pair of trousers; so I had to hang around for three solid hours, which was not at all good for me and made me feel ill for the rest of the day. — That is the

---

[1] The year, which on internal evidence is certainly correct, is written on the verso in another hand. Early in July Beethoven left Heiligenstadt for Nussdorf, where he remained until the middle of October. He lived in the Greinerhaus, in the Kahlenbergerstrasse 26, a house which still exists.

[2] In 1817 July 7th fell on a Monday. Hence Letters 786 and 787, dated July 9th, were written on Wednesday.

[3] Taken from Nohl II, no. 168 and *TDR* IV, 486.

sort of thing one has to put up with in households run by servants! — As long as I am ill, I really ought to be associating on a different footing with quite different people. Much though I usually like solitude, yet at the moment it distresses me, the more so as with all the medicines and the baths I have to take it is hardly possible for me to occupy myself as I used to do. Furthermore, there is the distressing prospect that perhaps I may never be cured. I myself am inclined to distrust my present doctor who has finally pronounced my condition to be caused by a *disease of the lungs*.[1] I shall have to think over the question of a housekeeper. If, despite this utter moral rottenness of the Austrian state, one could feel certain even to some extent of being able to find some honourable person, everything would be easy, but — but — !!!

Now I have a great favour to ask of Streicher. Request him on my behalf to be so kind as to adjust one of your pianos for me to suit my impaired hearing. It should be as loud as possible. That is absolutely necessary. I have long been intending to buy one of your pianos, but at the moment that would be very difficult for me. Perhaps, however, it will be possible for me to do so later on. But until then I should like *to borrow* one of yours. Of course I don't want to do so without paying for it. I am prepared to pay you in advance what you usually receive for one, i.e. for six months in assimilated coinage. Perhaps you are not aware that, although I have not always used one of your pianos, since 1809 I have always had a special preference for them — Only Streicher would be able to send me the kind of piano I require — On the whole I find it difficult to bother anybody, for I am accustomed rather to do things for other people than to let other people do things for me — Whatever proposals you make to me in this connexion I will accept, and I will gladly comply with your conditions — Many thanks for the 20 gulden you lent me. The spoon is going to you too, for I am returning it herewith — I shall soon see you for a few minutes — My best greetings to all your family.

Your friend and servant

L. V. Beethoven

---

[1] Beethoven's doctor was at that time Dr. Jakob Staudenheim, whom he frequently miscalled Staudenheimer. Cf. Letter 381, p. 385, n. 2.

(786) *To Ferdinand Ries, London*

[*MS not traced*] [1]

DEAR FRIEND! VIENNA, *July* 9, 1817

The offers made to me in your welcome letter of June 9th are very flattering.[2] From this reply you will judge how greatly I value them. If it were not for my unfortunate infirmity on account of which I need a good deal of attention and have to face many expenses, particularly on a journey to a foreign country, I would accept the proposal of the Philharmonic Society *unconditionally*. But put yourself in my place, just consider how many more obstacles I have to overcome than any other artist, and then judge whether my demands are unfair. Here they are and I beg you to communicate them to the Directors of the aforesaid Society:

1) I shall be in London during the first half of January, 1818, at latest.

2) The two grand symphonies, which are entirely new, will then be ready and they will become and remain the sole property of the Society.[3]

3) For these symphonies the Society will pay me 300 guineas and 100 guineas for my travelling expenses, which, however, will far exceed that sum, since it is essential for me to have a travelling companion.

4) As I am beginning at once the task of composing these symphonies, the Society (after accepting my statement) will remit to me in Vienna the sum of 150 guineas, so that I may provide myself without delay with a carriage and make other arrangements for the journey.

5) I accept the conditions about not appearing with another orchestra or in public, about not conducting and about the preference to be given to the Society in similar conditions; and in view of my love of honour this was a foregone conclusion.

[1] Taken from *WRBN.* 169-171. This was the letter which Beethoven on July 7th requested Zmeskall to have written for him. See Letter 784.
[2] Portions of Ries's letter to Beethoven, dated June 9th, of which the Royal Philharmonic Society has a complete copy, are reproduced in *KFR* III, pp. 179-181.
[3] Beethoven was planning his ninth and, evidently, a tenth symphony.

6) I am to count on the support of the Society in organizing and promoting one or, if circumstances permit, several concerts for my benefit. Both the particular friendship of some Directors of your estimable assembly and, in general, the kind interest of all artists in my work guarantee the success of such an undertaking. And this makes me all the more eager to fulfil their expectations.

7) And now please obtain the acceptance or confirmation of the above statement in English, signed by three Directors and made out in the name of the Society.

You may well imagine that I am looking forward to making the acquaintance of that excellent Sir George Smart and to meeting you and Mr. Neate again. If only instead of sending you this letter I myself could fly over to London!

Your sincere admirer and friend
L. v. BEETHOVEN

(787) *To Ferdinand Ries, London*

[*Autograph in the possession of Julius Wegeler*] [1]

DEAR RIES, [VIENNA, *July* 9, 1817]

I embrace you with all my heart. I have purposely asked somebody else to write the above letter, so that you may read it all with greater ease and then expound it to the Society. I am convinced of your good intentions with regard to myself; and I hope that the P[hilharmonic] S[ociety] will accept my proposal. The Society may rest assured that I will exert myself to the utmost to perform as worthily as possible the honourable task entrusted to me by such a select company of artists — How powerful is the Society's orchestra, how many violins and so forth; and are there *one or two of each wind-instrument*? Is the hall large and resonant?

Your sincere admirer and friend
L. v. BEETHOVEN

---

[1] This short note in Beethoven's hand was enclosed in the preceding long letter to Ries written in another hand, i.e. Letter 786.

(788) *To Wilhelm Gerhard, Leipzig* [1]

[Autograph not traced] [2]

SIR!   NUSSDORF, *July* 15, 1817

You once honoured me with a request that I should set
to music a few of your anacreontic songs. As I was very busy,
it was more through physical impossibility than lack of courtesy
that I did not send you a reply. It was even more difficult to comply with your wishes, for those particular texts
you sent me were really the least suitable for singing.[3] The
description of a picture belongs to painting. And in this
respect the poet too, whose sphere in this case is not so re-
stricted as mine, may consider himself to be more favoured
than my Muse. On the other hand my sphere extends further
into other regions and our empire cannot be so easily reached —
My ill health, which has now persisted for about four years, is
partly to blame if I can only reply with silence to very many
suggestions which are put forward to me — Since last October,
1816 my ill health has become even worse. I contracted a
heavy feverish cold and resulting from it a disease of my lungs.
I am telling you all this so that you may not think me disobliging or misjudge me in some way, as many other people
do.

With kind regards, your devoted

LUDWIG VAN BEETHOVEN

[1] Wilhelm Christian Leonhard Gerhard (1780–1858), a Leipzig business
man who dabbled in writing poetry, had met Beethoven during a visit to Vienna
in 1816. Beethoven gave him his MS of ' Gretels Warnung ' (no. 4 of Op. 75), his
setting of a poem by Gerhard Anton von Halem. Gerhard had been writing
anacreontic poems which he published in 1818 in a collection entitled *Anakreon
und Sappho*.

[2] Taken from Nohl II, no. 170. The autograph of the letter was then in the
possession of Gerhard's daughter.

[3] So far as is known Beethoven never set to music any of Gerhard's poems.

(789) *To Frau Nanette Streicher, Baden*

[*Autograph not traced*] [1]

MY BELOVED FRIEND!   VIENNA, *July* 20, 1817
Owing to the bad weather I couldn't come in to town before Thursday, and you had already left — *What a prank* on the part of Frau von Streicher!!! [2] and for *Baden*???!!! So you are at Baden — — —
I have spoken to your husband. His sympathy for me has helped me and has also pained me; for Streicher very nearly shattered my resignation. God knows what is going to happen. But as I have always helped other people whenever I could, I am trusting to His being merciful to me — As for the housekeeper whom you know and have at any rate found to be honest, one might perhaps sample *her cooking* before she comes to me. But that can't be arranged until you come to town again, *and when will that be*? By the way, don't let yourself be *misled by your husband into playing certain marriage pranks* —
It's now time to see about the rooms. In the Gärtnergasse there are also rooms on the other side, where one would really enjoy an extraordinarily fine view. But all that depends upon your *return — Pray how did you have your letters to me delivered at Nussdorf?* —
Train your daughter carefully so that she may become a wife — Today happens to be Sunday, and if I am to read you out something more from the Gospel, then 'Love one another' etc., etc., etc. — I am closing this letter and I send you and your most excellent daughter my best greetings, and I trust that all your wounds will be healed.
If you go to the old ruins, remember that Beethoven has often lingered there. If you wander through the secluded fir-woods, remember that Beethoven has often poetized or, as the saying is, composed there.[3]
In haste, your friend and servant
L. V. BEETHOVEN

[1] Taken from *TDR* IV, 487-488.
[2] Here Beethoven is playing on the word 'Streich', which means 'prank', and on the name 'Streicher'.
[3] Beethoven is referring to the beautiful surroundings of Baden where he spent many summers.

NB. I am returning to Nussdorf today. Is there any commission I can carry out for you there? [1]

(790) *To Nikolaus Zmeskall von Domanovecz, Vienna*

[Autograph in the Nationalbibliothek, Vienna]

[NUSSDORF, *July* 23, 1817]

DEAR AND MOST EXCELLENT Z[MESKALL]!

I shall soon see you again in town. In the interest of economy I have a question to ask you, namely, what does one pay *now to have a pair of boots soled and heeled*? For indeed I have to pay my servant, who often walks into town and back, *for this.* —

Let me add that it drives me to despair to think that owing to my poor hearing I am condemned to spend the greater part of my life with *this* class of people, the most infamous of all, and partly to depend upon them —

Tomorrow morning the servant will call at your rooms for *a reply, but in a sealed cover* — I shall see you soon.

In haste, your friend

BEETHOVEN

(791) *To Franz Xaver Gebauer* [2]

[Autograph in the Musée de Mariemont]

VIENNA, *July* 26, 1817

If you do not return to me within eight days at latest this very same score of Nos. 4 and 5 of the *ballet music Prometeo* composed by me, then I will make a point of asserting my

---

[1] According to *TDR* IV, 488 this postscript was written on the top of the first page of the autograph.

[2] Franz Xaver Gebauer (1784–1822), born at Eckersdorf, near Glatz, in Prussian Silesia, became a music teacher in Vienna about 1810, and in 1816 was appointed choirmaster at the Augustinerkirche. He was one of the founder members of the Gesellschaft der Musikfreunde and in 1819 established his famous Concert Spirituel. See Hanslick, pp. 185-188. In his address on the verso of the autograph Beethoven describes him as 'Musikus bei dem Kaiserl. Königl. Orchester an der Wien'.

rights and lodging a claim with the authorities [1] —

All that you have to do is to hand in the score at Steiner's print-shop in the little Paternostergasse where you will be given a receipt — You ought to be ashamed of trying to swindle me or do me out of what belongs to me. Do not think that this is a mere threat. I will and must have back the score which belongs *to me* —

LUDWIG VAN BEETHOVEN

(792) *To Frau Nanette Streicher, Baden*

[*Autograph in the possession of Vizekonsul Fritz Hunziker*]

[NUSSDORF, *between July 22 and 27,* 1817]

MOST EXCELLENT FRAU STREICHER!

The enclosed letter should have been sent to you last Sunday, as you will see from the date [2] — In regard to Frau von Stein,[3] I must ask her not to let Herr von Steiner turn to stone, so that he may still be of use to me; or perhaps Frau von Stein should not be too much of a stone in respect of Herr von Steiner, and so forth and so on —

As to my health, well, it's certain that there are definite signs of improvement. But the chief trouble is still there; and I fear that it can never be removed — Most excellent Frau von Streicher, don't play any pranks on your little husband, but *in your dealings with everyone stick rather to your name of Frau von Stein*!!! I am spending next Wednesday and Thursday in town, where I shall again have a word with *Streicher.* I should like you to be here on account of the housekeeper, that is to say, as a secondary reason, though indeed I am delighted for your sake that you are enjoying the air of Baden. At the same time, when are you going to delight me again with your company at Nussdorf? — —

[1] See *KHV.* 102, according to which the autograph of the ballet music 'Die Geschöpfe des Prometheus', Op. 43, has not been traced. A copy of this work made by Gebauer with numerous corrections in Beethoven's hand is in the Nationalbibliothek, Vienna. But the copy is not complete, for nos. 4 and 5 are missing. Hence it can be assumed that Gebauer never returned those nos. to Beethoven.

[2] The 'enclosed letter' is obviously Letter 789, written on July 20th, which in 1817 fell on a Sunday.

[3] Nanette Streicher's maiden name was Stein. Cf. Letter 692, p. 628, n. 1.

My best greetings to your dear daughter and to Herr von St[reicher] —

Your friend and servant

BEETHOVEN [1]

(793) *To Nikolaus Zmeskall von Domanovecz*

[Autograph in the Nationalbibliothek, Vienna]

DEAR ZMESKALL!   VIENNA, *Wednesday, July* 30, 1817

I have reconsidered the question and have come to a different conclusion. After all, it might hurt Karl's mother to have to visit her child at the house of a stranger ; and in any case it is a less charitable arrangement than I like. So I am letting her come to me tomorrow.[2] A certain Bihler, tutor to Puthon's family, will be there too. If you could come to me about six o'clock, but not later, I should be extremely delighted. Indeed I *most earnestly* beg you to do so, for I like to inform the Landrechte who has been present at these meetings. As you know, a *Court Secretary* is more acceptable to them than *a person without a character, but full of character* [3] — Well, all jesting apart, if you do come, you will really *do me a great service*, apart from the fact that I am fond of you — So I shall expect you for certain.

Your friend and admirer

L. VAN BEET [4]

NB. I insist that my *jest* shall not be misinterpreted [5] —

---

[1] The autograph lacks the musical addition quoted in all the printed versions of this letter. The owner of the autograph suggests that the missing portion was added to the 'enclosed letter', i.e. Letter 789. It runs in translation as follows :

Where are my blankets ?

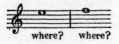

[1] In *KHV*. this musical quip is listed WoO 205ᵈ.
[2] Beethoven was in Vienna on Wednesday and Thursday, July 30th and 31st.
[3] Beethoven is probably alluding to an immoral person like his sister-in-law. Zmeskall was a Court Secretary.
[4] Remainder of signature torn off.
[5] This postscript is added at the side of page 3.

(794) *To Frau Nanette Streicher, Vienna*

[Autograph not traced] [1]

DEAR FRAU VON STREICHER!   [NUSSDORF, *July*, 1817]
    Forgive me if I perhaps offended you with my mission
today — My poor health and, in consequence, my situation,
which in this respect is really very distressing, prevent me from
thinking out things as carefully as I used to do — When I see
you I will explain this more clearly — I hope to see you soon —
Your friend
BEETHOVEN

    Please let me have the bed-clothes. Forgive me, but I am
feeling exhausted.

(795) *To Dr. Johann Bihler*

[Autograph in the collection of the late Stefan Zweig]

DEAR B[IHLER]!   [VIENNA, *July*, 1817]
    Doctor Sassafrass,[2] whom I told you of, is coming at noon
today. So please turn up at my home too — In order that
you may not lose your way, I am giving you the numbers of
the house and the floor, so that you may see everything in
front of you before you drop in — At no. 1241 on the 3rd
floor [3] lives this poor, persecuted and despised Austrian musical
drudge.

BEETHOVEN

---

    [1] Taken from Nohl II, no. 171 and *KFR*, no. 720.
    [2] See *KFR*, no. 748, note, where the suggestion is put forward that by Dr.
Sassafrass Beethoven meant Dr. Malfatti and his numerous prescriptions. Sassa-
fras is a small tree, the bark of which is used for medicinal purposes.
    [3] It has not been possible to identify this address. From 1795 to 1821 this
no. was on the Schottenbastei near the Pasqualati house, no. 1239 on the Mölkerbastei. If the address given by Beethoven is correct, he must have lived there for
a very short time. In any case, if the presumed date is correct, he was then at
Nussdorf and came into Vienna only occasionally.

(796) *To Frau Nanette Streicher*

[Autograph not traced] [1]

[VIENNA, *July*, 1817]

I will come to you early today. Do let me know where you hand in your letters here for Nussdorf and at what place in town *they should be handed in for Nussdorf?* [2] —

In haste, your friend

BEETHOVEN

(797) *To Frau Nanette Streicher, Vienna*

[Autograph not traced] [3]

[NUSSDORF, *July*, 1817]

Please — please send a
message to the washerwoman,
so that I may have the laundry
on Sunday.

It was not forgetfulness — for I am far more inclined to forget what I *owe to myself than what I owe to others* — it was only my desire not to overburden the servant, because on the last occasion he had so many errands to do — Here is the gulden which you were good enough to give the washerwoman; the spoon, which the servant is returning with thanks, was also put out in my apartment in the Landstrasse when I left it to come here. But the last time it was too much for him to cope with, so he is only taking it today —

In haste, your friend and servant

L. V. BEETHOVEN

All the best greetings to your
family and especially to
Streicher.

---

[1] Taken from *TDR* IV, 487.
[2] Beethoven probably wrote this note in the Landstrasse, then a suburb of Vienna.
[3] Taken from Nohl II, no. 167 and *TDR* IV, 494.

(798) *To Frau Nanette Streicher*

[*Autograph not traced*] [1]

[VIENNA, *July*, 1817]

I felt very ill yesterday and still do so today. I am going to Nussdorf. I don't know whether I shall come on Tuesday — God be with you —

L. v. BEETHOVEN

(799) *To Frau Nanette Streicher*

[*Autograph not traced*] [2]

[VIENNA, *July*, 1817]

It was impossible to call on you yesterday, my dear lady — I was far too busy — Today I have had *a fresh plaster put on the nape of my neck* — Oh necessity, notes are better than *needs* and *necessity*.[3] I must repeat my enquiry where you *hand in your letters here for Nussdorf*, and I must entreat you to answer it, really on account of my poor nephew who sometimes finds himself among Hottentots who don't know how to send his letters to me — I hope to see you today.

In haste, your friend

BEETHOVEN

(800) *To Cajetan Giannatasio del Rio*

[*Autograph in the Staats- und Universitätsbibliothek, Hamburg*]

[VIENNA], *August* 14, 1817

P.P.

Unfortunately, the day before yesterday I received your communication too late, for she had already been here.[4] Otherwise I would have shown her the door, as she deserved.

---

[1] Taken from *TDR* IV, 495.
[2] Taken from Nohl II, no. 173 and *TDR* IV, 487.
[3] As usual, Beethoven is playing on the words 'Not' (need) and 'Note' (note).
[4] Beethoven is referring to Karl's mother.

My warmest thanks to Fräulein N[anni] [1] for the trouble she has taken in writing down that woman's gossip. Although I am usually an enemy of all tittle-tattle and idle talk, yet that is important for us, for I shall hand over tomorrow to H[err] v[on] S[chmerling] [2] your communication as well as a letter which she has written to me. *A word about untidiness during the recent incident connected with her* may have slipped from me *in her presence.* But I have not the slightest recollection of having written *about you.* It was merely an attempt on her part to embitter *you against me* in order by so doing to obtain and gain more from you, just as formerly she retailed to me all sorts of things which you had said against me. But I pay no attention to her chatter — This time I wanted to see whether she could perhaps be reformed by a tolerant and more gentle attitude, and I informed H[err] v[on] S[chmerling] of my intention. But it came to nothing. For indeed on *Sunday* I had immediately decided to adhere *to my original strictly severe attitude which was necessary*, since she had rapidly infected Karl with some of *her poison* — In short, we must now keep to the zodiac and allow her to see K[arl] only twice a year and then hedge her round so closely that she can't hand him in secret even a pin, whether at your school or at my home or at any other third place, that is immaterial. This time I really believed that if I fully complied with her wishes, that would encourage her to reform and to recognize my absolute unselfishness — Perhaps I shall see you tomorrow. Frau v[on] G[iannatasio] can keep the stockings and also whatever shoes he requires. I will send the money for these to your house — In any case please buy Karl at once whatever he needs and purchase everything without asking me. But, without waiting for the end of the quarter, please inform me each time of the amount, which I shall then refund at once. I will see that Karl has a new tail-coat for the coming examination —

One thing more. She pretends that she *obtains information from a person in your house —*

---

[1] Anna (Nanni), the younger of Giannatasio del Rio's two daughters, was born in 1792. She was married on February 6, 1819, to the lawyer Leopold von Schmerling. For this occasion Beethoven composed his 'Hochzeitslied', WoO 105, which has survived in two versions. See *KHV.* 568.

[2] I.e. Leopold von Schmerling, the lawyer, who afterwards married Anna Giannatasio del Rio.

If you can't allow Czerny to accompany Karl to your house, well, the arrangement will have to be cancelled. *Look before you leap!* Karl must not have any other conception of her than the one I have already instilled into him, that is to say, to honour her as his mother. But he *must certainly not imitate her in any* way; and moreover he must be warned not to do so.

Yours
L. v. BEETHOVEN

(801) *To Sigmund Anton Steiner*

[Autograph in the Beethovenhaus, Bonn, H. C. Bodmer collection]

[VIENNA, shortly after August 14, 1817]

Here is the quintet *for the L[ieutenan]t G[enera]l's office.*[1] I shall soon know what conditions to lay down for this work. Herr Kaufmann must not be told anything about it, because the day after tomorrow I will write him a letter which will put an end to the whole affair. For Herr K[aufmann] *only provided me with the occasion to undertake this complete revision*[2] — I am making the L[ieutenan]t G[enera]l's office a present of it and as a return I shall request in due course some shooting and *advancing*;[3] and herewith punctum —

The G[ENERALISSIM]O
(in thunder and lightning, but a little more
subdued than usual)[4]

[1] Beethoven's arrangement of his C minor pianoforte trio, Op. 1, no. 3, as a string quintet for two violins, two violas and cello. The autograph is dated August 14, 1817. This work was published, not by Steiner, but by Artaria in February, 1819 as Op. 104. See *KHV.* 286–287.

[2] Apparently this Herr Kaufmann, probably an amateur musician, had arranged the pianoforte trio, Op. 1, no. 3, as a string quintet and shown it to Beethoven who, however, preferred to make his own arrangement. See Unger's note to his no. 62 and *KHV.* 287.

[3] I.e. some money.

[4] The address in Beethoven's hand on the verso is: 'To the devil's office of the L[ieutenan]t G[enera]l'.

(802) *To Nikolaus Zmeskall von Domanovecz*

[*Autograph in the Nationalbibliothek, Vienna*]

[VIENNA, *August* 17, 1817]

DEAR AND BELOVED Z[MESKALL]!

Alas, I have had bad luck again with another servant and have *probably been even robbed* — On the 4th I gave him 14 days' notice. But he gets drunk, stays out of the house for nights on end and is so shockingly rude and insolent that I should much prefer to get rid of him even sooner. So I should like to pay him for 14 days and chuck him out at once. Well, the question now is whether, if I get rid of him in that way, I shall be obliged to pay him for the previous days from the 1st of this month or from the 4th until the day (which could be tomorrow) when I pay him for 14 days? — His financial month begins with the calendar month and ends with it too — Forgive me, dear Z[meskall], but kindly let me have your reply tomorrow morning by your servant — I hope to see you soon.

Ever your friend

L. v. BEETHOVEN

My address is Landstrasse no. 268, second floor.

Please do not say anything to your servant about what I have written. I will take the necessary steps in due course.[1]

(803) *To Xaver Schnyder von Wartensee, Lucerne* [2]

[*Autograph in the Zentralbibliothek, Lucerne*]

SIR!   VIENNA, *August* 19, 1817

You have remembered that you were once with me in Vienna and have given me written proofs of your remem-

---

[1] These two sentences are written on the verso of the autograph.

[2] Xaver Schnyder von Wartensee (1786–1868), born at Lucerne, was a Swiss composer and pianist. He first visited Vienna in 1812, when he made the acquaintance of Beethoven, Czerny, Schuppanzigh and other eminent musicians. About 1817 he took a post as music teacher at Frankfurt am Main, where he remained more or less for the rest of his life. He composed symphonies, operettas, numerous songs, sacred and secular choral works.

brance. Such an action on the part of a noble and superior human being does me good — Continue to raise yourself higher and higher into the divine realm of art. For there is no more undisturbed, more unalloyed or purer pleasure than that which comes from such an experience — You once wished to see me completely absorbed in the contemplation of the splendid natural beauty of Switzerland, and I myself desire it. If God restores my health which during the last few years has deteriorated, I hope yet to be able to carry out this plan — The bearer of this letter, H[err] v[on] Bihler, who is travelling with his pupil von Puthon, ought to expect, even without my introduction, a friendly reception from you. Meanwhile I will fondly imagine that you attach great importance to my having introduced him to you ; and I will urge you to comply with my request to allow him to enjoy your favour as much as possible.

Your friend and servant
L. v. Beethoven

(804) *To Hans Georg Nägeli, Zürich* [1]

[Autograph in the Beethovenhaus, Bonn, H. C. Bodmer collection]

Sir !   [Vienna, *c. August* 19, 1817] [2]

Although one art and another and one artist and another, even though they may be separated, ever tend to meet, so I think that for this very reason I ought to take this opportunity of reminding you of our former association. And since I cannot believe that I have done anything which might have held you back or repelled you from me, I am therefore convinced that I ought not to let slip the opportunity afforded to me by one of my friends H[err] v[on] Bihler (who is travel-

---

[1] Hans Georg Nägeli (1773–1836), born near Zürich, was a Swiss writer, composer and music publisher. He founded his own publishing firm at Zürich, where in 1803–1804 he published the first edition of Beethoven's pianoforte sonatas, Op. 31, nos. 1-3. In 1825–1826 Nägeli published his lectures on music with very flattering comments on Beethoven's compositions. For a full description of Nägeli's many activities see *FRBH* I, 443-445.

[2] This undated letter of introduction to Nägeli was probably written on the same day as the preceding one to Schnyder von Wartensee, Letter 803. It was first published in the *Beethoven-Jahrbuch*, 1953/54, p. 42.

ling with his pupil Puthon) in order to ascertain whether you are really actuated more by *attraction than by repulsion* in regard to myself. Should it be the former, then most earnestly do I request you to give a warm reception to the bearer of this letter and to welcome him in a friendly manner. Should you wish to evoke some of your Swiss musical spirits in order to intoxicate him in every respect by means of *nature and art* in your country, then I shall be delighted to await my friend's account of such entertainment. It affords me much happiness to assure you of my regard; and I hope that you also remember me with pleasure.

Your most devoted

LUDWIG VAN BEETHOVEN

(805) *To Nikolaus Zmeskall von Domanovecz*

[*Autograph in the Nationalbibliothek, Vienna*]

DEAR KIND Z[MESKALL]!   [VIENNA, *August* 21, 1817]
I am sorry to hear of your indisposition —As for me, I often despair and would like to die. For I can foresee no end to all my infirmities. God have mercy upon me, I consider myself as good as lost — I must speak to you about other matters as well. This servant *is a thief*, I have no doubt about it. He must go. My health demands that I have *meals at home* and greater comfort. I should like to have your opinion about this — If the present state of affairs does not cease, next year I shall not be in London, but probably in my grave — Thank God that I shall soon have finished playing my part —

In haste, yours

L. VAN BEETHOVEN

NB. Please buy me a quarter [1] of green stiffened taffeta, but it must be *green* on both sides. It is incredible that [2]

---

[1] Beethoven probably means a quarter of an ell.
[2] The remaining two lines of the autograph are illegible owing to fading of ink.

(806) *To Frau Nanette Streicher, Baden*

[Autograph not traced] [1]

[NUSSDORF], *Monday, August 25,* [1817]

The enclosed note was written on Saturday.[2] But I had some necessary business to do in town on Friday, became overheated and then felt ill yesterday, which was Sunday; and today I am still far from well — How one feels when one is uncared for, without friends, without everything; left entirely to oneself, and even suffering, all that can only be known from experience. I shall probably come into town tomorrow. Then I shall see you and we can discuss many matters.

In haste, yours

BEETHOVEN

NB. You would do well to give the bearer of this note the laundry list, adding a few friendly words to me, but in a closed cover — Do engage immediately the man you know of until we have considered the question of the *housekeeper* —

(807) *To Frau Nanette Streicher, Baden*

[Autograph not traced] [3]

[NUSSDORF], *August 26,* [1817]

DEAR FRAU VON STREICHER!

I was delighted to receive your invitation which I am accepting. I cannot trouble you today and tomorrow, for in spite of the bad weather I must go into Vienna — Your patent piano certainly does not need my approval, but for my own sake I have long desired to make its acquaintance — In a few days I shall send someone to find out when you will

---

[1] Taken from Nohl II, no. 180 and *TDR* IV, 489-490.
[2] This note, written on August 23rd, has not been traced.
[3] Taken from Nohl II, no. 181 and *TDR* IV, 490.

be at home and I shall then give myself the pleasure of visiting you.

Ever your friend
BEETHOVEN

I have received the letter from *Elise Müller*.[1]

(808) *To Frau Nanette Streicher, Baden*

[Autograph in the Beethovenhaus, Bonn, H. C. Bodmer collection]

DEAR FRIEND,   [NUSSDORF, *after August* 26, 1817]

I am willing to look at this instrument with you tomorrow. At what time tomorrow? That I can discuss with you this afternoon when I go to see you. But I must ask you to be patient with me. In my present circumstances I can no longer *behave* as *I used to behave*, although my name is still *Beethoven* [2] —

(809) *To Frau Nanette Streicher, Vienna*

[Autograph not traced] [3]

BELOVED FRIEND!   [NUSSDORF, *August*, 1817]

As I am uncertain whether you are available today, I am sending my best and warmest greetings to you and yours. I have left my rooms for others which are a little better. Would you undertake just to advise me how I could now eat and drink well, and usually at home?! — The servant lost or — [4] a pair of stockings from my former laundry — Please give him the night-shirts. It is quite safe to do this, for I have told him that he must replace any article he loses —

---

[1] Elise was the very musical daughter of Dr. Wilhelm Christian Müller of Bremen. See Letter 1035. Letters from her and a present for Beethoven, received in January, 1817, are mentioned in Nohl, *op. cit.* p. 136.

[2] This pencilled note is not signed.

[3] Taken from Nohl II, no. 174 and *TDR* IV, 495.

[4] If the original letter had a dash here indicating a word omitted, then Beethoven obviously implied that the pair of stockings had been stolen. See p. 704.

Perhaps I shall see you soon — Please think now and then of a poor, ailing Austrian musical drudge.

In haste, your friend and servant

L. v. Beethoven

(810) *To Frau Nanette Streicher, Vienna*

[*Autograph not traced*] [1]

[Nussdorf, *August*, 1817]

Under what a great obligation are you putting me, beloved friend; and I have become so poor that there is no way in which I can repay you. — I shall come into town on Monday or Tuesday when we will discuss the rooms. Don't you think that those on the other side of the Gärtnergasse would be better after all? And the rent would be the same as that of the ones opposite — My warmest thanks to Streicher for his trouble. Please ask him to continue his efforts. Surely God will again enable me sometime to repay good with good, since the opposite is what grieves me most of all. I am sending you the laundry and also eleven gulden which I still owe your washerwoman — Don't let the servant go to the washerwoman — As for a new servant, I think that, since I have given this one notice, for the moment I should abide by what I have done. *Whoever it be whom* we have to thank for all the articles we have lost, his otherwise unsatisfactory behaviour and the way in which he has slandered the servants with respect to their *Chief* and many other things which have occurred have made me lose confidence in him at one fell swoop; and I am inclined to regard *him* as the culprit rather than anyone else. Please tell *him* that you thought that *a pair of short socks had been lost. This is plain from the letter which you wrote to me about them.* He always refers me to *you* and says that you had found *the stockings.* The washerwoman took in two pairs of stockings, exactly as the two *laundry lists, yours and mine, have proved. If she had not received them, then she would have either cancelled one pair or sent a message to say that she had only received one.* Nothing of the kind was done; so I am convinced that she gave him two pairs of stockings, which she certainly received, and that *he* alone is responsible for their loss.[1] Wherever he happens to be, he bawls about my *distrust* of him and invents things which have never happened, merely in order to clear himself and to get people to put in a good word for him again, so that he may be retained in my service. I only intended to ask you about the stockings when I should have an opportunity. But I had completely forgotten all about them; and it is only because of his chattering that you have had to listen to my remarks about this rubbish. In any case *what he apologizes about most of all*, that he certainly perpetrates. *That* is my experience of him and I never say anything without being absolutely convinced — Away with him — You told me about somebody who, so far as you knew, could come to me on the first day of next month. As it is hard for these people to have to wait *a whole month* for their wages, *I will pay him 2 gulden, 20 kreuzer a day* as long as I am here at Nussdorf. If he wants to cook for himself, I mean, just for himself, he can use my *wood.* As he will have to go into town twice or even three times a week, I will compensate him for those errands as well in a suitable way, for instance, *whatever it costs to have a pair of boots soled and heeled* — Perhaps the servants here would provide him with his board; but with my present servant *they want to have as little to do as I* — No doubt nothing can be done about the housekeeper until I come into town — Well, thanks be to God that I have safely survived those experiences by *the sweat of my brow.* May God grant that I shall not have to talk, write or think anything more about them. For in the sphere of art swamp and slime are of even more use to a man than all that damned nonsense!!![2] —

All good wishes, and cherish some regard for your friend

BEETHOVEN

My warmest greetings
     to Streicher and his wife.

---

[1] Cf. Letter 809.
[2] Beethoven is evidently alluding to the disorders in his household.

(811) *To Nikolaus Zmeskall von Domanovecz, Vienna*

[*Autograph in the Nationalbibliothek, Vienna*]

DEAR ZMESKALL!   [NUSSDORF, *August*, 1817]
It is very necessary for me to have as full a description as possible of your residence *and also to know at what time you are to be found?* Somebody has to deliver something to me; and for safety's sake I should like to direct him to you. If you neither see nor hear anything of me, put it down to exceptional circumstances. I shall soon see you at your rooms or at mine, namely, at the residence of your friend

L. v. BEETHOVEN

(812) *To Frau Nanette Streicher, Baden*

[*Autograph not traced*] [1]

DEAR FRIEND!   [NUSSDORF, *Summer*, 1817]
So that you may not misjudge me, I am sending you herewith three Dutch ducats which you can give your worthy cousin in Cracow [2] to be changed. Will you settle immediately what you have disbursed and the washerwoman's bill. Then you can let me have the remainder at Nussdorf as soon as I send for it.

In haste, your grateful

BEETHOVEN

(813) *To Frau Nanette Streicher, Vienna*

[*Autograph not traced*] [3]

[NUSSDORF, *Summer*, 1817]

BELOVED FRAU VON STREICHER!
Please give the blankets to the bearer of this letter, but don't listen to his gossip, for that fellow is not to be trusted — And please also be so kind as to see that the washerwoman

---

[1] Taken from *TDR* IV, 491.   [2] See Letter 899, p. 763.
[3] Taken from Nohl II, no. 177 and *TDR* IV, 489.

delivers the laundry on Sunday at latest. The state of my shirts, two of which are now in rags, and of numerous other articles of clothing, makes me long for the return of my laundry — By the way, please do not think that I fancy that any article has been lost through any negligence of yours. Such a suspicion would hurt me. Don't draw any conclusions about my opinions in general from the chatter of bad servants — As soon as we meet I shall tell you about another servant or about any other household arrangements I am making — I must have my cooking done at home, for owing to these bad times there are so few people here in the country that it is difficult to get any meals at the inns, and still more so to find the kind of food that is wholesome and good for me.

In haste, your friend and servant

L. v. BEETHOVEN

(814) *To Georg Friedrich Treitschke*

[*Autograph not traced*] [1]

[VIENNA, *Summer*, 1817]

MOST EXCELLENT FELLOW! MOST POETICAL AND MOST IMAGI-
NATIVE WRITER!

Kindly send the manuscript of the song in A major [2] to Steiner in the little Paternostergasse — There are a few mistakes in the engraved copies. After the mistakes have been corrected — you may, should you wish to do so, have the manuscript returned to you immediately by Steiner —

Your friend

BEETHOVEN

I thank you for the
    copy of your poems.

---

[1] Taken from Aloys Fuchs's transcript in the Benedictine Abbey, Göttweig.
[2] WoO 147. Cf. Letter 782, p. 682, n. 4.

(815) *To Frau Marie Pachler-Koschak* [1]

[Autograph in the Gesellschaft der Musikfreunde, Vienna] [2]

[VIENNA, *Summer*, 1817]

I am delighted that you are sparing us another day. We will make a great deal more music. Surely you will play for me the sonatas in F major and C minor, won't you? [3]

I have not yet found anyone who performs my compositions as well as you do; and I am not excluding the great pianists, who often have merely mechanical ability or affectation.

You are the true fosterer of my spiritual children —

(816) *To the Archduke Rudolph, Baden*

[Autograph in the Gesellschaft der Musikfreunde, Vienna]

YOUR IMPERIAL HIGHNESS!   NUSSDORF, *September* 1, 1817

I have been hoping all this time that I should be able to betake myself to you at Baden. But my ailing condition still persists; and although in some respects there is an improvement, yet my complaint is still not absolutely cured. What I have taken and am still taking to cure it are medicines of all kinds and in all forms. Well, at last I must abandon the hope I so often cherished of making a complete recovery — I hear that Y.I.H. is looking wonderfully well; and though it is quite possible to draw therefrom wrong conclusions about excellent health, yet I hear people talking about the improvement in Y.I.H.'s condition, and in this I certainly do take the most lively interest. I hope too that when Y.I.H. returns

---

[1] Marie Leopoldine Koschak (1794–1855), born at Graz, became a distinguished pianist who also composed. In 1816 she married Dr. Karl Pachler, a lawyer at Graz. In the summer of the following year she visited Vienna where she made the acquaintance of Beethoven. She was again in Vienna in 1823, and on parting from Beethoven on September 27th she received from him a musical farewell of two bars, listed in *KHV.* as WoO 202. For an excellent account of her association with Beethoven see *FRBH* II, pp. 1-3. Cf. also Letter 334, p. 346, n. 1, and Nohl, *op. cit.* pp. 155-156.

[2] This note is written in pencil.

[3] Probably Op. 54 and Op. 13. The latter is the early 'sonate pathétique', dedicated to Prince Karl Lichnowsky.

to town I shall be able to assist you in the sacrifices you make
to the Muses — Surely God will hear my prayer and will once
more liberate me from so many calamities, seeing that since
my childhood I have served Him trustfully and have performed
good actions wherever I could.   Hence on Him alone I place
my reliance and hope that in all my manifold miseries the
All-Highest will not let me utterly perish —

I wish Y.I.H. all the good and beautiful things that can
be conceived; and as soon as Y.I.H. has returned to town,
I will immediately betake myself to you.

Your Imperial Highness's

faithful and most obedient servant

L. v. Beethoven

(817) *To Nikolaus Zmeskall von Domanovecz, Vienna*

[Autograph in the Nationalbibliothek, Vienna]

Dear Z[meskall] !   [Nussdorf, *September* 9, 1817]
    Owing to a chill I am now feeling very much worse.   I
couldn't *find a carriage* here; and though usually I am very
fond of walking, on account of my condition I couldn't go in
on foot.   In a few days you will receive the quintet,[1] which
you may perform at your own place whenever you like — I now
know what it feels like to move daily nearer to my grave, and
without music.

In haste, yours

L. v. Beethoven

I shall see you during the next few days, as I must go into
town to see the *doctor*.

(818) *To Nikolaus Zmeskall von Domanovecz*

[Autograph in the Nationalbibliothek, Vienna]

Dear Z[meskall] !   [Vienna, *September* 10, 1817]
    Let the question of the rehearsal rest for a bit.[2]   Today
I must pay another visit to the doctor, of whose stupidity

---

[1] Probably Op. 104.   Cf. Letter 801, p. 698, n. 1.
[2] Possibly the rehearsal of the quintet, Op. 104.

I am now getting thoroughly tired — Thanks for your chronometer — We must see whether with its help one can measure to all eternity. Surely no other instrument could rival the *lightness* and *legibility of yours* — Meanwhile we must have a meeting about this. Although there is naturally greater mathematical accuracy in a watch, yet formerly during the little experiments you made when I was present, I really found that your c[hronometer] had some advantages; and I hope that we *shall make a complete success of it.* I shall see you soon —

Your friend
BEETHOVEN

(819) *To Nikolaus Zmeskall von Domanovecz*

[*Autograph in the Nationalbibliothek, Vienna*] ¹

DEAR Z[MESKALL],   [VIENNA, *September* 11, 1817]
The reply from London arrived yesterday, but it is in English.² Don't you know anyone who could translate the letter for us even orally? —

In haste, your
BEETHOVEN

(820) *To Nikolaus Zmeskall von Domanovecz*

[*Autograph in the Nationalbibliothek, Vienna*]

[VIENNA, *September* 14, 1817]

I am better, my dear Z[meskall], but I cannot visit you until tomorrow afternoon — Today I am busy hunting for rooms and inspecting them; so you would come here to no purpose — Tomorrow I will look you up myself or you will have word from me — With my thanks,

your
BEETHOVEN

NB.   My profound thanks to Ribini.³

---

¹ This note is written in pencil.
² The Philharmonic Society's reply had reached Beethoven on September 10th. It amounted to a refusal of his offer put forward in his letter to Ries of July 9th. See Letter 786.   ³ This postscript is added at the side of the note.

(821) *To Frau Nanette Streicher, Vienna*

[*Autograph not traced*] [1]

[NUSSDORF], *September* 25, 1817

In spite of wind and rain I managed to be here at seven
o'clock this morning, although yesterday evening I tried to
set out for Nussdorf in the rain; but — *fire is quenched by
water* — *I have found the servant and the medicine as well* — but
not your letter — Yet I should have liked very much to read
your elucidatory remarks about game in housekeeping [2] — I
could still give notice to leave the rooms in the Gärtnergasse,
but we should have to calculate mathematically the distances
of both places from town — What do you think? And so
forth and so on. I should like your shoemaker to send *me
some good blacking which doesn't smear*, for my Fidelis [3] has *cheated*
me over the one he provided. In a few days *I will pay in town* his
bill of 27 gulden — If you would be so very kind as to send
me 25 gulden just for a few days, it would be very helpful.
I forgot to take yesterday the keys of my box, although I wanted
to cash some money — I should like to *read* something profitable about the game and the housekeeper — My best greetings
to your ladyship's well behaved daughter.

Tantus quantus lumpus [4]

L. v. BEETHOVEN

NB. We need a supply of dusters

as a preliminary contribution towards the future household.

---

[1] Taken from *TDR* IV, 491.
[2] Beethoven obviously means 'the cooking of game', which he much enjoyed
eating. [3] I.e. faithful servant.
[4] I.e. some sort of rascal.
[5] Probably a musical setting of the word 'Abwischfetzen', which means
'dusters'. It is not listed in *KHV*.

(822) *To Frau Nanette Streicher*

[*Autograph not traced*] [1]

[VIENNA, *September*, 1817]
I will let you have the reply this evening. I should prefer
it to be arranged, if possible, for Tuesday when in any case I
shall be rehearsing a quintet which I have arranged from a
sonata.[2]

In haste, your friend

BEETHOVEN

(823) *To Dr. Karl Pachler* [3]

[*Autograph in the Gesellschaft der Musikfreunde, Vienna*]

MY DEAR P[ACHLER]!   [VIENNA, *September*, 1817]
My doctor thinks that to travel for pleasure would be
very good for my health. So it may well be that I shall avail
myself of your offer. Of course I shall willingly bear my
share of the expenses; and at Graz I shall not have to be a
charge on anybody — Tomorrow and perhaps the day after
I shall still be in Vienna; and I am living in the Landstrasse,
no. 268, on the second floor [4] — You will always find me at
home in the morning, and certainly about eight o'clock —

Your friend

BEETHOVEN

(824) *To Frau Nanette Streicher, Vienna*

[*Autograph in the Beethovenhaus, Bonn*]

NUSSDORF, *October* 2, [1817]
I will come to you tomorrow afternoon. You would oblige
me very much if you would kindly tell the housekeeper to

---

[1] Taken from *TDR* IV, 495.
[2] Possibly Op. 104, Beethoven's arrangement of his pianoforte trio Op. 1,
no. 3 as a string quintet.
[3] Dr. Karl Pachler, a lawyer at Graz, had come to Vienna to fetch his wife.
Cf. Letter 815. Beethoven, though still at Nussdorf, had come into town for a
day or two.
[4] Beethoven had moved into these rooms in April in order to be near Karl's
boarding school. Cf. Letter 777.

come — Yesterday I worked out my future expenses with *someone who* gave me a most horrible picture of them — For board alone he calculated 2 gulden for the servant and 2 gulden for the housekeeper. On this calculation the servant with 20 gulden a month and the housekeeper with 120 gulden a year would together cost the sum of 1704 gulden a year? — Is that really possible? — God have mercy on us — All good wishes — I hope to find you tomorrow for certain. For I am coming into the *Landstrasse from the country solely for that purpose*.

In haste, your
L. v. BEETH [1]

(825) *To Frau Nanette Streicher, Vienna*

[Autograph in the Beethovenhaus, Bonn, H. C. Bodmer collection] [2]

[NUSSDORF], Monday, October 13, 1817

How gladly would I tell you that I have spent a few more peaceful days here, but it is not so — I must drain the bitter cup of all kinds of sorrows; and if only that would mean the end once and for all — I shall probably forfeit a sum of 800 gulden, thanks to a bad lawyer and an even worse *perjured — sham friend —* for the government has already stamped the *bond!* — Please send word today to our maid Trudel, keeper of our housekeeping, that tomorrow I am *leaving here* for good and that *therefore she must be at my rooms without fail.* We shall arrive about noon —

If you think that it is worth while to take over the door and the curtains, then I will take them, but as cheaply as possible. — Just send me a few lines in reply, so that I may know for certain that *the housekeeper is expecting me tomorrow.*

All good wishes, dear friend, from your [3]

---

[1] The remainder of the signature has been torn off.
[2] This letter was first published in the *Beethoven-Jahrbuch*, 1953/54, p. 57.
[3] The remaining words of the signature have been torn off under the seal. As the letters 'F R E' of the first word are still legible, the signature was probably 'Freund L. v. Beethoven'.

(826) *To Frau Nanette Streicher*

[Autograph not traced] [1]

[VIENNA, *after October* 15, 1817]

Yes, indeed, this whole household is still *without any hold* [2] and is exactly like an Allegro di Confusione — If I have read your note aright, you are going to give me the pleasure of a visit at half past four this afternoon, or do you mean half past two ? —

This point will have to be cleared up. So you must send off your little *carrier pigeon* once again. For today my women are washing themselves in the washing-trough, one after another. [3]

In haste, your friend

L. V. BEETHOVEN

(827) *To Frau Nanette Streicher*

[Autograph not traced] [4]

[VIENNA, *after October* 15, 1817]

Please accept from me, my dear Frau von Streicher, these six bottles of genuine eau de Cologne, which you cannot obtain here very easily for money. I hope that I shall see you soon, provided, that is to say, that the second flood is not approaching; at any rate we are bound to become watery, seeing that the sky is always showering on us.

In haste, your friend and servant

BEETHOVEN

---

[1] Taken from *KFR*, no. 679. Frimmel transcribed the autograph then in private ownership.

[2] Beethoven is playing on the words 'Haushaltung' and 'Haltung'.

[3] Beethoven means that he cannot spare one of his female servants to fetch Frau Streicher's reply.

[4] Taken from *TDR* IV, 492.

(828) *To Nikolaus Zmeskall von Domanovecz*

[*Autograph in the Nationalbibliothek, Vienna*]

DEAR ZMESKALL!   [VIENNA, *October* 28, 1817]
   Your famulus is using the wiles of the devil to avoid
taking away the wine — Forgive me about yesterday. I
wanted to come myself this afternoon to apologize. In the
predicament in which I am now placed I need *indulgence* in all
directions. For I am a poor, unhappy man —
                    In haste, as always your [1]

(829) *To Frau Nanette Streicher*

[*Autograph not traced*] [2]

[VIENNA, *Autumn*, 1817]
   I am busy sorting my papers and am considering among
other things what is necessary for the future change [3] — So
put it down to this alone that your accounts have not yet
been paid and that I have not been to see you. To do something like putting my papers in order, I need a *dreadful amount
of patience* which, however, when it does make its appearance,
anyone like myself *must hold on to*, because usually it is never
there. This, by the way, has also to do with utensils which
we require — Many thanks for your recommendation of the
new housekeeper and for your continual readiness to look
after our interests; *without your help* I should always distrust
every housekeeper. But when there are three it will be easier
to get to the bottom of everything — I hope to see you tomorrow or the day after.
                    In haste, your friend
                                   BEETHOVEN

[1] The autograph is not signed.
[2] Taken from *KFR*, no. 712.
[3] Beethoven was preparing to move into another house in the Landstrasse
It was in the Gärtnergasse, and he appears to have kept these rooms until 1819.

(830) *To Frau Nanette Streicher*

[Autograph not traced] ¹

[VIENNA, Autumn, 1817]

MOST EXCELLENT FRAU VON STREICHER!

As soon as you have read the first letter, please send it to me — I wrote to you recently in a hurry and may perhaps have offended you. But a few days after you had visited me with Winter ² I had a frightful attack of rheumatism, so much so that I am not going out again until *tomorrow or the day after.*

Your friend

BEETHOVEN

(831) *To Frau Nanette Streicher*

[Autograph not traced] ³

[VIENNA, Autumn, 1817]

I am not feeling well, so I can't go to you. Forgive me for sending you the 17 gulden so late; but on the whole I am still not yet straight. I really think that my household should be in a *better* state. The cooking alone is rarely up to my standard. I think that we require a *more sensible* person, for both of them are stupid.⁴ And I am very much annoyed about everything. By the way, don't have much to say to them, for talking will not improve matters and will only make them more angry with me. So far as I can see, that N[anni] needs someone *to supervise her.* Without that everything will *go wrong* — Please be so kind as to buy as many ells of the enclosed fustian (the thicker the better) as are necessary for two pairs of trousers, and *an extra ell.*

In haste, your friend

BEETHOVEN

---

¹ Taken from *KFR*, no. 729.
² Peter von Winter, the Munich Kapellmeister. Cf. Letter 173, p. 195, n. 2.
³ Taken from *TDR* IV, 496-497.
⁴ With a view to having Karl to live with him Beethoven had now started a household of his own with two female servants, Nanni the housekeeper and Baberl the kitchen-maid.

(832) *To Frau Nanette Streicher*

[Autograph not traced] [1]

[VIENNA, *Autumn*, 1817]

I am still feeling unwell and there is little comfort in my home. Yesterday and today I had really *horrid* meals. This person can't even think — However, when I see you I shall tell you all about her. I know that she means well; and probably both servants are not of the worst type. But N[anni], in particular, does not fulfil my requirements. I refuse to take any drastic and hasty action. But I fear that you would have far too much to do to introduce order and method into my household. What would happen if you fell ill or were away from home! — We must have somebody on whom we can rely without the assistance of other people — In any case it is a bitter experience for me to be placed in the position of having to use people of such different types — My heartfelt thanks for your purchase — As I have a good deal to do tomorrow I shall not see you until the day after. But I shall see you then provided I feel better.

In haste, your friend

BEETHOVEN

(833) *To Frau Nanette Streicher*

[Autograph not traced] [2]

[VIENNA, *Autumn*, 1817]

I had to pay dearly for your last interview. That N[anni] behaved to me afterwards *in such a way* that on Saturday I *flew into a rage*, after which explosion, I admit, she again behaved decently — But *your* intervention will not help *in the very least*. For the evil nature of this person and her *obstinacy* cannot be cured; and she has already forfeited my confidence — Moreover we must remember that the time is gradually approaching when Karl will *certainly* be living with me; and I fancy that

---

[1] Taken from *TDR* IV, 497.　　[2] Taken from *TDR* IV, 499.

you will agree that both these persons should be replaced by other and better servants.

Perhaps I shall see you tomorrow, but, *if not, certainly the day after.*

In haste, your friend
BEETHOVEN

(834) *To Cajetan Giannatasio del Rio*

[*Autograph in the Royal College of Music*]

VIENNA, *November* 1, 1817

P.P.

A change in my circumstances may well prevent me from leaving Karl at your boarding school after the end of the present quarter.[1] Thus I am obliged to give you notice *that I am removing him.* However painful this notice is to me, yet my straitened circumstances do not permit me to exempt you. Seeing that in normal conditions I would gladly hand you as a small token of my gratitude the amount for a whole quarter at the time when I remove Karl from your school, I should like you to consider my intentions in this matter to be *sincere and single-minded.* Meanwhile should I be in a position to leave Karl with you for the next quarter beginning in February, I will let you know this at once in January, 1818, and, what is more, at the beginning of the month. I must ask you *to do me this favour* and I trust that you will not let me ask in vain. Moreover, if my health is so completely restored that I can again *earn* more money, I will prove my gratitude to you in some additional way. For I know only too well how much you are still doing for Karl, that is to say, kindnesses which I cannot really expect you to perform. And indeed I must say that it pains me very much to have to confess my inability to reward you at the moment.

With the deepest regard I remain, as always, your friend
L. V. BEETHOVEN

---

[1] Karl was removed from Giannatasio del Rio's boarding school on January 24, 1818.

(835) *To Cajetan Giannatasio del Rio*

[*Autograph in the Beethovenhaus, Bonn, H. C. Bodmer collection*]

DEAR FRIEND!   [VIENNA, *November*, 1817]

As I have been very busy and, moreover, am not yet completely recovered from my indisposition, I have not been able to answer your friendly letter sooner — As to your offer, it deserves as much thanks as consideration. I must confess that already some time ago I too had *this idea* about Karl. At the moment, however, I am in the most unsettled circumstances. And that is precisely why I have taken my present decision and am now requesting you to agree to the following arrangement, namely, that I shall inform you during the last month of this quarter whether Karl can remain with you in future. In this way nothing will be done too hastily and no plans will be upset. Of course I am well aware that there could be no cheaper arrangement *than the one by which* Karl is at present at your boarding school, and particularly after your latest proposal; and that is precisely why in my letter I only wanted to mention how gladly in addition to the payment of the usual fee I would have shown you my gratitude in some special way. When I alluded to my being hard up, I did not mean to imply that I wished to spend less on Karl. On the contrary, I know that by any other arrangement his education would cost me more than it does at your boarding school. At the same time, every father has, so far as possible, some purpose in the education of his children; and so have I with Karl. Well, we shall soon find out what is *best* for K[arl], whether it is to remain with you on this or that new arrangement, or as formerly. Just now I certainly do not want to bind myself, as I wish to be able to act in this matter with complete freedom and entirely as Karl's interest demands. —

It is true that Karl costs me great sacrifices; but these I have just mentioned rather on *his* account. For who knows in what way his mother will some day succeed in influencing him? She is determined to resemble more and more the Queen of Night; for everywhere she is spreading the news that *I* have not paid nor am paying anything at all for Karl but that *she* has done and is doing everything. And since I am now mentioning her, I thank you for your really intelligent letter, which in any case will be useful to me. Please ask Herr Leopold von Schmerling to be so kind as to apologize for me to his brother [1] for not yet calling on him. As I was partly very busy and partly still indisposed it was really almost impossible for me to do so. When I think of this matter which we have so often discussed, I would rather call on him for any other purpose than about that question. She never sends me a message, so it is not for me to take the initiative about arranging a meeting with her son. In regard to the other story, I have heard in fact from other people that *in this case* only *force* can be applied. That is again costing me more money; and for that I have chiefly Dr. Adlersburg to thank. But since Karl's education must be arranged as far as possible independently of his mother and with a view to the future as well, that must be done too —

With kind regards, your sincere friend

L. v. BEETHOVEN

(836) *To Nikolaus Zmeskall von Domanovecz*

[Autograph in the Nationalbibliothek, Vienna]

[VIENNA, *December* 10, 1817]

Highly born and most excellent Court Secretary, chief despotic ruler over all the mines of Ofen and Burgundy!

It is impossible for me to come to you today. But do order the servant for tomorrow and kindly let me know at what time I am to be with you. Be sure to *arrange today* what is really necessary —

Well, I shall wait until tomorrow for you to fix the hour when I am to come to you — In haste, your very own

L. v. BEETHOVEN

---

[1] Probably Joseph von Schmerling, who held an appointment in the Court of Appeal. Cf. Letter 611, p. 561, n. 3.

LETTER TO THE ARCHDUKE RUDOLPH (December 31, 1817)
(*Autograph in the Gesellschaft der Musikfreunde, Vienna*)

LETTER TO THE ARCHDUKE RUDOLPH (December 31, 1817)—*cont.*
(*Autograph in the Gesellschaft der Musikfreunde, Vienna*)

(837) *To* [*Frau Nanette Streicher ?*] [1]

[Autograph in the Musée Grobet-Labadié, Marseilles]

[VIENNA, *c. Christmas*, 1817]

At this Holy season I would rather send you the Gospel than the housekeeping book [2] —

I am sorry about your son's misfortune [3]; and perhaps I shall see you today —

In haste, your friend

L. v. BEETHOVEN

(838) *To Frau Nanette Streicher*

[Autograph not traced] [4]

[VIENNA, *December* 27, 1817]

In the first place it is evident from all that has happened that unless you will be kind enough to undertake some sort of supervision I with my *infirmities* shall nearly always have *the same experience* with people of that type — What has greatly lowered both those persons in my estimation is their *ingratitude* to you. I fail to understand your other remarks about people *gossiping*. All I remember is that on one single occasion *I forgot myself* for a moment about a third matter, *but that was in the company of quite different people* — that is all I have to say about that — I for my part never pay attention nor listen to the gossip of the *rabble*. I have even given you hints about this without mentioning *one word* of what I have heard — away, away, away with everything of that kind —

On several occasions indeed I have sent N[anni] to you in the hope that you might forgive her; and since your last visit to me I have not only not scolded her, but I have not even spoken *a word, not another syllable* to her; and in that way

---

[1] The autograph is neither addressed nor dated. But on internal evidence this note was probably sent to Nanette Streicher, and at Christmastide.

[2] See the beginning of Letter 884, p. 748.

[3] Probably Johann Baptist Streicher, who on his father's death in 1833 became manager of the firm. See Appendix G (19).

[4] Taken from Nohl II, no. 195 and *TDR* IV, 497-498.

I have made my wishes sufficiently clear to her. For I must say that in the case of *people who have behaved in that way to you* I cannot draw a hopeful conclusion in regard to myself; and on the whole I don't care for either of them —

I am going to give B[aberl] notice today. Perhaps she will ask N[anni] to forgive her, since she has already taken a step in that direction. But in any case I must repeat that unless someone takes charge of this business *we shall not fare a bit better with any other servants* — At any rate I rely on your love of human nature which moves your inner spirit to do good. I can't do that, I can't meet you on the same terms. Unfortunately I realized this a long time ago. Nevertheless I trust that you will always be glad to act in my interest, to act in the interest of your friend and servant

L. v. BEETHOVEN

Note

N[anni] must have *someone* to supervise her. A *more sensible servant* who would not require this supervision would certainly *suit* us better, *although she too would require a certain amount of supervision.* Besides we don't want to indulge too much in reproaches, for 'each one of us *errs, though always in a different way*'.[1] Just engage the other one at once; and do forgive me for all the trouble I am giving you — As soon as you return from Klosterneuburg,[2] please be *very good to me*! — I have told N[anni] that I have *engaged a man servant.* Please let her continue to believe this.

(839) *To Frau Nanette Streicher*

[*Autograph not traced*][3]

[VIENNA, *December* 28, 1817]

N[anni] was to have given you the New Year tickets yesterday, but she didn't do it — The day before yesterday I

---

[1] See Letter 1541 to Karl Holz, where this quotation has been set to music by Beethoven in the form of a canon. In *KHV*. the canon is listed as WoO 198.

[2] A village near Vienna, on the right bank of the Danube, with a famous Augustinian Abbey.

[3] Taken from *TDR* IV, 498-499. The original letter contained Beethoven's visiting-card.

was busy with Maelzel, who is in a great hurry, because he is leaving Vienna very soon. Hence you will surely know in any case that, had I been free, I would certainly have rushed up to you again — Yesterday I saw your dear kind daughter at my home, but I was *so* ill that I don't remember very much about her visit.[1] The day before yesterday my splendid *servants* took three hours, from seven until ten in the evening, to get a fire going in the stove. The bitter cold, particularly in this house, gave me a bad chill; and almost the whole day yesterday I could scarcely move a limb. Coughing and the most terrible headaches I have ever had plagued me the whole day. As early as six o'clock in the evening I had to go to bed, where I still am. But I am feeling better. Your brother dined with me yesterday and has done me a very great kindness [2] — As you know, on the same day, that is to say, on December 27th I gave B[aberl] notice. I really cannot stand the low behaviour of those two women, and I shall be very much surprised if N[anni] behaves any better when the other one has gone. I doubt it. If she doesn't, we must *chuck her out* at once. She is too ill-bred, too *brutish* to be even a housekeeper. But the other one in spite of her looks is even *lower than a beast* — Since the New Year is upon us, I consider that five gulden will be enough for Nanni. After her *bad behaviour to you* I didn't give her *the cost of having her spencer* [3] *made — the other one does not really deserve any New Year gift.* In any case she has been given nine gulden in advance; and when she leaves I shan't be able to deduct more than four or five gulden at most from that sum. I should like to have *your advice about all this* — Well, you must accept my wishes for your welfare, wishes which are truly sincere. I am in so many respects your debtor that when I think of it I am frequently overcome by a feeling of shame.

All good wishes; and continue to bestow on me your friendship.

Ever your friend
L. v. BEETHOVEN

---

[1] Probably Sophie, the Streichers' eldest daughter.
[2] Matthäus Andreas Stein. Cf. Letter 420, p. 416, n. 1.
[3] This word for a close-fitting bodice worn by women was first used early in the 19th century.

(840) *To the Archduke Rudolph*

[*Autograph in the Gesellschaft der Musikfreunde, Vienna*]

YOUR IMPERIAL HIGHNESS! VIENNA, *December* 31, 1817 [1]
The old year is almost at an end and the new year is approaching. May Y.I.H. too have no sorrows but enjoy the greatest happiness that can be conceived. Those are my wishes for Y.I.H., which can all be comprised in this one wish. — If I may be allowed to talk about myself, well, my health is very shaky and uncertain; and unfortunately I am obliged to live at a great distance from Y.I.H.[2] But this is not going to prevent me from giving myself as soon as possible the pleasure of waiting upon you — I commend myself to your most gracious thoughts about me, even though I may not seem to deserve them. May Heaven shower special blessings on every day of your life for the good of so many other people.
But I shall ever be
Your Imperial Highness's
most obedient servant
LUDWIG VAN BEETHOVEN

(841) *To Frau Nanette Streicher*

[*Autograph not traced*] [3]

[VIENNA, *December*, 1817]
It would be well *for you, as it certainly would be for me, not to let my two servants notice that unfortunately I can no longer have the pleasure of going to see you.* For, if this arrangement were not observed, there might be *very disastrous consequences* for me, because it might seem as if in this respect you wished to detach yourself altogether — Please be so kind as to let me know what you have disbursed for me. I will send you the sum immediately with my warmest thanks. And please be so kind

---

[1] This date is added at the end of the letter in the form 'on the last day of December, 1817'.
[2] Beethoven was living in the Landstrasse, which was then a suburb of Vienna.
[3] Taken from Nohl II, no. 200 and *TDR* IV, 500-501.

as to let me know the *whereabouts of your silversmith's shop*? —
I have scolded N[anni], and the other one too, about their
behaviour to you. Nevertheless the younger one behaved
yesterday so *impudently* and *pertly* that I threatened, if she was
naughty again either to me or to other people, to turn her out
of the house *immediately*; you will notice that we are receiving
practically the *same* treatment *from both of them*. This propensity
is ingrained in their characters, and particularly in the really
evil character of the *younger one* — *You* are as little to blame
for this as I am — As soon as you can, give me the pleasure
of visiting me or dining with me —

Any small kindness on your part will be treasured in my
memory; and I shall always call myself your grateful

BEETHOVEN

(842) *To [Joseph Anton von Pilat?]* [1]

[*Autograph in the Staats- und Universitätsbibliothek, Hamburg*]

SIR! [VIENNA, *December,* 1817]

I hereby request you not to have anything inserted of
what Herr Maelzel may communicate to you, until he and I
call on you together — For several statements have already
appeared in the papers; and this is unpleasant for all who have
contributed to the work. Truly in such a beautiful and sacred
matter no one is first and no one is last, but all are equal. So
I should like you to be so kind as not to have anything inserted
until I have had the honour of speaking to you. This I will
do without fail either today or tomorrow —

I am, Sir, your devoted servant

LUDWIG VAN BEETHOVEN

[1] This letter, addressed by Beethoven to the editor of some influential newspaper in Vienna, may have been intended for J. A. von Pilat, who since 1811
had been editor of the *Österreichischer Beobachter*. For a note on Pilat see Letter
1217, p. 1072, n. 6.

(843) *To Tobias Haslinger* [1]

[*Autograph in the Beethovenhaus, Bonn, H. C. Bodmer collection*]

MOST EXCELLENT A[DJUTAN]T! [VIENNA, *December*, 1817]
Send me the fugue for a few hours.[2] I remember that
when writing it down I made one or two mistakes but afterwards forgot all about them — The little A[djutan]t will have
everything back this afternoon —
The etc., etc., etc., etc.

(844) *To Frau Nanette Streicher*

[*Autograph not traced*] [3]

[VIENNA, *December*, 1817]
I thank you. Things now seem to be greatly improving.
I am sending the *ear-trumpet* as well. Please let me have it
back tomorrow, for with its help I have gained a considerable
amount of information.

Your grateful

BEETHOVEN

[1] The address on the verso is: 'For the Adjutant (in person)'.
[2] Fugue in D major for string quintet, composed in November, 1817, as a
contribution to a collection of all Beethoven's works which Haslinger had begun
to copy in his own hand. This little work, Op. 137, was not published by Haslinger
until the autumn of 1827. The autograph is dated November 28th. See *KHV*.
417-418.
[3] Taken from Nohl II, no. 194 and *TDR* IV, 507.

(845) *To Ignaz Franz, Edler von Mosel* [1]

[*Autograph in the Nationalbibliothek, Vienna*]

SIR !   [VIENNA, 1817] [2]

I am heartily delighted to know that you hold the same
views as I do about our tempo indications which originated
in the barbarous ages of music. For, to take one example,
what can be more absurd than Allegro, which really signifies
merry, and how very far removed we often are from the idea of
that tempo. So much so that the piece itself means the *very
opposite of the indication* — As for those four chief movements,
which, however, are far from embodying the truth or the
accuracy of the four chief winds, we would gladly *do without
them.* But the words describing the character of the composition are a different matter. We cannot give these up. Indeed
the tempo is more like the body, *but these certainly refer to the
spirit of the composition* — As for me, I have long been thinking
of abandoning those absurd descriptive terms, Allegro, Andante,
Adagio, Presto ; and Maelzel's metronome affords us the best
opportunity of doing so. I now give you *my word* that I shall
never again use them in any of my new compositions — But
there is another question, and that is, whether by so doing
we are aiming at bringing the metronome into *general use,* a
thing which is so necessary? I hardly think so. Moreover I
have no doubt whatever that we shall be howled down as
tyrants. If only the cause itself were thus served, it would still be
better than to be accused of feudalism — Hence I fancy that the
best solution would be, particularly for our countries where
music has now become a national need and where every
village schoolmaster will be expected to use the metronome,
that Maelzel should try to sell a certain number of metronomes by subscription, and at a very high price.[3] Then as

---

[1] Ignaz Franz, Edler von Mosel (1772–1844) was a Viennese conductor,
composer and writer on music. He arranged and conducted the first concert
given in 1816 by the Gesellschaft der Musikfreunde, which he helped to found
in 1813. In 1820 he was appointed Deputy Director of the Court Theatres and
from 1829 until his death he was custodian of the Court Library. In 1827 he
published a book on the life and work of Antonio Salieri. See *FRBH* I, 429–430.

[2] This year is noted on the autograph in another hand.

[3] The words from 'and' to 'price' are added at the foot of the page.

soon as he has been covered financially by this number he will be able to dispose of the other necessary metronomes for the musical need of the nation so cheaply that we can certainly expect to see the greatest *universal use and distribution* of this commodity — It is clearly understood, of course, that some people must place themselves at the head of this movement in order to work up enthusiasm. You can certainly rely on me to do what lies in my power; and I look forward with pleasure to hearing what task you are going to allot to me —

With kindest regards I remain, Sir, your most devoted

LUDWIG VAN BEETHOVEN

(846) *To [Nikolaus Zmeskall von Domanovecz]* [1]

[*Autograph in the Nationalbibliothek, Vienna*]

[VIENNA, 1817]

I have seen nothing — I have heard nothing — Meanwhile I am always ready for it. The time I prefer most of all is at about half past three or four o'clock in the afternoon.

Your

BEETHOVEN

(847) *To Frau Nanette Streicher*

[*Autograph in the Beethovenhaus, Bonn, H. C. Bodmer collection*]

DEAREST FRAU V[ON] ST[REICHER]!　　　[VIENNA, 1817]

Something important that has happened prevents me from going to see you today. But I shall be with you before three o'clock tomorrow afternoon —

In haste, your friend

L. V. BEETHOVEN

---

[1] This undated letter bears no address. It is, however, included in the file of Beethoven's letters to Zmeskall in the Nationalbibliothek, Vienna.

(848) *To Frau Nanette Streicher*

[*Autograph in a private collection*]

DEAR FR[AU] V[ON] STR[EICHER]!   [VIENNA, 1817]
    Please do not be angry with me for not yet coming to see
you and for . . . . not yet thanking you . . . .[1] Meanwhile
I hope to see you tomorrow or the day after, any time after
three o'clock in the afternoon —

In haste, your sincere friend
BEETHOVEN

(849) *To Frau Nanette Streicher*

[*Autograph not traced*] [2]

[VIENNA, 1817]
    Forgive me. I have no scissors, no knife nor anything.
I think that the rags are too bad and that it would be better
to buy some linen — The neckcloths too need *to be mended* —
When we meet we will discuss this, and also my request for
your further forbearance.

In haste, your friend
BEETHOVEN

(850) *To Frau Nanette Streicher*

[*Autograph not traced*] [3]

[VIENNA, 1817]
    I have just received the medicine and I fancy that in a
few days I shall be completely cured. Thank you very much
for your sympathy, most excellent F[rau] v[on] Streicher. We
will discuss the question of the vest tomorrow, when I shall
have the pleasure of seeing you.

In haste, your friend
BEETHOVEN

---

[1] These dotted passages do not indicate omissions. They appear thus in the
autograph.   [2] Taken from *KFR*, no. 739.
[3] Taken from *KFR*, no. 742.

(851) *To Frau Nanette Streicher*

[*Autograph not traced*] [1]

[VIENNA, 1817]
I have only *one* emetic powder. After taking it should I drink *tea frequently*? Please let me have a pewter spoon —
In haste, your friend
BEETHOVEN

(852) *To the Archduke Rudolph*

[*Autograph in the Gesellschaft der Musikfreunde, Vienna*]

YOUR IMPERIAL HIGHNESS!   [VIENNA, 1817]
I thank you most warmly for your gracious interest in me. I am really better; and tomorrow I shall be able to enquire in person of Y.I.H. what arrangements you would like to make about your lessons *in the mornings*. For my doctor has strictly forbidden me to be out of doors *later* than six o'clock in the evening. In any case I know that Y.I.H. will gladly agree to have lessons in the morning —
Your Imperial Highness's
faithful and most obedient servant
L. v. BEETHOVEN

(853) *To the Archduke Rudolph*

[*Autograph in the Gesellschaft der Musikfreunde, Vienna*]

YOUR IMPERIAL HIGHNESS!   [VIENNA, 1817]
I had frequently resolved to enquire in person about the state of your health. But from week to week I myself had to remain on several occasions in my room and in bed; and that is again my condition at the moment. My most heartfelt desire is that Y.I.H.'s health may soon improve. As for

---

[1] From a facsimile of this letter in Shedlock II, p. 92. The autograph was then (1908) in private ownership. Nohl II, no. 166, attaches it as a postscript to Letter 873.

me, I hope that I shall not have to take a rest [1] as soon as you
are again recovered and able to make music —

Your Imperial Highness's
most obedient servant
LUDWIG VAN BEETHOVEN

(854) *To the Archduke Rudolph*

[Autograph in the Gesellschaft der Musikfreunde, Vienna]

YOUR IMPERIAL HIGHNESS!   [VIENNA, 1817]
    I have had to take medicine again today. Nevertheless
I thought that I should be able to enjoy the pleasure of waiting
upon Y.I.H. today. But unfortunately I feel weaker than I
did yesterday. I tried to go out, but had to turn back after a
few minutes. No doubt the very bad weather is partly responsible for my condition. I shall certainly have recovered my
health by tomorrow; and on Monday before six o'clock (as
I hear that this is now the most acceptable time for Y.I.H.)
I shall have the pleasure of presenting myself at Y.I.H.'s
residence. I do earnestly beg you still to cherish your most
gracious and favourable opinion of me —

Your Imperial Highness's
most obedient and most faithful servant
L. V. BEETHOVEN

(855) *To the Archduke Rudolph*

[Autograph in the Gesellschaft der Musikfreunde, Vienna]

YOUR IMPERIAL HIGHNESS!   [VIENNA, 1817]
    Today it is impossible for me to satisfy my most fervent
wish and to wait upon you. But I hope that tomorrow Y.I.H.
will permit me to betake myself to you at the usual hour —

Your Imperial Highness's
most faithful and most obedient servant
LUDWIG VAN BEETHOVEN

---

[1] Beethoven uses the word 'pausieren', which is the German musical equivalent for 'to observe a rest'.

731

(856) *To the Archduke Rudolph*

[*Autograph in the Gesellschaft der Musikfreunde, Vienna*]

YOUR IMPERIAL HIGHNESS!   [VIENNA, 1817]

Unless Y.I.H. sends me word not to come or would like me to come at some other time, I shall have the honour of waiting upon you at about five o'clock tomorrow evening. Why I have unfortunately not been able to comply sooner with my dearest wishes to be constantly in the company of Y.I.H., I shall best explain by word of mouth. I trust that the Lord will graciously hear my prayers and those of other people for your health and happiness —

Your Imperial Highness's
most obedient servant
LUDWIG VAN BEETHOVEN

(857) *To* [*Carl Czerny ?*] [1]

[*Autograph in the Gesellschaft der Musikfreunde, Vienna*]

[VIENNA, 1817]

The score of the symphony in E flat [2] by

BEETHOVEN

(858) *To Carl Czerny*

[*Autograph in the Gesellschaft der Musikfreunde, Vienna*]

DEAR CZERNY.   [VIENNA, 1817]

Karl is with me, but he is not feeling well. I request you, therefore, *to come to me* today, for in any case I must have a word with you about the lessons at the boarding school —

Your most devoted
LUDWIG VAN BEETHOVEN

---

[1] The autograph bears no address. Frimmel (see *KFR*, no. 783) presumes that the note was intended for Carl Czerny.

[2] The third symphony, Op. 55, known as the 'Eroica'.

(859) *To Carl Czerny*

[*Autograph in the Nationalbibliothek, Vienna*]

DEAR ZERNI!   [VIENNA, 1817]

Please come to breakfast with me tomorrow morning.
Breakfast will be ready at any time. There is something I
must talk to you about. Please bring the pianoforte arrangement of the symphony in F.¹ I would go to you, but it so
happens that the time when you are at home is the least convenient time for me —

Your friend

BEETHOVEN

(860) *To Frau Nanette Streicher*

[*Autograph not traced*] ²

[VIENNA, 1817]

I am glad that you *yourself* realize that it is impossible for
me ever to set foot in your house again — The enclosed note
was written this morning; I was about to send it to you when
yours was brought by your servant.

I look forward with pleasure to your visit on Tuesday
morning — You will certainly find me here — I know from
Karl's doctor that *his body* is in a sound condition; in regard
to his soul, that can only be left to Heaven.

In haste, your friend

BEETHOVEN

¹ Czerny made a two-pianoforte arrangement of the eighth symphony, Op. 93,
which was published by Steiner in 1817.
² Taken from *TDR* IV, 500.

(861) *To Frau Nanette Streicher*

[*Autograph not traced*] [1]

[VIENNA, 1817]

Many thanks, dear Fr[au] v[on] Streicher, for your latest kindness — I myself will go to Sieber [2] tomorrow afternoon and give him the remainder —
I shall soon have the pleasure of seeing you and Karl.

In haste, your friend

BEETHOVEN

(862) *To Frau Nanette Streicher*

[*Autograph not traced*] [3]

[VIENNA, 1817]

Very many thanks for the kindness you have shown me — I shall go to the S.[4] one of these days and find out all about the whole affair — As I am up to the eyes in business of all kinds, it has been almost impossible for me to see you — Karl sends you his compliments. We will visit you soon.

In haste, your friend

BEETHOVEN

Don't relinquish completely your post of chief Lady-in-Waiting. For you will always exert an uncommonly good influence.

(863) *To the House of Giannatasio* [5]

[*Autograph in the British Museum*]

HOUSE OF G[IANNATASI]O!   [VIENNA, 1817]

The Klavierschule is a — *general one* — that is to say, it is a kind of compendium — Let me add that I consider the

---

[1] Taken from *TDR* IV, 506.

[2] According to *TDR* IV, 506, Jakob Matthias Sieber was a dealer in fancy goods, whose shop was in the Graben, no. 1171.

[3] Taken from *TDR* IV, 507-508.

[4] The printed versions have 'zur S.'. As the autograph is not available, the present editor is inclined to think that the words may have been misread.

[5] The address on the verso is : 'For the whole patriarchy of the Giannatasios'.

Swiss one to be quite useful. But the *'graces'* [1] are by no means the term in ordinary usage —

In haste, the most devoted servant and friend
of the House of G[iannatasi]o

BEETHOVEN

(864) *To Cajetan Giannatasio del Rio*

[Autograph not traced] [2]

[VIENNA, 1817]

Karl has to be with H[err] B[ernard] [3] before four o'clock today. So please ask his teacher to let him go at about half past three — If this can't be arranged, then he will have to stay away from school. In the latter case I would fetch him at your boarding school, but in the former case at the University in the corridor upstairs. So that there may be no misunderstanding, please let me have a definite reply stating how this should be done — As you have the reputation of being partial, I will accompany Karl. If you don't see me, ascribe my absence to my grief which only now I am experiencing to the full in connexion with this terrible incident. [4]

In haste, your
BEETHOVEN

(865) *To Frau Nanette Streicher*

[Autograph not traced] [5]

[VIENNA, 1817]

MOST EXCELLENT FRAU VON STREICHER,

Although I hesitate wholly *to condemn him without further proof, it is not likely* that this servant is honest — In the meantime I am thinking of keeping him here *with the housekeeper*; what do you think? — It will certainly not be easy to find

---

[1] The German original is 'Gnaden', probably a term for grace-notes or ornaments.
[2] Taken from Nohl I, no. 163 and *KFR*, no. 606.
[3] For a full note on Joseph Karl Bernard see Letter 947, p. 812, n. 1.
[4] Karl had probably run away to his mother.
[5] Taken from *TDR* IV, 494.

someone else at once; and yet I fear that the *fellow* might have a bad influence on a *decent* person — I am sending you herewith the two keys so that you can have a look at everything. You can tell me whether it would be possible for the housekeeper to come here on Tuesday morning at the latest? — or perhaps even on Monday afternoon? — There are no *dusters* — not even here, for the supplies I provided two or three times are all used up — All good wishes, my beloved friend.

In haste, your friend

L. V. BEETHOVEN

NB.   Don't curse me for giving you so much trouble.

(866) *To Frau Nanette Streicher*

[Autograph in the Beethovenhaus, Bonn, H. C. Bodmer collection] [1]

[VIENNA, 1817]

This very morning I wanted to send a message to you, for the conduct of the housekeeper is shocking — I was given hardly any supper last night — She went off after ten o'clock and did not return until half past seven this morning — I did not go to Breuning — The housekeeper's departure terrified me so that I was already awake at three o'clock — My lonely condition demands the assistance of the police —

If by chance you are returning home today, do come to me quickly. You will find me at home after five o'clock. What a dreadful existence?!

Should you not receive this note today, then come the day after tomorrow, but very early in the morning —

In the greatest haste,

yours

---

[1] The autograph, which is not signed, was first published in the *Beethoven-Jahrbuch*, 1953/54, p. 58.

(867) *To Nikolaus Zmeskall von Domanovecz*

[*Autograph in the Nationalbibliothek, Vienna*] [1]

MY DEAR Z[MESKALL], [VIENNA, 1817]

I am fairly well. Since you, when you are in good health, are *always peddling*, I *can't find you*, however hard I may try. Meanwhile I shall enquire for you at your residence one of these days —

Ever your friend

BEETHOVEN

(868) *To the Archduke Rudolph*

[*Autograph in the Gesellschaft der Musikfreunde, Vienna*]

YOUR IMPERIAL HIGHNESS! [VIENNA, 1817]

An urgent affair prevents me from coming to you this evening as usual, unless, of course, I could come to Y.I.H. later, for instance, at about seven o'clock, if perhaps you are not going to the theatre — I await your command about this and I remain

Your Imperial Highness's
most obedient
LUDWIG VAN BEETHOVEN

(869) *To the Archduke Rudolph*

[*Autograph in the Gesellschaft der Musikfreunde, Vienna*]

YOUR IMPERIAL HIGHNESS! [VIENNA, 1817]

Please be indulgent to me just for a few days longer, first of all, because I am not well, and, secondly, because I must press on with and finish some necessary compositions which cannot be postponed; and unfortunately, they are of a kind from the composing of which I cannot easily break off — In

---

[1] This note, written and addressed on the verso in pencil, was evidently scribbled by Beethoven at Zmeskall's rooms.

any case, you are by now convinced that no bounds can be set to my zeal in your service. But a very exceptional incident prevents me at the moment from fulfilling my dearest wishes to serve you. In four days at the latest, however, I shall again have reached the point of being able to wait upon you —

Your Imperial Highness's
most obedient
LUDWIG VAN BEETHOVEN

(870) *To ?*

[Autograph in the Kestner Museum, Hanover]

[VIENNA, 1817]

I wonder would you be so kind as to let me know when I can speak to you this afternoon. I should much prefer the time to be about half past three — I think that after all we ought to be able to come to an agreement about the rooms —

Wholly your most devoted servant
BEETHOVEN

(871) *To Cajetan Giannatasio del Rio* [1]

[Autograph in the Royal College of Music]

[VIENNA, 1817]

As for the mother, she has expressly asked to see Karl *at my home*. That you have seen me wavering now and then and inclined to have more confidence in her you must attribute to my dislike of inhuman behaviour, the more so as it has been made impossible for her to do Karl any harm. Moreover you can easily conceive how intolerable all these worries and anxieties, into which I have been drawn on account of K[arl], frequently seem to a man accustomed to living as unconstrainedly as I do ; and one of these worries is this question

[1] No address is given on the autograph which appears to be an incomplete letter. But on internal evidence and since the autograph is included in this collection, it is safe to assume that the recipient was Giannatasio del Rio. Cf. p. 552, n. 2.

of his mother. I should be delighted *never* to have to hear anything more on this subject; and that is the reason why on the whole I avoid mentioning her. — As for Karl, I beg you to enforce the strictest obedience and *to punish him* immediately if he doesn't obey you (or any other persons whom he ought to obey). Treat him rather as you would treat your own child and *not* as a pupil. You will remember that I have already told you how during his father's lifetime he would only obey when he was beaten. Of course that was very wrong, but that was how things were done, and we must not forget it. — By the way, if you don't see me very often, attribute my absence to nothing but my lack of inclination for society. Sometimes this lack of inclination is more in evidence, sometimes less; and of course it might be regarded as a change in my opinions and feelings.[1] But that is not so. Even if there are unpleasant incidents I remember *only* and always what is good. So you must ascribe it solely to this iron age that I am not giving *more lively* expression to my gratitude to you for what you are doing for Karl. Yet God can change everything. And so my circumstances too can improve once more, in which case I will certainly hasten to show you how much I am ever with my kindest regards, your grateful friend

L. v. BEETHOVEN

Please read this letter with Karl.[2]

(872) *To Cajetan Giannatasio del Rio* [3]

[*Autograph in the Royal College of Music*]

[VIENNA, 1817]

I am sending you herewith, my dearest friend, through Karl his fees for the coming quarter. — I beg you to appeal even more strongly to his feelings and affections, since the latter, in particular, enable us to acquire all the virtues. And

---

[1] I.e. about other people.

[2] This request is written at the side of the last page of the autograph.

[3] No address is given on the autograph, but on internal evidence and since it is included in this collection, it is safe to assume that the recipient was Giannatasio del Rio. Cf. p. 552, n. 2.

however much the affectionate side of our nature may sometimes be derided and disparaged, yet our greatest writers, such as Goethe among others, consider affection to be an excellent virtue. Nay more, many people maintain that without affection no man can excel or possess any depth of character. Time fails me to write more about this; but when we meet we will discuss more fully my views on the method of dealing with K[arl] in this respect —

Your friend and servant

L. v. BEETHOVEN

(873) *To Frau Nanette Streicher*

[*Autograph not traced*] [1]

DEAR F[RAU] V[ON] STR[EICHER]!   [VIENNA, 1817]
   I am full of vexations today. It is impossible to enumerate them to you. But I hope to see you tomorrow — All good wishes. God watches over all of us!!
My compliments to your family.

In haste, your friend

BEETHOVEN

(874) *To Nikolaus Zmeskall von Domanovecz*

[*Autograph in the Nationalbibliothek, Vienna*]

[VIENNA, 1817]

Please do me the kindness, my dear Z[meskall], to ask your servant to look for another one for me whom I should like to engage. I give 20 gulden a month, and small and large livery. — You can let him know this or say nothing about it, whichever you consider advisable. Further, I should like the servant to be able to do a bit of tailoring — He need not be physically attractive. Even if he is a bit hunchbacked I should not mind, for then I should know at once the weak spot at which to attack him. You will do me a very great

---

[1] Taken from *TDR* IV, 494. Nohl II, no. 166 attaches Letter 851 to the above letter as a postscript.

kindness if you will give this commission to your servant, whose good offices I am not demanding free of charge —

Wholly your
B<small>EETHOVEN</small>

(875) *To [Nikolaus Zmeskall von Domanovecz ?]*

[*Autograph not traced*] <small>1</small>

[V<small>IENNA</small>, 1817]

Please be so kind as to send a message to your refined tailor. He has already had for a fortnight two pairs of trousers of mine, which would be a protection to me in this cold weather. But despite all my efforts I can't make him return them.

(876) *To Cajetan Giannatasio del Rio* <small>2</small>

[*Autograph in the Royal College of Music*]

[V<small>IENNA</small>, 1817]

No doubt your friend will have informed you that Karl is to be fetched tomorrow morning. His mother wants to place herself on a better footing with her neighbours, and so I am doing her the favour of taking her son to her tomorrow in the company of a third person. — This meeting takes place once every month. — I beg you neither to say nor to write anything more about what has happened, but to forget everything, as I have.

(877) *To Frau Nanette Streicher*

[*Autograph not traced*] <small>3</small>

[V<small>IENNA</small>, 1817]

All I can tell you is that I am better, though indeed last night I frequently thought of my death; but in any case

---

<small>1</small> Taken from *TDR* IV, 485, where the suggestion is made that Zmeskall may have been the recipient.

<small>2</small> The autograph bears neither the name of the addressee nor the date nor a signature. But on internal evidence and since it is included in this collection, it is safe to ascribe it and date it as above. Cf. p. 552, n. 2.

<small>3</small> Taken from Nohl II, no. 207 and *KFR*, no. 713.

741

such thoughts occur to me occasionally in the daytime as well —

As for the future housekeeper, I should like to know whether she has a *bed* and a chest of drawers? By bed I mean partly the bedstead, partly the bed itself, that is to say, the mattress and so forth. — And do have a word with her too about the laundry, so that we may be sure about everything. She will have to receive an advance payment, which I shall give her, of course, as well — About all else I shall get in touch with you tomorrow or the day after. My musical and unmusical papers are almost in order; that was one of the seven labours of Hercules. —

In haste, your friend

BEETHOVEN

(878) *To Carl Czerny*

[Autograph in the Gesellschaft der Musikfreunde, Vienna]

MY DEAR CZERNY! [VIENNA, 1817]

Please be as patient as possible with our Karl, even though at present he may not be making as much progress as you and I would like. If you are not patient, he will do even less well, because (although he must not know this) owing to the unsatisfactory time-table for his lessons he is being unduly strained. Unfortunately nothing can be done about that for the time being. Treat him therefore so far as possible with affection, but *be firm with him. Then there will be* a greater chance of success in spite of these really unfavourable circumstances where K[arl] is concerned — In regard to his playing for you, as soon as he has learnt the right fingering and can play a piece in correct time and the notes too more or less accurately, then please check him only about his interpretation; and, when he has reached *that point*, don't let him stop playing *for the sake of minor mistakes*, but point them out to him when he has finished playing the piece. Although I have done very little teaching, yet I have always followed this method. It soon produces *musicians* which, after all, is one of the chief aims of the art, and it is less tiring for both master and pupil — In certain passages, such as

I should like him also to use all his fingers now and then, and
in such passages too as

so that he may slip one finger over another. Admittedly
such passages sound, so to speak, as if they were 'played like
pearls (i.e. with only a few fingers) or like a pearl' — but
occasionally we like to have a different kind of jewelry. —
More of this some other time — I hope that you will take note
of all these suggestions in the affectionate spirit in which I
have ventured to make them and would like to have them
interpreted — As it is, I am and must still remain your debtor
— In any case may my sincerity serve as a guarantee to you
that so far as possible I shall soon discharge that debt. —

Your true friend
BEETHOVEN

(879) *To Carl Czerny*

[Autograph in the Gesellschaft der Musikfreunde, Vienna] [1]

DEAR CZERNY!   [VIENNA, 1817]
    Please do not *say* anything at Giannatasio's *about the
person* who dined *with us* on the day when you gave me the
pleasure of your visit. He has begged me not to mention his
name. When I see you some time I will explain *the reason
for my request* — I hope to be able to return in some special way
my thanks to you for the trouble you are taking with my
nephew. For I do not wish to remain in your debt for ever —

In haste, your friend
L. V. BEETHOVEN

---

[1] This note is written and addressed in pencil.

(880) *To Sigmund Anton Steiner*

[*Autograph in the Stadtbibliothek, Vienna*]

[VIENNA, 1817]

MOST EXCELLENT LIEUTENANT GENERAL!

Could I not have the copies of the sonata now [1] —

In haste, your

G[ENERALISSIM]O

[1] Possibly a reference to the A major pianoforte sonata, Op. 101, published by Steiner in February, 1817.

1818

1818

(881) *To Frau Nanette Streicher*

[*Autograph not traced*] [1]

[VIENNA, *January* 1, 1818]

Thank you for the interest you are taking in me — Things are really better — although today I had to put up with a good deal from N[anni] — But as a New Year wish I threw half a dozen books at her head — We are pulling out the leaves (by getting rid of B[aberl]) and even the branches, but we shall probably have to get at the *roots*, so that nothing more shall be left but the soil — I have an idea that I saw Sophie.[2] When I got home for the second time my pain was so severe that all I could do was to lie down on the couch — I hope soon to see you here or to see myself at your home.

In haste, your friend

BEETHOVEN

(882) *To Frau Nanette Streicher*

[*Autograph not traced*] [3]

In haste. [VIENNA, *January*, 1818]

N[anni] did not hand me your letter until yesterday evening; every day I long for the end of her stay in my home — I have caught another chill and have a violent cold and cough. I shall see you soon. Thanks for the cotton. As soon as the silver has been delivered you will receive it.

Your friend

BEETHOVEN

(883) *To Cajetan Giannatasio del Rio*

[*Autograph in the Beethovenhaus, Bonn, H. C. Bodmer collection*]

[VIENNA], *January* 6, 1818

P.P.

So that there may be no misunderstanding, I am taking the liberty of informing you most humbly that unfortunately

---

[1] Taken from *TDR* IV, 500.   [2] Cf. Letter 839, p. 723, n. 1.
[3] Taken from *TDR* IV, 505.

the arrangement must stand that my nephew leaves your excellent boarding school at the end of this month. In regard to the other proposal you very kindly made to me, here too my hands are tied, because other aims for the benefit of my nephew would thereby be completely defeated.[1] But I do thank you most warmly for your kind intention — Circumstances may well demand that Karl be removed even before the end of this month, and, as I shall probably not be here, by somebody whom I shall appoint for that purpose. I am telling you this in advance so that nothing in this arrangement may take you by surprise. Let me add that my nephew and I shall be grateful to you as long as we live. I have noticed that Karl is so already; and to me this is a proof that, although he may be thoughtless, there is nothing evil in his nature and, still less, that he has a bad heart. I am very hopeful about his future development, the more so as he has already spent almost two years under your excellent supervision [2] —

With sincere regards,
your friend
L. VAN BEETHOVEN

(884) *To Frau Nanette Streicher, Klosterneuburg near Vienna*

[Autograph not traced] [3]

[VIENNA, c. January 7, 1818]

I am delighted that you are willing to continue to take an interest in my domestic affairs, for without your help everything in that line would be quite hopeless. In the housekeeping book I am sending you there is a letter which I wrote to you some time before you went to Klosterneuburg — N[anni] is now much better so far as her behaviour is concerned; and I certainly don't think that her intentions are evil. Perhaps it will be possible to run *our establishment more satisfactorily* with the other maid. But you must not forsake me. You can easily see in the housekeeping book whether I

---

[1] Giannatasio del Rio had offered to continue Karl's education for a reduced fee.
[2] Karl left Giannatasio del Rio's boarding school on January 24, 1818. He had been there since February 2, 1816.
[3] Taken from *TDR* IV, 502 and *KFR*, no. 635.

have dined alone or had several guests or not been at home —
I don't think that Nanni is absolutely *honest*, apart from the
fact that she is also a disgusting *beast*. I now realize quite
clearly that people of that type must be ruled not by *affection but
by fear* — It is understood that the maid can come on Saturday
morning. But please be so kind as to let me know whether
Baberl is to leave on Friday morning or after dinner? The
housekeeping book alone will not tell you everything in detail.
In order to take stock as well of *what we have*, you must sometimes appear at our table *unexpectedly* as a recording angel —
I never dine at home now unless I have *a guest*, for I don't
want to buy so much for one person that three or four people
can have their meals out of it too — I shall soon have my dear
son Karl *living with me*, so it will be all the more necessary for
me to be economical — It is difficult for me to bring myself
to visit you. I know you will forgive me. I am very sensitive
and not accustomed to such treatment, and still less can I lay
myself open to any more of it — Do come and see me as soon
as you can, but send me word beforehand. I have many
things to discuss with you. Return the little book to me this
evening. Until the other person turns up, we will adopt a
sterner method; and with your kind and friendly help it
ought surely to be possible to get on in that way — In addition
to her bread money amounting to 12 kreuzer N[anni] gets
a roll in the mornings. If the kitchenmaid is to get one too,
then the morning rolls will amount to 18 gulden a year [1] —
All good wishes for your happiness. Fräulein N[anni] has
been quite different since I threw those half dozen books at
her head. Probably one landed by chance in her *brain* or in
her *evil heart*; at any rate we have a full-bosomed deceiver!!!

In haste, your

L. v. BEETHOVEN

[1] In his diary kept between January 3 and 16, 1818, Beethoven noted: 'The
kitchenmaid gets 60 gulden a year in wages and 12 kreuzer daily as bread money'.

(885) *To Frau Nanette Streicher, Klosterneuburg near Vienna*

[*Autographs of two fragments of this letter in the British Museum and of the latter portion in the Beethovenhaus, Bonn, H. C. Bodmer collection*] [1]

[VIENNA, *early January*, 1818]

As for B[aberl], she is leaving on Monday morning. So the other one can take up her duties at noon or *at about two or three in the afternoon*, at whatever time you think best. N[anni] asked me today *whether B[aberl] was staying*. I said *no*, and added that she could stay until *Monday morning at the latest.* By the way, I have good reason to think that N[anni] or the other one is still carrying on her spying tricks in your house — The day before yesterday in the evening N[anni] began to chaff me, in her manner which is characteristic of *all her filthy tribe*, about ringing the bell. So she did know that I had written *to you about that.* Yesterday morning they both resumed their devilish tricks. I made short work of them and threw the heavy chair beside my bed at B[aberl]. After that I had peace for the rest of the day. They always have their revenge on me whenever they deliver our letters or notice that something is going on between you and me — So far as N[anni]'s *honesty* is concerned, I fancy that it is not very strongly developed. *She has a sweet tooth* and that may account for a good deal — As soon as the other maid has arrived I will call in N[anni] *when you are present*, i.e. the next time you visit me, and express my doubts about the housekeeping book — *Monthly accounts* are of no use in my household unless a certain number of people dine with me every day; and, moreover, the purchase of supplies has made that impossible. But it is evident that I *alone* need almost as much as if two other persons were having meals with me — Apart from the two servants we shall probably be always *three* at table, since my Karl's tutor will always lunch [2] with me. I must be grateful to Heaven that everywhere I find people who, particularly at this

---

[1] The passages, the autographs of which have not been traced, have been taken from *TDR* IV, 502-504 and *KFR*, no. 636.

[2] The passages from 'lunch' to 'very best way' and from 'might still like' to 'shall soon' form the recto and verso of a fragmentary autograph in the British Museum.

time, are ready to help me. For instance, I have come across one of *the most distinguished professors at the University here* who is arranging and advising me in the very best way about *everything connected with Karl's education* [1] — If you happen to meet those Giannatasios at Czerny's, *pretend to know nothing whatever about what is being done about my Karl; say that it is not my practice to chatter about my plans, since any plan that one has chattered about becomes public property.* For those people might still like *to interfere even more; and I don't want those commonplace people either for my Karl or for myself* — That you willingly forgive N[anni] I can well understand, for that is also my inclination. Yet I can no longer regard her as anything but an *immoral person.* We shall soon see [2] how things proceed in other directions. But *usually* what has once happened between masters and servants can never be patched up — Please instruct and train the kitchenmaid who is now taking up her duties, *so that she may side with you and me against N[anni].* As a reward for doing so I will make her a present occasionally; but the other one need not know anything about this. In any case she won't have as *sweet a tooth* as N[anni] and B[aberl]. In short, the kitchenmaid must always behave as *the party in opposition* to N[anni]; and then N[anni]'s extraordinary sauciness, wickedness and vulgarity which, I admit, are now a little toned down, will also gradually subside. I assure you that what I have gone through with N[anni] far exceeds anything I *have ever suffered from the many servants* I have had — I have strictly forbidden N[anni] to receive any visitors who may call and especially those from the first floor.

And now I send you my most heartfelt wishes. As for the servants there is only *one opinion* everywhere on their *immorality,* to which all other misfortunes *in this city* can be ascribed. Therefore, so far as I am concerned, in this connexion you may never have to suffer or even expect an insult. I shall always acknowledge with gratitude the sacrifices which your friendship has made for me. I am only sorry that in all

[1] This was Professor Emmerich Thomas Hohler (1781–1846), writer and classical scholar. He was tutor to the family of Prince Schwarzenberg and later librarian to the same prince. He also taught Latin at Blöchlinger's boarding school.

[2] The autograph of the remaining portion of this letter beginning at 'see how things' is in the Beethovenhaus, Bonn, H. C. Bodmer collection.

innocence *I was the cause* of a slight disturbance in your
house — Instead of the clergy of Klosterneuburg I give you my
blessing —

In haste, your friend

BEETHOVEN

By the way, N[anni] asked me
   whether I had found somebody to
   replace B[aberl].   I said *yes*.

(886) *To Frau Nanette Streicher*

[*Autograph not traced*] ¹

[VIENNA, *January* 23, 1818]

True, I wrote to you recently that I felt *better*, but I am
not yet quite well.   Hence I have not been able to see you;
and now the carpenter has been here since yesterday — Karl
is arriving tomorrow, and I was mistaken in thinking that
perhaps he would prefer to stay *there*.² He is in good spirits
and much livelier than he used to be; and every moment he
shows his love and affection for me.   In any case I hope that
you will see that *I* do not hesitate about undertaking something
I have once firmly resolved to do; and *it was so good*!

As for N[anni] and the entering of the kitchen utensils,
you are quite right; I shall think over today how it could be
done.   Perhaps I shall see you tomorrow or even today.

Her fortnight will have already expired on Monday.   The
question is whether she ought to leave on that day.   I should
be delighted.   She has done a lot of harm, for nothing is
safe from her wickedness and her meddling — We can let the
tutor come *whenever* we like.   In any case we can't talk over
and carry out anything together until N[anni] has left.   We
need only make the most necessary arrangements, since it is
quite certain that *I shall have to leave Vienna* either in the middle
of June or at the end of September ³ — All good wishes.   I
thank you for your sympathetic attention.

Your friend

BEETHOVEN

---

¹ Taken from *TDR* IV, 505.
² I.e. at Giannatasio del Rio's boarding school.
³ Beethoven was planning a visit to England.

FIRST PAGE OF A LETTER TO GEORGE THOMSON (February 21, 1818)

(Autograph in the British Museum)

CANON WRITTEN FOR CARLO SOLIVA (June 2, 1824)
(*Autograph in the National Museum, Cracow*)

(887) *To Cajetan Giannatasio del Rio*

[*Autograph not traced*] [1]

VIENNA, *January* 24, 1818

P.P.

I am not coming in person, because then there would
certainly be a kind of farewell; and farewells I have always
avoided.

Please accept my most sincere thanks for the zeal, integrity
and honesty with which you undertook the education of my
nephew — As soon as I can find a little time to call my own,
we will visit you. Let me remind you that on account of his
mother I should not like it to be too widely known that my
nephew is now living with me —

My greetings to you all and my thanks also to Frau v[on]
G[iannatasio] in particular, for the motherly care she has bestowed on my Karl.

With sincere regards

L. V. BEETHOVEN

(888) *To Frau Nanette Streicher*

[*Autograph not traced*] [2]

[VIENNA, *before January* 25, 1818]

I beg you, my dear friend, to settle that matter of the silver
plate which still remains to be dealt with. For it would have
to wait far too long before I can manage to see to it. First of
all, we ought to know whether we must go on spending money?
And how much? *In any case we are going to return the sugar
basin*; and I shall add *three coffee spoons* of my own. If we
could only obtain instead of these and without spending
much money two more dessert spoons and a light cream
spoon, then our needs would be met. For I, a poor Austrian
musical drudge, nay, one of the very poorest, must not think
of buying anything more — In haste — but with my best

---

[1] Taken from Nohl, no. 207 and *TDR* IV, 91.
[2] Taken from Nohl II, no. 206 and *TDR* IV, 506.

compliments and thanks for your and your daughter's exemplary behaviour.

Your friend
BEETHOVEN

For Frau von Streicher,
together with the account for silver, a silver sugar basin and three coffee spoons.

(889) *To Frau Nanette Streicher*

[Autograph not traced] [1]

[VIENNA, *January* 25, 1818]

It was not possible to visit you yesterday — I am looking forward with the greatest pleasure to seeing you this afternoon. At any rate N[anni] is going out; and in any case there must never be any meeting between *her* and *you*. Besides we could go out and buy the silver afterwards, for it is really necessary — After three o'clock N[anni] will have certainly left the house — I may be much mistaken but I fancy that today or tomorrow she will be leaving for good —

In haste, your
BEETHOVEN

C'est justement que j'entens, que la N[anni] demain s'en va sûrement.[2]

(890) *To Count Moritz Lichnowsky*

[Autograph not traced] [3]

MY MOST BELOVED FRIEND,   [VIENNA, *January,* 1818]
MY DEAR COUNT!

From the enclosed you will see how matters stand. I do not doubt that I shall be allowed, without my making great

---

[1] Taken from Nohl II, no. 205 and *TDR* IV, 504.

[2] According to Nohl, who transcribed the original letter, this postscript in French was written beside the address.

[3] Both Kalischer (cf. *KFR*, no. 766, note) and Thayer (cf. *TDR* IV, 85) had access to the autograph of this letter which was originally in the possession of Count Moritz Lichnowsky's daughter. There was no address on the autograph.

demands, to receive this instrument, particularly as it will soon arrive at Trieste.[1]   Bridi [2] has been commissioned by the Englishman [3] to deal with the business side — I am now awaiting the result of your kind efforts or investigations.   Then no doubt the best thing will be for me to apply in writing or verbally to His Excellency Count Stadion [4] himself — I hope that I shall soon have the pleasure of seeing you —

With deep love and admiration,

Your friend

BEETHOVEN

(891) *To Thomas Broadwood, London* [5]

[*Autograph not traced*] [6]

VIENNA, *February* 3, 1818

MON TRÈS CHER AMI BROADWOOD!

Jamais je n'eprouvais pas un plus grand Plaisir de ce que me causa votre Annonce de l'arrivée de cette Piano, avec qui vous m'honorès de m'en faire present, je regarderai comme un Autel, ou je deposerai les plus belles offrandes de mon esprit au divine Apollon.   Aussitôt cõe je recevrai votre Excellent Instrument, je vous enverrai d'en abord les Fruits de l'inspiration des premiers moments, que j'y passerai, pour vous servir d'un Souvenir de moi à vous mon très cher

---

[1] This was the six-octave grand pianoforte which Thomas Broadwood, a member of the firm of John Broadwood & Sons, had sent as a present to Beethoven on December 27, 1817.   See following Letter 891.

[2] Giuseppe Antonio Bridi (1763–1836), born at Rovereto, belonged to the Viennese firm of import merchants, Bridi, Parisi & Co.   His father, Dr. Antonio Giacomo Bridi (1721–1799), pianist and singer, enjoyed the friendship of Mozart, to whose memory the son erected a monument in the family park at Rovereto.

[3] I.e. Thomas Broadwood.

[4] Count Johann Philipp Karl Joseph von Stadion (1763–1824) was then Austrian Minister of Finance.   According to a notice in the *Wiener Zeitung* of June 8, 1818, Beethoven received his Broadwood pianoforte free of freightage and customs charges.   It is now in the National Museum, Budapest.

[5] The firm of Broadwood & Sons was founded in London in 1732 by Burkhard Tschudi from Switzerland.   His son-in-law John Broadwood (1732–1812), a cabinet-maker, carried on the business and was succeeded in turn by his sons James, who joined the firm in 1795, and Thomas, who joined it in 1807.

[6] Taken from the facsimile in J. S. Shedlock: *The Letters of Beethoven*, vol. ii, p. 103.   The original letter was then in private ownership.

B[roadwood], et je ne souhaits ce que, qu'ils soient dignes de votre instrument.

Mon cher Monsieur et ami recevés ma plus grande consideration de votre ami et très humble serviteur

LOUIS VAN BEETHOVEN

(892) *To George Thomson, Edinburgh*

[*Autograph in the British Museum*]

MONSIEUR THOMPSON   VIENNA, *February* 21, 1818
MON TRES CHER AMI

Mon copiste est malade, et voilà la raison pourquoi je vous envoie mes manuscripts, il me falloit prendre quelques Ducats de plus qu'ordinaire, parcequ'il était necessaire de copier moi même, et je perdûs quelque tems et sans cela la somē ordinaire n'est pas d'un si grande importance en consideration qu'il y a des chansons, qui ne reussent pas sans quelque peine, quoiqu'on ce n'entend pas en jouant et aussi en voyant par exemple comē No 2, on trouve bien vite des harmonies pour harmoniser des telles chansons, mais la simplicité, le caractère la Nature du chant, pour y reussir, ce n'est pas toujours si facile comē vous peut-être croyez de moi, on trouve un Nombre infinie des Harmonies, mais seulement une est conforme au genre et au caractère de la Mélodie, et vous pouvez toujours encore donner une douzaine ducats de plus, et pourtant cela ne sera pas vraiment payé, et si vous m'honorez avec des autres chansons, il me serait plus agréable, si vous m'envoyéz un grande nombre, puisqu'il s'en vaut plus de peine, d'y se donner. — il me falloit payer pour votre lettre du 25 Juin 1817 dix florins à la poste, j'ai à présent si reglé, que les Fries m'envoient toujours les lettres de vous, car il y en eut en quelquefois des confusions, parceque les Fries donnèrent les lettres à un tel et à un autre ainsi s'arrivât, que je reçus vos lettres quelque fois deux trois mois plus tard, que vous l'avez ecrites, mais comē la chose est à présent organisé, je tiens tous vos lettres sur le champ de Messieurs le Fries, que je trouve toujours bien complaisant — Il n'estoit pas possible de vous donner une réponse à votre lettre de 25

Juin, j'étais trop occupé et encore malade, et il est difficile de vous servir dans cet affaire, croyez moi, que je traite toujours en ami avec vous, mais contre les circonstances je ne sais agir, je vous fais un autre proposition je suis prèt de vous composer 12 overtures pour un honoraire de 140 Ducats en espece, je suis prêt de vous composer 12 Thèmes avec variations pour 100 Ducats en espèce, mais si vous voulez faire composer 12 overtures et 12 Thèmes avec variations *ensemble* ou à même temps j'étais en état de ne prendre plus pour les 12 overtures et les 12 Thèmes varies, que 224 Ducats, dans de telles petites choses, on n'est pas en état de gagner quelque chose autrement, qu'il soit un assez grande nombre, que alors procure un some considerable, voila come je parle franchement come un ami à un autre, je vous assûre, que je opprime bien souvent mon honneur seulement pour vous servir aussi a bon prix, qu'il m'est possible. — vous m'avez parlé d'un ode des paroles angloises sur la pouvoir de la Musique sur les passions [1] avec une traduction litterale en Allemand je l'accepterai avec le plus grand plaisir, et aussi je tacherai de la mettre en musique le plutôt, je vous prie bien de m'envoyer cette poême, mais pas par la poste qu'il soit à Messieurs le Fries et Compy, car autrecela il me coutoit trop, nous devons ici payer bien moins cher toutce, qu'en Angleterre, il y a encore chez moi des poèmes Angleterre, dont quelques sont fort belles, et j'aimerais de les mettre en musique. — encore j'y joint à mes propositions à l'egard des Variations et overtures que je vous enverrai d'en mon Manuscript, et la Copiature vous ne coute rien. — Dernièrement j'ai publié un nouveau simfonie en partition grave et aussi pour grand orchester. — Un fois quand le temps me ne presse pas come aujourd'hui, je vous ecrirai plus de ma Musique gravée — je crois que vous m'avez un fois écrit d'un autre Volume, que vous avez publiée des mes chansons, je vous en prie de me l'envoyer par occasion, aussi je vous remarque, que vous vous faites attention, d'y eviter la monotonie c'est a dire que vous mêlez les sérieux des tristes entre les gais etc en changeant les modes les mesures ausitot deux dur un moll un dur un moll un dur etc aussitot la Mesure C $\frac{2}{4}$ $\frac{6}{8}$, aussitot $\frac{6}{8}$ $\frac{2}{4}$ C, aussitot $\frac{2}{4}$ $\frac{2}{4}$ $\frac{6}{8}$ C etc. — Portéz vous

---

[1] William Collins's poem 'The Passions, an ode for music', which has been set to music by several English composers.

757

bien et me donnez le plaisir d'une reponse, parceque je sens toujours quelque plaisir d'entendre de vous des nouvelles. —
avec estime et vrai amitié votre
BEETHOVEN

(893) *To Frau Nanette Streicher*

[Autograph not traced] [1]

[VIENNA, *February*, 1818]

We were up early, both Karl and I, for the tutor had not *come home* during the night — So I cannot quite account for our untidiness which prevented you from coming to see us, although indeed we are in many respects frequently in that condition — Today my guest is one of the most eminent professors who is coming to see me about my Karl! [2] — I hope that I shall certainly see you this afternoon. I told the housekeeper to ask you about the pastry which you were once so kind as to make for us for the New Year — All good wishes — God help me, I appeal to Him in the last resort.
Your friend
BEETHOVEN

(894) *To Frau Nanette Streicher*

[Autograph not traced] [3]

[VIENNA, *c. February*, 1818]

I was just about to write to you when I received your letter with the silver; we shall discuss everything else. Karl is not allowed to go out yet, not for some days at any rate, and my household arrangements will keep me busy too for a few days. For all these reasons I have not been able to see you, but I hope to arrange to do so tomorrow or the day after. P[eppi] [4] is a *good* cook; and for this I must again express to you my infinite gratitude. If you will only continue to take

---

[1] Taken from *KFR*, no. 779 and *TDR* IV, 507.
[2] Probably Professor Hohler. See Letter 885, p. 751, n. 1.
[3] Taken from Nohl II, no. 208 and *TDR* IV, 505-506.
[4] The new cook. See Letter 904, p. 768, n. 2.

an interest in us now and then, the whole establishment may yet become tolerably comfortable and perhaps even something more. But it will be some days yet before I shall have everything absolutely straight. And for me this was a Herculean labour. May God grant that I shall be able again to dedicate myself entirely to my art. Formerly I used to be able to make all my other circumstances subservient to my art. I admit, however, that by so doing I became a bit crazy.

More of this when we meet — Karl sends you his greetings —

In haste, your friend and servant,

BEETHOVEN

(895) *To Ferdinand Ries, London*

[*Autograph not traced*] [1]

MY DEAR RIES! VIENNA, *March* 5, 1818

Notwithstanding my desire to do so, it has not been possible for me to go to London during this season. Please inform the Philharmonic Society that my poor health has prevented me from undertaking the journey. But I hope perhaps to make a complete recovery in the spring and then later in the year to avail myself of the offer the Society has made to me and to fulfil all its conditions.

Please request Neate on my behalf not to make any public use at any rate of the large number of works which he took from me, that is, until I come to London myself. Whatever his circumstances may now be, I have good reason to complain of his behaviour.

Botter has visited me a few times. He seems to be a good fellow and has talent for composition.[2] — I hope and trust for your sake that your happy circumstances may daily improve.

---

[1] Taken from *TDR* IV, 95.

[2] Cipriani Potter (1792–1871), English pianist, conductor and composer, had recently arrived in Vienna and was studying composition with Förster. After extensive travels in Germany and Italy Potter returned to London in 1821, was appointed Professor of the pianoforte at the Royal Academy of Music in 1822 and ten years later Principal of that institution, an office which he held until 1859. He was a sincere admirer of Beethoven's compositions and introduced the latter's pianoforte concertos to the English public in 1824 and 1825.

Alas, I can't say the same about myself. Owing to my unfortunate connexion with this Archduke I have been reduced
almost to beggary. I can't see people starving. I must help
them. So you can imagine that I suffer even more in this
way. Please write to me soon. If it is at all possible for me
to do so, I will leave Vienna even sooner, in order not to be
utterly ruined; and then I shall arrive in London during the
winter at latest.

I know that you will stand by an unfortunate friend. If
only I had been able to do so and if I had not been fettered
by circumstances, as I have always been in Vienna, I would
certainly have done far more for you — I wish you every
success. Give my greetings to Neate, Smart and Cramer —
although I hear that the latter is an adversary [1] of yours and
mine. Meanwhile I do know something about the art of
dealing with such people. And in London, I feel sure that,
all the same, we shall produce a pleasant harmony.

With all my heart I greet and embrace you.

Your friend

LUDWIG VAN BEETHOVEN

Many cordial greetings to your dear and (as I hear) most
lovely wife.[2]

(896) *To George Thomson, Edinburgh*

[Autograph in the Beethovenhaus, Bonn, H. C. Bodmer collection]

MONSIEUR THOMPSON   VIENNA, *March 11, 1818*
MON CHER AMI!

C'est deja du 12 Novembre 1814, que vous m'aves
accordè de votre propre Main pour chaque air Ecossais
quatre ducats en Espéce, mais helas bien occupè, lorsque j'ai
vous envoyés derniere fois les trois airs, et parce la un peu en
confusion, j'ai vous mis seulement, pour chaque air trois
ducats en Espéce, eh bien, j'ai encore quatre ducats en Espéce
de vous reçevoir, et que je vous pris de les m'assigner *chez*

---

[1] In Thayer's version the word is 'Contra-Subject'.
[2] Ries had married in 1814 Harriet Mangeon, a beautiful and accomplished
Englishwoman. She died at Königswinter in 1860.

Fries — Dans la Même lettre du 12 Novembre 1814 vous m'aves offert pour une ouverture *dix huit* Ducats, quant à moi je ne me souviens tout à fait, de vous aves ecrit de cette objet, mais j'espere, que vous trouves mes derniers offrandes justes et amicales, soyes persuadés, que je fais toujours mon possible pour vous prouver mon Attachement à votre personne — je passai, il y a quelques jours, quelque tems, pour liser votres lettres à moi, et je trouvai encore les poêmes anglaise, que vous m'aves envoyés un fois, j'ai presentai ces poèmes à un ami de moi, qui connait parfaitement l'angue anglaise, et qui est un de nos Traducteurs le plus grands, il à traduit les meilleurs poesies des auteurs anglais en Allemande, il trouvât quelques des ces poesies, qui sont fort belles, et m'encourageat de les mettre en Musique, j'espére, que vous trouves mes offerts si juste ainsi, qu'il est possible, quand je vous demande pour six chansons anglaises 54 ducats en Espéce, à present cõme j'ouis d'une santé rejouissante, je vous montrerai avec grand plaisir mon zéle de vous servir et de vous livrer tojours le plus belle de mon Art — quant a moi, je vous pris, de prendre de l'égard, que vous faites l'occasion avec votres cõmissions, ainsi, qu'elles me produisent quelquefois *des rondes sommes*, parcequ'on gagne seulement avec des Bagatelles, quand il y a un assés quantité — j'espére d'avoir bientôt de vous Nouvelles, et que vous aimés, de vous souvenir quelque fois

de votre ami, bien vous attaché

LOUIS VAN BEETHOVEN

(897) *To Frau Johanna van Beethoven*

[*Autograph in Yale University Library*]

VIENNA, *March* 29, 1818

So far as I am concerned, you have my full consent when selling your house to leave for the buyer the sum on the house of the 7000 gulden which belong to your son Karl.[1] *But the worshipful Landrechte must give their permission to enable you to*

---

[1] For the text of Caspar Carl's will see *TDR* III, 517-519. The house which Johanna, his widow, had inherited and the value of which was to fall eventually to her son Karl, was in the Alserstrasse.

guarantee to any prospective buyer that the capital of 7000 *gulden shall not be called in* [1] *for three or four years.* — In my opinion there is nothing harmful or unfair to your son Karl in such an arrangement. Hence I have not the slightest doubt that the worshipful Obervormundschaft will grant your request. As I have already stated, I can think of no objection whatsoever; and I hope and trust that the eminent Obervormundschaft will fully agree with me about this.

LUDWIG VAN BEETHOVEN
Guardian of my nephew Karl van Beethoven

(898) *To Ferdinand Ries, London*

[Autograph not traced] [2]

DEAR RIES!   [VIENNA, *before March* 30, 1818]
    I am only now recovering from a severe attack from which I have been suffering; and I am off to the country — I should like you to arrange to sell to a London publisher these two works, i.e. a grand sonata for pianoforte solo and a *pianoforte sonata which I myself have arranged as a quintet for two violins, two violas and a cello.*[3] No doubt it will be easy for you to get 50 gold ducats for the two works. (If you can get more, all the better. And surely it ought to be possible!!!!).[4] Provided the publisher informs me about what time he would like to bring out the two works, I could bring them out here at the same time. At any rate I should then make more than if I were to publish them only in Vienna — Furthermore, I could also publish a new trio for pianoforte, violin and cello if you could find a publisher for it [5] — In any case you are well aware that I have never done anything illegal. Therefore you can go ahead in London without endangering your honour or mine. As soon as he has received the works, the

---

    [1] I.e. left invested in the property. Evidently the house was mortgaged and the mortgage was not to be called in.
    [2] Taken from *TDR* IV, 119-120. Thayer transcribed the autograph then in private ownership in England.
    [3] Probably Op. 106 and Op. 104.
    [4] According to Thayer this bracketed sentence was added at the foot of the page as a NB.
    [5] This was a trio in F minor for which Beethoven made some sketches. See Nottebohm II, p. 345.

publisher will inform me when he intends to publish them, and then they can appear in Vienna as well — Forgive me if I am giving you a great deal of trouble. My situation is now so difficult that I have to resort to every means merely to enable me to preserve this dreary life. *Potter* says that Chappell [1] in Bond Street is one of the best publishers. Well now, I am leaving everything to you. But please let me have a reply as quickly as possible so that these works may not be left on my hands. — Do ask Neate not to produce in public any of the numerous works he took away from me, that is to say, until I come to London *myself.* I hope to do so next winter for certain. I must do this unless I want to become a beggar in Vienna — My best compliments to the Phil[harmonic] Society — I will write to you soon about several things; and again I beg you to reply very quickly.

Ever your true friend

BEETHOVEN

Many cordial greetings to your lovely wife.[2]

(899) *To Frau Nanette Streicher*

[*Autograph not traced*] [3]

[VIENNA, *Spring*, 1818]

From the attached document you will see how the matter stands — As your cousin from Cracow is going to be so helpful, he has only to ask at the Head Customs Office for Hofrat Anders [4] who will produce the necessary information, and to

---

[1] The publishing firm of Chappell was founded in 1811 by Samuel Chappell, J. B. Cramer and F. T. Latour. Cramer resigned in 1818 and Latour in 1826. After Samuel Chappell's death in 1834 his son William Chappell (1809–1888) took over the business.

[2] According to *TDR* IV, 120, the address on the verso with the postscript, all in Beethoven's hand, runs as follows:

A Monsieur
Ferdinand Ries
celébre compositeur

Chez B. A.   a
     Goldschmidt   Londres
        et Compagnie

Forgive the double address, due to my being confused.

[3] Taken from *TDR* IV, 87.

[4] Professor O. E. Deutsch has suggested Hofrat Bernhard Anders, Ritter von Porodim, who until 1825 drew a pension as a bank official.

give him many compliments from me, seeing that his lovely daughter is musical too. The main problem is *how to arrange for the Head Customs Office here to send an order to the Head Office at Trieste to have the instrument delivered here — As soon as I receive this order from the Head Customs Office here, I will give it to Henikstein & Co.*[1] *who are authorized to arrange for the delivery of the instrument.*[2]

In haste, your friend
BEETHOVEN

(900) *To the Archduke Rudolph*

[*Autograph in the Gesellschaft der Musikfreunde, Vienna*]

YOUR IMPERIAL HIGHNESS!   [VIENNA, *early May*, 1818]

I crave your gracious forgiveness for two misdemeanours, firstly, for not waiting upon Y.I.H. this morning, and, secondly, for having apologized for this omission so late — Last night I was again very ill, but this afternoon I feel a little better, and I hope that I shall be able to come to Y.I.H. again the day after tomorrow — The doctor has promised me that by the middle of June I shall certainly be quite restored to health. This I do desire, the more so in order that Y.I.H. may not be constrained to harbour any evil thoughts about me. My intentions are certainly of the purest and my ill health alone prevents me from carrying them out.

Your Imperial Highness's
most humble and most faithful servant
LUDWIG VAN BEETHOVEN

(901) *To Count Moritz Lichnowsky*

[*Autograph in the Library of Congress*]

DEAR FRIEND!   [VIENNA, *shortly before May* 19, 1818]

You recently sent to enquire of me whether I should be at home on the following day; and I sent a message to say

[1] For a note on Henikstein see Letter 984, p. 858, n. 2.
[2] The Broadwood pianoforte sent as a gift to Beethoven. Cf. Letter 890, p. 755, n. 1.

that I should expect you with the greatest pleasure on the following day; and, what is more, I waited for you that whole morning until half past one! — Has my worthy brother now arrived? I am very busy or I should have gone to you. I hope to be at Mödling in a few days.[1]

In haste, your sincere friend who loves you

BEETHOVEN

(902) *To Vincenz Hauschka*

[*Autograph in the possession of Fräulein Gertrud von Waldkirch*]

DEAR LITTLE HAUSCHKA![2]   [VIENNA, *May* 18, 1818]

Send me the score and the parts of the symphony in E^b [3] and do so today, if possible, for I am going into the country tomorrow. If the bearer can't find me tomorrow, he need only leave them below with the caretaker — About our other projects I shall soon have a talk with you. I am ready to undertake any task whereby I can serve the Gesellschaft des Musikvereins [4] with my meagre talents; and I am delighted that at least a beginning has already been made with the founding of a future conservatoire.[5]

Your true friend

BEETHOVEN

[1] According to his diary Beethoven settled at Mödling on May 19th. He had rooms in the Hafnerhaus, now Hauptstrasse 79, which still stands.

[2] Beethoven calls him 'Hauschkerl', using a Viennese diminutive.

[3] Op. 55, the Eroica symphony, the first movement of which had been performed at a concert given by the Gesellschaft der Musikfreunde on May 3, 1818.

[4] Beethoven means the 'Gesellschaft der Musikfreunde'.

[5] The Conservatoire was founded in 1817 and by 1821 was fully working.

(903) *To Vincenz Hauschka, Vienna*

[*Autograph in the Gesellschaft der Musikfreunde, Vienna*]

[MÖDLING, *early June*, 1818]

MOST EXCELLENT LEADING MEMBER OF THE CLUB OF THE
ENEMIES OF MUSIC OF THE AUSTRIAN IMPERIAL STATE! [1]

The only subject I have is a *sacred* one. But you want a
heroic subject. Well, that will suit me too. But I think that
for such a *mass* of people it would be very appropriate to mix
in a little sacred stuff.

Herr von Bernard would suit me quite well. But you
must also pay him. I am not mentioning myself. Since after
all you call yourselves friends of music, it's only natural that
you are prepared to do a good deal for the sake of music —!!!

Now all good wishes, most excellent little Hauschka. I
wish you an open stool and the finest commode. As for me, I
am rambling about in the mountains, ravines and valleys here
with a piece of music paper and scrawling several things for
the sake of bread and money. For such is the height I have
reached in this all-powerful former *land of the Phaeacians*[2] that

---

[1] This musical setting of 'Ich bin bereit' (I am willing) is listed in *KHV.* as
WoO 201.

In May, 1818, Hauschka was commissioned by the Gesellschaft der Musikfreunde to request Beethoven to compose an oratorio on a heroic subject. Beethoven agreed, and early in 1820 J. K. Bernard provided him with a text 'Der
Sieg des Kreuzes' which, however, he never set to music. See Letter 947,
p. 812, n. 1.

[2] Cf. p. 457, n. 5.

in order to gain some leisure for a great work I must always
scrawl a good deal beforehand for money so that I can keep
alive while I am composing the great work — Let me add
that my health has greatly improved and that if the matter
is urgent I can easily contrive to serve you —
    Well,

ich bin be - rei - - - - - t!   ich bin be -

A - - - - - - - men!

- rei - - - - - - - - - t!

    If you consider it necessary to have a word with me, write
to me and I will then make all the arrangements for our
meeting — My best regards to the society of the enemies of
music and so forth.

In haste, your friend
BEETHOVEN [1]

(904) *To Frau Nanette Streicher, Vienna*

[Autograph not traced] [2]

MÖDLING, June 18, 1818

MOST EXCELLENT FRAU VON STREICHER!

    I have not been able to reply to your last letter sooner.
I would have written to you a few days before the servants
were chucked out, but I was still hesitating to take the decision

---

[1] The verso has the following address in Beethoven's hand :
    'To Herr von Hauschka,
    leading member of the club of
    the E[nemies] of the Austrian I[mperial]
    State and also Grand Cross of
    the Order of the Violoncello, and so forth
    and so on —'

[2] Taken from Nohl II, no. 213 and *TDR* IV, 509-511. According to Thayer,
the autograph of this long letter was in the possession of the Austrian pianist Ernst
Pauer (1826–1905), who had inherited it from his father, a son-in-law of Nanette
Streicher.

until I noticed that Frau D.[1], in particular, was preventing Karl from confessing everything; '*He really ought to spare his mother*' she told him; and Peppi[2] backed her up. Of course they didn't want to be discovered; both of them have joined forces quite shamefully and allowed Frau van Beethoven to make use of them; both have accepted presents of coffee and sugar from her, and Peppi has been given *money*, and the *old woman* presumably too. For there is no doubt whatever that she *herself went to Karl's mother*. Moreover she told Karl that *if I dismissed her* from my service, *she would go at once to his mother*. She said this on one occasion when I reprimanded her for her behaviour with which I frequently had cause to be dissatisfied. Peppi, who often listened to what Karl and I were talking about, seemed to be tempted to confess the truth. But the *old woman taxed her with being stupid and roundly abused her* — Hence Peppi's attitude hardened again and she tried to put me off the scent — The story of this horrible treachery may have been going on for almost six weeks; and both these women would not have got off *so lightly* had they been dealing with a less magnanimous person. Peppi got from me nine or ten gulden for chemise cloth. She borrowed this money but later on I gave it to her. So instead of 60 gulden she has had 70. Indeed she could have done without those despicable briberies. In the case of the old woman, who on the whole behaved worst of all, hatred may have been a contributory cause, for she always believed that she was being kept down (although she has had higher wages than she deserves). But just from her *sneering expression one day* when Karl was embracing me, I suspected *treachery* and thought how shameful and how mischievous such an old woman could be. Just imagine, two days before I came out here[3] K[arl] went to his mother in the afternoon without my knowledge; and both the old woman and P[eppi] knew about it. Listen, however, to the triumph of a grey-haired traitress. When I was driving out here with her and K[arl], I was talking to K[arl] in the carriage about this, although I did not yet know all; and when I expressed my fear lest we should

---

[1] Evidently the new housekeeper, the 'old woman', who according to an entry in Beethoven's diary had taken up her duties on June 8th.
[2] The new cook.　　　　　　　　　　[3] On May 19th.

GEORGE THOMSON (1757–1851)
From the water-colour drawing by William Nicholson (*c.* 1816)
(*Scottish National Portrait Gallery*)

not be safe even at Mödling, she exclaimed that '*I had only to rely on her*'. Oh, what infamy! Only twice, including this occasion, have I come across *such behaviour* in human beings of an otherwise venerable age — When I dismissed them both several days previously, I had put down in writing for them that neither should dare to accept from Karl's mother any present for him. Peppi, without considering whether she was at fault, secretly tried to revenge herself on K[arl] who had admitted everything. They both knew this, because I had noted down on that piece of paper *that everything had been discovered* — After that I expected them both to beg my pardon. But instead of that they both, one after the other, played nasty pranks on us. Well, as a change for the better was not to be expected in the case of such hardened sinners and as every moment I had to expect some new act of treachery, I decided to sacrifice my bodily well-being and my comfort to the welfare of my poor Karl who had been so misled, and I marched them out of the house *as a warning* to all future servants — I could have made the testimonial less favourable, but so far from doing that I put each of them down for a full six months, although it was not so in fact. I never *revenge myself*; whenever I must act *against* other people, I only perpetrate *against them* what necessity demands, so as to protect myself against them or to prevent them from doing any further harm. — I am sorry to have lost Peppi, for indeed she used to be honest. So I gave her an even more favourable testimonial than the one I gave to the old woman; besides, she seems to have been more or less led astray by the old one. But that P[eppi] has had a bad conscience is obvious from her saying to K[arl] that '*she didn't dare go to her parents any more*'; *and I fancy that she really is still at Mödling* — I had been noticing signs of treachery for a very long time; and then on the eve of my departure I received an anonymous letter, the contents of which filled me with terror; but they were little more than suppositions. Karl, whom I pounced on that very evening, immediately disclosed a little, but not all. As I often give him a good shaking, but not without valid reason, he was far too frightened to confess absolutely everything. We arrived here in the middle of this struggle. As I frequently reprimanded him, the servants noticed it; and the old traitress, in particular, tried to prevent *him from confessing the truth*. But as I gave Karl a solemn promise that everything would be forgiven him if only he would confess the truth and as I reminded him that lies would plunge him into an even deeper abyss than the one into which he had already fallen, everything came to light. Well, if at this point you add the data about the servants which I previously gave you, you will have a clear idea of the whole disgraceful story of these two traitresses — K[arl] has done wrong, but — a mother — a mother — even a bad mother is still a mother. — And in so far he must be excused, especially by me, since I know *only too well* his intriguing and passionate mother — The parson at Mödling [1] is well aware that I know all about him, for K[arl] had already told me. Presumably he was not fully instructed and possibly he will take care, which means that Karl will not be ill-treated by him; for on the whole he seems to be a rather rough fellow. Well, that is enough for the time being. But as K[arl]'s virtue is now being tested, for there is no virtue without temptation, I am purposely letting all this pass until it happens again (which indeed I do not think likely), when I shall give His Reverence such a merciless drubbing with countless spiritual flails and amulets and with my exclusive guardianship and the privileges connected therewith that the whole parsonage will quake with it — This affair has given me a dreadful heart attack from which I have not yet completely recovered — Now to the subject of our household, which requires your help — You surely know how much we need it. Don't let yourself be intimidated; such a thing can happen anywhere. But if it has once happened and one can hold up the incident as a warning to all future servants, then it is not likely to happen again — You know what we need, perhaps the Frenchwoman and whatever you can find in the way of a housemaid. Good cooking is our chief requisite — also with a view to economy. For the time being we have a person who cooks for us, it is true, but badly. I can't write any more to you today. At any rate you will see that *on this occasion* I couldn't have done anything else, for things had gone too far — I am not inviting you out here yet, since

[1] Johann Baptist Fröhlich, who gave lessons to Karl for about a month. See *TDR* IV, 97, 546 and 548-549.

everything is in confusion. *Still it won't be necessary to take me to the madhouse* — I may as well tell you that even in Vienna I was suffering terribly on account of this business; and that is why I just kept to myself — All my best wishes. Don't mention anything of all this, for, if it were known, unfavourable opinions might be formed about K[arl]. And *I alone*, knowing all the forces at work here, can testify *in his defence* that he has been most dreadfully misled. — Please send us soon a comforting letter about the art of cooking, laundering and sewing. I am feeling very ill and shall soon need something to restore my stomach.

In haste, your friend
BEETHOVEN

(905) *To Frau Nanette Streicher, Vienna*

[*Autograph not traced*] [1]

[MÖDLING, *July*, 1818]

You have no conception of what is going on — First at home and then later on and so forth. We have a housemaid and, what is more, she is not as elephantine as Peppi but much smarter; and I hope that she is honest too. This can't be said of the housekeeper; and we should like to have a better one. But it is wiser to keep her until we have secured a better one — and therefore there is time enough to find a better one. The enclosed letter is to be delivered at Herr Giannatasio's school in the Zimmerplatz no. 379. At any rate I think that is the correct number. — Over the doorway is written in gilt letters 'Boarding School'. But it should be called '*Warping School*' [2] — I beg you most earnestly to send your little girl there at about eleven o'clock tomorrow and tell her *to ask for this Herr Langer* [3] *and to give him the letter in person*. He must not know that either *you* or *I* have sent it — When I see you and tell you everything you will be very much surprised to hear of my recent experiences. My poor Karl

---

[1] Taken from *KFR*, no. 788 and *TDR* IV, 512. The letter is addressed 'To Frau von Streicher together with a parcel'.

[2] Beethoven plays on the words 'Erziehung' (education) and 'Verziehung' (bad upbringing).

[3] Presumably a master at Giannatasio del Rio's boarding school.

was talked over, but only for a moment. There are human brutes indeed — and one of them is the parson here, who ought to be thrashed.[1]

In haste, your friend
BEETHOVEN

You can't send the message to Langer until eleven o'clock on Friday, for he is not there on Thursday — I don't know your number. That is why I have to send this letter by a former non-commissioned officer — I am hoping soon to have confirmation of your having received this without my having received anything.[2]

In haste, your B.

(906) *To Sigmund Anton Steiner, Vienna*

[Autograph in the Deutsche Staatsbibliothek, Berlin] [3]

MÖDLING, August 12, 1818 [4]

Forgive me, dear Steiner, for troubling you with the following matter. We are coming into town the day after tomorrow and shall be there as early as seven a.m. Owing to the two holidays [5] we must leave on the same day, for Karl has still to prepare for his second examination with the teacher here; and precisely on account of these holidays the teacher can give him most of his attention [6] — But in connexion with the *life certificate for Karl* I must again go into town, and that costs both too much time and too much money. For in general I dislike travelling by mail coach, which has this particular disadvantage that, whatever day you take it, in the mail coach it is always *Friday*; and, though I am a good Christian, one Friday in the week is enough for me — If you can do so,

---

[1] I.e. J. B. Fröhlich.

[2] According to *TDR* IV, 512, this paragraph is written at the top of the first page of the autograph. The last sentence, which in the original is unintelligible, seems to suggest a misreading of the autograph.

[3] Not available. Taken from Unger, no. 67.

[4] According to Unger, who transcribed the autograph, Beethoven dated this letter October 12th, but the recipient endorsed it with the remark 'received August 13, 1818'.

[5] Saturday, August 15th, which was Assumption Day, and Sunday, August 16th.

[6] According to Unger this clause is added at the foot of the page.

please send a message to the *Chorführer* or *Brautführer* (the devil knows the name of that parson) and ask him to be so kind as to give us Karl's life certificate at any time in the afternoon of that day. Perhaps he might do this at seven in the morning, as soon as we arrive; but he would have to be punctual, for Karl has to attend his first examination at half past seven. Therefore *it must be either at seven o'clock in the morning or at any time in the afternoon.* We will call to see you about this in your shop before seven in the morning and we are looking forward to further visits.

In haste, and asking your forgiveness as well,

your amicus ad amicum

BEETHOVEN

(907) *To Frau Nanette Streicher*

[*Autograph not traced*] [1]

[VIENNA, *August*, 1818] [2]

BELOVED FRAU VON STREICHER!

Czerny has just been here — and I shall be with him this evening. But I don't yet know whether I shall be with you tomorrow. Some devils of human beings have again played such a trick on me that I don't care to be in human society — Karl has an examination at eleven o'clock tomorrow; so he can't come with me. But perhaps we shall see you tomorrow afternoon.

In haste, your friend

BEETHOVEN

[1] Taken from *KFR*, no. 743 and *TDR* IV, 507.

[2] See *TDR* IV, 507, where Thayer suggests this date on account of the reference to Karl's examination, possibly the entrance examination to the Akademisches Gymnasium.

(908) *To Joseph Schreyvogel* [1]

[*Autograph in the Institute for Russian Literature, Academy of Science, Leningrad*]

[VIENNA], *written at home on November* 24, [1818]

MOST HONOURED HERR VON SCHREYVOGEL,

I send you herewith the theatre tickets through Herr von Bernard [2] with a request to let me have some fresh ones. If hitherto I have not frequented the theatre as often as formerly, my poor health is chiefly the reason. But now I am feeling better and shall be able to take more interest in the theatre — I would very gladly have composed something again for it, but as *unfortunately I have to* consider the payment, since *my income* has *no value* whatever,[3] things are truly difficult. As you are aware, I have never demanded any payment for trifles — my sole desire is that your *merits* too should be recognized at last. Rest assured that I esteem you very highly, however little value you may attach to my opinion. At the same time there is an affinity between spirits from which, I fancy, nobody can detach himself.

With sincere regards,

your most devoted

BEETHOVEN

[1] Joseph Schreyvogel, alias Thomas West or Karl August West (1768–1832), was a well-known Viennese writer who, after studying in Vienna and Jena, became Secretary to the Court Theatres in 1802. He resigned this post in 1804 in order to devote himself entirely to the Bureau des Arts et d'Industrie which he had founded with Jakob Hohler and continued to direct until 1811. In 1814 he again became Secretary to the Court Theatres under Count Dietrichstein and continued in this office until 1824. Schreyvogel is frequently mentioned in the Conversation Books.

[2] For a full note on J. K. Bernard see Letter 947, p. 812, n. 1.

[3] One of Beethoven's favourite puns on the word 'Gehalt' which means 'income' and 'substance' or 'value'.

(909) *To Carl Czerny*

[*Autograph in the Beethovenhaus, Bonn, H. C. Bodmer collection*]

DEAR CZERNY!   [VIENNA, 1818] [1]
Do me the favour to play in the Grosser Redoutensaal the day after tomorrow the Adagio and Rondo of my concerto in E♭.[2] If you do, you will lend lustre to the whole concert — As the choruses have not been sufficiently rehearsed, it is not possible to perform more than one of the hymns [3] — I hope that you will not refuse my request —

As always, your friend
BEETHOVEN

(910) *To Carl Czerny*

[*Autograph in the Gesellschaft der Musikfreunde, Vienna*]

MY DEAR AND BELOVED CZERNY!   [VIENNA, 1818] [4]
I have learnt this very moment that you are in a situation such as I really never suspected. I wish that you would have confidence in me and that you would just tell me how some things might perhaps be improved for you (this is no vulgar desire on my part to patronize you). As soon as I can breathe freely again I must see you. Rest assured that I esteem you and am willing to prove this to you any moment by acting in your interest.

With sincere regards, your friend
BEETHOVEN

---

[1] See Nohl I, p. 186, note. Nohl quotes a passage in Zellner's *Blätter für Musik*, 1857, no. 59, in which Czerny, according to his own statement, was requested by Beethoven in a letter to play the E♭ concerto, Op. 73, at one of his last concerts in the Grosser Redoutensaal in 1818. Czerny stated that he had given this letter to Cocks, the London music publisher. Czerny refused Beethoven's request on the grounds that having to earn his living by giving pianoforte lessons he had been giving these lessons daily for more than twelve hours and had therefore greatly neglected his own pianoforte playing. Whereupon he received from Beethoven the sympathetic letter which follows, i.e. Letter 910.

[2] Op. 73.
[3] Probably certain numbers of the Mass in C, Op. 86.
[4] See preceding Letter 909.

(911) *To Carl Czerny* [1]

[Autograph in the Gesellschaft der Musikfreunde, Vienna]

[VIENNA, 1818]

Landstrasse, Gärtnergasse No. 26, second floor, first staircase [2] —

The time was too short, dear Czerny, to invite you any sooner.

(912) *To [Carl Czerny ?]* [3]

[Autograph in the Gesellschaft der Musikfreunde, Vienna]

[VIENNA, 1818]

Let Karl leave about eight o'clock, for my servant must come home early —

Your
L. v. BEETHOVEN

(913) *To Carl Czerny*

[Autograph in the British Museum]

DEAR CZ[ERNY],   [VIENNA, 1818]

Forgive me for worrying you with this letter, but I don't know Z's number.[4] — So please forward the letter to Z. immediately. — I am, as always, still deeply in your debt.

L. v. BEETHOVEN

[1] The address on the verso of this pencilled note is written in ink in another hand.

[2] Beethoven appears to have moved into these rooms in April, 1818. The house no longer exists.

[3] This pencilled note bears no address. But it was probably sent to Carl Czerny who was then giving pianoforte lessons to Beethoven's nephew.

[4] Possibly the residence of Zmeskall or, more likely, Zizius. Cf. Letter 104, p. 123, n. 3.

(914) *To Carl Czerny*

[Autograph in the Gesellschaft der Musikfreunde, Vienna]

[VIENNA, 1818]

Don't go to *Karl* today, dear Czerny, for something has happened to us. But he hopes to see you, as I do, the day after tomorrow for certain —

I will visit you soon — Meanwhile I remain your grateful friend

BEETHOVEN

(915) *To ?*

[Autograph in the Deutsche Staatsbibliothek, Berlin]

[VIENNA, 1818]

What kind of stamped paper does one require in order to write out a receipt for *600 gulden*? —

(916) *To the Archduke Rudolph*

[Autograph in the Gesellschaft der Musikfreunde, Vienna]

YOUR IMPERIAL HIGHNESS!   [VIENNA, 1818]

On Sunday I was already indisposed and since then I have had to stay in my room — But as every day I thought I was feeling better and should be able to go to you, I did not send you word — for I considered it to be of too little importance to Your Imperial Highness. Today, however, I am better, so much so that I shall certainly have the honour of waiting upon you tomorrow — In any case I trust for the sake of Y.I.H.'s good health which, we all desire, that the arcanum — may be a true arcanum [1] —

Your Imperial Highness's
most obedient and most faithful servant
LUDWIG VAN BEETHOVEN

[1] I.e. a nostrum, elixir or panacea.

777

(917) *To Cajetan Giannatasio del Rio*

[*Autograph not traced*] [1]

[VIENNA, 1818]

Please look up the date on which Karl entered your boarding school. The enclosed receipt may provide you, I think,
with some information about this. I have not got the date
or the year. Unless my memory plays me false, it was in
February 1816 that you took Karl into your boarding school.[2]

Please send me the correct particulars about this by tomorrow, for I need them. Indeed I never thought that I
should find myself in the predicament of having to give an
account of my generous behaviour. Hence I did not bother
to keep many of the receipts. But as this appears to be the
case with Karl's mother, I must have this document.

With kindest regards, your friend

BEETHOVEN

(918) *To Carl Czerny*

[*Autograph in the Gesellschaft der Musikfreunde, Vienna*]

HERR VON CZERNY!   [VIENNA, 1818]

Be so kind as to return to me the score of the Pastoral
symphony [3] today or tomorrow at latest, for I need it —

LUDWIG VAN BEETHOVEN

(919) *To Carl Czerny*

[*Autograph in the Gesellschaft der Musikfreunde, Vienna*]

[VIENNA, 1818]

Here are all the parts and the score — The parts which
have not yet been corrected must be checked. As they were
copied in a hurry, no doubt there are very many mistakes in
them —   In haste, your friend

BEETHOVEN

---

[1] Taken from Aloys Fuchs's transcript in Tübingen University Library.
[2] Karl entered the boarding school on February 2, 1816.   [3] Op. 68.

(920) *To Count Moritz Lichnowsky*

[*Autograph not traced*] [1]

DEAR AND BELOVED COUNT!   [VIENNA, 1818]

I have just received this written statement which I am sending on to you herewith. I have done my best to persuade the writer to be very modest about me; and you too will be pleased with it — I will visit you again one of these days. Rest assured that my friendly affection and regard for you could not be exceeded and will ever persist, quite unchanged.

Love your friend
BEETHOVEN

In haste, in haste. Prestissimo.

(921) *To the Archduke Rudolph*

[*Autograph in the Gesellschaft der Musikfreunde, Vienna*]

YOUR IMPERIAL HIGHNESS!   [VIENNA, 1818]

I know that you will graciously forgive me for not waiting upon Y.I.H. today, but on account of my cough I dare not go out in this weather.

Tomorrow the weather cannot possibly be as bad as it is today. So I shall certainly enjoy what is for me the greatest pleasure, i.e. when I can again show my zeal in the service of Y.I.H.

Your Imperial Highness's
most faithful and most obedient servant
LUDWIG VAN BEETHOVEN

(922) *To Tobias Haslinger*

[*Autograph in the Stadtbibliothek, Vienna*]

[VIENNA, 1818]

The engravers are very unmusical. One can see from all the work they have done that you used to have better ones —

---

[1] Taken from Aloys Fuchs's transcript in Tübingen University Library.

The list of errata must now be done from the copy printed on poor paper — Please return to me the copy corrected today with the one corrected from it (which will be the last proof, I hope) — I have not yet received the separate parts corrected and should also like to see these as soon as possible — the Adjutant is requested to pay attention to everything I have marked so that my orders may be duly carried out.

volti subito.[1]

More presto, prestissimo, so that the list of *peccata* may be sent off — Pay especial attention to the marks in the Andante
——————— —————— — In regard to the misunderstanding

of the grace notes, NB: 𝄽 ♪, you must not put instead

of these a slur, such as ⌒ or ⌣. Faugh, the devil take you — In future the proofs must be done on better and *more satisfactory* paper, so that one may make them out more easily — The devil take you! God protect you [2] —

(923) *To Tobias Haslinger*

[*Autograph in the Stadtbibliothek, Vienna*]

Very bad behaviour! —   [VIENNA, 1818]
The Scottish songs will follow, and they are numbered, that is to say, the pianoforte part is with the vocal parts; [3] and it is the Adjutant's duty to see which can be engraved forthwith in this order. In regard to the pianoforte part, it must be shown to me each time when three songs are ready, that is to say, the poems as well, because some trifling points perhaps, on account of the expression of the German poetry, may have to be altered here and there — The *Lower House* is requested to send to the *Upper House some quills (cut, of course),*[4] *and also some sealing-wax and pencils, seeing that the Upper House has pro-*

---

[1] I.e. P.T.O. Page 2 begins here.
[2] The autograph has no signature.
[3] Probably WoO 156, which Steiner did not publish. See Letters 1012 and 1022. See also Unger's note to his no. 73.
[4] This bracketed reminder is added at the foot of the page.

vided the Lower House with all these commodities — The ever
slovenly Adjutant is admonished to be on his best behaviour —
The

(924) *To [Tobias Haslinger?]*

[*Autograph in the Stadtbibliothek, Vienna*]

[VIENNA, 1818]

Is there no letter for me from Frankfurt apart from the
one which the Lieutenant General sent to Baden by Herr
Giuliani? [1]

(925) *To Tobias Haslinger*

[*Autograph in the Stadtbibliothek, Vienna*] [2]

WORSHIPFUL A[DJUTAN]T'S OFFICE !   [VIENNA, 1818]
You are requested to send red pencils for marking — We
are hoping for the best behaviour, less ill will, etc. etc. etc.

(926) *To [Sigmund Anton Steiner?]*

[*Autograph in the Stadtbibliothek, Vienna*]

[VIENNA, 1818]

His Majesty, on his own supreme initiative, has commanded
that Maelzel's metronome be introduced into the Ministry of
Finance, so that the *tempo of the finances may be determined* by
means of this instrument — See the Allgemeine Kaiserl.
Österreichische Musik Zeitung.[3]

---

[1] Possibly Mauro Giuliani, the famous guitar-player. See Letter 1245,
p. 1094, n. 1. The allusion to Baden might place this note in an earlier year,
e.g. 1816.   [2] This unsigned note is written in pencil.
[3] This note bears no signature.

(927) *To Nikolaus Zmeskall von Domanovecz*

[*Autograph in the Beethovenhaus, Bonn*]

MOST EXCELLENT Z[MESKALL]!   [VIENNA, 1818]

Please do not think of *household equipment* at the moment,
for debts are now our primary concern; and debts resemble
inspiration in this respect, i.e. one must make use of the moment
at once, whenever a noble work can be completed. Besides
I have so many other extremely necessary things to purchase
that nothing will be left for household equipment. So do
leave off altogether, dear Z[meskall], for in a few days I may
perhaps have to ask you for the sum, seeing that I have not
yet collected everything due to me from L(ondon) and that I
always hasten to discharge my debts.

BEETHOVEN

I can't come to the Schwan tomorrow, for I am dining
with Johann Browne.[1]

(928) *To [Nikolaus Zmeskall von Domanovecz?]* [2]

[*Autograph in the Gesellschaft der Musikfreunde, Vienna*]

[VIENNA, 1818]

Please have the chocolate prepared. We have taken the
supreme decision to have breakfast with you; and important
matters are going to be dealt with — We shall be with you
at eight o'clock sharp —

[1] This remark is added at the top of the first page of the autograph. The
person referred to is doubtless Graf Johann Georg von Browne-Camus. Cf.
Letter 50, p. 57, n. 1.

[2] This unsigned autograph bears no address; but it is in the file of letters from
Beethoven to Zmeskall and may have been intended for the latter.

(929) *To Count Moritz von Dietrichstein*

[*Autograph in the State Archives, Třeboň*]

DEAR AND BELOVED D[IETRICHSTEIN],   [VIENNA, 1818]

Since I cannot make any contribution whatever to the mending of the amateur machine which is definitely ruined,[1] I resigned yesterday and immediately informed Herr G. Herzi [2] — of my decision by returning the tickets — Where *arbitrary arrangements are the rule*, an honourable person can *no longer* be responsible *for anything* — It is understood, of course, that I am no longer to be regarded or counted on as an active participant.

If you are sensible, you will copy me and resign too — Honour forbids one to belong to that association any longer —
Ever your friend and admirer
BEETHOVEN

Everything I did was done to please you and also because I thought that something good might come of it — To please you I put up with many things which otherwise I would never have tolerated — But now it is finished — Never speak to me again of such a *wretched institution*.[3]

(930) *To Frau Nanette Streicher*

[*Autograph not traced*] [4]

[VIENNA, 1818]

The female criminal in question was informed today of her sentence — On hearing it she behaved almost like Caesar

[1] This was a Society of Amateurs (Dilettanten-Gesellschaft), probably identical with the Vereinigte Privat-Musik-Gesellschaft which was established in 1818. The latter's founder and first conductor was Anton Scherrer, who was succeeded in 1821 by Friedrich Klemm. The first concert of this society was given in the Landhaussaal on June 28, 1818, and, according to Hanslick, p. 162, concerts were held on Sunday afternoons in the hotel 'Zum Römischen Kaiser'. This society had some connexion with the Gesellschaft der Musikfreunde, of which Dietrichstein was a leading member.

[2] It has not been possible to decipher the full name.

[3] This long postscript is written on the second page to the left of the signature.

[4] Taken from *KFR*, no. 604 and *TDR* IV, 501.

after the dagger thrust of Brutus, the only difference being that Caesar was speaking the truth and she was expressing wicked spite ¹ — The kitchen-maid seems to be more useful than the former *naughty beauty*. The latter has never put in an appearance — a sign that she never hoped for a *good testimonial*, which, nevertheless, I had intended to give her — Now I still have to find a new housekeeper. But please think everything over as carefully as possible. She must be a good cook for the sake of our digestions. Further, she ought to be able to turn her hand to mending shirts and so forth, but not in the state; ² she ought to have as much intelligence as is necessary to provide *adequately* for the requirements of our ³ persons and at the same time *economically* on account of the condition of my purse. The new kitchen-maid made a really wry face about carrying wood. But I trust that she will remember that even our Redeemer had to drag his cross to Golgotha — I shall probably see you tomorrow.

In haste, your friend

BEETHOVEN

(931) *To Frau Nanette Streicher*

[*Autograph not traced*] ⁴

[VIENNA, 1818]

I entreat you in haste, with haste and by haste, to request Streicher to see that we shall be alone today at about noon.

In the most hurried haste, your friend

BEETHOVEN

---

¹ According to Suetonius, Caesar called out 'Et tu, Brute'. In Plutarch's *Life of Caesar* Caesar threw his cloak over his face and sank at the foot of Pompey's statue. It has been suggested that the female criminal may have thrown her apron over her head.

² An allusion to the internal political difficulties of the Austrian Empire.

³ Here *TDR* has 'mehrerer' (several) and *KFR* has 'unserer' (our).

⁴ Taken from *TDR* IV, 508.

BEETHOVEN
From the oil portrait by Ferdinand Schimon (1818/19)
(*Beethovenhaus, Bonn*)

(932) *To Frau Nanette Streicher*

[*Autograph not traced*] [1]

DEAR FR[AU] V[ON] STR[EICHER], [VIENNA, 1818]

Please do not say a word to anyone about my decision to appoint a *tutor* for Karl. I am asking this so that no harm may be done either to *him* or to *Karl* before the matter has been quite settled — For my own existence I need better care and more service; and for that I require a *housekeeper*. Since we have found a good tutor, we certainly don't require the Frenchwoman [2] now. For, after all, Karl must have *scholarly* instruction in French, and our Frenchwoman would certainly not be equal to that. On the other hand, a *tutor* and a *governess* would cost *too much*. But I have just heard that one can get a housekeeper for 100 gulden a year *with* board and lodging. Think it over and advise and help your poor suffering friend

BEETHOVEN

(My most affectionate admonishments [3]
to Streicher)

[1] Taken from Nohl II, no. 179 and *TDR* IV, 504.
[2] Particulars of this person are not forthcoming. She may have been Karl's governess for a very short time after he left his boarding school in January, 1818.
[3] In the original German the word used is 'Mahnungen'. Possibly Beethoven is referring to an order given to Streicher.

1819

1810

(933) *To the Archduke Rudolph*

[*Autograph not traced*] [1]

VIENNA, *January* 1, 1819

All that can conceivably be comprised in a wish, all that can conceivably be called profitable, such as welfare, happiness and blessings, are included in the wish I have expressed for Y.I.H. today. May this further wish of mine for myself be graciously granted by Y.I.H., namely, that I may continue to enjoy the favour of Y.I.H. — A terrible event took place a short time ago in my family circumstances, and for a time I was absolutely driven out of my mind.[2] To this alone you must ascribe the fact that I have not called upon Y.I.H. in person nor reported on the masterly variations of my highly honoured and illustrious pupil who is a favourite of the Muses.[3] I dare not express my thanks either verbally or in writing for this surprise and for the favour with which I have been honoured. For I am *too lowly placed* and unable, however ardently I may intend or desire to do so, *to repay you in the same coin.* May Heaven be pleased to lend an especially favourable ear to my prayer and to grant my wishes for the health of Y.I.H. In a few days I hope to hear Y.I.H. yourself perform the masterpiece you have sent me; and nothing can delight me more than to assist Y.I.H. to take as soon as possible the seat on Parnassus which has already been prepared for Your Highness.

Your Imperial Highness's
   most obedient servant in affection and deepest reverence
                                LUDWIG VAN BEETHOVEN

[1] Taken from Köchel, no. 38.
[2] Early in December, 1818, Karl had run away to his mother. See Nohl, *op. cit.*, pp. 167-168.
[3] The Archduke Rudolph's 40 pianoforte variations, preceded by an adagio introduction in G minor on Beethoven's theme 'O Hoffnung' (WoO 200). The autograph of Beethoven's theme has the statement 'componirt im Frühjahr 1818 in doloribus, etc.'. The Archduke's variations were published by Steiner in December, 1819, with a dedication to Beethoven.

(934) To Nikolaus Zmeskall von Domanovecz

[Autograph in the Nationalbibliothek, Vienna]

DEAR ZMESKALL,   [VIENNA, January 20, 1819]

I do earnestly beg you to lend me just for today the copy of the two *violoncello sonatas* engraved by *Simrock*.[1] I have not yet seen either of them, since, for some reason unknown to me, he never sent me a single copy. I will visit you soon.

In haste, your friend

BEETHOVEN

(935) To Ferdinand Ries, London

[Autograph in the Beethovenhaus, Bonn]

MY DEAR RIES!   VIENNA, January 30, 1819

Only today am I able to reply to your last letter of December 18th. Your sympathy does me good. At the moment it is impossible for me to travel to London, because I am involved in so many kinds of affairs. But God will assist me to go to L[ondon] next winter for certain; and I shall also bring the new symphonies with me. I am expecting to receive very soon the text of a new oratorio which I am composing *for the music club* here; and no doubt this work will serve our purpose in L[ondon] as well.[2] Do all you can *for* me. For I need your help. Commissions from the Philharmonic Society would have been very welcome to me. But the *reports which Neate has sent me in the meantime about the virtual failure of the three overtures* have greatly distressed me.[3] *In Vienna not only did each overture in its own way* please the audiences but the E♭ major and C major overtures even made a great sensation.[4] The fate of these compositions at the hands of the P[hilharmonic] S[ociety] I cannot understand — You will have

---

[1] Op. 102, published by Simrock in March, 1817. In January, 1819, Artaria brought out a new edition with a dedication to the Countess Erdödy.

[2] This oratorio, which Beethoven never composed, was to be on a text 'Der Sieg des Kreuzes' by J. K. Bernard. The author delivered it to Beethoven in the spring of 1820.

[3] Op. 113, 115 and 117.   [4] Op. 117 and 115.

now received the quintet which I arranged myself and the sonata.[1] Do see to it that both works, and especially the quintet, shall be engraved immediately. Things can proceed a little more slowly in the case of the sonata. At the same time I should like it to appear within two or three months at latest. I did not receive the earlier letter from you which you mentioned. Hence I did not hesitate to dispose of both works in Vienna also — but by that I mean : only for Germany. Meanwhile it will be three months too before the sonata is published in Vienna. But do make haste with the quintet. As soon as you remit the money to me here, I will send you a written statement for the publisher declaring that he is the owner of these works for England, Scotland, Ireland, India, France and so forth. You will receive by the next post the tempo markings of the sonata according to Maelzel's metronome. De Smith, courier to Prince Paul Esterházy,[2] has taken with him the quintet and the sonata. By the next opportunity you will receive my portrait too, since I hear that *you really desire to possess it.* —

All good wishes. Be fond of me who am your friend

BEETHOVEN

All lovely things to your lovely wife ! ! !   (From me) ! ! ! ! !

(936) *To Cajetan Giannatasio del Rio*

[Autograph in the Royal College of Music] [3]

[VIENNA, *January*, 1819]

I shall let you know tomorrow, my very dear G[iannatasio], when you can come to me. Unfortunately I have not been

---

[1] Op. 104 and the Hammerklavier sonata in B♭ dedicated to the Archduke Rudolph and published by Artaria in September, 1819, as Op. 106.

[2] Prince Paul Esterházy, son of Prince Nikolaus Esterházy, for whom Beethoven wrote in 1807 his Mass in C major, Op. 86, was then Austrian Envoy to England. Cf. Letter 373, p. 375, n. 1.

[3] This pencilled note was first published by C. B. Oldman in *Music and Letters*, vol. xvii, no. 4, October 1936, p. 334. He suggests a connexion with the wedding song composed by Beethoven for Giannatasio del Rio's second daughter Anna on the occasion of her marriage to Leopold Schmerling on February 6, 1819. There are two autograph versions of this song with chorus, WoO 105. See *KHV.* 567-569.

able to get to your song.   But I will try to compose the parts
for it *tomorrow*.   I have been very busy with a great many
things which have had to be sent off recently to London.
And my delay should be ascribed to this. —

In haste, your friend
BEETHOVEN

(937) *To Johann Baptist Bach* [1]

[Autograph in the Beethovenhaus, Bonn, H. C. Bodmer collection]

SIR !   [VIENNA, *c. February* 1, 1819]
    It is obviously of great importance to me that I should
not be placed *in a false position*.   That is why the written statement which I am delivering is so long-winded.[2]   In regard to
the future education of my nephew, I am extremely glad that
I have arranged the *present best possible one*, which means that
the *future one is already included in it*.   But if my nephew's welfare
should necessitate a *change*, I shall be the *first* not only to propose it but also to *carry it out* — There is *no* self-interest in my
being a guardian.   But I want *by means of my nephew* to establish
a fresh memorial to my name.   I do not *need my nephew*, but
he needs me — Gossip and defamatory language are unworthy
of a man who wishes to raise himself.   And what is one to say
when that kind of talk extends even to the question of one's
laundry ! ! ! — I could be very sensitive, but *the just man must be
able to suffer injustice also*, without swerving *in the very least* from
what is right.   In this spirit I will endure every test and no one
shall make me waver — Whoever tries to remove my nephew
entirely from me will have to shoulder a great responsibility.
Disastrous consequences, both *morally* and *politically*, would be the
result for my nephew.   I *recommend* his welfare *to you* and *fully*

---

[1] Johann Baptist Bach (1779–1847) was a distinguished Viennese lawyer who
in 1820 was appointed to a professorship at Vienna University.   Bach was closely
associated with Beethoven in the protracted litigation about the latter's guardianship of his nephew.   Bach took part in and is frequently mentioned in the con-
versations preserved in the Conversation Books, some of which have been edited by
Georg Schünemann in three volumes (Berlin, 1941–1943).
[2] For this written statement, dated February 1, 1819, see Appendix C (9).

792

entrust you with it.   *My actions* must be *my recommendation for him, not for myself.*

      With kindest regards, your most devoted

                                  BEETHOVEN

    As I have been very busy and also rather unwell, *my document* will surely *be considered with indulgence.*

(938) *To Ferdinand Ries, London*

            [Autograph in the possession of Julius Wegeler]

                      VIENNA, *March* 8, 1819

    Mistakes which perhaps have been made in the parts of the quintet.[1] —

Violino primo. In the first Allegro. Part 1. Bar 106.

Part 2. Bar 68.

Part 2. Bar 207.

In the Andante. Variation 5. Bar 2.

Violino secundo. First Allegro. Part 2. Bar 1.

    [1] Op. 104, Beethoven's own arrangement of his pianoforte trio, Op. 1, no. 3, was published by Artaria in February, 1819. In his letter to Ries of January 30 (Letter 935) Beethoven informed him that he had given to de Smith, courier of Prince Paul Esterházy, Austrian Envoy in London, copies of this work and of the pianoforte sonata, Op. 106. Possibly after the courier's departure Beethoven discovered a number of mistakes in a duplicate copy which he had retained or in the proof-sheets of the original edition published in Vienna.

Ditto.   Part 2.   Bar 21.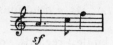

Ditto.   Bar 55.

Andante.   Variation 4.   [Bar 11].

V[ariation] 5.   [Bar 9].

Ditto.   Coda.   Bar 2.

Ditto.   Coda.   Bar 11.

Finale.   Part 1.   Bar 66.

Violino Secundo.   Part 1.   Bar 143.

Ditto.   Part 2.   Bar 262.

Viola prima.   Finale.   Bar 32.

Finale.   Part 2.   Second ending.
     Bar 1.

Part 2. Bar 64.

Ditto. Bar 70.

Viola secunda. Allegro.
Part 2. Bar 113.

Andante. Variation 2. Bar 7.

Variation 3. Bar 4.

Finale.
Part 2. Bar 88.

Part 2. Bar 215.

Part 2. Bar 240.

Violoncello. First Allegro.
Part 1. Bar 123.
If there is a trill on this note marked +,
then it must be deleted. —

First Allegro.
Part 2. Bar 19.

Ditto. Bar 102.

Violoncello.
First Allegro.
Bar 112.

Andante.
Variation 3.
Part 2. Bar 5.

cresc - - - - - -

Ditto. Coda. Bar 6.

Finale.
Part 1. Bar [15].

Part 2. Bar 109.

Part 2. Bar 160.

Don't forget me. There must be a terrible lot of mistakes in the sonata.[1] Next post-day you will receive the list.[2] Everything was written very quickly. Schlemmer, my copyist, is getting old and he is a poor devil[3] — indeed all of us here are poor devils — At last the Archduke Rudolph is assuming his office of Archbishop of Olmütz, to which he was appointed some time ago — But it may be a very long while before there is an improvement in my situation; and yet I am exhausted by so many hardships which until now have been afflicting me and still persist — My best greetings to your wife, to Neate and to Smart —

In haste, your

BEETHOVEN

[1] Op. 106.   [2] See Letter 939.
[3] See Letter 973, p. 844, n. 4.

(939) *To Ferdinand Ries, London*

[Autographs in the Beethovenhaus, Bonn, H. C. Bodmer collection, and the Fitzwilliam Museum, Cambridge] [1]

[VIENNA, *c.* March 20, 1819] [2]

Bar 31
♮ before B   [3]

Bar 34
♭ before B

Ditto [4]
Bar 82
the o is
omitted

Bar 87
♮ before G

Bar 90
♮ before G

Bar 89
♮ be-
fore G
♮ — — —

Bar 94
♮ be-
fore G
♮ — — —

Bar 98
♮ before A

Bar 112
Instead of
a 𝅗𝅥 there
must be a
crotchet 𝅘𝅥 in
both cases.

Bar 117
♮ before F

Bar 124

Bar 129

Bar 141
♮ before B

Bar 145
♮ before B

---

[1] This list of corrections to the copy of Op. 106 sent to London, is not complete. It consists of two autograph fragments, the first of which is in the Beethovenhaus, Bonn, H. C. Bodmer collection, and the second (with Beethoven's letter to Ries) in the Fitzwilliam Museum, Cambridge. The connexion between the two fragments was discovered in 1956 by Dr. Dagmar Weise of the Beethovenhaus, Bonn ; and her theory has been proved by the fact that both autographs have the same watermark.

[2] The London postmark on this undated letter is April 6, 1819.

[3] The first fragment begins with this correction to Bar 31 (Beethoven's numbering) of the Scherzo of Op. 106.

[4] Before this entry another correction and comment have been heavily scrawled out.

Bar 165
Here
there is
a ♯ before D
which must
be deleted —

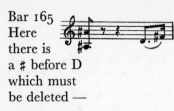

No. 3 Adagio $\frac{6}{8}$

Bar 13
♮ before G
× ♮ before G
× 3 :

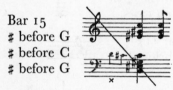

Bar 15
♯ before G
♯ before C
♯ before G

Bar 21
♮ before
G
♮ before ♮
G

Bar 22
♮ before G
♮ — —
♮ before G
♮ — C

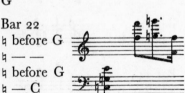

Bar 23
♯ before C
♯ — G

Bar 40
♮ before F

Bar 56
♯ before F

Bar 71
ped.

Bar 75
+ ♮ before B
+ ♭ — A
+ dot after + ped. + o

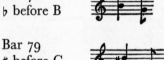

B + ped.
+ o + ped. + o
♭ before A

Bar 76
♭ before B

Bar 79
♯ before G
♯ — D
The ♯ at ×
must be removed

Bar 82
perhaps this
was not
copied cor-
rectly

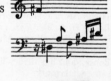

Bar 87
× C sharp

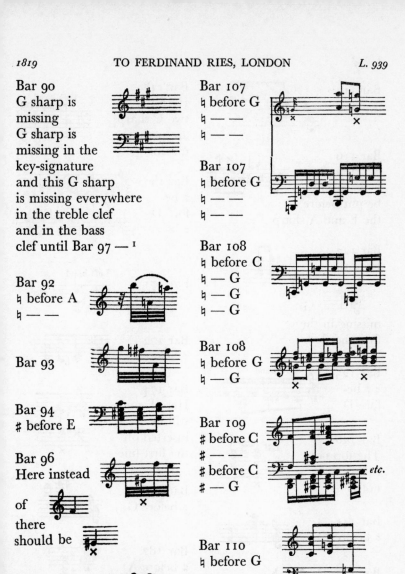

Bar 90
G sharp is
missing

G sharp is
missing in the
key-signature
and this G sharp
is missing everywhere
in the treble clef
and in the bass
clef until Bar 97 — [1]

Bar 92
♮ before A
♮ — —

Bar 93

Bar 94
♯ before E

Bar 96
Here instead

of

there

should be

Bar 102
♯ before E

Bar 105
♯ before E
♯ — —

Bar 107
♮ before G
♮ — —
♮ — —

Bar 107
♮ before G
♮ — —
♮ — —

Bar 108
♮ before C
♮ — G
♮ — G
♮ — G

Bar 108
♮ before G
♮ — G

Bar 109
♯ before C
♯ — —
♯ before C
♯ — G   *etc.*

Bar 110
♮ before G

Bar 111
♯ before G
♯ — —

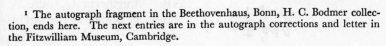

[1] The autograph fragment in the Beethovenhaus, Bonn, H. C. Bodmer collection, ends here. The next entries are in the autograph corrections and letter in the Fitzwilliam Museum, Cambridge.

Bar 114
× G
× A

Bar 119
× Here the
F sharp must
be put before
the E and A sharp

Bar 122
Here the

 is

missing in the
first chord

Bar 125
♮ ♯ be-
fore D

Left hand

Bar 126
The top note
is F sharp,
not G —

L.H.
×

Bar 141
♮ before E

Bar 144

× ped. u. c.　× ped. u. c.

Bar 146

Bar 148
Here the
two C sharps
are perhaps
missing

Left hand
× ×

Bar 169
♯ be-
fore D
♮ — —

×　　　　×

Bar 171
♮ before C

Left hand
etc.

Bar 172
♯ before C

Bar 174
Here E must
still be
inserted on
the first line

×

Bar 176
♮ before G

Bar 182
♯ before A

Largo. Fourth movement.
Allegro.

♯ before B.  etc.

NB. Furthermore, the c
should be added at the beginning of the Allegro; and,

moreover, in two bars the bar-lines | | are omitted — and in the Allegro the × before F sharp is missing.

Immediately after the Allegro there should again be Tempo Primo, which has been omitted —

Here the ♮ before D is missing

Allegro
risoluto
Bar 7
The notes
must be
as here.

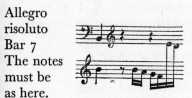

Bar 37
D♭ and B♭

Bar 50
♭ be-
fore G

Bar 53
♭ be-
fore A

Bar 59
♭ be-
fore D

Bar 68
♭ be-
fore

♮ be-
fore G

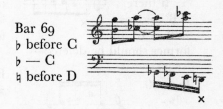

Bar 69
♭ before C
♭ — C
♮ before D

Bar 71
♭ before C

Bar 72
♭ before the trill

Bar 73
♭ before C

Bar 85
× F
dot after
♩ •

Bar 92
♮ before D

Bar 95
♭ before A

Bar 114
The trill is
continued.

Bar 103
Here the
grace notes of
the two trills
are missing.

Bar 115
grace note

Bar 105
× If there
is B♭ here as
well as E♭, the
former should be deleted—

Bar 116
♮ be-
fore G
♮ be-
fore G
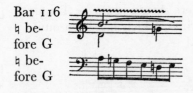

Bar 108
♮ be-
fore E

Bar 153
♮ before E

Bar 110
♭ before E

Bar 184
Here the
semiquavers

must be marked downwards
and upwards exactly
as they are here —
and the rests for
the left hand added.

Bar 107
♮ before E

Bar 108
♮ before E
♮ — —

Bar 188
• after B
• — D

Bar 108
and Bar 109

Bars 111 and
112

Bar 189
♮ be-
fore A

Bar 195
♮ be-
fore C
× D

Bar 214
♯ be-
fore G

Bar 219
♭ before A
♭ — B

Bars 2[3]5 and 2[3]6
Here the key-
signature is
wrong, I
think, and the bar
divisions not
right

Bar 262
♮ before D

Bar 276
♭ before E

Bar 273
♭ before B

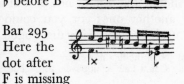

Bar 295
Here the
dot after
F is missing

Bar 299
♯ before F

Bar 305
♭ be-
fore E

Bar 306
♭ before E

Bar 323
♮ before E
× grace
notes to be
drawn
downwards

Bar 334
× B♭ in-
stead of A

Supplementary.
In the last movement Allegro
risoluto

Bar 2[0]8
Here the
quaver rest
is missing.

In the second move-
ment Adagio

Bar 115
Instead of

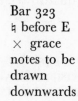

there should be D sharp

In the first movement Allegro　Third movement Scherzo

Bars 381 and 382　　　　　　Bar 93

Here the two ⌢ ties are missing, and in front there is a ♮ which must be deleted — [1]

♮ before G

♮ — —

In the fourth movement marked LARGO the following indication should be added to the title : NB : per la misura si conta nel Largo sempre quattro semicrome cioè ♪♪♪♪ [2]

DEAR R[IES],

I do beg you to pardon the trouble I am giving you. But I cannot understand how so many mistakes have crept into the copy of the sonata. Haste may partly account for it, and the fact that the copyist did not do the work himself but had it copied by somebody else. It was only when the copy made here was played through that the mistakes were discovered ; and perhaps several of them have already been corrected. Have the bars counted and marked from 10 to 20, to 100, to 200 and so on ; and then it will be easy to correct everything quickly. Just let me know how much this costs you... I cannot yet send you the tempi because my metronome is broken ; and I shall not have it back for a few days — The inaccurate copying is probably due in part to the fact *that I can no longer employ my own copyist, as I used to.* Circumstances are the cause of this ; and may God help me ! — until the Archduke R[udolph] finds himself in a better position, which may not happen for *a whole year.* It is just terrible to think how all this has come about, and how my income has vanished ; and as yet no one can say what will happen before the end of the present year — Should the sonata not be suitable for London, I could send another one ; or you could also omit the Largo and begin straight away with the Fugue

---

[1] This correction refers to bars 365 and 366 of the first movement.

[2] Beethoven's Italian indication means : Count four semiquavers throughout the Largo.

, which is the last move-
ment; or you could use the first movement and then the
Adagio, and then for the third movement the Scherzo —
and omit entirely no. 4 with the Largo and Allegro risoluto.[1]
Or you could take just the first movement and the Scherzo
and let them form the whole sonata. I leave it to you to do
as you think best. At the moment it would be most inconvenient for me to compose a new sonata, because I am very
busy with other things. The sonata was written in distressful
circumstances, for it is hard to compose almost entirely for
the sake of earning one's daily bread; and that is *all* I have
been able *to achieve*. About my going to London we shall
correspond some other time. It would certainly be the only
way to extricate myself from this miserable and anxious situation, where I am *never in good health* and can never do *what
I could do* if I were in better circumstances — I shall postpone
all arrangements about the publication of the sonata *in Vienna*
until you write to me.[2] But I beg you to do so soon and also
to send me the money and at the same time to inform me
when the sonata is to *appear in London,* so that I may then act
here accordingly. The s[onata] ought certainly to be published in London as soon as possible, for the Viennese publisher
has really been kept waiting too long. Further, I will send
the English publisher immediately the statement confirming
that this composition is his property *for England*. No doubt the
quintet has already been engraved.[3] —

In haste, your friend

BEETHOVEN

[1] This sentence has been reconstructed by the present editor from the leaf
which is badly torn on the right and left sides near the top. In his quotation from
the Fugue Beethoven has mistakenly put a trilled crotchet.

[2] Op. 106 was published by Artaria in September, 1819. According to an
article on *Contemporary English Editions of Beethoven* by Paul Hirsch and C. B. Oldman,
published in *The Music Review*, vol. XIV, no. 1, February, 1953, it was published
in London in two parts as Op. 88 by the Regent's Harmonic Institution in (1819?).

[3] According to Hirsch and Oldman, *op. cit.* p. 12, this quintet, Op. 104, was
published by E. Lavenu in (1820?).

(940) *To Ferdinand Ries, London*

[*Autograph not traced*] [1]

[VIENNA, *April* 16, 1819]

Here, dear Ries! are the tempi of the sonata.[2]

First movement Allegro, but only Allegro; you must remove the Assai.

Maelzel's metronome ♩=138

Second movement Scherzoso.[3] M[aelzel]'s metronome ♩=80

Third movement. M[aelzel]'s metronome ♪=92
Here I must point out that the first bar has still to be inserted, that is to say:

Bar 1

Fourth movement. Introduzione. Largo. Maelzel's metronome ♪=76

Fifth movement. ¾ time.

and the last movement: Maelzel's metronome ♩=144

Forgive these muddled indications. If you knew how I am placed, you would not be surprised, nay rather, you would be amazed at what I still manage to do in spite of everything. At last the quintet need not be held up any longer and can appear shortly.[5] But the sonata must not appear until

---

[1] Taken from *WRBN*. 176-178.   [2] Op. 106.
[3] Now Scherzo. Assai vivace.
[4] The first two bars of the Allegro risoluto.
[5] Op. 104 was published by Artaria in February, 1819.

I have finally received a reply from you and the fee for which I am longing. De Smith is the name of the courier through whom you have received both the quintet and the sonata — Please send me an early reply. More news very soon!

In haste, your

BEETHOVEN

(941) *To Matthias von Tuscher* [1]

[Autograph in the Beethovenhaus, Bonn, H. C. Bodmer collection]

DEAR T[USCHER],   [VIENNA, *Spring*, 1819]

As I have another copy of Goethe, please ask your dear wife to accept this one which I send herewith (and to which the volume you received from me belongs) as a friendly remembrance from me — I shall see you before half past nine today. Don't forget about *Schmerling*, for by reason of your knowledge you can certainly exert much influence on this affair.

Your friend

BEETHOVEN

(942) *To the Archduke Rudolph*

[Autograph in the Gesellschaft der Musikfreunde, Vienna]

YOUR IMPERIAL HIGHNESS!   [VIENNA, *Spring*, 1819]

I am greatly distressed to hear that you are again indisposed. I trust that this will be only a temporary relapse. Probably the still uncertain spring is responsible for it — Only yesterday I wanted to bring you the variations. They really should be brought boldly to the light of day; and perhaps people will venture to approach Y.I.H. about this [2] — I very much regret that I can only have *pia desideria* [3] for Y.I.H.'s

---

[1] Matthias von Tuscher, born in 1775, was a Magistratsrat (Municipal Councillor) in Vienna at the time of Beethoven's prolonged dispute with his sister-in-law, and in March, 1819 became co-guardian and then sole guardian of Beethoven's nephew for about four months. He was also a member of the committee of the Gesellschaft der Musikfreunde and had a good tenor voice. In May, 1814, he requested Beethoven to set to music a farewell song written by J. v. Seyfried. It is listed in *KHV.* 564-565 as WoO 102. On the autograph, now in the Paris Conservatoire, Beethoven wrote: 'von L. v. Bthvn um nicht weiter — Tuschirt zu werden', meaning 'in order not to be touched up any more'.

[2] Cf. p. 789, n. 3.   [3] Pious wishes.

well-being. But I trust that the power of the Aesculapii will in the end win the day and bestow on Y.I.H. permanent good health —

Your Imperial Highness's

most obedient

L. v. BEETHOVEN

(943) *To the Philharmonic Society, Laibach*

[Autograph in the Beethovenhaus, Bonn, H. C. Bodmer collection]

VIENNA, *May* 4, 1819

I know how to value the honourable proof which the worthy members of the Philharmonic Society have given me of their recognition of my slight achievements in musical art by appointing me an honorary member of their Society and by sending me the diploma relating to this through the Magistratsrat von Tuscher.[1] In due course as proof of my appreciation I shall have the honour of arranging for an unpublished work of mine to be sent to the Society by the said Magistratsrat von Tuscher.[2] Let me add that whenever the Society may require my services, I shall always be willing to give them.

The most devoted honorary member of the Philharmonic Society,

LUDWIG VAN BEETHOVEN

(944) *To Ferdinand Ries, London*

[Autograph in the possession of Julius Wegeler]

DEAR RIES!   VIENNA, *May* 25, 1819

I have neither heard of you nor seen a letter from you, although I have sent you the quintet and the sonata; still

---

[1] Beethoven's diploma is dated March 15, 1819. See Dr. Friedrich Keesbacher, *Die Philharmonische Gesellschaft in Laibach, 1707–1862* (Laibach, 1862). After many struggles to survive the Society ceased to exist in 1921.

[2] There is no evidence that Beethoven ever sent an unpublished composition to the Philharmonic Society of Laibach. But the Society possessed a copy of the Pastoral symphony, Op. 68, in another hand with corrections and the title entered in Beethoven's characteristic red pencil writing. See *KHV*. 162.

less have I received a farthing for these compositions [1] — I think that the metronome markings of the tempi of the sonata are still missing.[2] These I will send on the next post-day. Meanwhile I have been afflicted with more cares than I have ever had to face in all my life and, what is more, thanks to my too great kindnesses to other people —

Go on composing diligently. My dear little Archduke Rudolph and I play your compositions too ; and he says that my former pupil is a credit to his master —

Now all good wishes. As I hear that your wife is beautiful I must kiss her now merely in thought, but I hope to have that pleasure in person next winter — Don't forget about the quintet and the sonata and *the money*, I mean to say, *the honorarium* (avec où sans honneur ! ! ! !).

I hope to have excellent news from you very soon, not in allegro tempo, but veloce, prestissimo — The bearer of this letter to you is an intelligent Englishman.[3] His fellow-countrymen are for the most part splendid fellows with whom I should very much like to spend some time in their country.

Prestissimo — Responsio il suo amico ed maestro

BEETHOVEN

(945) *To George Thomson, Edinburgh*

[*Autograph in the British Museum*]

VIENNA, *May* 25, 1819

MON CHER AMI !

Vous écrivez toujours facile, très facile — je m'accomode tout mon possible, mais — mais — mais — l'honoraire pourroit pourtant être plus difficile, ou plutôt pesante ! ! ! ! Votre ami Monsieur Smith m'a fait grand plaisir a cause de sa visite chez moi — en hâte, je vous assure, que je serais toujours

---

[1] Op. 104 and 106.

[2] Beethoven had sent these metronome markings to Ries. Cf. Letter 940.

[3] This was John Smith of Glasgow, a friend of George Thomson's. Cf. Schünemann I, pp. 48, 49 and 55. On the verso of the autograph there is this remark in another hand : 'The gentleman who brought this committed it to the care of a friend, who unfortunately mislaid it and found it again only two days [ago]. Edinburgh, 28 Oct. 1819.' See Letter 982, p. 856.

avec plaisir de votre service — comme j'ai à present votre Adresse par Mr. Smith, je serai bientôt en Etat de vous écrire plus ample — l'honoraire pour un Thème avec variations j'ai fixé, dans ma dernière lettre à vous par Messieurs le Fries, a moien dix Ducats en or c'est, je vous jure malgré cela seulement par complaisance pour vous, puisque je n'ai pas besoin, de me mêler avec de telles petites choses, mais il faut toujours pourtant perdre de temps avec de telles bagatelles, et l'honneur ne permet pas, de dire à quelqu'un, ce qu'on en gagne, — je vous souhaite toujours le bon gôut pour la vraie Musique et si vous crie facile — je crierai difficile pour facile ! ! ! ! !

Votre ami
BEETHOVEN

(946) *To the Archduke Rudolph*

[Autograph in the Gesellschaft der Musikfreunde, Vienna]

YOUR IMPERIAL HIGHNESS!   [VIENNA, *May*, 1819]

Please be so gracious as to acquaint His Imperial Highness the Archduke Ludwig [1] with the following circumstances. Y.I.H. will remember that I spoke to you about the necessity of removing my nephew from Vienna on account of his mother. I had decided to hand in a petition on this question to H.I.H. the Archduke Ludwig. But so far no obstacle has been placed in the way of such a move, since all the authorities, through whom this matter must pass, *are in favour of it*, including the chief authorities, i.e. *the Court police, the Obervormundschaft and also the guardian*, all of whom entirely agree with me that for the moral welfare of my nephew nothing would be more profitable than to remove him as far as possible from his mother. Moreover at Landshut everything is very well arranged for the training of my nephew, because the worthy and celebrated Professor Sailer [2] would superintend everything

---

[1] The Archduke Ludwig (1784–1864) was an elder brother of the Archduke Rudolph.

[2] Johann Michael Sailer (1751–1832) had been Professor of Theology at Landshut University since 1800. In 1826 this University was transferred to Munich. Sailer, who later became Bishop of Regensburg, is frequently mentioned in the Conversation Books.

pertaining to his education and because I too still have some relatives there.[1] So doubtless the most desirable results for my nephew would be realized. Since, as I stated, I have not yet come across any obstacle, I have refrained from troubling H.I.H. the Archduke Ludwig in any way whatsoever. But I hear that my nephew's mother wants to have an audience of H.I.H. the Archduke Ludwig in order to *oppose* my plan. She will not scruple to indulge in all kinds of calumnies *about me*. But I trust that these will be easily disproved by my moral character, which is publicly recognized. And I assume that even in this respect I may request, without fear of refusal, Y.I.H.'s recommendation to His Imperial Highness the Archduke Ludwig *on my behalf*. What sort of person my nephew's mother is can be gathered from the fact that the courts have declared her to be quite incapable of being entrusted with any kind of guardianship over her son. *All the intrigues she has woven* in order to ruin her poor child, can only be ascribed to her depraved character — Hence in all quarters there is *unanimity* on this point, namely, that the child must be removed from Vienna and thus be entirely out of reach of her influence — Such is the nature and unnatural character of this affair. So I entreat Y.I.H. to intervene with H.I.H. the Archduke Ludwig and to ensure that he shall not listen to the defamatory statements of this mother who would plunge her child into an abyss from which he could never be rescued. Justice which in our just Austria is meted out to every party will not exempt *her*; and precisely *this justice* is also quashing all her remonstrances — One of the chief considerations which have made the judges decide to remove her son as far as possible from her is a religious precept connected with the fourth commandment. And certainly one must bear in mind the difficult position of the guardian and instructor who must not infringe this commandment; and the necessity that the son must never be induced to ignore or break this commandment — There has been no lack of forbearance and magnanimity to enable this unnatural mother to reform herself, but in vain — Should it be necessary I will deliver to H. I. Highness the Archduke Ludwig a discourse on this subject. Whereupon after the favourable intervention of my most gracious lord, His Imperial

[1] It has not been possible to identify these relatives of Beethoven.

Highness the Archduke Rudolph, I shall certainly expect a
dispensation of justice —

Your Imperial Highness's
most obedient servant
LUDWIG VAN BEETHOVEN

(947) *To Joseph Karl Bernard, Vienna* [1]

[Autograph in the Beethovenhaus, Bonn, H. C. Bodmer collection]

DEAR B[ERNARD],   [MÖDLING], *Sunday, June* 6, 1819 [2]
Here at last is the decision brought to me by a third
member of the town militia. Apparently the *latter* has favoured
us; and *for that we must thank* our friend Br. P.[3]
It is all easily refuted. No. 3, *the supreme sanction* will
win the day — Please exert yourself just a little so that I may
have on Tuesday *the petition* which I request you to draft
partly on the basis of my scrawl and partly on the basis of
what you know better and above all are also more conversant
with. At about half past one on Tuesday I shall fetch you
for dinner. I should like to deliver the petition to His I. H.
that same afternoon.[4] —
Assuring you of my warmest friendship I again entreat
you to let me have a strongly worded petition well supported
by reasons, a document which I can hand in at once on
Tuesday —

Your
BEETHOVEN

[1] Joseph Karl Bernard (1780–1850), writer, journalist and librettist, was born
in Bohemia and came to Vienna in 1800. He first had a post in the Court War
Council. In 1815 he began to write for the *Wiener Zeitung* and in 1818 became
co-editor of the *Wiener Zeitschrift*, a post which he held until January, 1820. In
October, 1819, he became chief editor of the *Wiener Zeitung* and at that time wrote
the text 'Der Sieg des Kreuzes' for the oratorio that Beethoven was to compose
for the Gesellschaft der Musikfreunde. Konradin Kreutzer set to music his
'Libussa', which was produced in 1822. Bernard's friendship with Beethoven
seems to date from 1816, when the latter placed his nephew at Giannatasio del
Rio's boarding school. This letter was first published in the *Beethoven-Jahrbuch*,
1953/54, p. 24.
[2] According to his diary Beethoven settled at Mödling for the summer on
May 12th.   [3] Possibly Baron Pasqualati.
[4] Probably Beethoven's petition to the Magistrat of July 5, 1819. See
Appendix C (10).

(948) *To the Archduke Rudolph, Vienna*

[*Autograph of the first portion in the Institute for Russian Literature
in the Academy of Science, Leningrad, and of the remaining
portion in the Gesellschaft der Musikfreunde, Vienna*]

YOUR IMPERIAL HIGHNESS!   [MÖDLING, *early June*, 1819]

I was not at home on the day when Y.I.H. graciously
sent me a message; and immediately afterwards I caught a
violent cold. Hence while lying in bed I am paying my
respects in writing to Y.I.H. — However numerous may be
the congratulations which have been pouring in to you, my
most gracious lord, yet I know only too well that this new
honour will not be accepted without *some sacrifices on the part of
Y.I.H.*[1] When I remember, however, what an enlarged sphere
of activity is going thereby to be opened to you and to your
fine and noble qualities, I too cannot but add my congratulations to the many others which Y.I.H. must have received.
There is hardly any good thing which can be achieved —
without a sacrifice; and it is precisely the nobler and better
man who seems to be destined for this more than other human
beings, no doubt in order that his virtue may be put to the test.

That is what I would like to sing now with all my heart, if only
Y.I.H. were quite restored to health. But your new sphere of
activity, the change, and the journeys to be undertaken later
on will surely restore Your Imperial Highness's priceless health
to the best possible condition very soon; and then I shall
develop the above theme with a resounding A—men or Halle-
lujah — As for Your Imperial Highness's masterly variations

---

[1] The Archduke Rudolph had been created Archbishop of Olmütz on June 4,
1819. He had been made a Cardinal on April 24th.

[2] Beethoven's musical setting of 'Erfüllung' (fulfilment) is listed in *KHV*.
706 as WoO 205[e].

I gave them the other day to be copied.[1] I noticed several little slips and I must remind my illustrious pupil 'La musica merita d' esser studiata'.[2] In view of Your Imperial Highness's truly fine talents and really excellent gifts of imagination it would be a pity not to press forward to *the very source of Castalia* ; [3] and on this expedition I offer to be your companion, as soon as Your Imperial Highness's time permits. Y.I.H. can thus create in two ways, both for the happiness and welfare of very many people and also for yourself. For in the present world of monarchs creators of music and benefactors of humanity have hitherto been lacking — And now a word about myself — Indeed I need your most gracious indulgence — I enclose two pieces on which I have written that I had in fact composed them last year before Your Imperial Highness's name-day.[4] But despondency and several distressing circumstances and my very poor health at that time had made me *lose courage* to such an extent that it was only in a state of great nervousness and diffidence that I could even approach Y.I.H. from Mödling where I was staying. By the end of my stay my health was better, it is true, but very many other sorrows assailed me. Meanwhile in my writing-desk there are several compositions which bear witness to my having remembered Y.I.H.; and I hope to work them all out under more favourable conditions — The meaning of Your Imperial Highness's command that I should come, and again your intimation that Y.I.H. *would let me know when I should do so*, I was quite unable to fathom, for I never was, am still not, and never shall succeed in being a courtier. And to myself I seem to be exactly like Sir Davison in 'Maria Stuart' when Queen E[lizabeth] places her death sentence in his hands.[5] I hope that I shall be allowed to visit my most gracious lord as I used to do. God knows my innermost [6] soul; and, however much appearances may perhaps be against me, everything will be cleared up one day *in my favour* — The day on which a High Mass composed by me will be per-

---

[1] The Archduke's 40 pianoforte variations on Beethoven's theme 'O Hoffnung', WoO 200.   [2] Music deserves to be studied. Cf. p. 674.

[3] I.e. the fount of poesy and music.

[4] April 17, 1818. The two pieces are the first two movements of the B♭ sonata, Op. 106, the composition of which was begun in the autumn of 1817.

[5] Beethoven is referring to Schiller's 'Maria Stuart', Act IV, Sc. 11.

[6] The autograph of the second portion, from this word until the end, is in the Gesellschaft der Musikfreunde, Vienna.

formed during the ceremonies solemnized for Your Imperial Highness will be the most glorious day of my life; and God will enlighten me so that my poor talents may contribute to the glorification of that solemn day [1] —

With an expression of my deepest gratitude I am sending you the sonatas; but the cello parts are missing, I think, because I couldn't find those parts at once.[2] Since it is a fine specimen of engraving I have taken the liberty of including an engraved copy of them as well as a violin quintet [3] — To the two pieces in my handwriting composed for Y.I.H.'s name-day I have added two more, the second of which is a grand Fugato, really amounting to a grand sonata,[4] which will soon be published and which was long ago dedicated entirely *in my heart* to Y.I.H.; *and indeed Y.I.H.'s most recent achievement is not in the least responsible for it.* I beg you to forgive me for writing and I implore Our Lord to let his blessings flow down in rich measure on the head of Y.I.H. Y.I.H.'s new profession which so fully embraces the *love of humanity* is certainly one of the finest; and in it Y.I.H. both as *a human and a spiritual* leader will always provide the finest example.

Your Imperial Highness's
most obedient and most faithful servant [5]

[1] A reference to Beethoven's intention to compose his ' Missa Solemnis ', which he had possibly begun.
[2] Op. 102.   [3] Op. 104.
[4] I.e. the Adagio and the final movement of Op. 106. The whole sonata was published by Artaria in September, 1819, with a French title and the dedication to the Cardinal-Archbishop of Olmütz.
[5] The signature has been cut off.

(949) *To [the Gesellschaft der Musikfreunde, Vienna ?]* [1]

[Autograph in the Isabella Stewart Gardner Museum, Boston, Massachusetts]

SIR!   MÖDLING, *June* 15, 1819

I am in bed and cannot therefore embark at once on a lengthy disquisition on the subject of the oratorio [2] — But in a few days I shall write to you or have a talk with you about it. I hereby acknowledge in my own handwriting the receipt of the 400 gulden V.C.[3] —

With kind regards, your most devoted

BEETHOVEN

(950) *To Joseph Karl Bernard, Vienna*

[Autograph in the Beethovenhaus, Bonn, H. C. Bodmer collection]

DEAR B[ERNARD],   [MÖDLING], *Wednesday, June* 16, [1819]

Please do complete the written statement.[4] You yourself must realize *how much unhappiness K[arl] has to bear*, and with a few strokes of the pen you can help him; and how much harm is being done by your delay! — Well, I must now eat humble pie at Giannatasio's or somewhere else in order to find a place for K[arl], for I will never send him again to that K[udlich],

---

[1] This short letter was first published in Sonneck, with a facsimile facing p. 92. Sonneck maintains that the words written on the verso are 'Für Oliva', whereas they are quite clearly 'in Vien' (Beethoven's way of spelling Wien). Obviously this letter written from Mödling was addressed, as was Letter 1260, to the Directors or, more probably in this case, to the Chairman or Secretary of the Gesellschaft der Musikfreunde. This famous Society was formed in 1812–1813 and was directed by a committee which included Hauschka, Castelli, Salieri, Zizius and Zmeskall. The Chairman was Landgraf von Fürstenberg the Deputy Chairman Georg Kiesewetter and the Secretary Joseph Sonnleithner.

[2] In 1815 Zmeskall was commissioned by the Executive Committee to ask Beethoven to compose an oratorio for the Society, which he agreed to do. At the request of the Society, J. K. Bernard wrote in 1819–1820 a text 'Der Sieg des Kreuzes', which Beethoven never set to music, partly because 'he found it uncongenial and partly because he was then engrossed in other work'.

[3] This was an advance payment of part of the fee which Beethoven was to receive for his composition. He was never asked to return it; and in 1826 he was made an Honorary Member of the Society.

[4] Probably the letter to the Magistratsrat enclosed in Beethoven's communication to Bernard, Letter 951.

who is either a *rascal* or a *weak fellow*!!!!! [1]   There is not much
difference between the one or the other whenever what
ought not to happen is allowed to happen!!!! —

I shall see you on Saturday. I have received a communication about the oratorio — I am now waiting for the whole
text, for how can I start work on it before then? Be on your
best behaviour, see that your best friends in their direst need
are always left in the lurch, etc., etc., etc., etc.[2]

All good wishes. I shall see you on Saturday.

Ever your
BEETHOVEN

(951) *To Joseph Karl Bernard, Vienna*

[*Autograph in the Beethovenhaus, Bonn, H. C. Bodmer collection*]

[MÖDLING, *early July*, 1819]

Here, dear B[ernard], is the letter to the M[agistrats] R[at].
It would be well for you to read it first and then seal it. In
any case you and I have *a B* in common — The best thing
would be for you to show *him* the enclosed letter which I
recently received from Giannatasio *and in any case* to agree
too that she shall be allowed to enjoy the half of the pension,
a portion of which was not drawn until 1818, although since
1815 my nephew has been paid for entirely by me. But this
relief must not be regarded as anything but a compensation
for the rights to his inheritance which my nephew has completely relinquished. Moreover without my consent and
assistance she would *never* have obtained even *that* — Karl
has not yet written a single word. So at a boarding school
*a son can behave towards his father exactly as he likes without being
punished for it*?!! God help him! — You have no idea how
much I am suffering on his account. What callousness and
ingratitude on the part of that young miscreant!! If you go
there, ask to see Karl so that you may hear what this boy,
who is entirely misled, has to say about me? — On no account

---

[1] In February, 1819, Beethoven had placed his nephew at the boarding school
of a certain Johann Kudlich in the Landstrasse. He removed him early in June
and after Giannatasio del Rio's refusal to have him back at his school, placed him
at Blöchlinger's boarding school on June 22.   [2] This is ironical.

must my brother be admitted, for he will *only* talk about all the things Karl can enjoy with him and so on, all those filthy statements which always set Karl on the wrong track ¹ — and it is desirable to make Karl realize that he is no longer to see such a vicious mother, who by means of God knows what Circean spells or curses or vows bewitches him and turns him against me, and whose one desire in any case has been to hasten his physical and moral ruin —

In haste, yours ²

With calmness ! ! !   I ask you, what would have happened to this calmness, if I had not destroyed it ? ! ! ³

(952) *To the Archduke Rudolph, Baden*

[*Autograph in the Gesellschaft der Musikfreunde, Vienna*]

YOUR IMPERIAL HIGHNESS !   MÖDLING, *July* 15, 1819

Ever since I was proposing to wait upon Y.I.H. the last time I was in town I have been very unwell. But I hope to be in a better state of health by next week when I shall immediately betake myself to Baden to visit Y.I.H. — Meanwhile I have been in town a few times to consult my doctor — The persistent worries connected with my nephew who has been morally almost completely ruined are largely the cause of my indisposition. At the beginning of this week I myself had again to assume the guardianship, for the other guardian had resigned after perpetrating a good many misdemeanours for which he has asked me to pardon him.⁴ The Referent too has resigned his office because, although he was really interested in our good cause, he was being publicly described as prejudiced.⁵ So this confusion persists, the end is not in sight, and I am without help or comfort. Everything I built up has

¹ The clause consisting of the words from 'for he' to 'track' is added at the foot of the page. Beethoven's brother wanted Karl to adopt his own profession, i.e. to become a pharmaceutical chemist.
² The letter is not signed.
³ Beethoven is evidently taking up a suggestion put forward by Bernard that he should keep calm about the whole affair.
⁴ Matthias von Tuscher resigned early in July.
⁵ A 'Referent' was an official who reported on the findings of a committee or acted as its secretary.

been blown down by a hurricane, as it were. Moreover the present proprietor of a boarding school where I have placed my nephew (he was a pupil of Pestalozzi) [1] thinks that it will be difficult for him and for my poor nephew to achieve his desired objective. And he is now of the opinion that by far the best solution would be to send my nephew abroad! — I hope that the health of Y.I.H., which is the health of one of those persons dearest to me, leaves nothing to be desired; and I am already looking forward to being able soon to be with Y.I.H. again and to prove to you my zeal to serve you —

Your Imperial Highness's
most obedient and most faithful servant
BEETHOVEN

(953) *To Franz Xaver Piuk, Vienna* [2]

[Autograph in the Beethovenhaus, Bonn, H. C. Bodmer collection]

SIR!   MÖDLING, *July* 19, 1819

Having learnt that you have undertaken to act as Referent in the question affecting my nephew, I am taking the liberty of expressing myself with frankness about a few points — Recently an attempt was made to make my nephew appear before a commission. That I cannot possibly allow. He is *innocent*, and that I can testify so far as he is concerned. The meagre support which the guardian I appointed received from the Obervormundschaft coupled with the mother's wicked intrigues is the only reason why my poor nephew and ward *has been put back in his studies for a whole year* — Well, that has now been done. But it is not advisable to summon *him* to appear, seeing that he must give evidence *against his mother*. Moreover on account of her frequent visits to him and his vacillating behaviour where his mother is concerned he might under the influence of her machinations even give evidence *against me*, as he has already done when misled by her wickedness. In

[1] Joseph Blöchlinger, at whose boarding school Karl was placed on June 22, 1819. For a full note on Blöchlinger see Letter 959, p. 829, n. 1.
[2] Little is known about Franz Xaver Piuk, who was a Magistratsrat and for a time acted as Referent in the litigation between Beethoven and his sister-in-law about the guardianship of the latter's son. Beethoven occasionally spells his name Piuck.

any case no boy in his 13th year should be brought before a court of law. 'Solum humanae faciei tegumentum decorum, modestia et verecunda.'[1] What is to become of modesty if so many witnesses to his shortcomings and mistakes, which have been caused entirely by his wicked mother, were to be brought forward ?!! Once more I repeat that he is *innocent of everything*. If the Obervormundschaft wants to have *information about what went on during the time when I had resigned my guardianship*, I am willing to provide it.[2] And in any case if *he* is to be questioned, it is obviously fitting that I should be at his side. *But it would be better* that *I* alone should explain everything about this, if necessary, seeing that I know best how the *threads* were knotted together — The poor misguided boy needs peace in order to recover his equanimity. That is the only thing that can *help him*. His faults and mistakes should be dealt with by a domestic court, that is to say, by myself and the person who is in charge of his education. — Peace and no *further opposition* to my well-considered decisions concerning his education — But the question now is how to settle the matter relating to the *meetings* between mother and son. I insist that they shall meet only *once* every two months, because in any case this mother must be for *him* both *morally and politically dead*. It is quite impossible *to reform her*. But *how much can be ruined where my nephew is concerned* ?!!! Here we must act with *unswerving perseverance*, we must take precautionary measures and hold the reins *as tightly as possible — any sign of inconsistency will bring its own punishment* — Giannatasio, at whose boarding school my nephew was educated continuously for two years,[3] even wanted to allow the mother to see my nephew only once in three months; and he would not even allow him to be taken to her house. Among the papers in the possession of the Obervormundschaft there must be a letter about this —

I am compelled to insist that we should abide by what the Landrechte have arranged in respect of *that* unnatural mother. It depends *on myself alone* to direct how and when

---

[1] It has not been possible to trace the source of this Latin quotation which means : 'modesty and a sense of shame are the only fitting covering of the human face'. The last word should be spelt 'verecundia'.

[2] On March 29, 1819 Beethoven resigned the guardianship in favour of Matthias von Tuscher, but from June, 1819 onwards he again considered himself to be the guardian.   [3] From February 2, 1816, until January 24, 1818.

she *is to see him.* Giannatasio would not even allow the meeting
to be in his house; and so it took place a few times at my
rooms. But that her maternal longing was not very great is
proved by the fact that for *a year and a half* she did *not* see him,
that is to say, during the period when he was at Giannatasio's
boarding school — Let me add that *in accordance with the laws
the mother was excluded both from the guardianship and from exerting
any influence on her son's education*; and as such too she was also
treated *by the Landrechte.* But when her wickedness and her
evil spirit reached their climax, I *asked that the matter should be
investigated and that the mother should be finally removed once and
for all*, seeing that she only wanted to sacrifice the welfare of
her child to her private hatred of me. Hence it was agreed
that the Landrechte should appoint a commission; and in
that case it was quite *right* that my nephew too should be
summoned. Despite all the defamatory statements made by
the mother and her abettors, no accusation could be brought
against me. But the discussion turned on the little word
'van'; and I had sufficient personal pride to declare that I
had *never* worried *about my nobility* — And that is how we came
to the worshipful Magistrat [1] — Here a party *in favour of* the
mother was immediately formed. No consideration was given
to the fact that *two parties cannot exist in this matter.* For surely
nowhere in the world could I be placed on the *same* level as a
person *who has been handed over to the criminal courts* — Spare
me the narration of the horrible details — sapienti pauca [2] —

(954) *To Joseph Karl Bernard*

[*Autograph in the Beethovenhaus, Bonn, H. C. Bodmer collection*]

[VIENNA, *c. July* 20, 1819]

. . . in the letter from Karl to Karl [3] you will find the
monthly sum for B[löchlinger].[4] — I desire to inform him that

---

[1] See p. 1374, n 1.

[2] 'Sapienti pauca' is a variant of 'sapienti sat'. The text in Terence's
'Phormio', III, iii, 8, is 'dictum sapienti sat est', i.e. 'A word is enough for the
wise'. In the above quotation Beethoven evidently wants to say: 'A few words
are enough for the wise'. The autograph breaks off here.

[3] Beethoven obviously meant to say 'from me to Karl'.

[4] See Letter 959, p. 829, n. 1.

provided I see that there is no disturbance until the end of October, I shall then pay him for the half year — Not a word about our [1] and intentions — Do arrange to go there the day after tomorrow at latest, for B[löchlinger]'s month finishes on the 22nd — The best thing would be to resign the guardianship without choosing anyone and to leave Karl entirely to his fate. For already he is an utter scamp and is most fit for the company of his own mother and my *pseudo*-brother.[2]

(955) *To the Archduke Rudolph, Baden*

[Autograph in the Gesellschaft der Musikfreunde, Vienna]

YOUR IMPERIAL HIGHNESS !   MÖDLING, *July* 29, 1819

I was indeed distressed at receiving the report of Y.I.H.'s fresh indisposition ; and, as I have had no further definite news, I am extremely anxious — I was in Vienna in order to collect in Y.I.H.'s library what was most useful for me. The chief purpose is *rapid execution* united to a *better understanding of art*, wherein *practical considerations*, however, may of necessity admit certain exceptions ;[3] in which connexion the older composers render us double service, since there is generally real artistic value in their works (among them, of course, only the *German Händel* and *Sebastian Bach* possessed genius). But in the world of art, as in the whole of our great creation, *freedom and progress* are the main objectives. And although we moderns are not quite as far advanced in *solidity* as our *ancestors*, yet the refinement of our customs has enlarged many of our conceptions as well. My eminent music pupil, who himself is now competing for the laurels of fame, must not bear the reproach of being one-sided — et iterum venturus judicare *vivos* — et *mortuos*.[4] — Here are three poems. Perhaps Y.I.H. might choose one of them to set to music. The Austrians are now aware that the *spirit of Apollo* has come to life again in the

---

[1] In the autograph a word is omitted here. The letter is a fragment.

[2] The last two sentences of this letter beginning at 'The best thing' are scrawled in pencil and the word 'pseudo' is heavily underlined.

[3] The words from 'united' to 'exceptions' are added at the foot of the page.

[4] Quoted from the Nicene Creed, but with the omission of 'est cum gloria' after 'venturus', i.e. 'and will come again in glory to judge the living and the dead'.

Imperial dynasty. From all sides I am receiving requests to obtain something composed by you. *The editor of the Moden-zeitung* ¹ will send Y.I.H. a *written* request. I trust that *I shall not be* accused in any quarter of *taking bribes* — At *court and no courtier, why, the possibilities are infinite*? ? ! ! ! *His Excellency the Obersthofmeister raised a few objections* when I wanted *to select the music in Vienna.*² It is not worth while to trouble Y.I.H. with this in writing. But let me just say this, that by such behaviour many a talented, good and noble person would let himself be put off from associating with Y.I.H., unless he had the good fortune to have intimate knowledge of your excellent qualities of mind and heart — I wish Y.I.H. a very, very quick recovery and for *myself* some news *to set my mind at rest.*

Your Imperial Highness's
most obedient and *most faithful servant*
L. v. BEETHOVEN

(956) *To Joseph Karl Bernard, Vienna*

[Autograph in the Beethovenhaus, Bonn, H. C. Bodmer collection]

DEAR B[ERNARD] !   [MÖDLING, *late July*, 1819]
I tried to find you yesterday evening after O[liva] had brought me your letter. But you were away, though O[liva] assured me with absolute conviction that I should find you at home — Of course I immediately wrote to Blöchl[inger] ³ at the tavern yesterday evening, telling him that he must on no account bring Karl to the Ober-Arsch Hinterschaft.⁴ I had to give this letter to O[liva] so that he could be sure to deliver it today and early enough. I trust that he has done so — Of course I knew all about the mother, for she was seen going to B[löchlinger's]. I sent Oliva to him on purpose and it was I who ordered him, without disclosing, of course, that

---

¹ Johann Schickh (1770–1835), a Viennese draper, founded in 1816 the *Wiener Zeitschrift für Kunst, Literatur, Theater und Mode*, called the *Modenzeitung*, a periodical which he edited until his death. As supplements it had fashion plates, chiefly from French models, and sheet music, mostly songs. See *FRBH* II, 103-104.
² This was Count Ferdinand von Laurencin d'Armont, who was Oberst-hofmeister (i.e. Chief Steward) of the Archduke Rudolph.
³ For a note on Blöchlinger see Letter 959, p. 829, n. 1.
⁴ Beethoven's rather indecent joke about 'Obervormundschaft'.

I knew about it, to trounce Blöchlinger rather severely. A person who has written *such a letter to me* can certainly be given rather strong purgatives. I refuse to waste any more words by writing to Herr Blöchl[inger] on the subject of that pestilential female. This very day I will send him through Steiner the amount for the next month which expires on August 22nd. In the *present* circumstances in which we now find ourselves, inasmuch as that beast of a mother, it seems, can blow out everywhere her pestilent breath, I am not going to let myself in for a half-yearly payment. I heard from Oliva that Karl *asked* Blöchl[inger] *for permission* to write *me* a letter in Latin for my name-day [1] — Hence I am of the opinion that you should make it clear to K[arl] in the presence of Herr B[löchlinger] that I do not wish to receive *any letter* from him. He ought to have done that long ago and apologized to me for the wicked pranks which he was induced to perpetrate partly by his mother and partly by his own inclination. His stubbornness, his ingratitude and his callousness have so got the better of him that when Ol[iva] was there he never once even *asked for me.* Moreover when I took him for the first time to Blöchl[inger] and held his hand, he drew it from mine as soon as we approached the house, and he did the same thing again on a later occasion when I was there with Ol[iva] — Away with him, my patience is at an end, I have cast him out of my heart. I have shed many tears on his account, that worthless boy. Only if he *on his own initiative* finds the way back to me and only after I first have proofs that he has reformed his bad heart will I see whether I shall acknowledge him once more. My love for him is gone. *He needed my love.* I do not need his. And since he has been in that plague-ridden atmosphere and has *now gone there again*, I don't want to hear anything more about him, save that I am paying and otherwise providing for him —

I have sent word to the worthy Magistrat Dr.   [2] that my time does not permit me to go to him today, or I would have done so, but that I shall very soon have the pleasure of paying my respects to the Obervormundschaft — Now, however, I consider that it is necessary for us to put up

[1] August 25th.
[2] It has not been possible to decipher this word.

a strong defence. We should add to the document which the Archduke Rudolph has forwarded to the Archduke Ludwig a statement to the effect that I myself have taken over the guardianship, that the previous Referent resigned his appointment because he had been accused of partiality; in short, that the Magistrat were always forming a party against me and thereby upsetting my plans to educate my nephew and that, moreover, owing to their interference my nephew had lost a whole year of his studies; that my nephew, owing to their wretched gossiping and tittle-tattle and the hearing which the mother always obtains in that quarter, is constantly being summoned to appear and that I am frequently disturbed; and that they indulge in all kinds of intrigues *against me*, despite the fact that my nephew is being supported by me; and that, moreover, my worthy brother is also an accomplice (he has now bought an estate worth 20,000 thaler or gulden,[1] so you may easily conceive that he too can afford to bribe people), for he wants my nephew to become a chemist, and so forth. Hence we request you to agree either to both propositions, that is to say, that my nephew be allowed to go to Bavaria and that the Magistrat be reminded not to upset my plan of education *any more* and not to interfere in anything else, or to *the one* proposition or *the other*. You may address this communication to the Archduke Rudolph, to whom you may also hand it in person, in which case you could have a few words with him again and, incidentally, perhaps improve your acquaintance with him, which would not be a bad thing. I will give him full particulars of everything. Thus the Archduke is to add this written communication to the others previously sent to him. He *himself* is going to speak to the Emperor [2] — Now you can let me have a reply about this. In regard to K[arl], the statement is drafted in such a way that *he* is to hear it when you read out my letter. You understand, of course, that this is not what I *really* think (I still love him as I used to, but without weakness or undue partiality, nay more, I may say in truth that I often weep for him). My condition caused by my closed senses is in itself very hard;

[1] Johann van Beethoven purchased in July, 1819, a large estate at Gneixendorf near Krems.

[2] Franz I (1768–1835) had become Emperor of Austria in 1806. He was the Archduke Rudolph's eldest brother.

and then what revolting events and horrible compromises for such great sacrifices, which, by the way, those wicked people have contrived to disparage — You are well aware of what *I* think of Oli[va], but unfortunately in my isolated position I need people of that kind.[1] Furthermore, in respect of money he is an additional charge on me. It seems that he considers himself to be *in my pay.* How can I alter all that — Resignation — my health is very much affected so that as I write this I can hardly keep going — Well now, do go to Blöchl[inger]; it is distasteful to me to go to his house any more, because I can't endure those horrible compromises between myself and that person and because I *refuse* to discuss and disprove her gossip about me —

In haste, your
BEETHOVEN

(957) *To Joseph Karl Bernard, Vienna*

[Autograph in the Beethovenhaus, Bonn, H. C. Bodmer collection]

DEAR BERNARD!   MÖDLING, *August* 2, [1819]

Hardly had I begun to believe that Karl and I were going to enjoy a little peace at last when Oliva heard yesterday from Blöchlinger that K[arl]'s beastly mother had again handed in to the Magistrat a written statement directed against me, that the M[agistrat] had asked *her whom* she would like to have as guardian and that she had immediately *proposed my brother* — Blöchl[inger] got this information from a lawyer — as Oliva, whom I beg you to consult, will tell you — I think that when you have discussed the whole matter with Schmerling you should hand it over to the lawyer Dr. Krause,[2] whom Oliva knows, and that we should not lose a moment but should apply to the Court of Appeal at once. For, unless we do this, we shall neither obtain *peace* nor ensure Karl's steady progress — At the same time I am waiting for Steiner to send me a formal statement explaining how the

---

[1] Oliva plays a prominent part in these discussions with Beethoven recorded in the Conversation Books.

[3] According to Professor O. E. Deutsch this was probably Friedrich Heinrich Krausseneck, a lawyer and notary, who lived at Singerstrasse 894.

enjoyment of her full pension can be assured to her *on certain conditions* — I do beg you to make a point of going to Schmerling. For if those rascally Philistines were to remove me, what a disaster it would be for Karl and for this *brother* — In short, something must be done. For instance, do we know for certain whether after all that has happened the *guardianship* has again been entrusted to us? — My peace of mind has again left me and my condition is distressing. And is that *monster* to get the better of us after all?

In haste, your
BEETHOVEN

Krause lives near
you, and so does Schmerling.

(958) *To Joseph Karl Bernard, Vienna*

[Autograph in the Beethovenhaus, Bonn, H. C. Bodmer collection]

[MÖDLING, early August, 1819]
To be read out to Herr Blöchlinger during a lecture.[1]
Premise.
The boy has been placed at a boarding school so that he may have no, or extremely little, association with his mother. — And the conclusion? That the Landrechte have issued their own most appropriate order about this — and that a short time ago Herr von Blöchlinger was instructed by the Referent through the Obervormundschaft never to admit her — and how was this instruction followed? — Why, B[löchlinger] himself told Oliva that *she was free to enter* his house, that *I was not* the guardian, and so forth and so on; and, moreover, it has been proved that the mother has been admitted all this time — It would be strange if I could not show the door to someone whom I did not wish to have in my house — Giannatasio did not find it difficult to do this — If I had to conclude from the wrong statements which B[löchlinger] *made about me* in his first letter to me in which he declared that he was a newcomer to this affair, well, it was a reasonable and *not an unreasonable* conclusion — Hence I entreated him, precisely because he was a

---

[1] This sentence is written in pencil at the top of the first page of the autograph.

newcomer, *not to act on his own initiative* in this affair; and also
because I was obliged to attribute rather narrow views to a
man who could not exert a good influence on my nephew,
so much so that although for four weeks I had been sending
messages to the latter, begging him to write to me, nothing
had happened — and in many other cases too — A *man* deals
with education in accordance with the circumstances and the
principles arising therefrom. But in this case precisely the opposite has taken place. The opposition has always found a
sympathetic hearing, as can easily be proved by B[löchlinger]'s
first letter to me and by subsequent data — So I was perfectly
justified in asking him to be guided by the method which the
Obervormundschaft and I considered most suitable for my
nephew. That I was right to do so is again proved by the
subsequent communication to Frau Beeth[oven] which, first
of all, arrived too late and, secondly, was not drafted in a
manner according with my character. Why was my earlier
communication to her never dispatched? — Yet in spite of
all my efforts she continues to go to H[err] v[on] B[löchlinger]
— If I was very much annoyed that a man, whose address I
enclose, should have been refused admission for no particular
reason, for this I shall certainly gain *the applause of all reasonable
people.* For where it is a matter of health, everything else must
take second place; and the occasion when a good person does
us a kindness must *not* be brushed aside *in that way.* This man
was quite justified in complaining to me about B[löchlinger]'s
behaviour — For the time being I again insist that in accordance with the decision of the Obervormundschaft the mother
must on no account be admitted —

                                              BEETHOVEN

Indeed I was right to treat B[löchlinger]'s first letter as a
premise to the — conclusion —

(959) *To Joseph Blöchlinger, Vienna* [1]

[Autograph in the Library of Congress] [2]

SIR!   [MÖDLING, *before August* 19, 1819]

Despite the notice you have given me, I protest, first of all, against the letter which you have written to Fr[au] B[eethove]n without my approval — Secondly, I absolutely insist that the regulation formulated by the Obervormundschaft and by myself be unconditionally observed, i.e. that the mother shall not be allowed to see K[arl] any more. If she is, then legal proceedings will be taken against you as a *seducer of my nephew into low company* — Here is the letter which you wrote to *me* as if I were a schoolboy, thus displaying your ignorance of human nature. The fact that men of high standing are *not of your insignificant opinion* about miserable trifles, which are yet of some importance, is proved by the action of the Referent, H[err] v[on] P[iuk], who has made exhaustive *enquiries of my nephew* about the board and the lodging, in short, about all details concerning your boarding school. In this respect I have been true to my custom of never insulting a teacher equipped with the necessary qualifications, and so forth and so on — Not another word. As for your *regard* for me, which really rests on shallow foundations, seeing that on the other hand I am taxed with being unreasonable, my advice that you should *study logic a little more assiduously* seems to me *not at all unreasonable* — All kinds of people and, I may say, several of the most eminent men show me *their regard* and affection. Among them are even several of the most distinguished and most worthy men of your native land, with

---

[1] Joseph Blöchlinger von Bannholz (1788–1855), born at Gobelingen in Switzerland, came to Vienna in 1804, married in 1814 Henriette von Fischer, daughter of a Court Secretary, and in the same year opened a boarding school with thirty-two pupils in Count Chotek's palace in the present Josephstädterstrasse. In 1825 the school was removed to another building in the Favoritenstrasse. For an excellent account of Blöchlinger's connexion with Beethoven see Frimmel, *Beethovenstudien* II, pp. 109-119, and also *FRBH* I, 50-52.

[2] This letter was probably not sent to the addressee, although Beethoven has written on the top above the text the following direction: 'Für Hr. Flegel von Blöchlinger'. 'Flegel' means 'lout' or the like.

whom, however, I would never associate *you* [1] —

Instead of desiring to instruct men like me, fulfil your duties as teacher and impress more strongly on my nephew his duties and his obligation to me, who have been waiting for a letter from him for the last five weeks — truly barbarous treatment [2] — Well, God be with you —

Your faithful

LUDWIG VAN BEETHOVEN

(sole guardian of my nephew Karl van Beethoven)

(960) *To Joseph Karl Bernard, Vienna*

[*Autograph in the Beethovenhaus, Bonn, H. C. Bodmer collection*]

MÖDLING, *August* 19, [1819]

Addenda ————————

Karl's letter has just arrived. I am returning it herewith. In spite of what Herr B[löchlinger] has said, please *hand it back yourself to Karl* — There is no heart in it. He doesn't even express a wish to see me or speak to me; and indeed as long as I live he shall never see me again, for he is a monster; and his pestilential mother who has trained him to behave like that is again weaving intrigues with the head of the boarding school —

You may tell him that the correct procedure was to see me about the matter in question. Well, he would not have failed to do so, ass as he is, if he had had something to be rude to me about — Tell him too that whenever she does come, which should be as seldom as possible, she must send a message beforehand to say *when* she is coming, *mentioning the day and the hour* — and that he must not dare to let Karl leave the house to go to her. If he does, he will soon know what stuff I am made of — I don't want him to mention me again before Karl. In any case, on account of this monster of a mother all is lost.

---

[1] When writing this remark Beethoven was probably thinking of H. G. Nägeli and Schnyder von Wartensee, both of Swiss extraction. Cf. Letters 804, p. 700, n. 1, and 803, p. 699, n. 2.

[2] These three words are added at the foot of the page.

Pity me for having sacrificed so much for such a rabble —
Make haste with that document. Please, please do so —
Perhaps I shall see you one of these days for a few minutes.
Karl is not to write to me any more; away with him for ever.
I shall just provide the money —

NB. Get somebody to show you the letter when you are
there so that you too may read it [1] —

NB. I shall let her come as she is doing now, but only as
long as I am not in town [2] —

(961) *To Joseph Blöchlinger, Vienna*

[*Autograph in the Beethovenhaus, Bonn, H. C. Bodmer collection*]

SIR!   MÖDLING, *August* 27, 1819

You inform me that Frau van Beethoven is still trying
to create disturbances in your house. Well, all I can do as
the guardian and father of my nephew is to request you to
carry out to the letter the orders of the Obervormundschaft
and not to depart from them in any particular whatsoever.
For those authorities absolutely insist that his mother shall
not be admitted to see him; and to allow it would be an
infringement of the customary arrangements and of the regulations which have been laid down. As soon as I return to
town, the mother can then see her son occasionally *at my home*.
But both Herr von Blöchlinger and I must observe the regulations of the Obervormundschaft and must never depart from
them. Otherwise you, Sir, may find yourself in an unpleasant
situation.

I am, Sir, Your most faithful

BEETHOVEN

Guardian of my nephew Karl van Beethoven

---

[1] This NB. is added at the side of the first page of the autograph.
[2] This NB. is added at the side of the fourth page.

(962) *To Artaria & Co., Vienna*

[*Autograph in the Beethovenhaus, Bonn*]

MÖDLING, *August* 31, [1819] [1]

MOST EXCELLENT, HONOURABLE AND HIGHLY LEARNED [2]
GENTLEMEN!

The title is good and can be sent to Guttenbrun, to Otha-heite,[3] Calcutta, Pondicheri and, what is more, to Greenland and North America. But you must write *Grosze* instead of *Grosse*, for the latter is an Austr[ian] *provincialism*.[4] Hence that must still be altered —

Your etc., etc., etc.

LvB

(963) *To the Archduke Rudolph, Vienna*

[*Autograph in the Gesellschaft der Musikfreunde, Vienna*]

YOUR IMPERIAL HIGHNESS!   MÖDLING, *August* 31, 1819

Only yesterday did I hear the news of a *fresh recognition and glorification of your excellent qualities of mind and heart*.[5] I ask Y.I.H. to receive my congratulations and most graciously to accept them. For they come from my heart — and it is not necessary to look for them — I hope that my affairs also will soon take a turn for the better. So many misfortunes have again had a bad effect on my health, and I am not at all well; and for some time now I have again had to take medicine. Hence I can scarcely devote myself for a few hours a day to Heaven's most precious gift to me, that is, my art and the Muses. But I hope to complete the Mass and *in good time* too,

---

[1] Op. 106 with its German title 'Grosse Sonate für das Hammerklavier', published by Artaria, appeared in September, 1819.

[2] The autograph has 'geleert' (emptied) instead of 'gelehrt' (learned), a favourite joke of Beethoven's.

[3] I.e. Tahiti.

[4] This was merely a difference in spelling, not in pronunciation. This 'Austrian provincialism' was also a characteristic of Haslinger.

[5] The Emperor Franz I had conferred on the Archduke Rudolph, now Archbishop of Olmütz, the Grand Cross of the Order of St. Stephen. This was reported in the *Wiener Zeitung* of August 30th.

KETCH FOR THE CREDO OF THE 'MISSA SOLEMNIS', Op. 123, *c.* 1819/20
(*Beethovenhaus, Bonn*)

so that, if the arrangement still stands, it can be performed on the 19th.[1] At any rate I should really despair if owing to my poor state of health I were to be prevented from completing it by that date. But I trust that my most heartfelt wishes for the attainment of this object will be fulfilled — In regard to Y.I.H.'s masterly set of variations I think that they could be published with the following title, namely :

Theme or exercise set by L. v. Beeth[oven], on which forty variations have been written and dedicated to his teacher *by His Excellency the composer.*[2]

There are so many demands for this work ; and in the end this very creditable composition might be sent into the world in garbled copies. Y.I.H. yourself will not be able to avoid making a present of it here and there. So, in the name of Heaven, in addition to the many sacred orders which have now been bestowed on Y.I.H. and been made public, let the order of Apollo (or, to use a more Christian term, the order of St. Cecilia) be made public. No doubt Y.I.H. may perhaps accuse me of *vanity.* But I can assure you that, although this dedication is very precious to me and although I am really proud of it, that alone is certainly not my chief object — Three publishers have come forward in connexion with your work, Artaria, Steiner and a third one, whose name I can't recall. So assuming that only the first two deserve to be considered, to which of them should the variations be given ? I await Y.I.H.'s commands. In both cases the variations are to be engraved *at the expense of the publisher*, for both publishers have offered to undertake this — Well, the question now is whether Y.I.H. *is satisfied with the title* ? [3] As to whether the variations should be published, I think that Y.I.H. should certainly agree. If they are published, *Y.I.H. will describe it* as a misfortune ; but the world *will regard it as the reverse* — May God preserve Y.I.H. and ever continue to empty the cornucopia

---

[1] The 'Missa Solemnis', Op. 123, was not completed until late in 1822; and even until the summer of 1823 Beethoven continued to make certain additions. But the enthronement of the Archduke as Cardinal took place on March 20, 1820.

[2] In the autograph of this letter the title Beethoven suggests is surrounded by a circle forming a sort of cage. The Archduke's variations were published by Steiner in December, 1819. They were dedicated to Beethoven.

[3] In the original edition of the Archduke's variations the title is slightly different. See *KHV.* 701.

of His favours upon Y.I.H.'s sacred head — and may God continue to foster your gracious opinion of me —

Your Imperial Highness's

most obedient and most loyal servant

L. v. BEETHOVEN

My poor state of health will serve as an apology to Y.I.H. for my untidy letter — ¹

(964) *To Joseph Karl Bernard, Vienna*

[*Autograph in the Beethovenhaus, Bonn, H. C. Bodmer collection*]

[MÖDLING, *August*, 1819]

I cannot remain silent about the fact that ever since we became acquainted your behaviour has often distressed me. Apparently you like to listen to the flattery of wretched, miserable people so that you may then seem to be their protector. By so doing you injure your friends, because when adopting that kind of protective attitude you are determined to find everything right and even of the best. This present business again proves how greatly you have erred and how inconsiderately you have added fresh worries to my old vexations — This man is obviously a vulgar, I might even say, a very vulgar person — You have expressed your approval of his despicable ideas and you have betrayed your friend. Only too clearly did I notice how loosely everything connected with that wicked person was arranged. Oliva was not clever enough and you were not rude enough for that *non-Swiss* lout, for he is a lout, wherever he may come from ² — *Out of respect for me he talks about my unreasonableness* — What logic — On the other hand he again commends himself to *your good will* — this ought not to prove contagious in your case, because any action on the part of such a wretch *can do nobody any honour* — But — I must say that I have a suspicion that to me you are just as much an enemy as a bit of a friend — So my

¹ This remark is added on the verso of the letter.
² Blöchlinger, whose seemingly indulgent behaviour to Karl's mother infuriated Beethoven, was born in Switzerland and had been trained by the Swiss pedagogue Pestalozzi.

nephew is really supposed to harbour quite hostile feelings for me. And if that were the case, he ought to be allowed to continue to do so? — or attempts should be made to ascertain whether he *loves this cruel mother more than me*? You gave your approval to these despicable ideas of that miserable wretch of a pedagogue without ever considering how utterly false they were. Why, when we met in town a few days ago, you yourself gave me to understand very clearly that my nephew hated me — Oh, may the whole miserable rabble of humanity be cursed and damned [1] —

(965) *To [Joseph Karl Bernard, Vienna ?]* [2]

[Autograph in the Beethovenhaus, Bonn, H. C. Bodmer collection]

NB.   [MÖDLING, *August*, 1819]

I protest against the letter which B[löchlinge]r has written to Frau B[eethove]n *in my name*. He ought to have written at once when Herr R[eferent] P[iuk] reminded him that he must not admit her. But it was then far too late and it was done in such a clumsy manner. Moreover I never mentioned a word of this in my last letter to him — Then why did B[löchlinger] not write in his own name — as Giannatasio did, who certainly did not wish to have anything whatever to do with such a person — Double-dealing, hatred, fury with me on account of my *having told him what he ought to do, a reminder he indeed deserved* — that was what prompted him to write that letter. Revenge — on the part of that lout — Besides it is plain from Frau B[eethove]n's letter what a good understanding has been established between Herr and Frau B[löchlinge]r and herself. And it is clear too that he *did not want to come to an agreement with the Obervormundschaft and myself* — That ass, that trainer of horses — God save us. Should that boor dare to admit the mother again, then I will have him summonsed as a seducer of young people *into low company* —

LUDWIG VAN BEETHOVEN

[1] The autograph is not signed.
[2] This autograph may be a postscript to some other letter to Bernard or even to Oliva, with whom Beethoven was then closely associated.

(966) *To Joseph Karl Bernard, Vienna*

[*Autograph in the Beethovenhaus, Bonn, H. C. Bodmer collection*]

[MÖDLING, *c. end of August*, 1819]

Do ask Karl whether Dr. Hasenhut [1] *visited him every day* during his illness — and whether he received his *little blue jacket from Lind, who says that he sent it to him. No one* in the house *has yet* been able to find out whether Karl received it. Don't forget about the Archduke's title. Forgive me for being such a nuisance to you — Not a soul is to know about our document.[2]

Oliva has been here for a few days — What sort of supervision is there at Blöchl[inger]'s when that woman could sneak in as she did? Believe me, there is *nothing sound there.* In short, we are at exactly the same stage as we were before — Why did he not consult you or me — and what sort of man can he really be who has written to me in such a *vulgar way?* — You may treat Karl as you like. You may even let him write. But don't say anything more about that. A letter from him will consist as usual of heartless and callous hypocrisy and a cold expression of gratitude. He belongs, I feel sure, to the viper's breed of his bestial mother — Enquire how often she has been there now, and perhaps even without sending word beforehand, which would be quite typical of that unnatural mother.[3] I will then issue instructions stating what steps are to be taken. My trust in him has ceased to exist — In the end he may even let Karl leave the house. If he does that, then let the devil seize him.[4]

[1] Beethoven's version of the name Hasenöhrl. Dr. Alois Hasenöhrl attended Karl in May, 1819. Cf. *TK* III, 14.

[2] This pencilled sentence was obviously added later.

[3] In the original German the word is 'Rabenmutter'.

[4] The autograph is not signed.

(967) *To Joseph Blöchlinger, Vienna*

[*Autograph in the Beethovenhaus, Bonn, H. C. Bodmer collection*]

SIR!   [MÖDLING, *end of August*, 1819]

It is high time for you firmly to insist that K[arl]'s mother shall never again set foot in your house — In this connexion I request you to return to her immediately the gossiping letter she sent you yesterday and to inform her that she must never dare to set foot in your house. That is the way to talk to people of that stamp and that is how they should be treated. As guardian I am making you responsible (for it is I who am really responsible, and that I presume you will not dispute) ; and even if I were not responsible, anyone who has the slightest acquaintance with me would know what bounds it is necessary to set in this case — How can anyone expect me to be constantly trying to defend myself against the abominable defamations and wicked insinuations about me concocted by *that* depraved person ? K[arl] *ran away* twice on a secret understanding with her and both times he played *wicked pranks* and took refuge with *his unnatural mother*, but was taken away from her again on both occasions. And the other piece of gossip is full of exactly the same abominable lies. I find it impossible to take any further interest in that gossip ; and I request you, moreover, to forbid her to write to you. At the same time in my capacity of guardian I am enclosing a written statement *for you*, one which, by the way, you do not really require, since you have been instructed not only to refuse each time to admit her but also to refer her to the guardianship authorities.

No further written order from the Magistrat is necessary, since you have already received it from the mouth of the Referent. I am sending you my written statement solely in order that you may see that I really am the guardian, a charge from which no authority whatever can remove me —

Furthermore, a short time ago you let her call at your house again. That was quite contrary to our arrangement. Indeed I knew about it before you reported it to Herr von Bernard. For one of my acquaintances who lives in that neighbourhood had seen her. Herr von Oliva had *only an indefinite order* to speak to you about it.   This order, I am told, he did not carry out with great zeal.   That was to be expected, because all of us know that she, the mother, is a wicked woman. Moreover your previous misjudgment of me has still left you, so far as you are concerned, with a certain distrust of me. Well, however that may be, it is incumbent upon me as the guardian and the mainstay of my nephew to have full knowledge of all the arrangements which are being made in this matter — *Even at my request* Giannatasio would not *have her in his house*.   For he and his family thought her horrible ; and without any suggestion from me they detested her on account of her nasty remarks about me.   Indeed the whole family were, and still are, kind and helpful and friendly.   They always did justice to my character ; and I never had to defend myself against her wretched tittle-tattle, because they made it difficult for her ever to *enter the house* and eventually refused to have her there at all.   What she has dared to do in your house she would never have attempted there.   I gather, therefore, that you still behave far too amiably to her.   If not, how could she dare to write such letters to you — As you yourself must know, education demands the strictest consistency, and particularly, of course, in the case of the son of that unnatural mother — You could have acted with greater self-assurance long before you had received the permission of the Obervormundschaft, and all the more so now.   You see, the tables are turned and I can assure you that I have had *nothing to do with this*.   In the end *truth* will completely remove and wipe out all the poisonous brew of that Queen of Night — I am not at all satisfied with Karl's behaviour to me.   He is callous to me, an attitude which he has adopted ever since he has been with his mother, in fact since his last visit to her.   One can imagine what poison she must have instilled into him.   Hence the arrangement that nothing is to be said *against her* can really not be adhered to.   All that he can be reminded of is that he owes her some forbearance.   Since his childhood he himself has known what she is ; and at Giannatasio's boarding school she was always shown to him *in her true light*.   Even clergymen did not scruple to do likewise and acted in the same way, and now you have the O.V.[1] as an additional example for you

[1] I.e. Obervormundschaft.

to follow, since the Referent himself yesterday directed my nephew *to me alone* and urged him to obey me in every particular. Hence you too may tell him that the O.V. themselves have forbidden his mother to see him any more, and you may tell him why, and so forth. I presume that now you will not lack any arguments. I would rather not see him any more if he is going to persist in his present behaviour to me. Formerly, it is true, thanks to her evil influence he now and then forgot to be kind to me. But soon everything was again just as it used to be. My heart is lacerated. Do remember that I showered benefits on his father, whose life (he, by the way, thanks to that dreadful person was sent to an untimely grave) I thus prolonged for several years and that I have cared for his son more than for myself and that he has warmly thanked me for having freed and rescued him from his mother. And now this behaviour, heartless, callous, without the slightest indication of any affection or sympathy. To me his letter seems to consist of nothing but phrases and I very nearly sent it back to him. It was Bernard who prevented me from doing so — In this case no middle course is possible; for me *it is all or nothing*. For his progress and his happiness depend on me. I have even provided for his future, and not without personal sacrifices. All this confusion has made him stray from the right path and I even suspect that his mother may have made him swear *to show me no marks of love and affection*. She has already tried something like that. Hence it is necessary that he should be guided back once more to his former path and be with me. The only way to ensure this is to show him his mother exactly as she is. Her bad reputation and her wicked and immoral character will never make it desirable that he should be much in her company. Therefore I must once more implore you to be absolutely consistent, for without consistency nothing can prosper. It is asking too much *to expect me to nurture a viper in my bosom — Nobility of character must in its turn produce what is noble*; and virtue should merely tolerate vice but not hesitate to check its evil effects — I must insist that you cease to have any communication with her, either personal or in writing. I refuse to listen to another word about her. God, who has always helped me, will again reform the evil, wicked, but, I admit, only misguided heart of my nephew who may perhaps, unless we are careful, be doomed to future unhappiness.

Your most devoted
BEETHOVEN

(968) *To Joseph Karl Bernard, Vienna*

[*Autograph in the Beethovenhaus, Bonn, H. C. Bodmer collection*]

DEAR B[ERNARD],   [MÖDLING, *August*, 1819]

This is for the glaciers — you are at liberty to say what you like about that ice-house, in a few lines of your own [1] — But you must kindly add that on no account is Karl to accept anything whatever from her.[2] Yesterday he was wearing *a hat*, a new one, which she had again bought for him. Keep me away from that vulgar rabble. The arrangement with G[iannatasio] was after all the best one. I have to stand and face that wretched rabble like a poor sinner; and all these vulgarities are raked up and wrangled about — Owing to the present silence about everything that he has committed against me, chiefly under the influence of his wicked mother, Karl will think that his behaviour to me is being approved of or tolerated — Why, a person with moderately delicate feelings would have refused long ago to listen to and countenance that tittle-tattle both verbally and in writing. Since we, both *you* and I and I and you, now have the fullest experience of K[arl], the best course is for that *glacier* H[err] B[löchlinger] to be guided by us. — But all the time I feel that you have something more to tell me which might terrify me. One moment you consider that I ought to abandon K[arl] completely to his fate, the next moment you think that I ought not to do so — Perhaps you have concealed from me something which would terrify me. You need not do this. There is nothing that can terrify me more than what I have already — experienced, and, what is more, through Karl — So out with it, my heart is stout, stab me and wound me as much as you like — Well,

---

[1] This was Beethoven's description of Blöchlinger, on account of the latter's Swiss extraction, and the staff of his boarding school. This time he was possibly including his nephew on account of the latter's seemingly callous behaviour to his uncle.

[2] I.e. Karl's mother.

please have the letter to Blöchl[inger] delivered at once, here
is the tip for the messenger — God help me, I am so weary
of the company of human beings that I almost wish never
to see or hear anyone again —

Yours
BEETHOVEN

NB. Between ourselves Weissenbach [1] has sent me word
that he is willing *to take Karl*, but only on a permanent arrangement. That would be a very good thing. I detest that glacier
and ice-house.

(969) *To Joseph Karl Bernard, Vienna*

[Autograph in the Beethovenhaus, Bonn, H. C. Bodmer collection]

[MÖDLING, August, 1819]

Here — are my views — In any case I will bring you out
here on Sunday and we shall have a jolly time. For I trust
that veritas *non* odium parit [2] — I believe that when we meet
we shall be able to settle this scoundrelly business much more
easily, more conclusively and more definitely —

In haste, your friend
BEETN

That fellow used to be a riding-master like that Herr
Krauss,[3] whose wife's sister *he* has married —
Fish-oil.
And what barbarous indifference — So it doesn't really

[1] Dr. Aloys Weissenbach (1766–1821), born in the Austrian Tyrol, settled at
Salzburg as a surgeon in 1804. He was also a writer and a poet. In September,
1814, he visited Vienna and made the acquaintance of Beethoven whom he
greatly admired. He describes very fully his meetings with the composer in his
book, *Meine Reise zum Kongress. Wahrheit und Dichtung* (Vienna, 1816). He also
wrote the text of Beethoven's cantata 'Der glorreiche Augenblick', Op. 136.
Evidently Weissenbach was prepared to take Karl to Salzburg. See *FRBH* II,
413-417.

[2] The present editor is indebted to Mr. D. M. Low for an admirable note on
this quotation. 'Veritas odium parit' appears in Terence, *Andria*, I. i. 41. The
whole line runs 'obsequium amicos veritas odium parit' (deference begets
friends, truth begets hatred). The negation in Beethoven's version suggests that
he is quoting a theme for a disputation giving the pro and con.

[3] Not identified. Cf. p. 829, n.1.

matter whether my nephew is attached to me or to that wicked and depraved woman?! — From the supplementary document you will see clearly what my opinion is — Please let the Referent see it — and please inform Blöchlinger of these elucidations of mine. It is quite possible that I may drive in and call on Blöchlinger myself. Heaven help him if he dares to allow that unnatural mother to visit his school any more — I was *right*; but the *worst results* fall on *me* alone — All good wishes, *friend* and enemy.

Yours
BEETHOVEN

(970) *To Fries & Co., Vienna*

[Autograph in the Beethovenhaus, Bonn, H. C. Bodmer collection]

[MÖDLING, Summer, 1819]

P.P.

I take the liberty of enquiring whether any letters have arrived for me from Mr. Thomson of Edinburgh? At the same time I request you, if letters from him should be sent to you, to have the kindness to forward them to *the music publisher Herr Steiner off the little Paternostergasse in the Graben (making sure that they are properly closed)*, for I am now in the country and shall remain here until the end of October —

With kindest regards,

your most devoted
BEETHOVEN

(971) *To Joseph Blöchlinger, Vienna*

[Autograph in the Geigy-Hagenbach collection]

Enclosing 85 gulden V.C.   MÖDLING, *September* 14, 1819
SIR!

I have the honour to send you the amount for the next month beginning on September 22nd; and I am adding 10 gulden for unforeseen expenses, of which you will kindly send me an account on October 22nd. — *Only the following persons have free access to my nephew*, i.e. *Herr von Bernard, Herr von Oliva, Herr von Piuk, the Referent* —

Further, whenever anyone has to see my nephew, I will give the visitor each time a letter informing you about it. Then please be so kind as to let the visitor see him; for it is a long way to your boarding school. Moreover, it is a favour on the part of anyone who does this for me, such as, for instance, the truss-maker and so forth — *My nephew must never leave your house unless he has my permission in writing* — This injunction will also make it clear to you how to deal with the mother — I insist that *this order be most strictly observed*, since it is an order emanating from the Oberv[ormundschaft] and myself. However much I appreciate your other eminent gifts, I consider that you, Sir, are too *new to this business to be able to take things into your own hands*, as you have already done. In such a matter *credulity only causes confusion* — and in any case the result might testify rather *against* you than *in your favour*, a thing which *for the sake of your honour* I should not like to see — I hear that my nephew requires or desires several things from me. *He has only to apply to me for them.* Please be so kind as *to send his letters always to Herr Steiner & Co. at the Steiner print-shop in the Graben, I mean in the little Paternostergasse* —

Yours faithfully

L. v. BEETHOVEN

sole guardian of my nephew K. v. Beethoven

NB.   *The expenses connected therewith will be refunded on each occasion —* [1]

---

[1] The NB. probably refers to the last sentence of the letter.

(972) *To Karl Friedrich Zelter* [1]

[Autograph in the Goethe Museum, Düsseldorf, Kippenberg Foundation collection]

MY MOST HONOURED SIR!   VIENNA, *September* 18, 1819

It is not my fault that recently I let you down, as people say here.[2] Unforeseen circumstances deprived me of the pleasure of spending in your company some delightful and enjoyable hours which might also have been of advantage to our art. I am sorry to hear that you are already leaving Vienna the day after tomorrow. This year owing to enfeebled health my stay in the country has not been quite as beneficial as usual. I may come into Vienna again the day after tomorrow; and if you have not left by the afternoon I hope to tell you in person with my sincerest cordiality how highly I esteem you and how much I should like to enjoy your company.

In haste, your most devoted friend

BEETHOVEN [3]

(973) *To Herr Schlemmer, Vienna* [4]

[Autograph in a private collection]

DEAR SCHLEMMER!   MÖDLING, *September* 23, [1819]

Please be so kind as to come next Monday evening. I have not availed myself of the invitation but have stayed here

---

[1] Karl Friedrich Zelter (1758–1832) was a musician of note and equally famous for his friendship and long correspondence with Goethe. He started life as a mason, devoting his leisure to music, playing the violin, singing and composing. In 1800 he succeeded his master K. F. C. Fasch (1736–1800) as Director of the Berlin Singakademie. At first Zelter had little liking for Beethoven's music, but gradually his indifference gave way to an ardent enthusiasm for his compositions and personality. See *FRBH* II, 470-473.

[2] Steiner had arranged a meeting between Zelter and Beethoven at his shop. But neither put in an appearance.

[3] Zelter wrote on Beethoven's letter on the same day the following reply: 'The reason for my wishing to visit you at Mödling, my worthy friend, was to see once more that man who has given so much pleasure and comfort to good people, among whom I count myself. You welcomed us, so at any rate my attempt has not been altogether a failure. For I have seen your face. I have heard of the infirmity which oppresses you. I sympathize, for I suffer from a similar complaint. I return to my professional work the day after tomorrow. But I shall never cease to esteem and love you. Your Zelter.'

[4] Beethoven's most reliable copyist, who according to Breuning worked for him for thirty years. He died during the summer of 1823. See *FRBH* II, 120-122.

in order to be able to await the effects of the medicine. I seem
to be better — So I shall expect you next Monday for certain,
when everything can then go forward with all speed —

In haste, your devoted servant

BEETHOVEN

(974) *To Joseph Karl Bernard, Vienna*

[*Autograph in the Beethovenhaus, Bonn, H. C. Bodmer collection*]

[MÖDLING, *September,* 1819]

I have commissioned Oliva to enquire at my rooms whether
any orders or instructions *have come* from the Magistrat. I
consider it necessary to *find out from Schmerling* whether, since
the M[agistrat] has not replied, I am the guardian or not.
Or you might ask Dr. Krause, who lives in the Singerstrasse.[1]
You may tell Schmerling everything that has been done so
far — and you may say that the chief reason for my acting
thus is that Karl must see as little as possible of his depraved
mother — Isn't it scandalous that Karl has not yet written
to me? But indeed most heads of boarding schools in Vienna
behave like that. Cursed, damned, execrable, abominable
rabble of Vienna! I need hardly remind you that, since my
brother is also an accomplice, a good deal is being got out of
the M[agistrat] by *money.* Schmerling will know best how this
business should be tackled. Perhaps it might be necessary
too for us both to call on the Referent again — I hope to have
your assistance soon and some news as well —

In haste, but, as always, your true friend

BEETHOVEN

(975) *To Artaria & Co., Vienna*

[*Autograph in the Beethovenhaus, Bonn, H. C. Bodmer collection*]

[MÖDLING, *October* 1, 1819]

MOST EXCELLENT VIRTUOSI SENZA CUJONI![2]

We inform you of this and of that and of other things as well,
from which you must draw the best conclusions you can; and

---

[1] Cf. Letter 957, p. 826, n. 2.
[2] Beethoven is trying to say 'virtuosi senza coglioni', i.e. castrated or emascu-
lated virtuosi.

we request you to send us what is due to the composer, i.e. six (I repeat, six) copies of the sonata in B♭,[1] and also six copies of the variations on the Scottish songs.[2] Please send these to Steiner in the little Paternostergasse, who dispatches many other things to me — While cherishing the hope that you are behaving properly and acting within the law I am your etc. etc.

devoted

B.

(976) *To Joseph Karl Bernard, Vienna*

[Autograph in the Beethovenhaus, Bonn, H. C. Bodmer collection]

MÖDLING, October 10, [1819]

DEAR BERNARDUS NON

sanctus

Well, as you are coming on Wednesday, please bring Karl with you. Do see that he takes his cloak with him, for it is now becoming cool in the evenings — In regard to Salzburg I consider that for secrecy's sake the best arrangement would be for me to take Karl there myself.[3] The only drawback is that I cannot do this before November. I feel sure that he will easily make up when he gets *there* what is taught at that school. But first of all we must arrange that his mother shall not be allowed to go there; and for that reason Gastein too is a stumbling-block — and *then* the *school*?! What would happen if he were again to behave as he did at the University [4] — Perhaps a pass could be issued for the three of us, W[eissenbach], K[arl] and myself, and I could then stay here. If so, we should not have to apply again to the chief swindlers [5] first, and at the same time we should achieve

---

[1] Op. 106 was published by Artaria in September, 1819.

[2] Op. 105, six sets of variations on song themes, not all of them Scottish, with flute or violin accompaniment *ad libitum*, were published by Artaria in September, 1819. The English edition had appeared in July, 1819.

[3] I.e. to Dr. Aloys Weissenbach at Salzburg. He had offered to take Karl on a permanent arrangement.

[4] In the autumn of 1818 Karl attended the Akademisches Gymnasium in Vienna and had extra instruction in music, French and drawing. Early in December, however, he ran away to his mother, was brought back and was sent for a few days to Giannatasio del Rio.

[5] In the original the word is 'Oberhinterschaft', Beethoven's sarcastic description of the Obervormundschaft.

our purpose — What do you think? You can let me know on Wednesday, for when you are here we can leave Karl for a moment with W[eissenbach] — Blöchlinger still has a *valise* of mine. Please bring it with you, as I now intend to leave here soon — Everything connected with the rooms I am giving up is proceeding quite smoothly. I can leave everything there even after my departure. — What still remains to be done is to have my new rooms painted. Light green would be best for one's eyes but would cost, no doubt, a good deal, even if there were no decorations. You would do me a great kindness if you were to see whether the owner of my future rooms has really left? He should have everything cleared out by noon on the 13th. The rooms could be painted beforehand so that they would be dry in good time.[1] If you have no expert knowledge about this, then ask Steiner in the little Paternostergasse. But we must hurry — hurry — hurry — this is not a case of more haste less speed — Not a line from K[arl] as yet, nothing but *ill will*. As I have said before, the pestilent poison of his worthy mother which he imbibed during Tuscher's swindling period,[2] is still infecting him deep down — Meanwhile on Wednesday I shall be able to catch him out so that he will soon come to his senses again — Well, I am expecting you and Weissenbach who will bring K[arl] for certain. When you arrive I will refund immediately your *outlay for the carriage* and the toll dues as well. All good wishes.

In great haste, yours [3]

[1] In October, 1819 Beethoven moved into rooms in a house on the corner of Rauhensteingasse and Blumenstockgasse, called thus after the adjacent inn 'Zum Blumenstöckl'. In this house, Rauhensteingasse 3, which no longer exists, he appears to have spent the winter.

[2] Beethoven again uses the word 'Hinterschaft' instead of 'Vormundschaft'. Tuscher was sole guardian of Karl from the end of March to the beginning of July, 1819.

[3] The autograph has no signature.

(977) *To Sigmund Anton Steiner, Vienna*

[*Autograph in the Deutsche Staatsbibliothek, Berlin*]

DEAR STEINER !   MÖDLING, *October* 10, 1819

I left you a note the day before yesterday asking you to
come here before the auction of the house. You would really
be doing me a great kindness. The auction takes place on
the 13th, that is to say, already next Wednesday. Without
your advice I should not like to take any step in this matter.
In no wise must my capital be reduced by such a purchase,
for my nephew, who is going to adopt a scientific career, will
have to be supported, of course, in the event of my death, so
as to be able to continue his studies — If you have had the life
certificate made out by a notary, I will gratefully refund your
expenditure for this purpose —

I have told the

Honourable

Little Tobias [1]

about some var[iations] composed by the Archduke.[2] I proposed *you* for this purpose, because I do not think that you
will suffer any loss and because it is always an honour to
engrave something composed by such a Principe Professore [3] —
As for the non-commissioned officer,[4] please tell him that he
must not sell anything I told him about, I mean, until I come
into town. Moreover, he must not forget to inform the out-
going tenants and the female caretaker in the Landstrasse
that the bell and the window-shutters belong to me — Well
now, I hope to see you tomorrow or the day after. The morning
is the most convenient time, for we must have a word with
Herr v. Carbon,[5] and then have a look at the house. Afterwards, if necessary, you can also examine all the deeds at

---

[1] The two words 'Ehrenwerthen Tobiasserl' are scrawled across the page
with many flourishes.

[2] The Archduke Rudolph's forty variations for pianoforte on Beethoven's
theme were published at the end of 1819 by Steiner with a dedication to Beethoven.
Cf. Letter 933, p. 789, n. 3.

[3] Prince and Professor (of Music), i.e. the Archduke Rudolph.

[4] Probably Diabelli or some other employee of Steiner's firm.

[5] Franz Ludwig von Carbon, an Army captain, who owned house property
at Mödling, where Beethoven was thinking of buying a house.

JOHANN BAPTIST BACH (1779–1847)
From the oil portrait by the elder Johann Baptist von Lampi (1824)
(*Oesterreichische Galerie, Vienna*)

the Chancellery and finally give your verdict. For I shall be guided entirely by your opinion —
The enclosed letter is for Dr. Staudenheim. Please send it for certain tomorrow and, let me remind you, before half past three in the afternoon at latest, to Count Harrach's house in the Freyung.¹ But the non-commissioned officer must wait for a reply, and this reply must be posted to me immediately, i.e. tomorrow, so that I may have it on Tuesday.² I presume, of course, that you are coming on Tuesday. If so, you might very kindly bring the reply with you — Now do carry out my request tomorrow or the day after.

In haste, your friend and servant

BEETHOVEN

(978) *To the Archduke Rudolph, Vienna*

[Autograph not traced] ³

YOUR IMPERIAL HIGHNESS! MÖDLING, *October* 15, 1819
On account of the vintage not a single carriage was to be had at Mödling; and only today have I been promised one for tomorrow. Hence Y.I.H. will understand why I shall not have the honour (*and the pleasure*) of waiting upon you until tomorrow. I shall be with Y.I.H. punctually at half past three in the afternoon, for I now know that this is the most suitable hour and the one which Y.I.H. prefers — Y.I.H. will remember the written statement about the removal of my nephew from Vienna which you were so kind as to deliver to His Imperial H[ighness] the Archduke Ludwig. I most earnestly beg Y.I.H. to ensure that this document is returned to you, because I urgently need it *on account of the enclosures*. Indeed I should find myself in an exceedingly awkward position if these enclosures were not available. A fresh attack has been launched upon me by the venal Magistrat of Vienna acting in collaboration with my nephew's mother, so that,

¹ A square in the Inner City which owed its name to the right of sanctuary afforded by the Schotten-Kirche. Count Harrach's and Prince Kinsky's Palaces are in the Freyung.
² Beethoven was writing on Sunday. His letter is endorsed: 'Received from Mödling on October 12th'.
³ Taken from Frimmel, *Beethovenforschung*, February, 1913, no. 4, pp. 114-115. The autograph was then in private ownership.

although I am almost too exhausted to take any further steps in the interest of my nephew under such unworthy auspices, yet for the sake of my honour I must address myself to the Court of Appeal. The impudence, the vulgarity, the ignorance and the wickedness of this Magistrat have now reached the point that even Y.I.H., is, so to speak, almost an object of their attack as well. You will be amazed to hear this. On the other hand, the entire cabal is so brainless that one doesn't know whether to feel distressed or almost to die of laughing. I fancy that the result of this whole disgraceful story will be that Y.I.H. will most graciously have a testimonial written for me about two points in the statement. Y.I.H. will forgive me for again entreating you to be so kind as to have the written statement I sent you returned to me as promptly as possible — Steiner has now received Y.I.H.'s var[iations] and will himself express his thanks to you. By the way, it has just occurred to me that the Emperor Joseph travelled under the name of Count von Falkenstein.[1] This remark refers to the title. — Baumeister, as I have seen in the Gazette, has built his house in eternity[2] — Without laying the slightest claim to being a good *adviser*, I know someone who would fill this post in Y.I.H.'s household to your complete satisfaction — I am greatly looking forward to being with Y.I.H. tomorrow. I dreamt about Y.I.H. last night. Although no music was performed, yet it was a musical dream. But in my waking hours too I think of Y.I.H. The Mass will soon be finished — May Heaven empty the cornucopia of its blessings every day, nay, every hour, upon your illustrious head. As for me I am and shall remain until the last moments of my life

Your Imperial Highness's

most faithful and most obedient servant

L. v. BEETHOVEN

[1] Evidently the Archduke Rudolph was proposing to adopt the *nom de plume* of Count Falkenstein, which Joseph II had used on his travels in 1780. No doubt Beethoven had suggested some similar disguise for his royal pupil. In the end, however, the variations were published under the composer's name.

[2] Baumeister, the private secretary and librarian of the Archduke, had died on October 6th. As usual Beethoven took the opportunity of making a pun, this time on 'bauen', to build.

(979) *To Johann Baptist Bach*

[*Autograph in the Beethovenhaus, Bonn, H. C. Bodmer collection*]

Sir! Vienna, *October 27, 1819*

By now you will have received the written statement of Frau von Beethoven. That person is far too devoid of any moral worth for me to rebut her attacks upon me. His Imperial Highness, Eminence and Cardinal, who treats me as a friend and not as a servant, would, if necessary, promptly produce a testimonial both about my moral character and concerning that idle talk about Olmütz, not a word of which is true. So far as we all, including H.H. himself, know, he will spend at most six weeks there every year. It would be doing her far too much honour, however, to produce in addition proofs of the baselessness of her calumnies to such a person who is practically outside the law and who according to Paragraph 191, in view of the fact that she was brought before a criminal court, ought not be entrusted with any guardianship whatever —

The chief points are that I am to be recognized forthwith as the sole guardian. I am not accepting any co-guardian. Moreover, the mother is to be forbidden to associate with her son *at the boarding school*, because not enough attendants can be present to cope with *her immoral behaviour* and because she confuses the headmaster by the false details and lies which she serves up to him, and, what is more, seduces her son into telling horrible lies and making statements *about me*, and even fabricates accusations against me, making out that I am giving, or have given, him now too much and now too little. I can prove the truth of all my statements by means of witnesses [1] — But so that in this case humane treatment may still be observed, the mother may see her son now and then at my home in the presence of the headmaster and other distinguished persons — The L[and]r[echte] very sensibly issued an order on general lines about this to Herr Giannatasio at whose boarding school my nephew then was. Yet things came to such a pass that Giannatasio absolutely refused to have her at his house; and she, *in order to see her son*, had to come to my home where Herr G[iannatasio] brought the boy to me for that purpose — At

[1] This sentence is added at the foot of the page.

Giannatasio's boarding school she succeeded in persuading her son to contrive to be put in the second or third class at the examination, so that people could say that *I had not looked after him properly*; hence he was *put back a whole year in his studies.* The guardian whom I then appointed, Herr von Tuscher, issued to the head of the boarding school where Karl was being educated, a written order stating that he was no longer to allow the mother to see her son.[1] — But what happened after that was dreadful. My opinion is that you must hold firmly and steadfastly to the argument that I am *sole* guardian and that this unnatural mother must never see her son anywhere else but *at my home.* My well-known humane attitude, my education and my customary philanthropy guarantee that my behaviour to her will not be less noble than it is to her son. Moreover I think that we should endeavour to make everything quite brief and, if possible, make the Court of Appeal the authorities responsible for the guardianship. Since I have raised my nephew into a higher category, neither he nor I have anything to do with the M[agistrat]. For only innkeepers, cobblers and tailors come under that kind of guardianship.

As for his present maintenance, that is being, and will be, assured during my lifetime. For the future he has 7000 gulden V.C., of which his mother, during her lifetime, will have the usufruct; and also 2000 gulden (or a little more, because I have commuted this sum for him), the interest on which belongs to *him*; and 4000 gulden in silver *belonging to me* are lying in the bank. Since he is my sole heir, these sums form part of his capital. You see that in view of *his great talent*, which admittedly is not taken into account by the Vienna Magistrat, and since my nephew cannot earn his own living at once, he has been provided for in case I should die before he can earn, and to an extent which at the moment is *quite unnecessary* for him. To obtain these 2000 gulden for him cost me a large sum. The muddled procedure of that wretched M[agistrat] only made the expenses heavier. Those people are quite incapable of understanding *such an important matter*, still less of acting *in its interest* or on its behalf —

As the will was not exactly to the advantage of the son and

---

[1] This was Blöchlinger's boarding school.

as the Landrechte also decided that the son should never live
with his mother, I made everything as fair as possible, although
in connexion with the inventory she was already suspected
by the Landrechte of having embezzled money. *My sole care
was for his soul.* Therefore the whole estate jure crediti [1] was
left to her, without enquiring whether the debts which had
been quoted were correct, with the result that little remained
for the son; that is to say, the 2000 gulden V.C. which I have
just mentioned were all that could be obtained for him, together with the usufruct of the said sum. I invested this
capital in lottery tickets, a transaction which was very expensive, so that he might have a higher rate of interest. I then
helped his mother to obtain her pension and she relinquished
half of it in exchange for the whole estate jure crediti. Nevertheless, even before 1816 I had been providing for my nephew
and entirely at my own expense (if you recall the fact that on
account of her bad character she had to be forced by law to
make her contributions, you can easily guess the sums which
the boy was costing me). As I have already stated, even before
1816 everything was done at my expense (and owing to the
high cost of living at that time his education at the boarding
school was very expensive). This arrangement lasted until
1818 when Frau von Beeth[oven], who only then began to
enjoy her pension, refused to make any contribution. So she
had to be compelled by law to do so. That game cost me over
180 gulden V.C. —

Hence what I have received for my nephew's education
since May 1818 can be quickly computed. Moreover for the
last nine months I have not received one farthing of her
pension, because she deliberately refuses to draw it, fondly
imagining that by omitting to do so she will embarrass me
financially. Since I cannot obtain my share of the pension
until she *herself* has drawn it, I am thus always short of money
every six months — My nephew has never yet wanted for
anything. And indeed much more could be done for him if
only this guardianship nuisance could be removed. Nothing
has deterred me, no legal trickery, no obstacle, from constantly
caring for him in the same way — even when he had another
guardian, an arrangement which only increased my cares,

---

[1] I.e. by right of the creditor.

and even in spite of the mother's instigations of the boy *against me*!!! [1]   Yet I always remained the same.   Why, only yesterday, despite all the humiliation I have suffered, I wrote to the headmaster, to whom also I *myself* brought *him*, that I would continue to provide for my nephew and that on no account must he give him into the hands of that wretched Magistrat —

Judge now not only whether I deserve to be the guardian but also whether the name of father in the full sense of the word should not be applied to me, the more so as for several years I saved and lengthened by my generous support the life of his unfortunate father, unfortunate on account of his horrible wife — I thought that if I gave you a few particulars they might be of some use to you and might enable you to deal with this question.   Forgive me for being so long-winded. You must attribute it to the short time at my disposal.   For Cicero long ago apologized for the same misdemeanour by saying that he had *too little time to be brief* [2] —

Indeed the whole matter in itself is extremely distasteful —

I commend to you most warmly not only my own affair but also that of my nephew who is dear to me.

I remain with very special regards your most devoted

BEETHOVEN

Postscript

The mother's intention is to have *her son* to live with her so that she may enjoy her full *pension*.   For this purpose she has already intrigued in all quarters where her son has been settled, whether in my home or at the boarding school.   What I think about this you may gather from the fact that I have asked sensible men to advise me whether I ought to let her use the half of the pension entirely for herself and to regard it as my duty to make up the amount to the son out of my own pocket.   Their advice is *not to do so*, since she would only make too bad a use of the money.   Hence I have decided gradually to put by this sum for my nephew.   At any rate you will again realize in this case how unreasonably the

---

[1] The words from 'and' to 'me' are added at the foot of the page.

[2] It has not been possible to trace this quotation, which has also been ascribed to the younger Pliny.   The present editor is indebted to Mr. Rudolf Flesch for the discovery of an identical remark in Pascal's *Lettres provinciales*, No. 16 of December 4, 1656: 'Je n'ai fait celle-ci plus longue que parce que je n'ai pas eu le loisir de la faire plus courte'.

M[agistrat] has acted in wanting to remove my nephew entirely from me, seeing that if she dies the boy will lose that portion of the pension, and deprived of *my help* and support, may find himself in extremely necessitous circumstances —

(980) *To Johann Baptist Bach*

[*Autograph in the Beethovenhaus, Bonn, H. C. Bodmer collection*]

SIR !   VIENNA, *October* 27, [1819]

In any case I owed you another supplementary statement [1] — The half of the mother's pension amounts annually to 166 gulden 40 kreuzer A.C. The interest coupons of the 2000 gulden amount half-yearly to 27 gulden A.C. — Formerly, from 1816 to 1818, I received no contribution whatever. Besides you will see from the supplementary documents that this should be regarded as the mother's debt on account of the whole estate jure crediti and by no means as a particular favour bestowed on her son or on me — At his present boarding school (his former one was far more expensive) my nephew costs me for absolutely necessary education, or what are called yearly fees, 900 gulden with uniform and so forth. Moreover he is being given extra lessons, which until now was not possible, i.e. when the tailors' Obervormundschaft [2] were in control; and these extras raise the sum to at least 1300 gulden V.C. — Some bills will be available, and these will make everything clearer to you than my statement —

As it is very strange that it is now almost nine months since Frau B[eethoven] drew her pension, I am convinced that this omission is connected with those Oberv[ormundschaft], who are up to the neck in plots and intrigues. So yesterday I sent a stamped form for the last half year to the cashier who, moreover, was prepared to cash it, 'but the Liquidatur [3] noticed that the mother had not yet drawn her pension and that therefore the worthy guardian's share could not be paid. So he noted on the pension form that the draft already made out was not valid '.

[1] I.e. postscript. Beethoven is referring to the postscript attached to his letter. See Letter 979, p. 854.
[2] See Letter 1008, p. 875, n. 4.
[3] The cash office.

I think therefore that we must be on our guard and that you should use without delay all legal means to secure for us that half of the pension to which I am by right entitled. I believe that the safest method would be to impound her pension which she is to receive now and in future. But do act with all haste and speed, for, as you see, we are dealing with really wicked people — ¹

(981) *To Vincenz Hauschka*

[*Autograph not traced*] ²

[VIENNA, *November,* 1819]

I have not forgotten. Such matters cannot be hurried. I will keep my word.³

BEETHOVEN

(982) *To Ferdinand Ries, London*

[*MS not traced*] ⁴

DEAR RIES !   VIENNA, *November* 10, 1819

I inform you that the sonata has already been published, but only about a fortnight ago. For it is almost six months since both works, the quintet and the sonata, were sent to you — In a few days I will send you by a courier from Vienna engraved copies of both the quintet and the sonata ; and with their help you can then make all the necessary corrections in both works.⁵

As I had had no letter from you informing me that you had received these two works, I came to the conclusion that nothing was going to be done about them ⁶ — Remember

---

¹ This letter is not signed. The outcome of these two letters was Beethoven's second, but unsuccessful, application to the Magistrat, dated October 30, 1819. See Appendix C (11).

² Taken from Seyfried, *Studien,* 1832. *Anhang,* p. 23.

³ Probably a reference to Beethoven's undertaking to write an oratorio for the Gesellschaft der Musikfreunde. Cf. Letter 903.

⁴ Taken from *WRBN.* 180.

⁵ The B♭ pianoforte sonata, Op. 106, had been published in September, 1819, and the quintet, Op. 104, in February, 1819, both by Artaria.

⁶ Cf. Letter 944, p. 809, n. 3.

that thanks to Neate I have already suffered shipwreck this year! But I now want you to make sure of obtaining the 50 ducats, because I have counted on receiving them and really need a good deal of money. Well, I will close for today and merely inform you that I have almost finished a new grand Mass.[1] Let me know what you could do with it in L[ondon], but do write soon, very soon — and send me soon the money for the two works as well —

I will shortly write to you more fully.

In haste! Your sincere good friend

BEETHOVEN

(983) *To Joseph Karl Bernard*

[*Autograph in the Beethovenhaus, Bonn, H. C. Bodmer collection*]

[VIENNA, *middle of November*, 1819]

MOST EXCELLENT BERNARDUS NON SANCTUS,

One agrees or does one agree? —

I am returning herewith the written statement.[2] I think it is excellent. What I have added you may perhaps not pay any attention to. That is up to you. For in this case I cannot say 'Anche io sono pittore'[3] — But now I do most earnestly entreat you to have it copied, whether on a stamped sheet of paper or not, and on what kind of paper, I don't know. You must ask someone in the State Chancellery about this. It never occurred to me to do so, or I could have asked our Cardinal yesterday — His Eminence who, by the way, wanted to deliver the document immediately and in person,[4] — laughed heartily when I told him that the very person against whom the petition was really directed had been invited to protest against it. To this point, I consider, you might give

---

[1] The 'Missa Solemnis', Op. 123, was not finished until the late spring of 1823. In all likelihood Beethoven began to compose this work in 1819.

[2] Very probably Beethoven's application to the Court of Appeal, dated January 7, 1820. See Appendix C (14).

[3] 'I too am a painter', a remark erroneously attributed to Correggio who, according to Padre Sebastiano Resta, expressed himself in this fashion on first seeing works by Raphael in Rome. See Julius Meyer: *Correggio* (Leipzig, 1871), p. 23. The present editor is indebted to Mr. Cecil Gould for the additional information that the first published source for this story invented by Resta is Roger de Piles: *Abrégé de la vie des peintres*, 1699, p. 190.

[4] The words from 'who' to 'person' are added at the foot of the page.

857

even greater prominence. Likewise the worthy curator could be given another dig on the lines that the Landrechte have so little trust in him that I have had another man attached to me, namely Dr. Adlersburg, who enjoys the confidence of the Landrechte — And now go on living in does one agree and one agrees until nothing but agree agree agree agree one one etc. etc. can be heard [1] — As for the library, I hope soon, that is to say, in a short time, to be able to contribute something — A beginning has been made —

Your
BEETHOVEN

(984) *To Joseph von Henikstein* [2]

[*Autograph in the New York Public Library*]

VIENNA, *December* 1, 1819

I presume that you will forgive my importunity; and I also hope that my confidence in you will not offend you — At this very moment I have to face my greatest and heaviest expenses; and I have not yet received several payments which have been guaranteed to me. Certain factors and considerations do not allow me to have recourse to some means which I still have at my disposal —

There is no lack of security, if you should still intend to be so kind as to assist me in this temporary embarrassment — Herr v[on] Oliva will explain everything to you; and I hope that you will not refuse me this favour which from your point of view, it is true, must seem rather strange [3] — For my part I will prove to you most readily, in whatever way my small powers are equal to the task, how welcome to me your desires will be.

I am, Sir, your most devoted servant —

LUDWIG VAN BEETHOVEN

[1] Beethoven is ridiculing the official language of the document.

[2] Joseph, Ritter von Henikstein (1768–1838) was the eldest of three brothers who were wholesale merchants. He was a member of the Gesellschaft der Musik-freunde, had a good bass voice, and played the cello and the mandoline.

[3] This request for financial assistance is discussed with Oliva in a Conversation Book for November and December, 1819. See Schünemann I, pp. 104-105.

(985) *To the Archduke Rudolph*

[*Autograph in the Gesellschaft der Musikfreunde, Vienna*]

YOUR IMPERIAL HIGHNESS! VIENNA, *December* 19, 1819
Immediately after my last visit to Y.I.H. I began to feel ill. I informed Y.I.H. of this, but, as a change was taking place in my household arrangements, Y.I.H. received neither this letter nor another one in which I craved Your Supreme Highness's indulgence. For I had to press on quickly with some work, which meant that unfortunately the Mass too had to be set aside — Y.I.H. must ascribe all this to the pressure of circumstances. This is not a suitable time to explain everything. But as soon as I consider that the right moment has arrived, I shall have to do so, lest Y.I.H. should pass an undeservedly hard sentence upon me — My heart is always with Y.I.H. and indeed I hope that in the end circumstances will change to such an extent that I shall be able to contribute very much more than hitherto to the perfecting of your great talent. I think that Y.I.H. has already perceived my good intentions at any rate and will certainly be convinced that only insuperable obstacles can separate me from my most beloved and most amiable Prince, who has completely won my heart — It was only yesterday that I heard of the mistake about the two letters. I am delivering this one myself, as I have no trustworthy person in my service — I will call at half past four this afternoon — My perpetual gratitude for Y.I.H.'s charming letter to me. When Y.I.H. expresses your *regard* for me, this can but increase and intensify my love of all that is good —
I kiss Y.I.H.'s hands and remain Y.I. Highness's faithful and most obedient servant

L. v. BEETHOVEN

(986) *To the Countess Anna Marie Erdödy*

[*Autograph not traced*] [1]

VIENNA, *December* 19, 1819
Best wishes for all that is good and beautiful to my dear
beloved friend, who is precious to me,
from her true friend and admirer
L. v. BEETHOVEN
In haste, on December 19, 1819.
I will soon come myself.

(987) *To [Sigmund Anton Steiner?]*

[*Autograph in the Deutsche Staatsbibliothek, Berlin*]

[VIENNA, 1819]
Please send to Herr Artaria & Co. for six copies of the
sonata in B♭ and the var[iations] on Scottish songs.[3]

(988) *To the Archduke Rudolph*

[*Autograph in the Gesellschaft der Musikfreunde, Vienna*]

YOUR IMPERIAL HIGHNESS!   [VIENNA, 1819]
Owing to certain legal proceedings in connexion with
my nephew and because I am unable to alter the hour already
fixed for this purpose, I must unfortunately forgo the pleasure
of waiting upon Y.I.H. this evening. But tomorrow I shall
not fail to be with Y.I.H. at half past four — In view of the

---

[1] From a copy in the Stadtbibliothek, Vienna, and from Schöne, no. 4, where,
however, the musical phrase is slightly different.

[2] On December 31, 1819, Beethoven sent to the Countess Erdödy the three-part
canon 'Glück, Glück zum neuen Jahr' (WoO 176), the opening notes of which
resemble those of this phrase. See *KHV.* 681.

[3] Both these works, Op. 106 and Op. 105, were published by Artaria in
September, 1819. Beethoven's receipt sent to Artaria for the fee of fifty ducats
paid for Op. 105, is dated June 8, 1819.

nature of this affair I know that you will be indulgent to me. May Heaven put an end to it once and for all, for my heart is suffering bitterly and cruelly.

Your Imperial Highness's
most faithful and most obedient servant
L. v. BEETHOVEN

(989) *To Karl van Beethoven*

[*Autograph in the New York Public Library*]

DEAR K[ARL],   [VIENNA, 1819]
I cannot see you today, as I have so much to do — I lost my wallet yesterday evening. Fortunately there was not very much in it. But I am in a difficulty today, because it was the only money I had. So I should like you most politely to request H[err] v[on] Blöchlinger to lend me ten gulden V.C. just for today. Tomorrow morning I shall be able to draw some of my own money and will immediately refund this sum with thanks —

Your faithful father

(990) *To Joseph Karl Bernard*

[*Autograph in the Beethovenhaus, Bonn, H. C. Bodmer collection*]

[VIENNA, 1819]
I have forgotten whether the Director of the L.I.[1] wanted to know only the *number of sheets* or whether he asked to see the score as well? — And what is the name of that man? Please do not come tomorrow, for it is impossible for me to fit in a visit from you. But on *Sunday*, if you are not invited to some better place, do give me the pleasure of dining with us —

Your friend
BEETHOVEN

[1] Possibly Lithographisches Institut, as suggested by Max Unger in his catalogue of Dr. H. C. Bodmer's collection of Beethoveniana (Zürich, 1939), p. 10.

(991) *To Joseph Karl Bernard*

[*Autograph in the Beethovenhaus, Bonn, H. C. Bodmer collection*] ¹

DEAR FRIEND!   [VIENNA, 1819]
    This is just to inform you that it was all a false rumour
about Karl's staying out at night. But this gossip will make
him careful. For he now sees how thoughtless behaviour can
give rise to malicious and even mendacious talk — I have no
paper, so I must be brief — I am still hoping for the best —
silence is necessary — You can announce me, I shall be received
with courtesy, and, moreover, I will not ask any questions —
                                        In great haste, your
                                                        BEETHOV

(992) *To [Johann Baptist Bach?]*

[*Autograph in the Stadtbibliothek, Vienna*]

                                                    [VIENNA, 1819]
    Forgive me, but do act, as far as possible, with energy
and speed. When dealing with such people a man of honour
can only use *force* — In haste.
                    With kindest regards, your most devoted
                                                        BEETHOVEN

    By the way, perhaps it may also be necessary to obtain
orders from superior officials to prevent his removal by force.
    NB. I will send you Frau B[eethoven]'s address this very
day. She no longer owns a house, so we can only refund
ourselves with some of her pension.
    In this case it must be a question of veni, vidi, vinci.²

    ¹ This note is written in pencil. The last two letters of the signature are
missing.
    ² This sentence is written on the verso of the autograph. The letter, which
bears no address, was probably intended for J. B. Bach. Beethoven frequently
misquoted familiar sayings, such as the one in this sentence. Cf. Letter 651, p. 593,
n. 8.

(993) *To the Archduke Rudolph*

[*Autograph in the Gesellschaft der Musikfreunde, Vienna*]

YOUR IMPERIAL HIGHNESS!   [VIENNA, 1819]

I have the honour to send you herewith by the copyist
Schlemmer Y.I.H.'s masterly variations. I myself will call
on Y.I.H. tomorrow and I already look forward to being able
to serve my eminent pupil as his companion in a glorious
undertaking —

> Your Imperial Highness's
> most humble and most faithful
>   L. v. BEETHOVEN

(994) *To Willibrord Joseph Mähler*

[*Autograph in the possession of Ferdinand de Goldschmidt-Rothschild*]

DEAR MÄHLER!   [VIENNA, 1819]

You will think me a wind-bag. But it is merely owing to
forgetfulness that you have not yet received these trifles from
me. I will see you as soon as I can do so. My best regards
to my relations.[1]

> Your friend
>   BEETHOVEN

(995) *To the Archduke Rudolph*

[*Autograph in the Gesellschaft der Musikfreunde, Vienna*]

YOUR IMPERIAL HIGHNESS!   [VIENNA, 1819]

Unfortunately I have only myself to blame. I went out
yesterday for the first time and seemed to be fairly well. But
I was only convalescent and I forgot, or was not careful, to
return home early; and so I have had to cope with another
attack. I think, however, that if I stay at home today, I shall
again be in good health tomorrow; and I certainly hope to

---

[1] Possibly Mähler was going to Krems where Johann van Beethoven had
recently bought an estate at Gneixendorf in the vicinity. If so, this note must have
been written after July, 1819.

be able to wait upon my most revered and illustrious pupil —
I beg Y.I.H. not to forget Handel's works, since these will
certainly always afford the most excellent food for your highly
developed musical soul which, moreover, is bound ever to
overflow with admiration for that great man.

> Your Imperial Highness's
> faithful and most obedient servant
> LUDWIG VAN BEETHOVEN

(996) *To the Archduke Rudolph*

[Autograph in the Gesellschaft der Musikfreunde, Vienna]

YOUR IMPERIAL HIGHNESS!   [VIENNA, 1819]

All this while I have been a semi-invalid, but I have
been carrying on as well as I can — I am desperately sorry
to hear of Y.I.H.'s attack, the more so as I knew nothing
whatever about it.   If I had, I would certainly have hastened
to you to enquire for you in person and to ask whether I could
not, by some means, alleviate to a certain extent your sufferings — Since Y.I.H. desires it, I will certainly visit tomorrow
my dearest, my one and only and most gracious lord!! —

> Y.I.H.'s
> faithful and most obedient
> L. V. BEETHOVEN

(997) *To the Archduke Rudolph*

[Autograph in the Gesellschaft der Musikfreunde, Vienna]

YOUR IMPERIAL HIGHNESS!   [VIENNA, 1819]

Most profoundly do I regret that I am unable to wait
upon you today, not only on account of the bad weather
which increases the catarrh from which I am suffering, but
also because I am very much rushed with composing something which must be sent off by a certain *opportunity* — I shall
wait upon Y.I.H. most certainly tomorrow and, what is more,
I suggest *about five o'clock in the afternoon*, since Y.I.H. yourself,
so far as I can see, is always busy.   I shall be delighted to
spend a few hours with Y.I.H.   If Y.I.H. approves, please
have a message sent out direct to the bearer of this note — I

BEETHOVEN

from the lithograph by Joseph Kriehuber after the oil portrait by Joseph Stieler (1819/20)

(*Historisches Museum der Stadt Wien*)

hope that this dull sky will become more cheerful at last and our souls and bodies too.

Your Imperial Highness's
faithful and most obedient servant
BEETHOVEN

(998) *To Tobias Haslinger*

[Autograph in the Beethovenhaus, Bonn, H. C. Bodmer collection]

[VIENNA, 1819]

For the Adjutant's Office —
The non-commissioned officer [1] is to be instructed to appear in the Landstrasse at the Goldene Sonne on the second floor with a suitable body of men [2] tomorrow at half past nine, I repeat, at half past nine, I again repeat, *half an hour* after nine o'clock.

Volti subito.[3]

(999) *To Joseph Stieler* [4]

[Autograph in the Beethovenhaus, Bonn] [5]

MY VERY DEAR STIELER!　　　　　　　　[VIENNA, 1819] [6]
　　It is impossible for me to come to you today. But I shall be with you tomorrow at eleven o'clock precisely — I know that you will forgive me —
　　In haste. With kindest regards, your most devoted

BEETHOVEN

[1] Possibly Diabelli or some other employee of Steiner's firm.
[2] Beethoven means 'an adequate sum of money'.
[3] I.e. P.T.O. The letter, which is written in a bold, clear hand, is not signed.
[4] Joseph Stieler (1781–1858) in his day was a celebrated portrait-painter, who lived at Munich. In 1816 he came to Vienna where he stayed until 1820. See *FRBS.* I, 88–99 and Frimmel, *Beethoven im zeitgenössischen Bildnis*, 1923, pp. 41–45.
[5] The note is written in pencil.
[6] The date suggested in another handwriting on the autograph is 1817–1818, but Stieler's autograph endorsement on the back of the portrait is 1819. See illustration facing page 864.

(1000) *To [Sigmund Anton Steiner ?]*

[Autograph in the Stadtbibliothek, Vienna] [1]

[VIENNA, 1819]

It is right and proper that you should notify the composer, as you are now doing, when the works are to appear *for certain* ; and you must not publish anything without first having obtained his veto. But when people who don't understand enough about this dare to say that no more proof-reading is necessary, the composer cannot then use the big stick. For that is the official right of the beadle —

(1001) *To Nikolaus Zmeskall von Domanovecz*

[Autograph in the Beethovenhaus, Bonn, H. C. Bodmer collection]

[VIENNA, 1819] [2]

I cannot [be responsible] either for the good fortune (if the *painter* considers it so) to have drawn me, or for the misfortune to have *made a bad drawing* of me [3] — But as he attaches so much importance to *my face*, which is really not so very significant, then *in God's name* I will sit for him, although I regard sitting as a kind of penance — Well, so be it — But why you should attach so much importance to my doing this, I can hardly understand and, what is more, refuse to understand —

Vale Domanovetz
BEETHOVEN

Good God! How pestered one
is when one has such a wretched
face as I have.

---

[1] The autograph has neither a signature, nor a date, nor the name of the addressee.

[2] It is impossible to establish even an approximate date for this letter. The signature is in German script, a fact which might point to an earlier year than 1819. Frimmel (see *FRBS.* I, 79-81) suggests 1818, the year in which Klöber did his portrait of Beethoven.

[3] Here Beethoven is playing on the verbs 'zeichnen' and 'verzeichnen'. The words in square brackets have been added by the present editor.

(1002) *To Artaria & Co.*

[Autograph in the Stadtbibliothek, Vienna]

[VIENNA, 1819]

Most respectfully do I request you to send to Professor von Weissenbach by the bearer of this note the two copies of the sonata in B♭ and the two sets of variations ¹ which I marked for him at your firm.

Your most devoted
BEETHOVEN

(1003) *To Artaria & Co.*

[Autograph in the University Library, Bonn]

MESSIEURS!   [VIENNA, 1819]

Be so kind as to send me four copies of the sonata in B♭ and three to five copies of each of the sets of variations ² — As for the publication of His Imperial and Royal Highness's composition, well, that is not my fault.³ The next work, however, is intended for you, if you behave properly!!! (signum exclamationis).⁴ The devil take you, God protect you —

your
L. v. BEETHOVEN
who is ready to serve you, etc. etc. etc.

¹ Op. 106 and, possibly, two of the early sets of pianoforte variations published by Artaria, such as WoO 71 and WoO 73; or Beethoven may be referring to the two volumes of Op. 105, published by Artaria in September, 1819.

² Op. 106 and 105. Beethoven means each of the two volumes of variations published by Artaria in September, 1819, as Op. 105. See *KHV*. 290.

³ Evidently a reference to the publication of the Archduke Rudolph's forty variations for pianoforte solo on Beethoven's theme 'O Hoffnung' (WoO 200), which Artaria had offered to undertake. Steiner published this work in December, 1819. See *KHV*. 701.   ⁴ I.e. exclamation mark.

1820

1820

(1004) *To [Johann Baptist Bach ?]* [1]

[*Autograph not traced*] [2]

[VIENNA, *January*, 1820]

You see what the result has been. So please be so kind as to find out there whether they are expecting *us today* at five o'clock in the afternoon, for I cannot present myself unaccompanied and, moreover, you yourself have full knowledge of all the circumstances ; or, even better, *on Monday* at five o'clock, since they would like to give you a brief account of everything — If this note doesn't find you at home, then it will doubtless find you at your office. Let me know the result, whether it is to be today or *Monday* aftern[oon].

Let me know this afternoon whether I am to send a message again to your office ? —

(1005) *To Peter Joseph Simrock, Bonn*

[*Autograph not traced*] [3]

DEAR SIMROCK ! VIENNA, *February* 10, 1820

As I have been very busy, only now can I reply to your last letter to me. I have not received from you anything about a plan for the publication of my collected works. Please let me have it very soon, for I have already had several communications about this, which, however, do not seem to me to be practicable in the long run. Such an undertaking could certainly be carried out most satisfactorily by your firm — You want to have some of my compositions. So I am letting you have particulars of what I could probably give you and

---

[1] According to Sonneck, pp. 2-6, this letter is neither signed nor dated nor addressed. But on internal evidence it was probably directed to some legal adviser such as J. B. Bach or Dr. Adlersburg.

[2] Taken from the facsimile in Sonneck, p. 2. The autograph was then in private ownership.

[3] Taken from Schmidt, pp. 22-24. According to Schmidt, p. 24, the autograph of this letter was given to Brahms in June, 1876, by F. Simrock of the Berlin firm. Brahms himself made a copy of it which he gave to Simrock.

am quoting the fee at the same time. You know in any case that I don't charge you more than anyone else — For instance, 25 Scottish songs with English words and with accompaniments for piano, violin and violoncello (both the latter ad libitum).[1] Among these airs or songs there is a duet; and four of them have choruses. Perhaps you could publish them in both languages, English and German — Moreover they are easy, all of them are provided with ritornellos at the beginning and the end and occasionally in the middle, and they might be useful for small domestic circles — The fee is 60 gold ducats — Eight themes with variations for pianoforte and one flute ad libitum, including six themes based on Scottish songs and one Russian; the other two themes being Tyrolese songs (which are also easy) [2] — The fee is 70 gold ducats.

Grand variations on a well known German waltz — which, however, I cannot yet promise you and for which, if you want to have it, I will let you know the fee [3] —

As for the Mass, which will soon be performed, the fee is 125 louis d'or [4] — It is a big work — But I must beg you to let me have a reply about this in a few weeks at latest, for, if not, I shall be the loser, since I shall be delayed in giving the work to other publishers. If the plan for you to publish my collected works were agreed upon, then I should much prefer to give you not only those works but others also, since they would be safest in your hands — As for Karl, I have not been able to send him even to Landshut to the celebrated and worthy Professor Sailer. You may imagine how people would scream about Bonn. They would immediately turn this bonna into a mala [5] — In this connexion the Chinese and Japanese, who never let anyone leave their respective countries, have the advantage over our culture, since at any rate another

[1] Op. 108.

[2] Op. 107. Ten sets of variations on airs for pianoforte with flute or violin accompaniment *ad libitum*. Nos. 2, 4, 6, 8, 9, 10 are Scottish, nos. 3 and 7 are Russian and nos. 1 and 5 are Tyrolese. Simrock published these in August/September, 1820. When Beethoven offered them he had only composed eight. Nos. 6 (Scottish) and 7 (Russian) were added later to make ten. See *KHV.* 297-299.

[3] Op. 120. This appears to be Beethoven's first reference to his composition of the Diabelli variations, which were dedicated to Antonia Brentano and published by Cappi & Diabelli in June, 1823. See *KHV.* 348-352.

[4] Beethoven's 'Missa Solemnis' was not finished until the spring of 1823. See *KHV.* 359-366.

[5] I.e. good into evil.

religion, another language and other customs might offend them. But what is one to say about being prevented from leaving one province to go to another where the religion and everything are *exactly the same or, if not, perhaps even better*?!!! My most gracious Lord, the Archbishop and Cardinal, has not yet got enough money to pay his chief Kapellmeister what is right and proper; and this state of affairs will probably last for some time yet — Therefore one must earn one's bread elsewhere. Bearing this in mind and remembering that, as has so frequently happened, I have allowed my arable field to lie fallow, I again request you to send me replies to all my questions Presto or, rather, Prestissimo, so that I may press on with my task in the right way — You need add no further address than the name of your friend. I receive all my letters in that way.

BEETHOVEN

(1006) *To Johann Baptist Bach*

[Autograph in the Beethovenhaus, Bonn, H. C. Bodmer collection]

SIR !   [VIENNA, *before February* 18, 1820]
    In a few days you will receive from me a written state-
ment containing information about Frau B[eethoven] —

	about the behaviour of the Magistrat
„	about the certificates
„	about what I have done for my nephew
„	about his property [1] —

Will you please have this document copied so that it can be forwarded to Herr von Schmerling [2] and Herr von Winter [3] — It is of no little interest to learn how people in Vienna can treat a man who only wants to do what is right, and at the same time can disregard the welfare of an innocent creature. —

---

[1] This is Beethoven's famous Denkschrift (memorandum), dated February 18, 1820. For a translation of this document see Appendix C (15).
[2] Probably Joseph von Schmerling, who was an Appellationsrat (Councillor of Appeal).
[3] See Letter 1010, p. 877, n. 1.

Has the report of the Magistrat already reached the Court of Appeal? Now let us deal with something else. I am told that in the suburb where I am living one must give notice by the 16th of this month to quit an apartment one has occupied since February 2nd, the Feast of the Purification or Candlemas.

Please send me just a few lines of information about this. In any case I am going to spend the whole summer in the country and require at most a room as a pied-à-terre in town.[1] And whatever happens I do not intend to keep on this apartment next year.[2] You surely realize how much I dislike troubling you. I hope, therefore, that you will forgive me for putting this question to you? — I am frequently unwell, or I would have called on you before now —

M[atthias] v. Tuscher has been to see me. An old friendship cannot be ignored. He has acted weakly, I admit. But under authorities of that type only a *guardian like myself, who provides the money*, can have the casting vote. If you want to speak to him, he could give you some information about many other points. He has now recovered his health. You will find him in his bureau, or *boureau*,[3] any morning between ten and twelve o'clock —

In haste, I remain with kind regards

BEETHOVEN

(1007) *To Joseph Karl Bernard*

[*Autograph in the Beethovenhaus, Bonn, H. C. Bodmer collection*]

DEAR BERNARD! [VIENNA, *shortly after February* 18, 1820]

When I happened to be alone again today in these surroundings which make me feel confused, only then did the right conception of my memorandum dawn upon me.[4] Without wishing to deck myself out in borrowed plumes I think

---

[1] Beethoven went to Mödling on May 1st and remained there until nearly the end of October.

[2] In October, 1820, Beethoven moved into rooms in the Landstrasse, called 'Das grosse Haus der Augustiner', no. 244.

[3] Beethoven is either poking fun at Tuscher's French pronunciation or humorously suggesting that his office atmosphere resembles that of an executioner's abode.

Cf. Letter 1006, p. 873, n. 1.

I ought to leave it entirely to you, since you can say in a few words as much as, or even more than, I can say on several sheets. Hence you may deal with everything exactly according to your own views which are sounder than mine. If you do this, the question will then be presented to the judges more forcibly and intelligibly. The only thing is that it must be finished soon. Imagine that you are acting in the interest of Karl's happiness and with the possibility of restoring my peace of mind, if *he* is to be left to me, and, what is more, that you are doing this for the *last time* — I repeat, do exactly what you like with my raw material, exactly what you think right. In any case you write more clearly than I do and the copy would soon be ready —

Your friend and admirer

BEETHOVEN

(1008) *To [Joseph Karl Bernard?]*

[*Autograph in the Beethovenhaus, Bonn, H. C. Bodmer collection*]

[VIENNA, *February,* 1820]

. . [how] could I have made a better choice for the welfare of my nephew than to accept as co-guardian Herr von Peters, who not only possesses all the requisite knowledge but will also show real devotion to and love for the good cause [1] — What better and happier choice could I possibly have made? — And yet what talk we had to listen to about fine clothes, of which Frau B[eethoven] has accused me, and on a former occasion the statements that I was supposed to be in love with Frau B[eethoven] and so forth. Is that kind of talk suitable for an Obervormundschaft or, to put it more plainly, do those people indulge in that kind of tittle-tattle? [2] At any rate it is not suitable for me, nor for Herr von Peters, nor for my [nephew],[3] though it may certainly be so for ale-house keepers, cobblers and tailors [4] —

[1] I.e. Hofrat Karl Peters. Cf. Letter 734, p. 651, n. 1.
[2] The words from 'or' to the end of the sentence are added at the foot of the page.
[3] This word has been added by the present editor. The fragmentary autograph is neither addressed nor dated nor signed.
[4] Beethoven is referring to the Magistrat (Municipal Council). Cf. Letter 980, p. 855.

875

Moreover in regard to the mother the principle had always been laid down that on account of her immoral behaviour my nephew should never visit her house — Thanks to the establishment of this principle and to her exclusion by the Landrechte from the co-guardianship it is now clear what the procedure should be in regard to the association of the son with his mother — Sapienti pauca [1] — but we have to deal with very many facts — — Appeal!! Appeal!! Appeal!!

(1009) *To* ?

[*Autograph in the Beethovenhaus, Bonn*] [2]

[VIENNA, *February*, 1820]

. . . neither housekeeper nor wife, excessively addicted to finery, so lazy and slatternly that when my poor brother happened to be in constant pain from his disease even I had to admonish her to work — Why, shortly before his death she drew 200 gulden without his knowing anything about it. Although I could never defend, still less approve, *her actions*, yet I warded off my brother's anger from her. If one remembers that any vexation endangered the life of that poor fellow, one can imagine what sort of character she has — During his last illness she tried in every possible way to conceal his serious condition from me. I knew nothing about a will having been made. But I got wind of it. If the original document is really the one I saw, then some passages must have been crossed out. I took the matter up with my brother, as I positively refused to be associated with so bad a woman in such an important question as the education of the child, or to be connected in any way with Dr. S[chönauer],[3] because I knew that she was constantly going to see him and because

---

[1] A variation of 'Sapienti sat', meaning here 'a few facts are enough for the wise'. Cf. Letter 953, p. 821, n. 1.

[2] This fragment of a letter or of a draft of a letter about Beethoven's sister-in-law Johanna may have been written before February, 1820, when the famous memorandum was completed.

[3] Dr. Schönauer was a Viennese lawyer whom Beethoven's brother Carl had appointed his executor.

he seemed to me to take *her part* too warmly — Everything relating to the guardianship was entered in the legal document exactly as I . . .

(1010) *To Karl Winter* [1]

[Autograph in the Beethovenhaus, Bonn]

SIR !   [VIENNA], *March* 6, 1820

I have the honour to inform you that I have written a memorandum consisting of information about Frau van Beethoven, about the Magistrat, about my nephew, about myself and so forth; and that I will send it to you in a few days.[2] *I thought* it was due to myself to disclose the baselessness of so many libellous statements directed *against me* and also to expose the intrigues of Frau v. Beethoven *against me* to the detriment of her own child, and, moreover, to place the behaviour of the Magistrat in its true light. You, Sir, will see from this information about the M[agistrat] that they never dealt with the matter *in a businesslike way* and that *without my knowledge* they summoned *my nephew with his mother*. According to his own assertion my nephew, *instigated and misled by his own mother*, was there compelled to make *several untrue statements about me* — Furthermore, my information will bring to light a *written document* which exposes the shifty and prejudiced behaviour of the M[agistrat] and shows how greatly they contradicted *themselves* when they nominated F[rau] v[an] B[eethoven] as a guardian. Again, my information will prove that after H[err] v[on] Tuscher whom *I myself* had selected as guardian, had resigned the guardianship, the M[agistrat] again accepted *me as the guardian*, since among other things they also invited me to choose another guardian. But I did not consider that at all advisable in view of the fact that my nephew during the period when I had resigned the guardianship, had only suffered considerable *harm*. For among several other disadvantages he was even faced with being encouraged to do so badly on purpose in his examination that he had

---

[1] Karl Winter, who died in 1827, was then an Appellationsrat (Councillor of Appeal).
[2] For a translation of Beethoven's memorandum see Appendix C (15).

to remain in the same class at that school for a whole year. What an irreparable loss! During the same period too he had a violent haemorrhage which, if I had not come to his rescue, might have almost cost him his life. H[err] v[on] Tuscher was not directly responsible, of course, for these happenings, seeing that he had far too little support from the Obervorm[undschaft] and for that reason could never act with the necessary energy with which I, for instance, as *uncle, guardian and financial supporter* could take up these matters — You, Sir, will gather from these few particulars that not much trust can be placed in the report of the M[agistrat]. Indeed one can gauge the strong support which Frau v[an] B[eethoven] found in that quarter from the fact that forthwith and *against the orders of the Supreme Landrechte*, according to which she was *excluded* from the guardianship, she was even *nominated a guardian*. The result of all this is that I must request you to take a deposition *both from myself and, if necessary, from my nephew* about certain accusations which may have been levelled against *me* — I consider, it is true, that the unnatural event of my being denied the guardianship of my nephew is hardly possible, since *from every point of view* this would only be to the disadvantage of my nephew, apart altogether from the fact that such a contingency would certainly provoke the disapproval of our civilised world. People should bear in mind that for over five years I have been the chief support of my nephew and in the most liberal way. For two years he was at a boarding school entirely at my expense; and it was only after that time that a small contribution was made, not more than a yearly sum of 450 gulden V.C. at the exchange rate of 250.

But for almost fourteen months I have received *nothing* of that contribution. Nevertheless a few accounts which I am enclosing will prove how liberally I have always provided for my nephew — Only in the event of my not being granted the guardianship with a co-guardian should I have to abandon my nephew to his fate. However much this would grieve me, yet I should then consider myself exempted from the duty *of taking any further interest in him* — But as soon as I am again accepted as the guardian with my helpful co-guardian, then I will provide for him most unselfishly and, as hitherto, bear all the expenses *in future as well* — Nay more, I have already made provision for him in the event of my death; and for this purpose there is a sum of 4000 gulden A.C. belonging to me now in the Austrian National Bank, which has been earmarked as a legacy for him. Moreover on account of my social connexions I can be very useful to him everywhere; and also my relations with His Imperial Highness the Archbishop of Olmütz entitle me to hope for several desirable favours from him, which like many other kindnesses will benefit my nephew as well — Finally, once more I urge you, Sir, to interest yourself in my nephew's weal and woe. I am placing my confidence in a man who is not only gifted but also kindhearted; and I trust that all will redound to my advantage. For nothing will ever make me believe that such a treatment as that which the M[agistrat] have ruthlessly meted out *to me, the benefactor of my late brother and the support and mainstay of my nephew for over five years,* can be sanctioned or even approved in any higher quarter —

I remain, Sir, with my deepest regards, your most devoted servant

LUDWIG VAN BEETHOVEN

My *numerous occupations* will ensure for me your *indulgence,* Sir, in respect of my rather careless handwriting [1] —

(1011) *To Peter Joseph Simrock, Bonn*

[*Autograph in the Beethovenhaus, Bonn, H. C. Bodmer collection*]

MOST EXCELLENT FELLOW! VIENNA, *March* 9, 1820

You sent me through somebody a letter in which you promised to give me information about a plan for the publication of my collected works and at the same time asked me to let you have some new works of mine. I wrote to you about this a short time ago.[2] But since our letter posts are known

[1] In a Conversation Book covering the second week of March, 1820 (see Schünemann I, pp. 325-326) there is an entry to the effect that something had been delivered to Herr Winter, who had kept the messenger, a footman of the Archduke Rudolph, waiting and had then declared that he could neither give him an answer nor enter into any correspondence. This is possibly a reference to Beethoven's memorandum. [2] Letter 1005, p. 871.

to be not of the most reliable kind, or perhaps the revolutionary upheavals in your part of the world may be causing tiresome delays in the delivery of letters in Vienna as well, I am taking this favourable opportunity of informing you briefly of the contents of the letter I sent you. — First of all, please give me particulars of your plan to publish my collected works — As to musical compositions I offer you the following: eight short works with variations on Scottish, Tyrolese and Russian themes for pianoforte and a flute ad libitum [1] for a fee of 70 gold ducats; [2] 25 Scottish songs with opening and closing ritornellos with accompaniment for pianoforte and for violin and violoncello ad libitum, for a fee of 50 gold ducats; [3] several of these songs have choruses and there are also some duets among them; a grand Mass for a fee of 125 louis d'or [4] — But please let me have a reply to all these points as quickly as possible because, if I don't hear from you, I will give these works to other people — Just send the reply to Frankfurt to the address which will be communicated to you from there.[5]

In haste, your friend
BEETHOVEN

(1012) *To Nikolaus and Peter Joseph Simrock, Bonn*

[Autograph in the Beethovenhaus, Bonn, H. C. Bodmer collection]

DEAR HERR SIMROCK! VIENNA, *March* 14, [1820]

I received your letter yesterday and am replying to it today — The eight themes with variations and also the Scottish songs *can be your property* for Germany, Italy, France, and Holland, in short, for the whole Continent [6] — Scotland and England are excluded; but the arrangement with them is on the following lines — In my contract with the English publisher I have *reserved to myself the right to publish on the Continent as well* and, what is more, *to my advantage, all the works which*

---

[1] The words from 'for' to 'libitum' are added at the foot of the page.
[2] Op. 107. In the end Beethoven added two more, making them ten.
[3] Op. 108. In Letter 1005, p. 872, Beethoven asked sixty ducats. See also Letter 1012.
[4] The 'Missa Solemnis', Op. 123.
[5] As usual, Franz Brentano at Frankfurt am Main was forwarding these letters.
[6] Op. 107 and 108. Simrock published only Op. 107.

he is receiving from me. Well now, as soon as the *English or, rather, the Scottish publisher* receives the said works from me, he is to inform me *of the date when he is going to publish them.* I shall then make my arrangements on the Continent accordingly and later fix the time for whatever publisher takes on the works. In this way the latter can bring his property to the light of day at the same time as the Scottish publisher [1] — Artaria and Steiner too have already engraved some works of mine in this way. Obviously in this transaction neither party is the loser. Indeed in the case of Steiner I have already had the experience that although he took Scottish songs from me in this way as far back as three years ago,[2] yet, because the *translator* has been so dilatory, he has *not yet* published them. Besides, he is not the slightest bit concerned about the matter ; and so far not a note of them has appeared anywhere else.[3] All that he had to do was to take the precaution of *announcing them in the newspapers* — The greatest demand for the Scottish songs is *in Scotland* itself.[4] There is not much demand for such works in England, where people are already satiated with far too many of them — In Germany, on the other hand, people seem already to be more prepossessed in their favour, because the songs by reason of their simplicity have more profound feeling than the usual songs of this type — Well, on *this occasion* I must still fix the time for your publication, since on account of my many tasks and distractions I have not been able to attend to this until now — Reckoning from the day on which you receive these two works you may have four to five months in which to publish them ; and, if necessary, I can let you have another month, that is, in all, half a year. But I should prefer the publication to be sooner. Let me know, therefore, how much time you require for your part of the work. But now I must entreat you to reply as quickly as possible, stating whether you are prepared to take these two works for the fee quoted in my first letter and also

---

[1] The words from 'as' to 'publisher' are added at the foot of the page.
[2] Twelve Scottish songs, WoO 156, seven of which were published by Thomson during Beethoven's lifetime. J. B. Rupprecht translated these songs which, however, Steiner never published. See *KHV.* 651-655.
[3] The words from 'and' to 'else' are added at the foot of the page.
[4] Some of the songs in this collection, WoO 156, were published by Thomson in 1822, 1824 and 1825. These are fully discussed in Hopkinson and Oldman, *op. cit.*

whether you are willing to accept the other conditions. For if you don't reply quickly, it will be too late for me to publish them here or elsewhere, and I shall be the loser — I have just noticed that you have already agreed to pay me a fee of 130 ducats for the two works.[1] Hence it is merely a question of agreeing to the other points about which you cannot have any scruples, inasmuch as your ownership is guaranteed to you for the whole Continent. If three or four months give you sufficient time for the publication of both these works, I can arrange this too, because for at least ten years I have been in friendly relations with the Scottish publisher and neither he nor any German publisher has suffered any loss from this method of doing business — About remitting the fee, well, you can arrange for it to be sent to Herr Franz Brentano at Frankfurt where you will also receive good copies of both works. But now, for the reasons set forth above, I await your reply *Presto or, rather, Prestissimo* — I will soon write to you about the plan for publishing my collected works, which seems to me practicable, and also about the Mass, the fee for which I will reduce as much as possible. On the whole you will never find that in this respect my demands are excessive.

Well, I can't remember whether I have written to the *father* or to the *son*. Never mind, I embrace both with all my heart.

Your friend

B<small>EETHOVEN</small>

(1013) *To Nikolaus Simrock, Bonn*

[Autograph in the Beethovenhaus, Bonn, H. C. Bodmer collection]

D<small>EAR</small> H<small>ERR</small> S<small>IMROCK</small>!   V<small>IENNA</small>, *March* 18, 1820

I am not sure whether in my last letter I expressed myself sufficiently clearly about every point — So I am sending you just a short letter to inform you that, should you find it necessary, I can certainly extend the time limit for the publication of the variations, i.e. make it longer than six months [2] — In

---

[1] I.e. seventy ducats for Op. 107, and sixty ducats for Op. 108. Cf. Letter 1005, p. 872.

[2] Op. 107, published by Simrock in September, 1820. The words from 'i.e.' to 'months' are added at the foot of the page.

regard to the Mass, I have given this question careful consideration and I could let you have it after all for the fee of 100 louis d'or which you have offered me, provided that you will perhaps agree to a few conditions which I shall propose and which, I am inclined to think, you will really *not* find unacceptable. Here we have already examined the plan for the publication and we certainly think that it can be carried out very soon, but with *certain modifications*. It is very necessary that it should be carried out very soon. So I shall hasten to suggest to you as soon as possible the necessary alterations — As I know that business men like to save postal expenses, I am adding here two Austrian folk-songs to refund you for your expenditure. You may do what you like with them. I have written the accompaniments — I am inclined to think that a hunt for folk-songs is better than a man-hunt of the heroes who are so highly extolled —

DAS LIEBE KÄTZCHEN

DER KNABE AUF DEM BERGE [1]

[1] The beginning of this second folk-song has been lost owing to the autograph having been torn.

My copyist is not here at the moment. I hope you will have no difficulty in reading them — You could have several folk-songs of this kind from me; and in exchange you might do me some other favour —

In haste, yours

BEETHOVEN

ouvres la lettre avec bien de ménagement.[1]

(1014) *To Ernst Theodor Amadeus Hoffmann, Berlin* [2]

[*Autograph in the Universitätsbibliothek, Tübingen*]

SIR!   VIENNA, *March 23, 1820*

I am taking the opportunity afforded me by Herr Neberich [3] of making myself known to such a gifted person as you are — Moreover you have written about my humble self. And our *weak Herr Starke* [4] showed me in his album some lines of yours

[1] This reminder is added on the verso in Beethoven's handwriting. The letter contained his copy of the folk-songs. See *KHV*. 665.

[2] E. T. A. Hoffmann (1776-1822), born at Königsberg, was a painter, a composer and a writer, whose short stories and newspaper articles enjoyed a great popularity in his day. Since 1810 he had been eulogizing Beethoven's compositions both in his literary and in his journalistic writings. Beethoven composed his canon, 'Hoffmann, sei ja kein Hofmann', on E. T. A. Hoffmann. See *KHV*. 684, where the canon is discussed and listed as WoO 180.

[3] Cf. Letter 619, p. 568, n. 2.

[4] Friedrich Starke (1774–1835) was an excellent musician who, during the Napoleonic wars, was the Kapellmeister of the 33rd Austrian Infantry Regiment. He gave pianoforte lessons to Beethoven's nephew until Czerny took charge of his musical education. Starke later edited a *Wiener Pianoforteschule* in which nos. 7-11 of Beethoven's 'Bagatellen' first appeared. Although no letters from Beethoven to Starke are recorded, they were close friends from 1812 until Beethoven's death, and Starke is frequently mentioned in the Conversation Books. In this sentence Beethoven is playing on the German words 'schwach' (weak) and 'stark' (strong).

about me. So I am bound to think that you must take some interest in me. Allow me to tell you that this interest on the part of a man like you who is endowed with such excellent qualities is very gratifying to me. I send you my best wishes and remain, Sir, with kindest regards, your most devoted

BEETHOVEN

(1015) *To Moritz Schlesinger, Berlin* [1]

[Autograph in the Beethovenhaus, Bonn, H. C. Bodmer collection]

SIR! VIENNA, *March 25,* 1820

I remember your visiting me at Mödling and desiring to have some of my works. If I remember rightly, you asked me to let you have smaller rather than larger compositions. Just now I am about to publish several works from which I offer you the following two, because I consider them the most suitable for you — 25 Scottish songs with pianoforte accompaniment — (violin or flute and cello — the violin or flute and cello are ad libitum). Each song is provided with opening and also closing ritornellos ; and several of them are for two or three voices and with choruses. The texts are by the best English poets. These could with advantage be translated into German and published with both English and German texts [2] — Eight themes (including Scottish, *Russian* and Tyrolese) for pianoforte with variations, each of which forms a little work in itself, with a flute ad libitum.[3] For the 25 Scottish songs I am quoting you a fee of 60 gold ducats, and for the eight themes with *easy* variations for pianoforte and a flute ad libitum a fee of 70 gold ducats.

I cannot agree to any reduction in these fees — You will have these works as your property for the whole Continent;

---

[1] Moritz Adolf Schlesinger (1798–1871), eldest son of the Berlin music publisher Adolf Martin Schlesinger (see Letter 1021, p. 891, n. 1), opened his own publishing house in Paris in July, 1821. He had visited Beethoven at Mödling in the summer of 1819. For an excellent account of the Schlesinger family of music publishers and of their association with Beethoven see Max Unger, *Ludwig van Beethoven und seine Verleger*, 1921, pp. 24-40. The above letter is the first extant one to the Schlesinger firm.

[2] Op. 108. The German edition of this work was published by A. M. Schlesinger of Berlin in July, 1822.

[3] Op. 107. Simrock published this collection in September, 1820.

England and Scotland are excluded.   But an arrangement
has been made whereby I am to refrain from publishing these
works in those two countries until I know when you are publishing them on the Continent —
This time I should like to see some speed in the procedure
of publishing the aforesaid works.   I request you, therefore,
to acquaint me quickly with your views on this subject.[1]   For
if you don't, I shall be wasting my time — Awaiting a very
early reply I remain your most devoted

BEETHOVEN

NB.   It is not necessary for you to put any other address
than 'To Ludwig van Beethoven in Vienna'.

(1016) *To the Archduke Rudolph, Olmütz*

[Autograph in the Gesellschaft der Musikfreunde, Vienna]

YOUR IMPERIAL HIGHNESS!   VIENNA, *April* 3, 1820
So far as I remember, when I wanted to wait upon you
I was informed that Your Highness was indisposed.   But I
went on Sunday evening to enquire, because I had been assured
that Y.I.H. would not leave on Monday.   In accordance with
my habit of not waiting about for long in the antechamber, I
hurried off quickly after receiving this information, although
I noticed that the footman wanted to say something more.   I
was distressed to hear on Monday afternoon that Y.I.H. had
really gone off to Olmütz.[2]   I admit that this news produced
in me an extremely painful emotion.   But my conviction that
I had not done anything wrong soon persuaded me that just
as such incidents frequently occur in similar moments of our
mortal life, here was another instance of the same phenomenon.
I fully understood that Y.I.H., who was excessively overwhelmed
by ceremonies and by your many new experiences, would not
have much time at O[lmütz] for anything else.   Otherwise
I would certainly have hastened to anticipate Y.I.H. in the

---

[1] According to a note on the autograph a reply was sent to Beethoven on
April 11th.
[2] In 1820 April 3rd fell on a Monday.

matter of writing — But now I should like Y.I.H. kindly to inform me how long you have arranged to stay at O[lmütz]. I was told here that Y.I.H. would return to Vienna about the end of May. A few days ago, however, I heard that Your Highness would remain at O[lmütz] *for a year and a half*. On that account perhaps I have already taken the wrong steps, *not in respect of Y.I.H.*, however, but in respect of myself. But as soon as I receive some information on this point, I shall explain everything more fully. By the way, I do beg Y.I.H. to pay no attention to some reports about me. I have already heard in Vienna several remarks, which one might describe as gossip, with which people fancy that they can be of service even to Y.I.H. Since Y.I.H. calls me one of your precious possessions, then I can say with confidence that Y.I.H. is to me one of the most precious objects in the whole world. Even though I am no *courtier*, yet I think that Y.I.H. has got to know *this much about me*, that it is no mere frigid interest that attaches me to you, but a true and deep affection which has always bound me to Your Highness and has ever inspired me ; and I might say in truth that Blondel has been found long ago and that if there is no Richard for me in this world, then God will be my Richard — It seems that my idea of forming a quartet will certainly be the very thing. Even if similar arrangements are generally made at O[lmütz] on a large scale, yet by means of your quartet wonderful things might be achieved for music in Moravia — If, as the above reports declare, Y.I.H. is to return to Vienna in May, I advise you to save up your spiritual children until then, because it would be better if I were first to hear them performed by yourself. But should your stay at Olmütz be really so prolonged, I shall be extremely delighted to receive them and I shall endeavour to guide Y.I.H. to the highest peak of Parnassus.

God keep Y.I.H. in perfect health for the benefit of humanity and, especially, of those who admire you ; and I beg you to be so kind as to delight me soon again with a letter. At any rate Your Highness is convinced of my readiness to comply at all times with your wishes.

    Your Imperial Highness's
       faithful and most obedient servant
                          L. v. BEETHOVEN

(1017) *To Carlo Boldrini* [1]

[Autograph in the Beethovenhaus, Bonn, H. C. Bodmer collection]

MOST EXCELLENT FALSTAFF! [2]   [VIENNA, *April* 8, 1820]

Most respectfully do I request you to send me a copy *of each of the two works for pianoforte and flute with variations* [3] — As for the receipt, you will receive that tomorrow. So I do beg you to dispatch them with all due speed — Give my compliments to Herr Artaria and thank him also for having been so kind and obliging about advancing money to me. But I have already received the sums due to me from abroad and therefore do not require any money at the moment — All good wishes, Sir Falstaff, do not be too dissolute; but read the Gospel and be converted — Let me add that we are most sincerely attached to you —

BEETHOVEN

(1018) *To Karl Pinterics* [4]

[Autograph in the Beethovenhaus, Bonn, H. C. Bodmer collection]

[VIENNA, *shortly after April* 8, 1820]

DEAR HERR VON PINTERICS!

I inform you that the Civil Senate have been instructed by the Supreme Court of Appeal to acquaint me with its decision, which gives me full satisfaction [5] — Dr. Bach acted

[1] Carlo Boldrini, who was employed in the music publishing firm of Artaria from 1807, was a partner from 1811 until about 1824, when he seems to have left it. He is supposed to have died in 1850.

[2] The address on the verso in Beethoven's handwriting is:
'An Ritter John Falstaff,
        abzugeben bei H. Artaria
    et Compagnie'.
Like Schuppanzigh, whom Beethoven also called Falstaff, Boldrini was uncommonly stout.

[3] Op. 105, published by Artaria in September, 1819. Beethoven obviously means a copy of each of the two volumes of this work. Each volume contained three sets of variations.

[4] Karl Pinterics was private secretary to Count Ferdinand Pálffy. He had a good bass voice, was a competent pianist and collected engravings. He was also closely connected with the Schubert group. He died in 1831.

[5] Beethoven had been informed of the decision in his favour reached by the Court of Appeal on April 8, 1820.

for me in this affair; and this *brook* [1] was joined by the sea with thunder, lightning and tempest. Hence the brigantine of the Magistrat had to suffer there a complete shipwreck —

Your most devoted

BEETHOVEN

(1019) *To Nikolaus Simrock, Bonn*

[*Autograph in the Beethovenhaus, Bonn, H. C. Bodmer collection*]

MY DEAR HERR SIMROCK! VIENNA, *April* 23, 1820

I sent off the variations to Herr Brentano at Frankfurt on April 22nd and am now waiting to receive from him the fee of 70 ducats for this work [2] — I sent you two more themes with variations; so you now have ten sets and can thus exchange one theme or any other, which may not perhaps please you or seem to suit your purpose, for one of the extra ones. [3] By the way, I am not asking anything more for them, since I have composed many of these trifles; and if you want to engrave the two extra ones, I have no objection either and shall not accept any extra fee for them — Later on you can do me a favour in some other way — You have four or even five months in which to publish them, and perhaps even longer; I shall not fail to make enquiries about that — I had many corrections to make, for my usual copyist happened to have too much to do for our Court; and the one I employed for the var[iations] was not sufficiently familiar with my handwriting which *frequently* produces only very sketchy 𝅘𝅥𝅮𝅘𝅥𝅮𝅘𝅥𝅮𝅘𝅥𝅮𝅘𝅥𝅮𝅘𝅥𝅮 *etc.*, and these might hardly be described even as *little notes*. The ordinary copyists are mostly *needy people* and much prefer fine juicy *notes* with which they can get along more quickly [4] —

I will send you something about the Austrian dialect, which will explain it; [5] and, by the way, if you would like to have them, I will send you several songs of the same kind

---

[1] Beethoven is playing on the word 'Bach', which means 'brook'.
[2] Op. 107.
[3] Beethoven added to the original eight sets two more, nos. 6 and 7, a Scottish air and a Russian one.
[4] Here Beethoven is playing on the words 'Not' (need) and 'Note' (note).
[5] The words from 'which' to 'it' are added at the foot of the page.

with accompaniments. They are just suitable now and then *for the multitude.*[1] But for these I will ask you to send me something different, for instance, a loaf of *black rye bread* — You have engraved many scores, I fancy. If only I knew which ? Then I would ask you to send me some for my nephew. — I have also enclosed the mail coach receipt for the ten sets of variations, which have been dispatched, to Herr Franz Brentano in a letter I wrote to him today [2] — You will receive the Mass by the end of May or the beginning of June.[3] So please remit the 100 louis d'or to Herr F[ranz] Brentano, to whom I will send the work.

In haste, your friend
BEETHOVEN

This is Ecossais and not Italienne

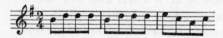

as is stated in the manuscript.[4]

(1020) *To Johann Speer, Mödling* [5]

[Autograph in the Beethovenhaus, Bonn, H. C. Bodmer collection]

SIR !   VIENNA, *April* 26, 1820

I inform you that I shall arrive at Mödling at the end of April or on May 1st at latest, and I request you to be so kind as to have the rooms thoroughly dusted and scrubbed, so that everything shall be clean and quite dry as well. Please do not forget to have the balcony made right. For that work I shall pay you immediately on my arrival the extra 12 gulden V.C.

---

[1] Evidently more Austrian folk-songs. Cf. Letter 1013, pp. 883-884.
[2] This letter has not been traced.
[3] The words from 'or' to 'June' are added at the foot of the page.
[4] This reminder is written on the verso. It refers to no. 3 of Op. 107, the autograph of which (no. 3) has disappeared : actually it is a Russian air and correctly described as such in *GA* 14/116, although *NV* describes it as 'Air de la petite suisse'. See *KHV.* 298.
[5] The address on the verso in Beethoven's handwriting is :

Für Johann Speer
in Mödling, No. 116

which I promised to give you as well as the rent we arranged —
With best wishes for everything that is good and pleasant,
I remain your most devoted
BEETHOVEN

(1021) *To Adolf Martin Schlesinger, Berlin* ¹

[*MS not traced*] ²

VIENNA, *April* 30, 1820

P.P.

I have very little time at my disposal — So I have the
honour to inform you that when your letter of April 11th
arrived, the Scottish themes with variations had already been
given away — The publisher who took them made no difficulties about doing so.³ But in order to show you that I value
my connexion with you, I am giving you the following elucidations of the points to which you object —

You will see from the following song which I am sending
you that the text is English and not old Scottish. All the
songs have violin and violoncello accompaniment to the
pianoforte part — The former are for two voices ad libitum.
Most of these songs are for one voice, but several are duets,
others trios, others with choruses. There are 25 in all ⁴ — They
are quite easy compositions and therefore eminently suitable
for performance in small circles of music-lovers — According
to my arrangements with English publishers I am entitled to
sell for the whole Continent, but only after a fixed date, the
works I send off to England ; and, what is more, they may be

¹ Adolf Martin Schlesinger (1769–1839) began his career in 1795 as a book-
seller in Berlin. In 1810 he established his music publishing firm which after his
death was carried on by his third son Heinrich (1807–1879), who owned it from 1844
until 1865. He also founded in 1824 the *Berliner Allgemeine Musikalische Zeitung*
which under its first editor, A. B. Marx, became a very influential organ. During
the previous year the firm had been moved to fine premises in Unter den Linden.
Schlesinger's eldest son, Moritz (Maurice), established his own publishing firm in
Paris in 1821. Cf. Letter 1015, p. 885, n. 1. During Beethoven's lifetime A. M.
Schlesinger published Op. 108, 109, 110, 111, 132, 135 and WoO 18.
² Taken from Unger, no. 105. The letter was written in another hand and
signed by Beethoven.
³ Op. 107, published by Simrock.
⁴ Op. 108. A. M. Schlesinger published the first German edition in July, 1822.

published by another publisher on the Continent before they appear in England — I have the same agreement about the 25 songs I have offered you — Indeed many years ago I sold a similar collection, which chiefly on account of the many obstacles raised by the publisher has never appeared, and of which as yet not a single copy of the foreign printed version has reached us [1] — Well, you will see from all this that there is no cause for your anxiety — Besides, these songs are old Scottish melodies, which no doubt will be sold out only in Scotland, and for which you can therefore hope for a good sale perhaps in England as well — Why I have to be so long-winded with you is because this kind of business arrangement is still new to you. For in Vienna and in all the rest of Germany people know about my foreign arrangements and every publisher complies with them. So much for your right of ownership. — As to the translation, I cannot believe that in Berlin you haven't several linguists who know English and even the old Scottish tongue. In fact I feel sure you have more than we have here — Still, if you really wish to have the translation undertaken here, then in order to do you a favour, I will provide you with an efficient translator, who has already greatly distinguished himself in similar work and who is quick and not too expensive [2] — I fancy that the whole work could be done for 15 ducats — a sum which you could refund to me when you are sending me my fee —

Well, if after all I have said you are prepared to take this work, be so kind as to write to me about it by *return of post* — In accordance with your proposal you could send me the fee payable at sight in Vienna — and I would then send off to you immediately a correct copy of the songs with English texts, merely in order not to hold up your work of producing the edition — If you want to have the translation, it will follow very soon and will fit the music perfectly —

I am fixing the time-limit for publication at three or four

[1] No doubt Beethoven is referring to the twelve English songs mentioned in his draft contract with S. A. Steiner of April 19, 1815. See Appendix F (6). This collection, WoO 157, was published by Peters in 1860. During Beethoven's lifetime Thomson published six of these songs, in 1816, 1822 and 1824/25.

[2] Probably Beethoven had J. B. Rupprecht in mind. But in the end Schlesinger commissioned Dr. S. H. Spiker (1786–1858), the Librarian of the Royal Library, Berlin, to do the translations of Op. 108. His name also appeared on the title-page of the second edition.

months from now, by the end of which period you should easily manage to have the work ready [1] —

Furthermore, I will gladly let you have new sonatas — but not at a lower price than 40 ducats each. Hence a work consisting of three sonatas would cost 120 ducats — Moreover we might perhaps undertake several works, even greater ones, perhaps trios or quartets — Kindly let me have your opinion about this suggestion, so that, should an opportunity arise, I may bear you in mind —

Finally, I am awaiting your reply about the songs by return of post. For now that we are beginning to do business with one another, I gladly give you the preference over all the others who have already applied to me about those works — If this first offer should not suit you, you must express yourself quite freely about it and not fear that by so doing you will offend me — Then perhaps later on we might embark on several undertakings —

With kindest regards, your most devoted

L. V. BEETHOVEN

(1022) *To Sigmund Anton Steiner*

[Autograph in the Beethovenhaus, Bonn, H. C. Bodmer collection]

DEAR STEINER! [VIENNA, *April*, 1820] [2]

I really do wish that you would publish the three overtures.[3] I will do everything in my power to promote the success of this undertaking. *Go ahead* — The Scottish songs too you could soon obtain from Rupprecht.[4] I should very much like to have them published so that I could also bring their sequel to the light of day —

You will soon receive a *musical interest* [5] and I am working daily for your early *complete satisfaction* with the others; and

---

[1] The German edition of Op. 108 was not published until July, 1822.

[2] This date is noted on the autograph in another hand.

[3] Op. 117, 115 and 113, i.e. Nos. 10, 11 and 12 on the list sent to Steiner in April, 1815. See Appendix F (6). Op. 113 appeared in February, 1823, Op. 115 in April, 1825 and Op. 117 in July, 1826.

[4] Rupprecht was evidently translating the twelve songs (WoO 156) which Steiner did not publish.

[5] I.e. payment in the form of a musical composition.

I have reason to hope that I shall be able to arrange this
very soon — You might kindly send me *your subaltern* tomorrow
morning, but very early, at about seven or eight o'clock, for
I should like to second him to the reserve at M[ödling] ¹ —
I shall see you soon — Continue to be well disposed to your
friend

BEETHOVEN

(1023) *To Nikolaus Simrock, Bonn*

[Autograph in the Beethovenhaus, Bonn, H. C. Bodmer collection]

MY DEAR HERR SIMROCK !   VIENNA, *May* 24, 1820
I hope that you have received the letter I sent to you
from here to the address you gave me at Frankfurt.² But
I mentioned on a cover that if you had left Frankfurt my
letter should be forwarded to you.³ In this very letter I
informed you that instead of eight sets of variations I had sent
you ten, but that I was not asking that the fee should be
increased.⁴ I told you also that I had sent to Herr Franz
Brentano at Frankfurt the receipt stating that this manuscript
had been safely handed in and informing him too that the
manuscript had been delivered here to the post. I considered
that in this way I was shortening the transaction, namely, by
sending him the manuscript and asking you to remit the fee
for it to him — Well, the manuscript is now at Frankfurt and,
what is more, has been lying there for a considerable time,
for it is now a month since it was dispatched ⁵ — Now I
should like you to apply immediately to Herr Franz Brentano
at Frankfurt and settle the whole business — I have too little
time to tell you anything more except that I have sent you
only the variations which you asked for, but have already
disposed of the songs in another quarter.⁶ At the same time I

¹ Beethoven went to Mödling on May 1st and remained there until the end
of October.
² Letter 1019, dated April 23rd.
³ This cover has not been traced.
⁴ Op. 107.
⁵ According to Beethoven's statement in his letter of April 23rd the manuscript
was sent off on April 22nd. Cf. Letter 1019, p. 889.
⁶ I.e. to A. M. Schlesinger in Berlin who published them as Op. 108.

must tell you that in this transaction you started off with quite unwarranted prejudices —

In haste, your friend

BEETHOVEN

Please settle this
business soon —

(1024) *To Adolf Martin Schlesinger, Berlin*

[*MS. not traced*] [1]

[VIENNA, *May* 31, 1820]

[Curieuse lettre sur ses ouvrages. Il leur accorde le droit de vendre ses compositions en Angleterre, y compris les airs écossais, aux conditions indiquées par lui. Il s'engage à leur livrer dans 3 mois trois sonates pour le prix de 90 florins qu'ils ont fixé. C'est pour leur être agréable qu'il accepte un si petit honoraire].

'Je suis habitué à faire des sacrifices, la composition de mes oeuvres n'étant pas faite seulement au point de vue du rapport des honoraires, mais surtout dans l'intention d'en tirer quelque chose de bon pour l'art.'

(1025) *To Tobias Haslinger, Vienna*

[*Autograph in the Deutsche Staatsbibliothek, Berlin*]

[MÖDLING, *c. May*, 1820]

MOST EXCELLENT LITTLE ADJUT[AN]T!

I have taken on a bet of 10 gulden V.C., I repeat ten gulden V.C., that it is not true that you have had to pay 2000 gulden as compensation to Artaria for the publication of Mozart's works (which, moreover, have already been pirated everywhere and sold in pirated copies) [2] — I would certainly like to know the truth. I really cannot believe it. But if this injustice has indeed been perpetrated against you, then 'O

---

[1] Taken from the sale catalogue of Gabriel Charavay, Paris, May 1881, no. 17.

[2] Steiner had been publishing since 1818 Mozart's works for pianoforte with accompanying instruments. See Köchel-Einstein's Thematic Catalogue (Leipzig, 1937), pp. 913-914.

dolce contento'[1] I must pay the 10 gulden —
Let me know the truth about this —
All good wishes and do behave like Christians —

Your

BEETHOV[EN]

(1026) *To Nikolaus Simrock, Bonn*

[*MS. in the Beethovenhaus, Bonn, H. C. Bodmer collection*][2]

VIENNA, *July* 23, 1820

I was delighted to receive your charming letter of July 10th. What you say in it about the publication of the variations is quite in order — I received the fee very quickly through Herr Brentano, and in future we shall keep to this method — You are quite right in thinking that here people prefer Brabantine thalers to ducats, but in Frankfurt, on the other hand, people pay for one ducat two thalers in F. 2.45 E.Z. Hence Herr Brentano was right too — In any case the question need not be mentioned again. As for the louis d'or I too know of no others but those at two ducats or F. 9.12 20 F basis, or F.11 E.Z. — and this was the rate I expected for the fee for my Mass which was intended for you — As in this case too everything is in order, I assure you that you will receive the Mass next month — Therefore please make arrangements for there to be no delay in my receiving the fee of 100 louis d'or at Frankfurt — I have reduced the price for you very considerably, a thing I would not willingly do for another publisher; and when doing so I was really mindful of our old friendly relations — Hasten, therefore, to remit the fee. I for my part am sending you the Mass by one of my friends who is going to Frankfurt. I am directing it to Herr Brentano and commissioning the latter to forward it to you as speedily as possible. By the same opportunity you will receive too the document about your ownership of the variations and the numbering of the work —

---

[1] 'Oh, sweet satisfaction.' Beethoven is obviously quoting the contemporary Italian version of the passage in Mozart's 'Die Zauberflöte', Act I, sc. 17, beginning with 'Das klinget so herrlich', sung by Monostatos and the slaves, when Papageno drives them away with his magic bells.

[2] Written in another hand and signed by Beethoven.

About the publication of my collected works I intend to write to you soon in very great detail. The subject demands rather careful consideration — Needless to say, I hope that we shall come to an agreement on all points; and I regard this undertaking as a fresh opportunity for cementing our friendship. Give my best greetings to your wife — I send you my compliments and remain your devoted friend

LUDWIG VAN BEETHOVEN

(1027) *To the Archduke Rudolph, Vienna*

[*Autograph in the Gesellschaft der Musikfreunde, Vienna*]

YOUR IMPERIAL HIGHNESS!   MÖDLING, *August* 3, 1820
I have just received the letter you intended for me in which Y.I.H. yourself informs me that you are coming to Mödling — With all my heart I thank Y.I.H. for this attention. I wanted to hasten into town tomorrow in order to wait upon Y.I.H., but no carriage was to be had. I hope, however, to secure one for next Saturday when I shall immediately call on Y.I.H. early in the morning [1] — In regard to the sacrifices which Y.I.H. desires to offer to the Muses under my direction, I will make suggestions to Y.I.H. when I see you — I am really delighted to know that Y.I.H. is again in my neighbourhood. My sole wish is that I may be able fully to contribute to the fulfilment of all that Y.I.H. desires of me — May Heaven bless Y.I.H. and make all that you have planted grow and prosper. —

Your Imperial Highness's
most obedient and most faithful
L. V. BEETHOVEN

[1] See the following Letter 1028, which Beethoven wrote from Vienna on Saturday, August 5th.

(1028) *To Nikolaus Simrock, Bonn*

[Autograph in the Beethovenhaus, Bonn, H. C. Bodmer collection]

MY DEAR OLD PAPA!   VIENNA, *August* 5, 1820

I have this moment come in from the country and am replying to your last letter. I am very busy; and my most gracious lord, the Cardinal, is here too. So things are rather hectic — When publishing the variations just keep to the number I gave you.[1] Admittedly a few subsequent works ought to have appeared by now in my part of the world, but circumstances have prevented this, a thing which often happens in similar cases. But I have really quoted other numbers in order that you may certainly not be held up — The document about the ownership will arrive at Frankfurt with the Mass. But indeed you must not worry about this — In regard to the publication of my collected works we here are inclined to think that it would be well to add a *new work* to each type of composition, for instance, to the variations a new work of that kind, and similarly to the sonatas, etc., etc. — As soon as you have received the complete résumé of our opinions on this question, you will then be able to disclose to us your views most conveniently — As for the scores you offer me for my Karl I shall certainly manage to make use of them later on; and I thank you for them — And in whatever ways I can be of service to you, you will always find me willing — I cherish the hope of being able perhaps to set foot next year on my native soil and to visit my parents' graves — My wishes for all that is beautiful and good to your wife and your family —

In haste, your friend

BEETHOVEN

NB. When sending letters to me, always direct them to the address you have used hitherto.[2]

[1] Op. 107.
[2] This NB. is added at the top of the third page of the autograph.

(1029) *To Nikolaus Simrock, Bonn*

[*MS in the Beethovenhaus, Bonn, H. C. Bodmer collection*] [1]

VIENNA, *August* 30, 1820

I am replying to your esteemed letter of August 12th. — The only alteration I desire to make in what you say in your letter about the payment of the 100 louis d'or guaranteed to me for my Mass is that, in order to avoid all differences in working out this sum, I am adopting the real value of an old shield louis d'or *at two ducats* and *the latter* at the scale of 9 in 20 — I am quite willing to forgo the gold standard and to keep to the par rate. But according to our arrangement, *the latter* makes up for it — So you will kindly place to my credit with Herr Brentano at Frankfurt 900 gulden (I repeat, nine hundred gulden) at the scale of 20 which I shall be able to draw as soon as this friend has received my manuscript —

What you say about the prospects of selling your edition of this Mass is not quite accurate — My first Mass, published by Breitkopf, was issued with a German text as well; and it is performed every year not only at Leipzig but also in all other Protestant towns.[2] Besides I flatter myself that this latest work of mine will certainly cause in the world of music the sensation it deserves and that therefore the first publisher, in view of the difficulty of pirating the engraved edition, will make a good profit, which I grudge to *you*, my dear friend! far less than I do to all other publishers —

I am only waiting to receive from you your agreement to the substance of this letter before having the copying completed and sending you my manuscript — So in the meantime make the arrangements about paying me the fee —

I will write to you soon about your offer to publish my collected works — Meanwhile I renew the assurance of my friendly regards —

Should you wish to have a German translation of the Mass,

[1] The letter is written in another hand, but the last four words and the signature are in Beethoven's handwriting.
[2] The Mass in C, Op. 86, published by Breitkopf & Härtel in October, 1812, with a German text by Dr. C. Schreiber.

let me know by return of post ; I will arrange for it to be done and will adapt it to my composition —

In haste, your friend

BEETHOVEN

(1030) *To Joseph Köferle, Vienna* [1]

[Autograph in the possession of Mrs. André Mertens] [2]

[MÖDLING, August, 1820]

. . . I enclose [a letter] to the chief accountant of the National Bank, from which you will see that you can also be admitted to this [—] [3] —

Do come to us on Sunday, we are looking forward. . . .

As to the b[ank] s[hares], I am relying absolutely on your judgment. The smaller the cut the better, but I fear that *a large cut* cannot be avoided [4] — In summer you will find this *Salzmann* [5] only at the Bank, for it would be too inconvenient for anyone to go out to *Döbling*. (Read the letter before you deliver it.)

In great haste, your friend

BEETHOVEN

DEAR HERR VON KÖFERLE !

My kind uncle has already written to you that he is expecting you on Sunday, so I am merely writing in haste to say that I too, as you must surely know, am looking forward to your visit with great pleasure. Please deliver the letter to Salzmann if you consider it necessary.

Your
C[ARL] V[AN] B[EETHOVEN]

[1] Joseph Köferle was an official in the Government Finance Department who also gave lessons to Karl during the latter's stay in Blöchlinger's boarding school. See *FRBH* I, 282-283.

[2] The autograph is a fragment, a single leaf written on both sides. The first two sentences of this translation form one side, the remainder the verso.

[3] An underlined illegible word.

[4] After this sentence several words are obliterated.

[5] Cf. letter 743, p. 658, n. 1.

(1031) *To Anton Dietrich, Vienna* [1]

[*Autograph in the Stadtbibliothek, Vienna*]

DEAR HERR DIETRICH! [MÖDLING, *Summer*, 1820]

Please do not be annoyed with me, but unfortunately I cannot manage today, for I am sorry to say that I remembered too late that you would be coming. Give me the pleasure of visiting me tomorrow. You will find me in during the whole morning.

Your most devoted
BEETHOV [2]

(1032) *To the Archduke Rudolph, Vienna*

[*Autograph in the Gesellschaft der Musikfreunde, Vienna*]

YOUR IMPERIAL HIGHNESS! MÖDLING, *September* 2, 1820

I had not been feeling well since Tuesday evening, but I hoped that by Friday I should certainly have the great pleasure of paying my respects to Y.I.H. I was mistaken, however, and only today am I able to inform Y.I.H. that I certainly hope to be able to wait upon Y.I.H. next Monday or Tuesday, when I shall call very early in the morning [3] — My indisposition is to be ascribed to my having taken a seat in an open post chaise so as not to miss seeing Y.I.H. During the day it rained and when I drove out here it was almost *cold.* Nature seems indeed to have taken umbrage at my foolishness or audacity and to have punished me for my stupidity — May Heaven bestow on Y.I.H. everything that is good, beautiful, sacred and blessed, and grant me your gracious favour! —

[1] Anton Dietrich (1799-1872), a young Viennese sculptor, whose bust of Beethoven, done in 1821, is now in the Vienna Akademie der Bildenden Künste. Several reproductions of this not very successful bust were made by Dietrich himself during the following years; and he also did a drawing of Beethoven. See Frimmel, *Beethovenstudien*, II, pp. 103-107 and the same writer's work on *Beethoven im zeitgenössischen Bildnis*, 1923, pp. 49-52. See illustration facing page 1265.

[2] The last two letters of the signature are missing. The note is written in pencil.

[3] Beethoven wrote this letter on Saturday.

But may this favour be granted only on the foundation of justice! —
Ever Your Imperial Highness's
most obedient and most faithful servant
L. v. BEETHOVEN

(1033) *To Adolf Martin Schlesinger, Berlin*

[*MS in the Beethovenhaus, Bonn, H. C. Bodmer collection*] [1]

VIENNA, *September* 20, 1820

I assure you that the amount of the bill of exchange drawn on you has been duly paid — Only persistently poor health has prevented me from finishing sooner the proof-reading of the copies of the songs.[2] Moreover the English and Scottish poems had to be copied by a linguist who is very busy; and here too everything was held up — Hence there has been a delay in dispatching the songs, which, however, will be sent off to you by the next mail coach; and on this you may count with absolute certainty — Everything will go more quickly in the case of the three sonatas [3] — The first is quite ready save for correcting the copy, and I am working uninterruptedly at the other two — My health is completely restored and I will make every effort to fulfil my obligations to you as soon as possible.

After dispatching the last two sonatas I will then draw on you again for the sum of 50 ducats in order to wind up this transaction once and for all — I hope that we shall soon co-operate again in some undertaking —

And now I must ask you to excuse the delay — I send you my greetings with all due respect and devotion.

LUDWIG VAN BEETHOVEN

[1] Written in another hand and signed by Beethoven.
[2] Op. 108.
[3] Of the late pianoforte sonatas, Op. 109 was published by A. M. Schlesinger in November, 1821, Op. 110 and 111 by the Berlin and Paris Schlesingers in 1822.

(1034) *To Johann Speer*

[*Autograph not traced*] [1]

[MÖDLING, *October*, 1820]

Kindly let me know the terms in connexion with the sale of your house, because, as I have already told you, I fancy that one of my friends might be prepared to buy it.

First of all, we must know

1) your valuation of the house together with the vineyard, etc. ?
2) the arrangements you have made with the vineyard employee who under you has been entitled to the proceeds of the vineyard and to the ground floor of the house ?
3) the mortgage on the house and how much has still to be paid off?

In short, please let me have accurate and detailed information on all these points. The buyer whom I would introduce to you might be very meticulous. At the same time he would be willing to comply with your wishes in many respects.

I cannot tell you how long I shall be here, for I myself am not yet certain. But I am always at your disposal for anything that may be useful or helpful to you whenever you care to ask me.

Yours sincerely,
BEETHOVEN

NB. I waited today until half past ten, but as no one came I went out.

---

[1] Taken from Frimmel, *Wiener Zeitung*, June 19, 1919, p. 2.

(1035) *To Dr. Wilhelm Christian Müller, Vienna* [1]

[Autograph in the Beethovenhaus, Bonn, H. C. Bodmer collection] [2]

[MÖDLING, *before October* 26, 1820]

I presume that you will forgive me for not being able to wait for you today. A chance event which is extremely distasteful to me, deprives me of the pleasure of seeing you. Perhaps you will stay on for a few days more. This I shall certainly hear from F[rau] v[on] Streicher; and then I will request you to give me the pleasure of seeing you at my home — The fact that I am just moving back to Vienna is partly responsible for our failure to meet; and it will take me several days more to get straight —

Your most devoted
BEETHOVEN

(1036) *To Artaria & Co.*

[Autograph in the Beethovenhaus, Bonn, H. C. Bodmer collection]

VIENNA, *October* 26, 1820

HIGHLY BORN HERREN ARTARIA, FALSTAFF [3] & KOMPAGNIE,

Most politely do I request Herr von Oliva to hand over the sum of 300 gulden, the whole amount of which will by now have arrived in Vienna. As I happened to be busy moving into town, I could not have the honour of expressing my thanks to you and, in particular, to Sir John Falstaff —

Your most devoted servant
BEETHOVEN

---

[1] Dr. Wilhelm Christian Müller (1752–1831), living at Bremen, was a writer and an enthusiastic lover of music, who with his daughter Elise (cf. Letter 807) met Beethoven in Vienna in 1820. In 1824 he published a book about his travels, *Briefe an Deutsche Freunde*, which included a description of his meeting with Beethoven. Cf. Letter 807, p. 703. See *FRBH* I, 436-437.

[2] This note is written in pencil.

[3] Carlo Boldrini, who was a partner in the firm. Cf. Letter 1017, p. 888, n. 1.

(1037) *To Nikolaus Simrock, Bonn*

[Autograph in the Beethovenhaus, Bonn, H. C. Bodmer collection]

MY DEAR SIMROCK!   VIENNA, *November 28, 1820*

I received your last letter while I was still in the country. When His Imperial Highness the Cardinal had left the country to return to his residence in Vienna and I had to go to him in town two or three times a week during the whole summer, my country life which is very precious to me was not a little disturbed. Not until October was I able to make up to some extent for the country life which I had missed. It was during that period that your letter arrived. But as I was moving about, now here now there, I did not manage to read it for some time. Since I understand nothing whatever about business affairs, I was waiting for my friend who, however, has not yet arrived in Vienna. Meanwhile I had to learn from other people that I shall be losing at least 100 gulden A.C. With my usual frankness I must confess to you that previously I could have had a fee of 200 gold ducats in Vienna. Yet we gave the preference to your offer, because according to the particulars quoted to us 100 louis d'or were supposed to be worth more. It is too late now to cancel the arrangement, since the firm which was to get the grand Mass has commissioned another big work from me, and since I too should not like to appear as if I had had to refuse an offer which I had already accepted — all of which you will find quite natural. As soon as the German text has been completely written out in the Mass, I will send it to you through Herr v[on] Brentano at Frankfurt, to whom you can then remit the 100 pistoles, as you have stated, instead of louis d'or. The translation is costing me at least 50 gulden V.C. I trust that you will add this amount at any rate to my fee — and so requiescant in pace — I would rather write 10,000 notes than one letter of the alphabet, particularly when it is a question of taking money *in this way* and not *in that way*. I trust that you in turn will treat me all the more favourably in the publication of my collected works which, as you know, I have very much at heart. Since Bonn is regarded as a foreign town, the publication there may greatly extend *my leave of absence* abroad, which I do desire. My wishes for all that is good and beautiful to Wegeler and his whole family. As soon as I find a handsome Bohemian drinking goblet I will send him *another one.*[1]

In haste, your

BEETHOVEN

(1038) *To Franz Brentano, Frankfurt am Main*

[*Autograph in the Beethovenhaus, Bonn*]

SIR!   VIENNA, *November* 28, 1820

Your good nature encourages me to hope that you will not refuse to have this enclosure forwarded to Simrock.[2] For in it I have expounded my views about the whole question. Nothing can be done now but to accept what he offers, namely, the 100 pistoles. As to what you as a business expert can obtain for me in addition by the *valuation* of the money, well, of course, I am convinced beforehand of your honourable intentions. My situation at the moment is difficult and distressing. But the *last person* to whom one should *write such a thing is a publisher* — Thank God, I myself am not to blame for it. The chief cause has been my excessive devotion to others, including that weak Cardinal who has led me into this swamp and who is unable to extricate himself — As soon as the translation is ready, I shall again trouble you by sending you the Mass. When that time comes, please give a little attention, if possible, to my advantage in this matter as compared with that of the Jewish publisher.[3] Would I were in a position to be able to perform some service for you or yours —

I remain, Sir, with sincere regards, your friend and servant

BEETHOVEN

Forgive my seemingly careless scrawl, but I have written this in a hurry — My greetings to all your family —

---

[1] Cf. Letter 661, p. 602, n. 4.
[2] I.e. Beethoven's letter to Simrock, Letter 1037.
[3] Adolf Martin Schlesinger of Berlin.

(1039) *To Artaria & Co.*

[*Autograph in the Beethovenhaus, Bonn, H. C. Bodmer collection*]

VIENNA, *December* 17, 1820

HERREN ARTARIA & KOMPAGNIE,

I thank you most warmly for the 750 gulden A.C. which you have advanced to me and for which I have sent you a receipt with the guarantee of His Imperial Highness the Cardinal; and I again request you, since I am in danger of losing one of my eight bank shares, to advance me another 150 gulden A.C., which I undertake to refund to you in three months from today at latest. But in order to prove my gratitude to you, I give you herewith a written undertaking to make you the owner of one of my compositions, consisting of one, two or several movements, without laying claim to any fee whatsoever for it.[1] —

Ever your most willing
BEETHOVEN

(1040) *To Carlo Boldrini*

[*Autograph in the Beethovenhaus, Bonn, H. C. Bodmer collection*]

DEAR POLDRINI![2]   [VIENNA, *December* 20, 1820]

I do earnestly request you not to postpone dealing with the matter with which you have been entrusted. The man is ill. He lives in the Adlergasse, 1st floor, at the Twelve Apostles (opposite the house of Count Deym)[3] — Should you have any objection perhaps to advancing the 150 gulden to me, I should prefer you to tell me so. In that case I shall doubtless find someone who will do me this favour. I should by no means take your refusal amiss — But should you wish to do me this favour, please redeem the share at once. Interest has been paid up to January 18th — But I shall be only too glad to recover the share immediately and I shall not mind that insignificant loss — Let me remind you too about my visiting

---

[1] There is no evidence that Beethoven gave Artaria a work of this kind.
[2] In the autograph Boldrini's name is spelt thus.
[3] The words in brackets are added at the foot of the page.

card — it should be quite simple, i.e. Ludwig van Beethoven. I require some for my New Year greetings — I will defray the cost at once — Please, please make haste and redeem the share.

Your friend
BEETHOVEN

The dividend period has already arrived; so I too require the share and have already had unpleasant scenes with S[teiner] about it. I will tell you more when we meet.

(1041) *To Joseph Lind*

[Autograph in the Beethovenhaus, Bonn, H. C. Bodmer collection]

DEAR LIND !   [VIENNA, 1820]

Please do me the kindness either to send me somebody who will take my *measurements* properly or to come yourself. I need a new body belt. This one is no good; and owing to the sensitive condition of my abdomen it is quite impossible for me to go out without a strong protecting belt. Today also I shall be at home all day. —

Your friend
BEETHOVEN

(1042) *To Joseph Friedlowsky* [1]

[Autograph in the Beethovenhaus, Bonn, H. C. Bodmer collection]

MY DEAR F[RIEDLOWSKY],   [VIENNA, 1820]

As I am not dining at home today, you would only take the walk to no purpose. But please give me the pleasure of *lunching with me tomorrow.* I shall expect you about half past one; and I am greatly looking forward to seeing you again at my home —

Your friend and servant
BEETHOVEN

---

[1] Joseph Friedlowsky was a renowned Viennese clarinettist, who according to Schindler was born in 1775. He taught the clarinet in the Gesellschaft der Musikfreunde and played in the orchestra at the Theater an der Wien. He was still performing in 1825. Beethoven had a high opinion of his musicianship. See *FRBH* I, 152-153.

(1043) *To Ignaz Moscheles* [1]

[*Autograph in the Beethovenhaus, Bonn, H. C. Bodmer collection*]

[VIENNA, 1820]

Please let me have the two overtures and also the other separate parts of a third one, which I gave you —

BEETHOVEN

(1044) *To Johann Sina* [2]

[*MS not traced*] [3]

DEAR SINA,   [VIENNA, 1820]

Be sure to come this evening. For Heaven's sake come!

(1045) *To Joseph Karl Bernard*

[*Autograph in the Universitätsbibliothek, Tübingen*]

DEAREST FRIEND!   [VIENNA, 1820]

Fortunately I found someone yesterday who knows Hofbauer [4] well and her also. Hence we shall arrive at some result in this matter. He is going to hand over the money to her this very day, so please send it back to me. I will have a

---

[1] Ignaz Moscheles (1794–1870), born at Prague, became a distinguished pianist, conductor and composer. He came to Vienna at an early age to study with Salieri and Albrechtsberger, and, according to his own statement, he enjoyed Beethoven's friendship from 1808 to 1820. During this period, however, he was often absent from Vienna on concert tours. He repeatedly gave pianoforte recitals in Vienna and from 1815 to 1825 he vied in popularity with Hummel. Moscheles settled in England in 1826. In 1841 he published an English translation of Schindler's biography of Beethoven with editorial notes and certain additions. See *FRBH* I, 425–428.

[2] Johann Sina, born in 1778, had been the second violin in the Razumovsky quartet. When Schuppanzigh after his return from Russia in 1823 formed this quartet again, Sina for a time played the second violin. In 1841 Schindler came across Sina in Paris where the latter was actively promoting the performance of Beethoven's works.

[3] Taken from *FRBH* II, 182.

[4] It has not been possible to identify this person who is said to have been the father of Johanna van Beethoven's second child, a daughter, named Ludovica. See also Letter 1259, p. 1103.

word with the doctor too, but I have forgotten *his name*. So please write it down for me. I am not very well or I should have come to see you. —

Your friend
BEETHOVEN

Vous pouves donner l'argent a cette femme.[1]

(1046) *To Johann Baptist Wallishausser* [2]

[Autograph in the Beethovenhaus, Bonn, H. C. Bodmer collection]

[VIENNA, 1820]

I send my greetings to the two Herren Vallis and Hauser and also to the Herren Hauser and Vallis and especially to H[err] v[on] Vallishauser and I request them most politely to inform me whether the following calendar can be obtained from them, namely : 'Gemeinnütziger und erheiternder Kalender für das österreichische Kaisertum etc., im Verlage bej A. Strauss im Komptoir des österr. Beobachters — Dorotheen Gasse no. 1108', and how much it costs ? [3] —

With my most polite compliments to the Herren Vallis and Hauser and so forth and to Herr von Vallishauser

I remain ever your most devoted servant

BEETHOVEN

[1] Written on the verso beside the address to J. K. Bernard. It evidently refers to the bearer of the note.

[2] Johann Baptist Wallishausser, a Viennese publisher, who in 1819 had started a bookshop and printing works in the Neuburgergasse, no. 1177.

[3] The correct title of this calendar is 'Gemeinnütziger und erheiternder Hauskalender für das Oesterreichische Kaiserthum, vorzüglich aber für Freunde des Vaterlandes, oder Geschäfts-, Unterhaltungs- und Lesebuch für Jedermann'. It was edited by Franz Sartori and printed by Anton Strauss in Vienna and was first published in 1819.

(1047) *To Frau Arlet* [1]

[*Autograph not traced*] [2]

EXTRAORDINARILY EXCELLENT PEOPLE! [VIENNA, 1820]
Kindly send me two and a half bottles of Austrian white
wine at 3 gulden a bottle, one pound of fine sugar and one
pound of ordinary sugar, and also one pound of fine coffee.
The whole parcel should be thoroughly wrapped and strength-
ened with a state seal — I hope to see you soon ed a pagare i
conti [3] — All good wishes to Herr Arlet.
In great haste and at top speed,
yours
BEETHOVEN

(1048) *To Anton Ungermann, Commissioner of Police* [4]

[*Autograph in the Deutsche Staatsbibliothek, Berlin*]

[VIENNA, 1820] [5]
Herr von Schindler [6] must not be mentioned, of course,
before those two persons, but most certainly *I* can —

[1] On June 21, 1818, Ignaz Arlet, Joseph Stieblitz and Joseph Sähnel acquired
the tavern 'Zum schwarzen Kameel' in the Bognergasse. They retired from
business in 1832.
[2] Taken from Frimmel: *DKMZ*, 1891, 18, 2.
[3] I.e. and to pay the bills.
[4] It has not been possible to identify this official.
[5] This approximate date is noted in Schindler's handwriting on the top of
the unsigned autograph. Schindler adds that the note is a postscript to a long and
detailed letter to Ungermann about Johann van Beethoven's wife, of whose
immoral behaviour Beethoven strongly disapproved. See letter 1078.
[6] For a full note on Anton Felix Schindler see Letter 1081, p. 951, n. 1.

1821

(1049) *To Carlo Soliva, Milan* [1]

[*Autograph in the Beethovenhaus, Bonn, H. C. Bodmer collection*]

MONSIEUR!   VIENNA, *February* 9, 1821

Vous me pardonnerés, de ne vous pas avoir ecrit plutôt, mais étant toujours trop occupé — je recevrai votre dedication avec le plus grand plaisir, et si je suis en état, de vous être utile ici en quelque cas, vous me trouveres toujours prêt —
En attendant
    Monsieur
        je suis votre ami et serviteur
                    BEETHOVEN

(1050) *To Adolf Martin Schlesinger, Berlin*

[*Autograph in the Koch collection*]

SIR!   VIENNA, *March* 7, 1821

You have probably formed an unfavourable opinion of me. But you will soon think better of me when I tell you that for six weeks I have been laid up with a violent attack of rheumatism. However, I am better now. But you will understand that many plans had to be set aside for the time being. I shall soon make up for lost time — Well now, let me just give you a brief outline of what is most necessary. Opus 107 is to be written on the songs.[2] If I remember rightly, the names of the *English authors*, which include those of Lord Byron, Scott and so forth, were not added. You will soon

---

[1] Carlo Evasio Soliva (*c.* 1792–1853), Italian composer, who lived at Milan until he was given an appointment at the Warsaw Conservatoire in 1821. For a full account of Soliva's career see Albert Sowinski: *Les Musiciens polonais et slaves* (Paris, 1857), pp. 506-507, where a dedicatory sonnet by George Sand is quoted. The work which Soliva dedicated to Beethoven was a 'Grand Trio concertant pour Piano, Harpe ou deux Pianos et Alto' published by Artaria, Milan. A copy is now in the Gesellschaft der Musikfreunde, Vienna. See also Letter 1297, p. 1131.

[2] This is a slip of Beethoven's, for Simrock had published Op. 107 during the summer of 1820. In the end the twenty-five Scottish songs published by A. M. Schlesinger in July, 1822, were given the opus no. 108. See Letter 1052, p. 919, n. 2.

receive them — You are at liberty to make the dedication to
the Crown Prince of Prussia.[1] Although I had intended the
work for someone else, yet in this case I will defer to your
wishes — But as to the sonata which you must have received
a long time ago, I request you to add the following title together with the dedication, namely,

Sonata for the
Hammerklavier
composed and
dedicated to
Fräulein Maximiliana Brentano [2]
by Ludwig van Beethoven
Opus 109   [3]

Would you agree to add the year as well? I have often
wanted this, but no publisher would do it.[4]

The other two sonatas will soon follow [5] — and I shall
inform you of the fee in good time — I have not got your
letters beside me. But if I remember rightly, you wanted to
have some other works as well. If you send me particulars
about these soon, I can then make my arrangements and create
what is desirable for my art and also for me and for you and
for the public; and I can do this also to suit my convenience —
I wish you all that is to your advantage. You will probably
be able to read my manuscript. If you find that proof-reading
is necessary, please send me proofs both of the songs and of
the sonatas. But the manuscript of the songs must be sent
with them. This manuscript, I admit, is only a very hastily
written copy of my own manuscript, which, however, I do
not possess. —

All good wishes, most honoured Sir, from your most devoted

BEETHOVEN

---

[1] The Crown Prince (1795–1861) became in 1840 Friedrich Wilhelm IV.
But Schlesinger dedicated Op. 108 to Prince Anton Heinrich Radziwill (1755–
1833), who was also a composer of merit and to whom Beethoven later dedicated
his Op. 115.

[2] For a note on Maximiliane Brentano see Letter 1062, p. 931, n. 3.

[3] Schlesinger published this sonata in November, 1821.

[4] Beethoven's wish was carried out in the case of only one of his compositions,
his 'Missa Solemnis', published by Schott in 1827 as Op. 123.

[5] The pianoforte sonatas, Op. 110 and 111, were first published by A. M.
Schlesinger's eldest son Moritz (Maurice) Schlesinger in Paris in 1822.

(1051) *To Nikolaus Simrock, Bonn*

[*Autograph in the Beethovenhaus, Bonn, H. C. Bodmer collection*]

DEAR SIMROCK !   VIENNA, *March* 14, 1821

Well, you will most probably receive the Mass at Frankfurt in the middle of April or at the end of April at latest.[1] In spite of my best intentions it has not been possible to let you have it any sooner — I was confined to bed for six weeks, during which time I was not allowed to attend to any work; and I am still continuing to take various medicines. The same fate befell the translator [2] and all the people I know in my neighbourhood. That strange and terrible winter in Vienna, of which people in our native districts [3] have no conception, is responsible for this state of things — As the translator was overwhelmed with other literary tasks, I had to be patient, the more so as I have good reason to be better pleased with the work he produces than if the Mass were to find its way into some translators' factory. Our Protestants have tired long ago of such factories, since their products have too little in common with the true original text. My translator is himself a musician, is thoroughly familiar with my own ideas about the Latin text and being a competent writer is able to produce an ideal translation. You will learn his name when I send you the Mass.

And now let me ask you to keep calm, because you will be amply rewarded for having had to wait. All good wishes. As I am up to my eyes in work, I am merely sending you this information so that you may not imagine that things are different from what *they really are* — My cordial greetings to you and yours. If you see Wegeler, give him my very best wishes. I know that instead of being a Government Councillor he won't be a bit of *Government rubbish*,[4] examples of which

---

[1] The words from 'or' to 'latest' are added at the foot of the page.

[2] Possibly J. B. Rupprecht, of whose work as a translator Beethoven had a high opinion.

[3] Beethoven is referring, of course, to the Rhineland where he was born.

[4] Beethoven is playing on the German words 'Rat' (councillor) and 'Unrat' (rot).

I have come across — I am still hoping to visit Bonn this summer —

In haste, your friend
BEETHOVEN

(1052) *To Adolf Martin Schlesinger, Berlin*

[*Autograph not traced*] [1]

SIR !   DÖBLING, *June* 7, 1821

As I was still absent from Vienna, I unfortunately received your parcel only a few days ago. I then fancied that with the kind help of Herr Lauska [2] I could finish the proof-reading soon, in fact, very quickly. So far as I have been able to see from a cursory glance, the copy of the sonata seems to be almost quite correct.[3] But the first and second proofs should have been done in Berlin from this copy and then sent to me. Thus there are now very many mistakes to *correct, including some really serious ones*; and I shall probably have to give them numbers so that they may all be recognized without fail in Berlin — The proofs can be handed *to the mail coach* this day week; and that will most certainly be done — You will soon receive the other   sonata.[4] My health is still very shaky and will probably remain so until I can betake myself to the watering-place where the doctor has ordered me to go — The names of the authors of the songs will be sent to you with the proofs [5] — I think I have mentioned all that is necessary for today. I have far too many things to deal with. I send you my best compliments and sign my name respectfully as your most devoted

BEETHOVEN

[1] Taken from Unger, no. 107.

[2] Franz Seraph Lauska (1764–1825), born at Brno, became a pianist, composer and teacher of music. He was trained by Albrechtsberger in Vienna, then lived for a time at Munich and in 1798 settled in Berlin. On his way to Italy in 1821 Lauska spent some time in Vienna, where he made the acquaintance of Beethoven.

[3] Op. 109, which A. M. Schlesinger published in November, 1821.

[4] Op. 110. Apparently Frimmel, who first published this letter in the periodical *An der schönen blauen Donau*, 1888, p. 120, was unable to decipher the missing word or words.

[5] The MS of this list, written in another hand, of the names of the authors of the Scottish songs sent to A. M. Schlesinger is endorsed 'Döbling, July 3, 1821'.

PS. I know that Herr Lauska will not refuse my request to be so kind as to help me with the proof-reading of the songs.[1] I am exceedingly sorry that your work has been held up by my manuscript, although indeed I have already had manuscripts engraved here. Well, in future I will have everything copied and carefully checked!

PS. Kindly write the address to me as usual 'Ludwig van Beethoven in Vienna' and I shall then receive everything safely at my country address —

PS. Please do not publish the sonata until the corrections made in the proofs have been entered. For there are really far too many mistakes in it —

(1053) *To Adolf Martin Schlesinger, Berlin*

[*Autograph in the Beethovenhaus, Bonn, H. C. Bodmer collection*]

DÖBLING, *July* 6, 1821

You are now receiving, Sir! the corrected proofs.[2] I have never had a more difficult and tiresome task to cope with — The chief mistake we made was not to have the first proof corrected in Berlin, the result being that it was hardly possible to deal with the mass of mistakes here and there in the engraved copy. Now we must aim *at having the copy* (since my original manuscript was apparently not sufficiently legible) *absolutely correct, and this copy must be followed in every detail* — In the engraved copy some of the mistakes are marked in red pencil and some in red ink; but the bars are marked off with a gray pencil. In the manuscript copy the corrections are indicated in red ink — and the list of errata is also in red ink. It is quite possible that several mistakes are marked in the engraved copy which are not to be found in the list of errata. In that case *one need only consult the copy which is now the most carefully corrected one* and which renders my manuscript superfluous. *Let me remind you that an expert* should always lend a hand, for at least two or three proofs will be required before the engraved copy is absolutely

---

[1] Lauska had evidently returned to Berlin.
[2] I.e. of the twenty-five Scottish songs, Op. 108.

identical with the *manuscript copy* — Having bestowed on them the greatest and most infinite care I consider that I have now finished dealing with these proofs. I am asking Herr Lauska, to whom I send my compliments, to check them carefully —

In haste, Sir, your most devoted

BEETHOVEN

(1054) *To the Archduke Rudolph, Vienna*

[*Autograph in the Gesellschaft der Musikfreunde, Vienna*]

YOUR IMPERIAL HIGHNESS!   UNTERDÖBLING, *July* 18, 1821

I heard yesterday of Your Highness's arrival here which, however gratifying this might have been to me, has now proved to be a sad event for me, for it may be a rather long time before I can enjoy the happiness of waiting upon Y.I.H. I had been very poorly for a long time when finally *jaundice definitely* set in; and in my case it seems to be an extremely objectionable disease. I trust, however, that I shall have recovered sufficiently to be able to see Y.I.H. here before your departure — Last winter too I had the most violent attacks of rheumatism — a great deal of this is to be ascribed to my distressing situation, and particularly to my economic circumstances. Until now I have hoped to overcome the latter eventually by the most strenuous exertions. God who sees into my innermost heart and knows that as a man I perform most conscientiously and on all occasions the duties which humanity, God and Nature enjoin upon me, will doubtless rescue me in the end from my afflictions — The Mass will be delivered to Y.I.H. while you are still in Vienna. Y.I.H. will kindly spare me an enumeration of the reasons for the delay, inasmuch as such details could not but be, to say the least, unpleasant for Y.I.H. to hear — I would very gladly have written to Y.I.H. from here occasionally. But Y.I.H. had told me here that I should wait until Your Highness should write to me. Well, what was I to do? Perhaps it would have displeased Y.I.H. if I had not paid attention to what you had said. Besides I know that there are people who like to slander me to Y.I.H.; and this hurts me very deeply. So I often think that all I can do is to keep quiet until Y.I.H. desires to see or hear something of me. — I have heard that Y.I.H. is indisposed. I trust that your indisposition is not serious. May Heaven shower blessings in richest measure on Y.I.H. I hope that it will not be too long before I shall have the happiness of being able to tell Y.I.H. how much I am

> Your Imperial Highness's
> > most obedient and faithful servant
> > > BEETHOVEN [1]

(1055) *To the Archduke Rudolph, Vienna*

> [*Autograph in the Gesellschaft der Musikfreunde, Vienna*]

YOUR IMPERIAL HIGHNESS!   UNTERDÖBLING, *July* 18, [1821]

I have already written to Your Highness a fairly long letter which Schlemmer, my copyist, will deliver.[2] The day before yesterday I heard of Y.I.H.'s arrival. Whereupon I at once wrote the above-mentioned letter yesterday — How sad I am that *jaundice*, from which I am suffering, prevents me from hastening immediately to Y.I.H. and from being able to express in person and by word of mouth my delight at your arrival —

May the Lord of all things take Y.I.H. into His keeping for the benefit of so many people.

> Ever Your Imperial Highness's
> > most obedient servant
> > > BEETHOVEN

[1] Beethoven added his address, Unterdöbling, No. 11, at the end of the letter.

[2] Beethoven is obviously referring to the preceding letter (Letter 1054) of the previous day. Hence the above letter should have been dated July 19th.

(1056) *To Tobias Haslinger, Vienna*

[*Autograph in the Beethovenhaus, Bonn*]

Most excellent Fellow!   Baden, *September* 10, 1821
When I was being driven yesterday in a carriage to
Vienna, sleep overcame me and the more heavily as (because
I always get up early at Baden) [1] I had not really been sleeping
enough — Now while I was dozing I dreamt that I was travelling to very distant parts of the world, even to Syria and, in
fact, to India and back again, and even to Arabia; and in
the end I even got as far as Jerusalem. The Holy City made
my thoughts turn to the sacred books. So it is no wonder
that I then began to think of that fellow Tobias; and, naturally,
our little Tobias also and his pertobiassing had to cross my
mind. Whereupon during my dream journey the following
canon occurred to me:

As soon as I awoke, however, the canon had vanished
and not one note of it could I recall. But on the following
day as I was driving back here in the same vehicle (that of a
poor Austrian musical drudge) and was continuing yesterday's
dream journey while awake, behold, in accordance with the
law of the association of ideas, the same canon occurred to me.[2]

[1] Beethoven had moved to Baden on September 7th. He remained there
until the end of October.

[2] A similar creative process, that of composing poetry, is described by A. E.
Housman in *The Name and Nature of Poetry* (Cambridge, 1933), pp. 49-50. In both
cases there was an interval between the beginning and the completion and,
furthermore, the experience of being driven (Beethoven) and of taking a walk
(Housman) had to be repeated.

This time, as I was awake, I held on to it, as Menelaus formerly did to Proteus,[1] and only allowed it to transform itself into three parts.

All good wishes. I will soon let you have something about Steiner too, so as to show you that he has no stony heart.[3] All good wishes, most excellent fellow. It is our constant hope that you will not justify the title of publisher nor ever be embarrassed, but that you will continue to be publishers who are never embarrassed either when making a profit or when publishing — [4] Sing every day the Epistles of St. Paul, go every

---

[1] As described in the *Odyssey*, Bk. IV.

[2] The bass part of this canon is quoted again in Letter 1058, p. 925. This three-part canon is listed in *KHV.* pp. 685-686 as WoO 182.

[3] Possibly Beethoven intended to send Haslinger a canon on Steiner.

[4] Beethoven's usual pun on 'Verleger' (publisher) and 'verlegen' (embarrassed).

Sunday to Father Werner [1] who will tell you about the little book which will enable you to go straight to Heaven. You see how concerned I am about your spiritual welfare. Well, I shall ever remain with the greatest pleasure and from eternity to eternity

your most faithful debtor

BEETHOVEN

(1057) *To ?*

[*Autograph not traced*] [2]

BADEN, *September* 27, 1821

Forgive me, Sir, for taking the liberty of troubling you. I have commissioned the bearer of this letter, Herr von   ,[3] to cash or sell a bank note. As I know nothing about all the arrangements attending such a transaction, please be so kind as to let him have your advice and your views. A few illnesses contracted during the past winter and summer have slightly upset my private economy. Since September 7th I have been at Baden, and must remain here until the end of October. All this costs a good deal of money and prevents me from earning some as I used to. I should add that I am expecting money from abroad. But as the value of notes is now so high, I thought that this would be the easiest way of providing for myself for the moment. For later on I can purchase a new bank note to replace this one —

your friend

BEETHOVEN

(With all haste and speed)

You will easily realize what a genius I am in business matters.[4] After writing the enclosed letter, but before sending it off, I discussed the bank note question with a friend. I was reminded at once that I had only to cut off a coupon and the

---

[1] Friedrich Ludwig Zacharias Werner (1768–1823), born at Königsberg, first became a poet. But in 1814 he was converted to Roman Catholicism, was ordained priest and rapidly became a fashionable preacher.

[2] Taken from *WRBN.* 44-45.

[3] Possibly the name omitted is that of Schindler. See Letter 1081, p. 951, n. 1.

[4] According to *WRBN.* 45 this postscript was written on the unsealed cover which enclosed the letter.

whole affair would thus be settled. But I am delighted not to have to trouble you at all with this transaction – – – –

Yours
BEETHOVEN

(1058) *To* [*Ferdinand Piringer ?*] [1]

[*Autograph in a private collection*]

MOST NOBLE SIR,   [VIENNA, *November* 6, 1821]
     You are receiving herewith what you asked me for. My sole request is that when you no longer need it, you should close it and return it well sealed to this gentleman :

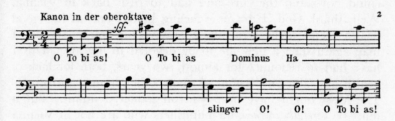

You will see from this that for eight months now I have received nothing. Now do please set things going with all speed and with great rapidity and prestissimo. If you do, you will again prove that you always (pardonnes moi le cochon) [3] keep time.

Most noble Sir,

We are, and ever shall remain, full of esteem and full of regard, nay more, with great esteem and with even greater regard

your amicus
BEETHOVEN BONNENSIS

[1] For a note on Ferdinand Piringer, to whom this letter may have been addressed, see Letter 1370, p. 1194, n. 2.
[2] For the three-part canon of which this is the bass part, cf. Letter 1056, p. 923.
[3] The paper is slightly torn and smeared with ink. Hence Beethoven's apology.

(1059) *To Franz Brentano, Frankfurt am Main*

[*Autograph in the Beethovenhaus, Bonn*]

BELOVED FRIEND!   VIENNA, *November* 12, 1821

Please don't think me a rogue or a thoughtless genius —
Since last year and until now I have been constantly ill.
Moreover, during the whole summer I was suffering from
jaundice, a complaint which persisted until the end of August.
On Staudenheim's orders I had also to betake myself in September to Baden. As in that part of the country the weather
soon became chilly, I started such violent diarrhoea that I
could not stand the cure and had to rush back to Vienna.
Well, thank God, I am now feeling better, and at last good
health seems to be returning to revive my spirits, so that I
may again start a new life to be devoted to my art. This I
have had to renounce for almost two years, both for lack of
health and also on account of many other human sorrows —
The Mass might have been sent off sooner, I admit. But it
must be *carefully checked*, for publishers who are not in Vienna
will certainly not make head or tail of my manuscript, as I
know from experience; [1] and a copy of that kind has to be
checked note by note before it can be engraved. Owing to
my many illnesses I could not manage to do this, the more so
as in order to keep myself alive I had also to finish off several
pot-boilers (unfortunately I have to describe them as such) —
I am inclined to think that I could still make another attempt
to induce Simrock to rate the louis d'or at a higher value,
particularly since from other quarters I have had several
enquiries about the Mass, about which I will certainly write
to you very soon. In any case do not doubt my integrity.
Frequently all I have in mind is that your kind loan should
be repaid as soon as possible — With sincere gratitude and
kindest regards,

your friend and servant
BEETHOVEN

[1] The words from 'as' to 'experience' are added at the foot of the page.

(1060) *To Adolf Martin Schlesinger, Berlin*

[*Autograph in the British Museum*]

SIR!   VIENNA, *November* 13, [1821] [1]

I see from your communication of October 13th that you have already sent off the sonata [2] and have not received the supplementary list of mistakes which I then forgot to enclose. Please therefore have these mistakes corrected in the plates, that is to say, where it is really obvious that the engraving is not *accurate*; and please send a printed supplementary list to me here. Perhaps too I could arrange with Steiner to have the mistakes corrected here before his copies are distributed — My persistent ill health is the reason why everything to a certain extent has become more wearisome to me; and that too is what happened in the case of the proof-reading. While I was doing it I was taken ill with jaundice and felt very poorly. Yet I exerted myself as much as possible in order to help you, and when doing so I forgot to send off in a supplementary list some further mistakes which I had discovered — My advice is, and please follow it to the letter, *to dispatch this supplementary list (of mistakes)* [3] *to all the places (to which you have sent copies)* [4] *and quickly too, with instructions to correct the copies in every respect with Indian ink and before they are distributed. In this way the matter will be dealt with most easily.* Please, please, please do follow this advice so that the work may appear as it should — As for the other two sonatas,[5] these will soon follow and, what is more, copied correctly. To enclose the manuscript would be too risky. For if some untoward mishap were to befall both manuscript and copy, the whole work would be lost. This is what happened the last time when on account of my ailing condition I had written down the *draft more fully* than usual. But now that my health appears to be

---

[1] The autograph is endorsed: Vienna, November 13, 1821, answered December 1, 1821. The letter was first published in an English translation by B. Schofield and D. Wilson in the *Daily Telegraph* of February 18, 1939 and later in the German original by the same editors in *Music and Letters* of July 1939, vol. xx, no. 3, pp. 236-238.   [2] Op. 109.

[3] The words in brackets are added at the foot of the page.

[4] The words in brackets are added at the foot of the page.

[5] Op. 110 and 111.

better, I merely jot down certain ideas as I used to do, and when I have completed the whole in my head, everything is written down, but only once —

I am taking this opportunity of writing to you *on the subject of the Mass*, about which you enquired. This is one of my greatest works and should you care to publish it, perhaps I might let you have it. The fee for it is 100 louis d'or (but not Friedrichs d'or nor pistoles), that is to say, the louis d'or reckoned at two gold ducats or, let us say, 200 gold ducats (or 900 gulden with valuation at the 20 gulden rate, V.C.) [1] I cannot take less, for that is the sum which others have already offered me ; and I am merely giving you the preference. But I must beg you *most urgently to send me a reply about this at once*, for this matter cannot be postponed any longer. You will kindly let me have *yes* or *no* in writing, but please do so *as soon as you receive this letter*. And now let me ask you to keep *this offer secret* — As to the order to Tendler & Co.,[2] please inform me at once when you have issued it to those gentlemen. It will be easier to dispatch the two sonatas to Berlin *in that way*, for all business transactions are a burden to me when I am constantly occupied with my art — Please do send your reply by letter post, so that I may be sure to receive it at once. The only address you need put is : *To Ludwig van Beethoven*.

In haste.

With kindest regards, your most devoted

BEETHOVEN

Be sure not to forget to arrange about the supplementary list of mistakes —

[1] This statement in brackets is added at the foot of the page.
[2] See Letter 1537, p. 1317, n. 3.

(1061) *To Adolf Martin Schlesinger, Berlin*

[*Autograph in the British Museum*] [1]

VIENNA, *November* 14, 1821

First movement, Bar 11.
The slur is missing.

First movement. Bar 13.
A semiquaver rest in the treble.

First movement. Bars 42 and
43. Both must be repeated, i.e.

Prestissimo. Bar 19.
The tie between F and F is
missing between the first
and second lines.

Prestissimo. Bar 37.
The tie between C and C between
the third and fourth lines must
be removed and the bar should be as here.

Prestissimo. Bars 136 and 137.
The ties between F and F on
the fifth line and between
G and G above the fifth
line must be removed
and the bars should be as here.

---

[1] The autograph was first published in an English translation by B. Schofield
and D. Wilson in the *Daily Telegraph* of March 4, 1939 and later in the German
original by the same editors in *Music and Letters* of July, 1939, vol. xx, no. 3,
pp. 238-239.
[2] These are corrections to the E major pianoforte sonata, Op. 109, published
by A. M. Schlesinger in November, 1821.

Last movement. Variation 1. Bar 10.
The B with the F and D is missing
and must be added.

Last movement. Variation 2.
Bar 29. ♮♯ before [F].

Last movement. [Variation 3].
A tie must be inserted between the last note B
and the first note B of
Variation 4, thus:

Variation 4. Bar 6 must
have D instead of B in
the bass, thus:

Variation 4. Bar 9.
♯ before G in the bass.

Variation 4. Bar 10.
♯ before D.

Variation 4. Bar 12.
♮ before A.

Variation 5. Bar 20.
♮♯ before F.

Variation 6. Bar 26.
♯ before D in the left hand.

Variation 6. Bar 45.
♮ before E.

Variation 6. Bar 29.
♮♯ before F.

Only yesterday did I receive the four copies intended for me. Admittedly many mistakes which I pointed out to you in my last communication through Tendler & Manstein [1] are not in them, but a few fresh ones have cropped up, such as, for example, the omission of two bars in the first movement, and so forth — You must now disregard completely the list I sent you recently and keep to this one, which is the latest and authentic one — I am attending to this so far as Vienna is concerned and also to the printing of additional copies — As to the Mass, I became muddled yesterday about louis d'or, because it so happened that I had to write to an address where they are current. *The fee* I am demanding is *really* 200 *gold ducats*; and again I ask you to reply at once, because I am postponing a decision solely on your account; and your hesitation spells loss to me. As to the sonatas, please make out the order too, specifying that the 60 ducats shall be paid to me here in gold also —

Thank God, my health is improving every day, and so I may hope that my mental powers will also become stronger — You will laugh a little at my business style. The fact is that I am extremely awkward in such matters and am accustomed to having everything attended to by a friend who is not here [2] —

In haste. With kind regards, your most devoted

BEETHOVEN

(1062) *To Maximiliane Brentano, Frankfurt am Main* [3]

[Autograph in the Koch collection]

VIENNA, *December* 6, 1821

A dedication!!! [4] Well, this is not one of those dedications which are used and abused by thousands of people — It is the spirit which unites the noble and finer people of this earth

---

[1] See Letter 1537, p. 1317, n. 3.
[2] Probably Schindler.
[3] Maximiliane Euphrosyne Kunigunde Brentano (1802–1861) was the daughter of Beethoven's staunch friends Franz and Antonia Brentano. She was very musical and Beethoven had already composed for her in 1812 his little pianoforte trio, WoO 39 (see *KHV.* 482). She married in 1824 Baron von Blittersdorf (1792–1861).
[4] I.e. the dedication of his pianoforte sonata, Op. 109.

and which *time* can *never* destroy.   It is this spirit which now speaks to you and which calls you to mind and makes me see you still as a child, and likewise your beloved parents, your most excellent and gifted mother, your father imbued with so many truly good and noble qualities and ever mindful of the welfare of his children.   So at this very moment I am in the Landstrasse — and I see you all before me.   And as I think of your parents' excellent qualities I have not the slightest doubt that you will have been and are being daily inspired to a noble imitation of them — The memory of a noble family can never fade in my heart.   May you sometimes think of me with a feeling of kindness — My most heartfelt wishes.   May Heaven bless your life and the lives of all of you for ever —

Cordially and ever your friend
BEETHOVEN

(1063) *To Adolf Martin Schlesinger, Berlin*

[Autograph in the Beethovenhaus, Bonn, H. C. Bodmer collection]

SIR !   VIENNA, *December* 12, 1821

I am just replying quickly to all the necessary points. *Arrangements have been made* with all these gentlemen for correcting the proofs. — The proof-reading of the songs will be completed as quickly as possible.[1]   But please *send them with the manuscript to Hensler*.[2]   For my own manuscript of these songs is practically only a sketch — And please be so kind as to send them to the Royal Legation or, at any rate, free of charge, for, as it is, we poor wretches in Vienna have to pay for almost everything *except the air we breathe* — Well, now let me deal with the Mass.   I really do consider it a great nuisance that you should wish to have the pianoforte arrangement and the copying of it included in the 200 ducats as well.   But in order to please you, I am putting forward the following suggestion, namely, that I shall be responsible for the pianoforte arrangement and for the copying of it and also for the copying of the score of the Mass, if you will add to the 200 ducats 100 gulden A.C.   You will doubtless find this a fair arrangement.   If you

---

[1] I.e. of Op. 108.
[2] For a note on Karl Friedrich Hensler see Letter 1286, p. 1123, n. 2.

agree, then there are no other difficulties to deal with.   But
please let me have a reply as quickly as possible, for people in
other quarters are urging me to come to a decision — In
regard to the payment of the fee, I propose that you send it to
the Senator Franz von Brentano at *Frankfurt am Main.* As
soon as this friend of mine informs me that he has received the
draft from you, then I will send you the Mass either to Berlin or
to Frankfurt am Main, i.e. to Herr von Brentano, who could
forward it to you.   Or if you do not trust us, then Herr von
Brentano could postpone payment of the fee to me until you
inform him that you have received the Mass.   But I am inclined to think that the first arrangement would be the simplest
and the best.   For there is no want of trust, I fancy, on either
side, between you and me.   The reason why I am asking you
to send the fee to Herr von B[rentano] in particular, is that
in any case I have sums to disburse and sometimes too to
receive and Herr von B[rentano] is such a kind, lovable and
unselfish fellow who would do this in the least expensive way.—
No doubt you will receive a sonata very soon, and also the
third one — I will let you know some other time about quintets and quartets — Well now, I must say good evening to
you, and in a great hurry — For this letter must go to the post
with all speed — Once more I beg you for an immediate
reply about the Mass, because I must make up my mind as
quickly as possible —
        I remain, Sir, with kindest regards, your most devoted
                                                          BEETHOVEN

(1064) *To Franz Brentano, Frankfurt am Main*

[*Autograph in the Beethovenhaus, Bonn*]

NOBLE FELLOW!   VIENNA, *December 20, 1821*
        I am waiting for a further letter about the Mass.   I will
send it to you immediately so that you may get the hang of
the whole affair.   In any case the fee will be made payable to
yourself; and then perhaps you will be so kind as to let me
discharge at once my debt to you.   My gratitude to you will
ever be boundless — I was too forward in not asking for
permission before dedicating one of my compositions to your

daughter Maxe.[1]   I would like you to regard this work as a token of my lasting devotion to you and your whole family — But do not put any wrong construction on this dedication, by fancying that it is a hint to use your influence, let alone to make me any reward — That would hurt me exceedingly. Yet if one insists on discovering reasons, then there are surely far more noble motives to which one can ascribe a dedication of that kind —

The New Year is about to begin.   May it fulfil all your wishes and daily increase your fatherly happiness in your children.   With all my heart I embrace you and ask you to remember me again to your excellent and exceptionally lovely Toni [2] —

I remain, Sir, with kindest regards, your

BEETHOVEN

I have already been offered both here and abroad 200 gold ducats for the Mass.   But I am inclined to think that I might perhaps obtain an additional sum of 100 gulden A.C. About this I am awaiting one more letter from abroad, which I will let you have at once.   Then we could put the whole question before Simrock, who will surely not expect me to lose too much.   Until then kindly be patient; and please don't think that you have behaved magnanimously to some worthless fellow.

[1] I.e. his pianoforte sonata, Op. 109.   Cf. Letter 1062.
[2] Franz Brentano's wife Antonia, née Birkenstock.

(1065) *To [Adolf Martin Schlesinger, Berlin ?*]

[*Autograph not traced*] [1]

[VIENNA, 1821]

Please let me have the book of the Scottish songs,[2] in the
form in which they are to be sent off immediately —
Thon [3]

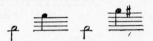

(1066) *To Sigmund Anton Steiner & Co.*[4]

[*Autograph in the Beethovenhaus, Bonn*]

[VIENNA, 1821]

I am requesting Geh'bauer [5] to let me have a few tickets
(two), for some of my friends want to go to this *hole-and-corner
musical performance* [6] — Perhaps you yourselves have some of
those *lavatory tickets*.[7]   If so, send me one or two —
Your amicus
BEETHOVEN

The score belongs to the chorus, of which that *peasant* [8]
has the parts.

[1] Taken from Kal., no. 979. The original note was then in the possession of
a descendant of the Schlesinger family.
[2] Probably Op. 108.
[3] This might be a part of Beethoven's signature.
[4] The address on the verso in Beethoven's hand runs as follows :
   An das berühmteste Musik Komtoir in Europa
      Steiner u. Company
         (pater noster miserere gässel).
[5] This is the form in the autograph. The meaning is 'go, peasant'. Beethoven
is referring to Franz Xaver Gebauer, the Viennese Kapellmeister, who in 1819
founded the Concert Spirituel. Cf. Letter 791, p. 691, n. 2.
[6] The original has 'Winkelmusik', meaning 'hedge-music' or the like.
[7] The original has 'Abtrittskarten', a variant of 'Eintrittskarten'.
[8] 'Bauer' in the original. Evidently Beethoven is playing on Gebauer's
surname.

(1067) *To Hofrat Karl Peters*

[*Autograph in the Royal College of Organists*] [1]

[VIENNA, 1881]

How are you? Are you well or unwell? How is your wife? — Allow me to sing something for you.

Canon

Sankt Petrus war ein Fels? Sankt

Canon

Bernardus war ein Sankt?? Ber=

How are your young princes? [3] If you are at home today, at about five o'clock in the afternoon, perhaps I shall call on you together with my *state burden*.[4]

In haste,

BEETHOVEN

(1068) *To Georg Friedrich Treitschke* [5]

[*Autograph in the Beethovenhaus, Bonn, H. C. Bodmer collection*]

EXTRAORDINARILY BELOVED FRIEND! [VIENNA, 1821] [6]

Let us begin with the primary original causes of all things, how something came about, wherefore and why it came about *in that particular way* and became what it is, why

[1] This autograph letter, purchased by John Ella in Vienna in 1846, was first copied in London by Thayer on March 7, 1861. In a letter written to Ella on the following day Thayer gives him a full account of Beethoven's close friendship with Karl Peters and J. K. Bernard. Thayer's letter is attached to the autograph in the Royal College of Organists.

[2] These two canons are listed in *KHV*. as WoO 175.

[3] Hofrat Karl Peters was tutor to the sons of Prince Lobkowitz. Cf. Letter 734, p. 651, n. 1.   [4] I.e. his nephew.

[5] The address on the verso in Beethoven's hand is: 'Für Seine wohl u. vortrefflich gebohrn H. v. Treitschke'.

[6] In all the German editions this letter is dated 1816. But Beethoven's signature in Latin script (the form he commonly used after 1817) and his reference to the Leipzig publisher C. F. Peters, who in 1822 began to make definite offers to him, provide sufficient evidence that the letter was written about that time.

something is *what it is*, why something *cannot be exactly so*!!! Here, dear friend, we have reached the ticklish point which my delicacy forbids me to reveal to you at once. *All that we can say is: it cannot be*!

With the greatest pleasure I will serve the Leipzig Bureau some other time.

All good wishes, my fine fellow, *you are calm indeed*, far too calm. What has become of your poetical thoughts and aspirations? All /∴\ good wishes! — We are, so far as possible, ever at your service.

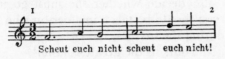

Scheut euch nicht scheut euch nicht!

Yours with kindest regards,

BEETHO[VEN] [3]

(1069) *To* ?

[*MS not traced*] [4]

[VIENNA, 1821]

. . . I thank you for your kindness and I feel certain that harmonies — will well up within me — In regard to — the musical ale-house, well, that is really established in itself for good and all by means of —

(1070) *To* ?

[*MS not traced*] [5]

[VIENNA, 1821]

P.P.

Kindly inform me whether I can still obtain all the numbers of this year's volume of your review, to which I should like to subscribe.

[1] In the autograph Beethoven gives the time-signature $\frac{2}{2}$ instead of $\frac{3}{2}$.

[2] This musical phrase is listed in *KHV*. as WoO 205f. The words mean 'Don't be afraid, don't hesitate'.

[3] The last three letters of the signature have been torn off.

[4] Taken from *KST*, no. 999, where it is quoted from an unspecified Stargardt catalogue.

[5] Taken from sale catalogue of Henrici, no. xvii, item 21.

(1071) *To ?*

[Autograph in the Conservatoire of Music, Leningrad]

[VIENNA, 1821]

Just read this, and let me tell you — the best arrangement would be to have *the district doctor*. One can't expect Braunhofer [1] to deal with this —

Tell the female bearer to arrange for the district doctor in the Alsergasse [2] to come when you are *at my home* today, so that we may also decide whether she must go into hospital and what interest should be taken in a person who has actually given notice during the first few days ? !

Yours in the greatest haste.[3]

The female bearer cooks

---

[1] For a note on Dr. Braunhofer, who attended Beethoven during the years 1820–1825, see Letter 1359, p. 1186, n. 1.

[2] The words 'in the Alsergasse' are added at the foot of the page.

[3] This autograph letter is neither addressed, nor dated, nor signed. Nothing is written on the verso.

1822

(1072) *To Bernhard Romberg* ¹

[*Autograph in the State University Library, Tartu*]

DEAR ROMBERG!   VIENNA, *February* 12, 1822

Last night I again *succumbed to the earache* which I usually suffer from during *this season. Even your playing* would only *cause me pain* today. So if you do not see me in person, put down my absence merely to that — Perhaps I shall feel better in a day or two and, if so, I shall still be able to say good-bye to you — By the way, if I have not called on you, just bear in mind the distance of my rooms and my almost ceaseless occupations, the more so as for a whole year I have been constantly ill and thus prevented from finishing many compositions which I had begun — and, after all, you and I do not need to pay one another compliments which really signify nothing — In addition to the full tribute of applause for your sublime art I wish you also the *ringing recognition of it in coins*, a thing we rarely see nowadays — If it is at all possible for me to do so, I will certainly contrive to see you and your wife and children, to whom I now send my heartfelt greetings —

All good wishes, great artist, I am ever yours

BEETHOVEN

(1073) *To Sigmund Anton Steiner*

[*Autograph in the possession of Pablo Casals*]

[VIENNA, *February*, 1822]

Please send me one copy of Meeresstille and Glückliche Fahrt ² and so forth for what has been promised ³; and at

¹ Bernhard Romberg (1767–1841), cellist, and his cousin Andreas Romberg (1767–1821), violinist, were in the Bonn Court orchestra from 1790 to 1793, when Beethoven first made their acquaintance. After touring with his cousin for many years Bernhard Romberg settled in 1805 as a solo cellist in Berlin, where from 1815 to 1819 he was Kapellmeister at the Prussian Court. He then resumed his tours as solo cellist and visited Vienna early in 1822.

² Two poems by Goethe set to music by Beethoven for a mixed choir with orchestral accompaniment. The work was published by Steiner in February, 1822, as Op. 112 and was dedicated to Goethe.

³ The original has 'für das Verbundene'; and Beethoven proceeds to pun on verbinden by adding 'dabei verbinde ich mich'.

the same time I undertake to correct the proofs in a few days. I am terribly busy and at the moment have no one to help me.

With the sincerest sincerity yours,

BEETHOVEN

(1074) *To Adolf Martin Schlesinger, Berlin*

[*Autograph in the British Museum*] [1]

SIR!   VIENNA, *April* 9, 1822

I have already written to you, I think, that the corrected proofs of the songs have been sent off from here.[2] But *owing to a hold-up the fresh copy of the last movement of the third sonata* is only being dispatched by tomorrow's mail coach.[3] As soon as you receive it *please mark it at once* so that *this copy may not be mistaken for the one you already have* ; *and destroy the latter immediately* — with regard to the Scottish songs, I have already written to you that it would be better to consult the poet about the long and short syllables, seeing that the latter have often fallen on *long* notes and the former on short ones. Admittedly there is some excuse for slips of that kind. If the poet were here, it would be an easy matter to settle. But at the moment I am so overwhelmed with work that it is impossible for me to do anything about it. No doubt Herr Zelter, who is a man well versed in poetry as befits a distinguished writer, would be able to help you to remove those little blemishes. I send him my best regards. As to the Mass I have already agreed to let you have the work itself *together with the pianoforte arrangement* for an honorarium of 650 Reichsthaler in Prussian currency. As to the costs of having the works copied, they will be fixed at as low a figure as possible. I should think that if you were to accept the following proposal as well, those costs would worry you even less. I am giving you in addition two

[1] The autograph was first published in an English translation by B. Schofield and D. Wilson in the *Daily Telegraph* of March 25, 1939 and later in the German original by the same editors in *Music and Letters* of July, 1939, vol. xx, no. 3, pp. 239-240.

[2] Op. 108.

[3] Op. 111, the C minor pianoforte sonata, dedicated to the Archduke Rudolph, was published by the Paris and Berlin Schlesingers in 1822.

songs,[1] for which I am not asking more than 45 gulden A.C. (although here I am paid eight gold ducats for every song I publish in the Modezeitung [2] and, what is more, all the numbers of this periodical have so far been sent to me every year and free of charge). And these 45 gulden A.C. added to the 650 Reichsthaler in Prussian currency would make a lump sum which would also be more gratifying to me. As soon as the draft has arrived here and been accepted I will immediately send the Mass to you and the songs as well. It will be necessary for you to make the draft payable at a reliable house in Vienna, such as Geymüller or the like —

Since the bill of exchange will have to be payable a month *after sight* (at last I now know what that means), it is high time to settle this transaction. So I await your instructions about this by return of post. The copying will be done most carefully so that it will not be necessary to send the copy backwards and forwards —

With kindest regards, your

BEETHOVEN

(1075) *To Adolf Martin Schlesinger, Berlin*

[*MS not traced*] [3]

SIR !   VIENNA, *May* 1, 1822

No doubt you have long ago received the Scottish songs [4] which were delivered here to Cappi & Diabelli [5] — with regard to the last movement of the third sonata, I am enclosing the receipt.[6] I assume that by now you will have received the sonata. I beg you once more to notify the receipt and

---

[1] Beethoven had added and then cancelled 'you are receiving them in manuscript'. It is difficult to say which songs Beethoven was offering.

[2] A Viennese periodical edited by Johann Schickh. Cf. Letter 955, p. 823, n. 1. Beethoven's song 'Das Geheimnis' (WoO 145) had appeared in the *Modenzeitung* for February 29, 1816, and another one 'So oder so' (WoO 148) in the issue of February 15, 1817.

[3] Taken from Kal., no. 834. Kalischer used a copy of the letter formerly belonging to Otto Jahn and deposited in the Berlin Library.

[4] Op. 108.

[5] In 1816 Pietro Cappi, nephew of Giovanni Cappi, had founded his own publishing firm in the Graben. Two years later he was joined by Diabelli and the firm became Cappi & Diabelli.

[6] Op. 111.

943

to destroy at once the copy you first received. As for the second sonata in A♭ I intend to *dedicate it to someone*, and I will let you have particulars about this in my next letter [1] — You are at liberty to dedicate the third sonata to anyone you like — Thank God, I am now in better health. As to the Mass, please settle up everything, I repeat everything, very soon, for other publishers too have expressed a desire to have it; and in Vienna especially, people have approached me several times about it. But I decided long ago that the Mass was not to be published *here*, because this work is of great importance to me — For the moment please just let me know whether you accept my last proposal about the Mass with the addition of the two songs.[2] Furthermore, in regard to the remittance of the fee, I prefer that this should not be deferred for longer than four weeks. On this I must insist, for two other publishers especially, who would also like to have the Mass for their firms, have been constantly pressing me for a definite answer for a very long time —

Now all good wishes for your welfare, and do write to me at once. I should be very sorry if *I were not able to let you have this particular work.*

With kindest regards, your most devoted

BEETHOVEN

(1076) *To Franz Brentano, Frankfurt am Main*

[*Autograph in the Beethovenhaus, Bonn*]

SIR !   VIENNA, *May* 19, 1822

You will be thinking Heaven knows what about my slovenly habits. But during the last four months I have again been constantly suffering from gout on my chest and have been able to do only very little work. At last the Mass will most certainly be delivered to you in Frankfurt by next month, let us say, the end of June. Cardinal Rudolph, who in general is very partial to my compositions, although so far I have had

---

[1] Although Beethoven intended to dedicate both Op. 110 and Op. 111 to Antonia Brentano (see Letter 1118), the former appeared without any dedication and the latter was dedicated to the Archduke Rudolph. But the Diabelli variations, Op. 120, were dedicated to Antonia Brentano.

[2] Cf. Letter 1074, p. 943, n. 1.

944

FERDINAND RIES (1784–1838)

From an engraving by Charles Picart (1821) after a lost portrait. There is a faint possi
bility that this engraving may be after an oil portrait of F. Ries by William Bradley
which was exhibited at the Royal Academy in May 1823. Efforts to find this
portrait have not been successful

(Edward R. Robbins, London)

no experience of his generosity, did not wish the Mass to appear
so soon; and I retrieved the score and the parts only three
days ago. The purpose of this was, as His Highness expressed
it, that I should suffer no loss from the publisher. At the
same time His Highness urged that the Mass should be dedicated to him. I am now having the score copied over again
for my own use and am checking it carefully. In my poor
state of health all this is rather *slow* — The Mass will be with
you in Frankfurt at the end of next *month* at the latest. Therefore Herr Simrock can remit to you by that date the fee we
have agreed upon. That is the quickest way, the more so as
at the moment I am finding everything a great strain — I
have received, it is true, even better offers in Vienna and also
from other quarters, but I have refused them all, because
although I shall be the loser, I have now given my word to
Simrock; and because, if only my health will allow me to
work, I will offer him several other compositions which will
enable me to compensate myself — and also because I could
make an agreement with him about the publication of my
collected works. *Since the winter here always nearly finishes me
off*, my health demands that at last I should leave Vienna for
a while.[1] The very friendly disposition you have so often
shown me leads me to hope that you will settle the whole
business in my favour.

With my sincere regards, your friend and servant

BEETHOVEN

(1077) *To Franz Brentano, Frankfurt am Main*

[*Autograph in the possession of Dr. Hans Wedig*][2]

VIENNA, *May* 19, 1822

If you think it advisable, forward this letter to Simrock,[3]
to whom I send my best regards — I will not weary you with
complaints, for that is all I could do. We are destined once

---

[1] From November, 1821 to May, 1822 Beethoven lived in the Landstrasse
no. 244, on the second floor. Early in May he moved to Oberdöbling, Alleegasse
135, where he remained until September 1st. He then went to Baden for about
six weeks and returned to Vienna in the middle of October.
[2] This unsigned note is almost certainly a postscript to Letter 1076.
[3] This letter has not been traced.

and for all to have both joy and sorrow, if only our share of sorrow does not become *too large.*

(1078) *To Johann van Beethoven, Vienna*

[*Autograph of letter not traced.*[1]   *Autograph of postscript in the
Gesellschaft der Musikfreunde, Vienna*]

[OBERDÖBLING, *May*, 1822]

I was hoping to see you for certain — but in vain — On Staudenheim's orders I must still continue to take medicine and must not move about too much — Instead of driving in the Prater today, please come along to me with your wife and your daughter [2] — My most ardent desire is that the good, which is always in evidence when we are together, should be achieved without let or hindrance. I have made enquiries about apartments. There are many suitable ones to be had; and you need not pay very much more than you have done hitherto. Considered merely from an economic point of view, the scheme would enable us both to save a good deal, apart altogether from the considerable pleasure it would afford us [3] — I have nothing against your wife. I only hope that she will realize how much could be gained for you too by your living with me and that all life's wretched trivialities need not cause any disturbances between us.

And now all good wishes. I hope to see you for certain this afternoon, when we could then drive out to Nussdorf. The drive would do me good too —

Your faithful brother

LUDWIG

Postscript. Peace, let us have peace.[4] God grant that the most natural bond, the bond between brothers, may not again

---

[1] Text of letter taken from Nohl II, no. 254 and Zekert, pp. 25-26. Both Nohl and Zekert transcribed the autograph, which was then in private ownership.

[2] Johann van Beethoven had married in November, 1812, Therese Obermayr, the daughter of a baker in Vienna. She already had an illegitimate daughter Amalie, born in January, 1807.

[3] During the winter 1822–1823 Beethoven and his brother had rooms in adjacent houses, Kothgasse 60 and 61. Beethoven lived in no. 60. The adjacent house belonged to Johann's brother-in-law, Leopold Obermayr, who was a baker.

[4] The autograph of this postscript beginning at the words 'Let us have . . .' is now in the Gesellschaft der Musikfreunde, Vienna.

be broken in an unnatural way. In any case my life will certainly not last very much longer. I repeat that I have nothing against your wife, although her behaviour to me on a few occasions has greatly shocked me. In any case owing to my indisposition which has now lasted for three and a half months I am very sensitive and irritable, I might even say extremely so. Away with everything that *cannot promote* my object, which is, that I and my good Karl may settle down to a kind of life that is particularly necessary and more suitable for me — Just have a look at my rooms here. You will then see the results, you will realize what happens, simply because when I am seriously indisposed I have to be *at the mercy of strangers.* I am not mentioning other matters which in any case we have already discussed —

If you come today, you could fetch *Karl. Therefore I am enclosing* this open letter to Herr v. Blöchlinger which you can forward to him immediately —

(1079) *To Carl Friedrich Peters, Leipzig* [1]

[*MS in the Beethovenhaus, Bonn, H. C. Bodmer collection*] [2]

SIR!   VIENNA, *June* 5, 1822

You have honoured me with a letter. But as I happen to be very busy and have been ailing for the last five months, I am replying only to its most essential points — Although I met *Steiner* a few days ago and jokingly asked him what he had brought me from Leipzig, he did not mention *a syllable* either about *your commission* or about *yourself.* But he urged *me* most insistently *to assure him* that I would give to *him alone both my present works and also my future ones* and, moreover, *to draw up a contract* with him about this. I refused — This incident will serve to explain to you why I frequently give

---

[1] After Ambros Kühnel's death in 1813 Carl Friedrich Peters took over the music publishing firm, which he directed until his death in November, 1827. Peters did not publish a single work of Beethoven's during the composer's lifetime.

[2] There are two versions of this letter, which are both in the H. C. Bodmer collection. One is a draft made by Beethoven and the other is the copy written in another hand, signed by Beethoven and sent to Leipzig. The latter is the version translated here. *TDR* IV, 294-252 gives this version and quotes some variants in the original draft.

the preference to other foreign or even to other native publishers. I like honesty and sincerity; and I maintain that an artist should not be shabbily treated. For alas! sad to relate, however glittering his fame may seem on the surface, yet the artist is not allowed to be Jupiter's guest in Olympus every day; unfortunately, vulgar humanity only too often drags him down against his will from those pure ethereal heights —

The *greatest* work which I have composed so far is a grand Mass with choruses, four obbligato voices and a large orchestra.[1] Several publishers have made offers for it. I have been offered 100 full weight louis d'or. Let me inform you that for this work I am asking at least 1000 gulden A.C. at the 20 gulden rate — and for that sum I shall also provide the pianoforte arrangement myself — Variations on a waltz for pianoforte solo (there are several variations) for a fee of 30 gold ducats (Viennese ducats).[2]

As to songs, I have some rather fine ones fully worked out, such as, for instance, a comic aria with full orchestra on Goethe's text 'Mit Mädeln sich vertragen'[3] and so forth, and again another aria of a similar type,[4] for each of which I am asking 16 ducats (a pianoforte arrangement too, if required) — then several songs worked out with pianoforte accompaniment, 12 ducats apiece, among which there is also a little Italian cantata with recitative — Among the German songs too there is one with recitative — For a song with pianoforte accompaniment 8 ducats — An elegy for four voices with the accompaniment of two violins, viola and cello for a fee of 24 ducats[5] — A chorus of Dervishes with full orchestra, 20 ducats.[6]

As to instrumental music I could let you have the following works: A grand march for full orchestra with a pianoforte arrangement for 12 ducats. It was composed for the tragedy 'Tarpeja'[7] — A romance for violin (solo with full orchestra)

---

[1] The 'Missa Solemnis', Op. 123.   [2] Op. 120.

[3] An aria for bass voice with orchestra on a poem by Goethe, not published in Beethoven's lifetime. It is listed as WoO 90 in *KHV*. 545-546.

[4] 'Prüfung des Küssens', an aria for bass voice with orchestra on a poem by an unknown author, not published in Beethoven's lifetime. It is listed as WoO 89 in *KHV*. 544-545.

[5] Op. 118, dedicated to Baron Johann Pasqualati, was published by Tobias Haslinger in July, 1826.   [6] Op. 113, no. 3.

[7] WoO 2a. It was not published in Beethoven's lifetime.

for 15 ducats — A grand trio for two oboes and an English horn (which could also be arranged for other instruments) for 30 ducats [1] — Four military marches for Turkish music; for these I will quote the fee if you desire — Bagatelles or trifles for pianoforte solo, the fee to be quoted if desired [2] — All the above works are finished — For a sonata for pianoforte solo, which you could have very soon, 40 ducats. For a quartet for two violins, viola and violoncello, which you could also have very soon, 50 ducats [3] — But what I have more at heart than anything else is the *publication of my collected works*, for I should like to arrange this during my lifetime. I have in fact received several offers about this. But there were objections which I found hard to overcome and conditions which I could not and would not accept. I would undertake to have the whole material ready in two years, or even, possibly, in a year or eighteen months, that is to say, provided I have the necessary help; I myself would prepare the whole edition and for each type of composition I would provide a new work; for instance, for the variations a new set of variations, for the sonatas a new sonata, and so forth, i.e. for each category in which I have composed some work I would compose a new one; and for the entire undertaking, everything included, I would demand 10,000 gulden A.C. at the 20 gulden rate. —

I am no business man and I would much prefer that in this respect things were different. But it is competition which, since things are as they are, guides and determines my attitude in this matter — Please keep this a secret. For, as you can already gather from the actions of those gentlemen, I should be exposed to many vexations. But as soon as some work of mine has been published by your firm, then I cannot be pestered any longer — It is my wish that a connexion should be established between us. For I have been assured that you are very good people to deal with. You would then realize that

---

[1] The romance for violin has not been identified. The grand trio is a set of variations on the duet 'Là ci darem' in Mozart's 'Don Giovanni', which was first published by Breitkopf & Härtel in 1914. It is listed in *KHV*. 467-468 as WoO 28.

[2] According to *KHV*. 347 Beethoven was thinking of nos. 1-6 of his Op. 119 (eleven bagatelles for pianoforte solo).

[3] Evidently Beethoven was proposing to compose these works. In *KHV*. 386 it is suggested that he was already working at his first late quartet, Op. 127.

I would rather have dealings with people of your type than with any others of the ordinary kind —

Please reply quickly. For I am now on the verge of deciding about the publication of several works.[1] If you are interested, kindly send me a copy of the list which you gave to Herr Steiner —

Awaiting an early reply I remain, with kind regards, your devoted

BEETHOVEN

(1080) *To* ?

[Autograph in the possession of Dietrich Fischer-Dieskau] [2]

[VIENNA, *June* 5, 1822] [3]

. . . everything be clear to you. In regard to the songs I thought that some sort of variation with choruses and instruments and a proper arietta would please you more than merely simple lieder. In any case it will be clear . . .

. . . from the foregoing remarks you will gather that I compose not merely *for money* but that I also like to pursue my artistic aims, and that from this point of view the fee I demanded was certainly small. — I request you . . .

[1] In his draft Beethoven added the following sentence, which was omitted in the letter sent to Peters: 'How sorry I am that Steiner, who has estimable qualities, has again on this occasion proved to be a *vulgar business man*'.

[2] The autograph is a fragment written on both sides of one sheet. It is obviously a portion of a letter to a publisher, possibly a postscript to the preceding Letter 1079.

[3] This date is in another hand.

(1081) *To Anton Felix Schindler, Vienna* [1]

[*Autograph in the Deutsche Staatsbibliothek, Berlin*]

[DÖBLING, *June* 18, 1822]

Please be so kind as to send me both the German and the French invitations to subscribe to the Mass. Some mistake seems to have been made either in the copies or in the wording of the invitation —

In great haste, your ami

LUDWIG VAN BEETHOVEN

(1082) *To Georg August von Griesinger, Vienna* [2]

[*Autograph in the Beethovenhaus, Bonn, H. C. Bodmer collection*]

[DÖBLING, *c. June* 20, 1822]

I am delighted to receive a few lines from you, and I will visit you as soon as I come into town. As I have now been ailing for five months I have to be careful about working at

[1] Anton Felix Schindler (1795–1864), born at Meedl in Moravia, is known chiefly for his long connexion with Beethoven as the latter's friend, amanuensis and first biographer. Schindler came to Vienna to study law, but all his leisure was devoted to music; and he became an excellent violinist and eventually leader of the orchestra at the Josephstadt Theatre. He first met Beethoven in March, 1814, and by 1819 was virtually his unpaid secretary and servant. For a short time in 1822 they lived in the same house. When, in the summer of 1825, Beethoven formed an intimate friendship with the gifted and lively Karl Holz (see Letter 1409), Schindler, who strongly disapproved and was possibly jealous of Holz, disappeared from the scene for over a year. But he faithfully attended his beloved master during the last four months of his life. After Beethoven's death Schindler left Vienna, became musical director at Münster and later at Aachen, and after a few years settled at Frankfurt, where he led a very retired life. He is now chiefly remembered for his life of Beethoven, first published at Münster in 1840. This was followed by *Beethoven in Paris*, 1842, and by a second edition of the original biography with additions in 1845. The work has a very personal tinge and many of his statements are deplorably inaccurate. But Schindler was so closely associated with Beethoven during the last ten years of his life that many passages in it are of absorbing interest. In 1845 Schindler's large collection of Beethoven MSS, Conversation Books, letters, etc., were sold to the Berlin Library in return for an annuity.

[2] Georg August von Griesinger (1769–1845), a German Government official and writer, was first tutor in various aristocratic families and lastly to the children of the Saxon Envoy in Vienna, who assisted him to join the Diplomatic Service. In 1804 Griesinger was appointed Counsellor at the Saxon Legation in Vienna. On June 17, 1822, he wrote to Beethoven (the letter is quoted in *KST*, no. 1012a) offering to act as intermediary for a resumption of business relations between Beethoven and Härtel and suggesting that the former should compose an opera.

my art — It has afforded me much pleasure to hear from you, a man of such distinction (in general — and particularly in connexion with Haydn's biography).[1]

With kindest regards, your most devoted

BEETHOVEN

(1083) *To Carl Friedrich Peters, Leipzig*

[Autograph in the Beethovenhaus, Bonn, H. C. Bodmer collection]

SIR!   VIENNA, *June* 26, 1822 [2]

This is just to inform you that I *agree to give* you the Mass together with the pianoforte arrangement for a redemption bond of 1000 gulden A.C. at the 20 gulden rate. You will receive a careful copy of the score by the end of July, perhaps even a few days before or after that date. As I am always very busy and have been ailing for the last five months and as obviously one must check works of that kind with great care, especially if they are to be sent away, I am no doubt a bit slower than other people. — In no circumstances will Schlesinger ever get *anything more from me*, because he too has played me a Jewish trick. In any case he is not one of the publishers who might have got the Mass. At the moment, however, the competition to secure my works is very keen; and for this I am grateful to the Almighty. For I have already lost a great deal. Moreover I am the foster-father of the destitute child of my deceased brother. As this boy of fifteen shows so much aptitude for general knowledge, not only do the acquisition of this learning and his maintenance now cost a good deal of money, but his future must also be provided for, since we are neither Indians nor Iroquois who, as everyone knows, leave all to the Lord God, and since a pauper's existence is always a sad one — I am keeping all our dealings secret, a thing which *in any case I much prefer to do*; and please treat my present connexion with you as a secret. I shall not forget to inform you

---

[1] Immediately after Haydn's death in May, 1809, Griesinger compiled his *Biographische Notizen über Joseph Haydn*, a short work which was published by Breitkopf & Härtel in 1810. A new edition of this book with a commentary by Dr. Franz Grasberger has been published by Paul Kaltschmid (Vienna, 1959).

[2] In the autograph the date is July 26, but on internal evidence the letter must have been written in June. Moreover it obviously precedes Letters 1085 and 1086.

when the time has come to talk. At the moment that is not at all necessary — In order to give you proof of my veracity, to a certain extent at any rate, I am enclosing this form written out by Steiner, whose handwriting you will recognize. It is rather difficult to decipher. I assure you *on my honour,* which next to God I value most highly, that I never asked Steiner to take commissions for me. It has always been my *chief principle* not to approach any publisher. This is not due to pride but because I have preferred to observe how far the field of my small talent would extend. I presume that Steiner has made this whole offer to you in *some artful way.* For I remember that *you very kindly delivered to me through Steiner some music from England.* Who knows but that for that very reason he hit *on this idea* and thereupon played *this trick,* suspecting perhaps that you would make me an offer — As to the songs, I have already sent you my views. I consider that for the three songs with the four marches the fee of 40 ducats is *not excessive* — you can write to me about this [1] — As soon as the Mass is ready I will let you know and then ask you to remit the fee to a banking house in Vienna where after receiving it I will immediately hand in the work. Let me add that I will make a point of being present when the work is handed in at the post office and that I will also ensure that the carriage shall not cost too much. I should like to hear soon about your plan to publish my collected works, for I am bound to have such an undertaking very much at heart — Well, I am closing this letter for today. I wish you everything that may redound to your advantage and I remain,

with kindest regards, your most devoted

BEETHOVEN

(1084) *To Ferdinand Ries, London*

[*Autograph in the Fitzwilliam Museum, Cambridge*]

[VIENNA], *July* 6, 1822

DEAR AND MOST EXCELLENT RIES!

As I have again been unwell for more than half a year, I have never managed to answer your letter. I received safely

---

[1] Cf. Letter 1079 for the many works which Beethoven offered to C. F. Peters in his first reply.

the 26 pounds sterling, for which I send you my warmest thanks. I have not received any portion of the symphony you have dedicated to me. It is best to send parcels of that kind to *Steiner & Co.'s art and music shop.* But send all letters direct to me and I shall receive them quite safely —

My greatest work is a grand Mass which I have recently composed, etc., etc. Today I have too little time, so can only add quickly what is absolutely necessary for me to tell you — I have composed two new sonatas for pianoforte solo which are really not very difficult.[1] I should be glad if you could obtain the same sum of 26 pounds sterling for these, for I can dispose of them in Germany as well without injuring either the English or the German publisher. *If you can get more, all the better.* But I do beg you not to keep me waiting so long again for an answer, because otherwise, if it is too late, I shall have to give them away at once both in Vienna and elsewhere —

Have you any idea what fee the *Harmony Society* would offer me for a grand symphony?[2] I am still toying with the idea of going to London, provided my health permits it, perhaps next spring?! — You would find in me the just critic of my dear pupil who has now become a great master. And who knows how many other benefits to art might result from our joint efforts? I am entirely devoted to my Muses, as I have always been; and in this alone do I find the joy of my life; and I also work and exert myself for others so far as I can; — Do write immediately, and in particular about the sonatas, a matter which is of great importance to me. *You* have two children and *I have one, my brother's son.*[3] But you are married, so that your two children do not cost you as much as *one child* costs me —

Now all good wishes. Kiss your beautiful wife for me until I can perform this solemn action *in person* —

Your warm-hearted friend

BEETHOVEN

NB. Do see that I receive the dedication, so that I too

---

[1] Op. 110 and 111.

[2] This appears to be the first mention by Beethoven in a letter of his plan to compose a ninth symphony, although there are extant sketches for the first movement and the Scherzo dating back to 1817–1818.

[3] The words 'my brother's son' are added at the foot of the page.

may have something to display; and this I shall do as soon
as I receive it.[1]

(1085) *To Carl Friedrich Peters, Leipzig*

[*Autograph in the Beethovenhaus, Bonn, H. C. Bodmer collection*]

S<small>IR</small>!   [V<small>IENNA</small>], *July* 6, 1822

Only now have I read your letter carefully. Thus I
notice that you would like to have some of the bagatelles for
pianoforte solo,[2] and also a quartet for two violins[3] and so
forth — As to the bagatelles, I charge 8 gold ducats apiece.
Some of them are rather long. You could also publish them
separately and with a German, and, possibly, more suitable
title, such as :—Kleinigkeiten No. 1, No. 2 and so forth or,
for instance, Kleinigkeiten separately No. 1 — Kleinigkeiten
No. 2 and so forth, in fact whatever you think best.

As to the violin quartet, which is not yet quite finished,
because something else intervened, it would be difficult for
me to reduce the fee I am asking you for this work. For it
is precisely for a composition of this kind that I am most
highly paid — and I should almost like to add, to the disgrace
of the general taste of the majority, which in the world of
art is often far inferior to that of individuals — But perhaps
I could let you have another quartet later on. In regard to
the ducat, you may calculate its value as 4 gulden, 30 kreuzer
at the rate of 20. It's all the same to me — As I can let you
have immediately not only the songs but also the marches
and the bagatelles,[4] I do request you to write to me *soon*
about this, so that I may not be the loser when allocating
the works. For I have been approached from several quarters
precisely about trifles of that kind. — Well, St[einer]'s procedure requiescat in pace.[5] He seems to have been very
anxious to get something out of me. I can't *excuse* methods

---

¹ This NB. is written on the left side of the second page of the autograph.
² Beethoven was evidently offering Peters some of the eleven bagatelles for
pianoforte solo, Op. 119, which were first published by Moritz Schlesinger in Paris
towards the end of 1823.   ³ Op. 127.
⁴ Cf. Beethoven's letter to Peters of June 5, 1822 (Letter 1079), where all
these works are enumerated.
⁵ I.e. may rest in peace.

of that kind, but — one must, whether one likes it or not, take people of that stamp as they are. If not, one would be living in a perpetual state of war. — I have already written everything to you about the Mass, an arrangement which must stand. Do not forget about the publication of my collected works — and so forth and so on. And now please let me have as soon as possible a reply about the other questions I have raised — I wish you all the good things you can imagine —

With kindest regards, your most devoted

BEETHOVEN

(1086) *To Johann van Beethoven, Gneixendorf*

[Autograph not traced] [1]

DEAR BROTHER!   VIENNA, *July* 22–26, 1822

I have not been able to write to you until now, because I have been exceedingly busy and hampered in every way by my living arrangements and my servants, both of whom are extremely unsatisfactory. As to my health, I feel better. For the last few days I have had to drink Johannesbrunnen water and take the powders four times a day; and now I am to go to Baden and take 30 baths. If I find it *possible* to arrange this, I shall go there about August 6th or 7th.[2] If only you could come for a few days and help me. But the dust and the heat would be too much for you. Otherwise you could spend eight days with me at Baden ad tuum libitum.[3] Here I still have to deal with the proof-reading of the Mass. I am to get 1000 gulden A.C. for it from *Peters* who is also taking some other minor compositions. He has already remitted 300 gulden A.C. to Vienna. I do wish that you could read the letters. But I have not yet drawn the money. Breitkopf & Härtel also have sent the Saxon chargé d'affaires to me about taking some of my works.[4] From Paris too I have received offers for my compositions, and from Diabelli in Vienna as well. In short,

---

[1] Taken from Nohl II, no. 245, and Zekert, pp. 28-29. Both Nohl and Zekert had access to the original letter, which in the former's time was in the possession of Karl's widow.

[2] Beethoven did not go to Baden until the beginning of September. He remained there for about six weeks.   [3] I.e. as you please.

[4] Beethoven is referring no doubt to Griesinger's letter. Cf. p. 951, n. 1.

there is a general scramble to secure my works. *What an unhappy, yet happy man* am I ! ! ! — And that *native of Berlin* too has turned up [1] — If only my health were restored, I might yet make a success of things —

The Cardinal Archduke is here and I go to him twice a week. I have no hope of generous treatment or money, I admit. But I am on such a good, familiar footing with him that it would hurt me exceedingly not to be pleasant to him. Besides I do believe that his apparent niggardliness is not his fault — Before I go to Baden I shall have to get some clothes, for, as you have already noticed, I am really very shabby even in respect of my shirts. Ask your wife what she thinks of this linen; an ell costs 48 kreuzer V.C. — Do come if you can, but not if it is a trouble to you. I will go to you in September with Karl if I don't go to the Cardinal at Olmütz. He is very anxious to have me — As to the apartments, since they have already been taken, well and good. But whether they are good for me too, that is a question? The rooms look out on the garden. Yet garden air is just the very worst air for me. Moreover the entrance to my rooms is through the *kitchen*, which is very unpleasant and not very good for my health— and now I have to pay a quarter's rent for nothing. To recoup myself Karl and I will come and stay with you at Krems, if possible, and live on the fat of the land until this sum has been made up, that is, of course, if I don't go to Moravia [2] — Do write as soon as you receive this letter. My greetings to your family. If I did not have to go to Baden, I would certainly have come to you next month. But nothing can be altered now. Do come if you can, for your presence would be a great relief to me. Write at once — All good wishes. With all my heart I embrace you and am, as always, your faithful brother

LUDWIG

---

[1] Offers for Beethoven's compositions had been made by Adolf Martin Schlesinger of Berlin and by his eldest son Moritz, now settled in Paris.

[2] To the Archduke Rudolph at Olmütz.

(1087) *To Johann van Beethoven, Gneixendorf*

[*MS in the Beethovenhaus, Bonn, H. C. Bodmer collection*] [1]

[VIENNA, *July* 31, 1822]

MOST EXCELLENT LITTLE BROTHER! HIGH AND MIGHTY LAND-
OWNER!

I wrote to you yesterday, but as I was exhausted by so
many exertions and tasks and as I was writing with a bad
quill, you may find the letter difficult to read. First of all,
let me know how quickly the posts go from your place to mine
and from mine to yours — I told you in my letter that the
Leipzig publisher is taking the Mass for 1000 gulden.[2] I only
wish that I could send you all the letters, but that would be
too inconvenient. It would be better if you were present at all
these negotiations, for I am inclined to think that I have let him
have some of the other trifles too cheaply. He has still to get four
marches for 20 ducats, three songs at 8 ducats apiece and four
bagatelles, at 8 ducats apiece.[3] In order to avoid tedious
formalities I have requested him to pay me the money in
silver. As he did not yet know, however, how many bagatelles
he would be getting, he immediately sent me a draft for 300
gulden, as you will see from the enclosed note. But now I
cannot send the bagatelles at once, because the copyist is
busy with the Mass, which is the most important task, and for
which, provided I inform Leipzig just a few days in advance
that the Mass is being dispatched from Vienna, I shall immediately receive the 1000 gulden, a sum which, had I so desired,
I could have had by now. From all I have said you may
gather how infatuated the man is with my work. At the same
time I should not like to lay myself open to certain charges.
And I should be delighted if you would let me know whether
you could spare a small sum, so that I may not be prevented
from leaving in good time for Baden where I must spend a

---

[1] Written by Karl and signed by Beethoven.

[2] Evidently a reference to his preceding letter of July 22–26 (Letter 1086), in
which Beethoven informed his brother of C. F. Peters's offer of 1000 gulden for the
Mass.

[3] Cf. Beethoven's first letter to C. F. Peters, dated June 5, 1822 (Letter 1079)
in which he enumerated several works.

month at least. You see that in this transaction there is no lack of security and that in September the 200 gulden will be refunded to you with my thanks. Please return the enclosed note immediately. Let me add that being a business man you always give good advice. The Steiners too are driving me into a corner. They insist on my giving them a written promise that I will let them have all my works. They are prepared to pay for every single proof-sheet. But I have stated that I refuse to make such an arrangement with them until they have cancelled the debt. With this in view I have offered them two works which I wrote for Hungary and which might be treated as a couple of short operas, from which, moreover, they took four numbers some time ago.[1] The debt is about 3000 gulden ; but they have been so low-minded as to add to this amount some interest, which I positively refuse to pay. Furthermore, I have shouldered a portion of the debts incurred by Karl's mother, for so long as Karl's prospects are not thereby endangered, I am glad to be as kind to her as possible. If you were here, these questions would soon be dealt with. Only necessity compels me to sell my soul in this way. If you could come here and go with me to Baden for eight days, that indeed would be splendid.[2] But you must let me know at once what you are proposing to do. In the meantime put your kitchen and your cellar in their best order, for in all likelihood I and my little son will make your estate our headquarters ; and we are nobly determined to eat you out of house and home. Of course I am referring now to our plans for September.

Now all good wishes, most excellent little brother ! Read the Gospel every day. Take to heart the Epistles of Peter and Paul. Travel to Rome and kiss the Pope's slipper. My warmest greetings to your family. Write soon. With all my heart I embrace you.

Your faithful brother
LUDWIG

I, secretarius, embrace you too with all my heart and hope to see you again soon.

KARL.

---

[1] Op. 113 and 117.
[2] Beethoven went to Baden on September 1st.

On *July* 31, 1822

NB. I am not enclosing the draft for 300 gulden A.C., because I am afraid lest something might perhaps happen to it.[1]

(1088) *To Johann van Beethoven, Gneixendorf*

[Autograph in the possession of Kommerzialrat Otto Reichert]

[VIENNA, *July*, 1822]

All the best greetings to your family.

The 300 gulden A.C. have been remitted to Meisl Bros. here.[2] But I should prefer, in case I need it, that you should make me an advance. For the Mass will be sent off by the 15th of next month at latest.[3]

NB.[4] The housekeeper is an *old child*. It is very difficult for me to manage with this woman. Her cooking is extremely poor, in fact it is hardly suitable for me; and she can scarcely *write* —

NB.[5] As soon as I write to Peters telling him to send me 1000 gulden for the Mass, I shall receive it at once —

NB.[6] After all, it would be better than to let H[err] Petrus at Leipzig notice qu'on a besoin de l'argent.

(1089) *To Johann van Beethoven*

[Autograph not traced][7]

DEAR BROTHER!   [VIENNA, *Summer*, 1822]

Do send over everything, including the manuscript of the bagatelles, for if you don't, I can't correct them[8] — As

---

[1] This dated postscript is written in Beethoven's hand inside a cover which undoubtedly belongs to the letter.

[2] See Letter 1141, p. 1004, n. 1.

[3] See Letter 1092, p. 962.

[4] The whole letter with its three postscripts is written on one page. This NB. is written upside down on the right side.

[5] This NB. is written upside down at the foot of the page.

[6] This NB. is written upside down on the left side.

[7] Taken from Nohl II, no. 243. Nohl transcribed the autograph then in the possession of Karl's widow.

[8] Johann was evidently in Vienna. The work referred to is the collection of eleven bagatelles for pianoforte solo, which was first published late in 1823 by Moritz Schlesinger, Paris, as Op. 119. See *KHV*. 342-347.

BEETHOVEN'S BROTHER, NIKOLAUS JOHANN VAN BEETHOVEN
(1776–1848)
From the oil portrait by Leopold Grosz (1841)
(*Historisches Museum der Stadt Wien*)

soon as I have received everything, then you can decide where I am to send the draft. It will be handed to the person whom you nominate for this purpose and he can collect the money and at the same time deliver the works.

Your faithful brother

BEETHOVEN

Herr Karl van Beethoven is authorized to take the music with him.

(1090) *To Johann van Beethoven, Vienna*

[*Autograph not traced*] [1]

MY DEAR BROTHER!   [DÖBLING, *Summer*, 1822]

Don't be impatient with me for giving you so much trouble — I hope yet to discover in what way I can prove my gratitude to you, to some extent at any rate — Please see that Karl brings his shoes when he is driving out to Döbling [2] — In my apartment at Karl's boarding school there is another side door in the room where there used to be a commode [3] — In the English pianoforte the screws beside the feet near the lyre below should be tightened by means of a spanner. No doubt you will need several people in the *Döbling hole* on account of the pianoforte. It would probably be best if it were carried — Now all good wishes. It would be very nice if you could come here on Sunday. For I am thinking of strolling off somewhere on Monday afternoon —

With all my heart I embrace you.

Your faithful brother

L. V. BEETHOVEN

[1] Taken from Nohl II, no. 239. According to his statement Nohl used a facsimile of the autograph.
[2] Beethoven had been at Döbling since the beginning of May, but came into Vienna occasionally. At Döbling he occupied rooms in the Alleegasse, no. 135.
[3] There seems to be some misreading here.

(1091) *To Antonio Diabelli* [1]

[*Autograph in the Beethovenhaus, Bonn, H. C. Bodmer collection*]

DEAR DIABELLI!   [VIENNA, *Summer*, 1822]
I looked them up yesterday, and today you may still
have the sixth in addition to the five bagatelles which you
have already seen. [2] For I really have a sufficiently large
supply to enable me to send off others instead of these — The
fee would be 50 ducats, the same sum which I also obtain
there for six specimens of this type of composition —
If this suits you, you can have them all this very day.
In haste, yours
BEETHOVEN

(1092) *To Carl Friedrich Peters, Leipzig*

[*Autograph in the Beethovenhaus, Bonn, H. C. Bodmer collection*]

SIR!   [DÖBLING] *August 3*, [1822]
I wrote to you some time ago about my health which is
not yet fully restored. I am taking baths and drinking mineral
waters and medicine as well. Hence my affairs are in a bit
of a muddle, the more so as notwithstanding all these draw-
backs I must compose. Proof-reading also takes up time —
In regard to the songs, the other marches and *bagatelles* I am
still uncertain what to choose. [3] But I shall be able to deliver
everything by the 15th of this month. I am awaiting your
decision about this, and for the time being shall not make use
of your draft. You will receive four of the bagatelles [4] — On
the basis of the fee we fixed they amount to 360 gulden at the

---

[1] Antonio Diabelli (1781–1858), born near Salzburg, received his musical
training in Bavaria and in 1803 came to Vienna where he gave lessons on the
pianoforte and the guitar. Later he was employed in Steiner's firm and in 1818
he and Cappi became partners in music publishing; and by 1824 he was publishing under his own name. Diabelli was also a prolific composer. He wrote the
waltz tune on which Beethoven composed his set of 33 variations for pianoforte
solo, Op. 120. See *FRBH* I, 107-108.
[2] Probably the first six of the eleven bagatelles published in 1823 by M.
Schlesinger, Paris as Op. 119.
[3] Cf. the list of works sent to Peters in Letter 1079, pp. 948-949.
[4] Probably four of the eleven bagatelles of Op. 119.

rate of 20 gulden. Just check that calculation carefully — I am not asking you to pay higher sums than other people. On the contrary, I have still quoted too low a fee for the songs. For my time is really far too precious. As soon as I know that the fee for *the Mass* and the other works has arrived in Vienna, then everything can be delivered by the 15th of this month — Forgive the casual way in which I am writing to you. You mentioned in your letter that you had already been let down. I too have been let down. *Please do not misconstrue such expressions as* 'my time is too precious' *and so forth.*[1] Well, after the 15th I still have to go to a watering-place near here.[2] So I am very anxious to be rid of all business affairs for a time — All the other points I will write about some day when I am a little less busy — You can have several bagatelles. But at the moment I am unable to state definitely how many I have — In great haste, with kindest regards, your most devoted

BEETHOVEN

NB.[3] Please do not put *a low construction* on anything I write — It *distresses me* — when I am obliged to bargain —

(1093) *To Artaria & Co.*

[*Autograph in the Beethovenhaus, Bonn, H. C. Bodmer collection*]

GENTLEMEN! [VIENNA, *August 22, 1822*]

As I am just now overwhelmed with work, all that I can tell you briefly is that, so far as I can, I will always return the kindnesses you have rendered me. As to the Mass, well, I have been offered 1000 gulden A.C. for it. My circumstances do not permit me to accept a smaller fee from you. All that I can do is to *give* you the *preference*. Rest assured that I shall not take from you *a farthing more* than the *others have offered* me. I could prove this to you in writing. You may think this over. But I must ask you to let me have a reply about this before *noon tomorrow*, for tomorrow is post-day, and my decision is

---

[1] This sentence is added at the foot of page 2.
[2] Beethoven went to Baden at the beginning of September. See Letter 1094, p. 964.
[3] The NB. is added at the side of page 3, near the foot of the page.

being awaited in other quarters as well — As to the 150 gulden A.C. which I owe you, I will also make a proposal to you. But, of course, they must not be deducted *now*, because I badly need the 1000 gulden — And now I must ask you to observe secrecy about everything connected with the Mass —

Ever your grateful friend

BEETHOVEN

(1094) *To Johann van Beethoven, Gneixendorf*

[Autograph in the Beethovenhaus, Bonn, H. C. Bodmer collection]

DEAR BROTHER!   VIENNA, *August* 31, 1822

No doubt you will have received by now my letter enclosing some papers. I left it with Steiner. Staudenh[eim] absolutely insists on my going to Baden. So I am off tomorrow or the day after at latest. In view of all this, I would have liked you to come to Vienna so that we could have discussed several matters and completed all the arrangements with Steiner. For they must engrave the 'Ruinen von Athen' by the end of October, when the theatre is to be opened; and as no agreement has yet been concluded, they certainly cannot begin the work [1] — In any case you could stay with me for a while at Baden, and the change would do you good — I am going straight to Baden and shall spend a day at the inn, during which time I will rent some rooms — All good wishes. With all my heart I embrace you. I am truly disappointed that I have not been allowed to go to you, which I should have preferred — All good wishes. With all my heart I embrace you.

Your faithful brother

LUDWIG

God be with you. Give my greetings to your family.

---

[1] Op. 113. Steiner published the score of the overture in February, 1823. But the first edition of the whole work in score did not appear until 1846, when it was published by Artaria. See *KHV*. 327-328.

(1095) *To Moritz Schlesinger, Paris*

[*Autograph in the Beethovenhaus, Bonn, H. C. Bodmer collection*]

SIR!   VIENNA, *August* 31, 1822

In the sonata sent here to Steiner there have still been found some mistakes of which you are being informed so that they may be corrected.[1] And please send me first a proof copy of the C minor sonata before you dispatch it.[2] For it is very unpleasant for me if my works come out so full of mistakes. The proof copy will be corrected here immediately and returned to you; whereupon you may then circulate the work throughout the world. I must insist that this be done, for, if not, it will be your own fault if your edition is pirated — And the *dedication* of the C minor sonata[3] is to be to his Imperial Highness the Cardinal, who has already been told about it. I have written it down for you and as soon as the proof copy arrives I will send you the dedication with the corrected copy or perhaps sooner by letter post — Although I wrote to your father and to you that the sonata in A♭ was to be dedicated to one of my friends, yet this has not been done[4] — Apparently I am to have several unpleasant experiences with you and your father, for when I was paid for the two sonatas here in Vienna I lost no less than 12 to 13 gulden A.C. For I happened to be ill and unable to fetch the money in person. Indeed I should have much preferred not to accept it at all than *to have to put up with* such insulting niggardliness, the like of which I have *never* experienced — I hope that you will send me without delay the proof copy of the C minor sonata so that it may be corrected here at once. If you don't, I cannot promise you that the consequences will not be unpleasant. — In great haste, your devoted

BEETHOVEN

NB.[5] I request you to send me six copies of the sonata which has been published and of the one about to be published.[6]

[1] Op. 110.   [2] Op. 111. Beethoven evidently means 'before you sell it'.
[3] The words from 'of' to 'sonata' are added at the foot of the page.
[4] Beethoven's first intention was to dedicate both Op. 110 and Op. 111 to Antonia Brentano.
[5] In the autograph the NB. is scrawled in pencil on the top of the first page over the date and the vocative.   [6] Op. 110 and 111.

These copies will not be sold. Only those artists who cannot pay and of whom there are millions, get these copies from me—

(1096) *To Tobias Haslinger, Vienna*

[Autograph not traced] [1]

MY DEAR HASLINGER! BADEN, *September* 5, [1822]
As I am living here in the waters of the Styx I need several things from the upper world. So I beg you and Steiner [2] to be kind enough to *lend* me for a few days the *four vocal parts of the march in E♭ from the Ruinen von Athen,*[3] and also *a score of the Schlacht von Vittoria,* both of which I will return in a few days — I must ask Steiner to go tomorrow afternoon to Bach's house where he can draw the 600 gulden A.C. The other 600 will also be delivered as quickly as possible to Dr. Bach — You can entrust everything to my dear Karl. If the Leipziger Zeitung could be understood and so forth and so on, if one could fathom it one would find — [4]
As always your friend and amicus
BEETHOVEN

(1097) *To Johann van Beethoven, Vienna*

[MS not traced] [5]

DEAR BROTHER! [BADEN], *Sunday, September* 8, 1822
We are rather anxious lest you should not be well, I mean, on account of your silence. Moreover this silence is causing

---

[1] Taken from Frimmel, *Neue Beethoveniana*, 2nd edition (Vienna, 1890), p. 125. In 1880 Frimmel copied the autograph then in private ownership.

[2] According to Frimmel, *op. cit.*, the words 'and Steiner' are added at the foot of the page.

[3] This was no. 6 of Op. 113 to which Beethoven made some musical and textual additions for its production at the opening of the newly rebuilt Josephstadt Theatre on October 3, 1822. It was published by Steiner in April, 1826, as Op. 114. For the same occasion Beethoven composed a new overture entitled 'Die Weihe des Hauses', which was published in score by Schott in December, 1825, as Op. 124.

[4] The meaning of this last sentence is so obscure that the present editor is driven to assume that it must have been misread by Frimmel.

[5] Taken from Zekert, pp. 31-32. The letter was written by Karl and signed by Beethoven.

me some embarrassment, because I don't know what has become of the commissions which you yourself undertook so lovingly. As for Simrock, he has written again for the Mass, at the old price, it is true. But if we were to write to him, I really believe that he would raise his offer. About my state of health I cannot declare with certainty that there has been a definite improvement. All the same I fancy that thanks to the good effect of the baths the trouble will be arrested, though not completely cured. Since we have received no letter from you and have had no news of you from any other source, we assume that you have now left. Well, in any case do send us a few lines, I beg you, wherever you may be. I am enclosing this letter to Herr Obermayr [1] so that, should you not be in Vienna, it may reach you at once. Today an overture of mine is being performed here ; and a grand historical tableau 'Stephen I', which suits it, is being produced.[2] Hensler [3] has sent us two free tickets and is behaving very amicably to us. Two women singers called on us today and as they absolutely insisted on being allowed to kiss my hands and as they were decidedly pretty I preferred to offer them my mouth to kiss.[4] Incidentally this is the shortest piece of news we can give you. Again I beg you to let me know at once whether you have exerted yourself and what you have done, so that I may know how I stand.

All good wishes,

your faithful brother LUDWIG,
who is the guardian of my little
rascal who is a minor.

All my best wishes to your family.

Owing to a slight cough I have been obliged to spend two days in bed, but am now quite well again and can therefore

---

[1] Leopold Obermayr, a baker, was the brother of Therese Obermayr whom Johann had married in 1812. Cf. Letter 1078, p. 946, n. 2.

[2] Probably the overture to Op. 117.

[3] For a note on K. F. Hensler see Letter 1286, p. 1123, n. 2.

[4] Almost certainly the famous singers Henriette Sontag (1806–1854) and Karoline Unger (1803–1877), who took the solo soprano and contralto parts in the performance on May 7, 1824, of Beethoven's ninth symphony and portions of his ' Missa Solemnis '. See his letter to H. Sontag, Letter 1289, p. 1125, n. 2.

return to my post of secretary to my dear uncle. Please be so kind as to let me know about my overcoat as well.

Your KARL who loves you dearly.

NB. My dear uncle requests you to observe when replying the tempo which is called prestissimo.

(1098) *To Nikolaus Simrock, Bonn*

[*MS in the Beethovenhaus, Bonn, H. C. Bodmer collection*] [1]

BADEN, *September* 13, 1822

MY DEAR AND BELOVED SIMROCK!

You are receiving this letter from Baden where I am taking the baths. For my illness, which has lasted two and a half years, is not yet completely cured. However much I should like to write to you about several matters, yet I must be brief and merely reply to your last letter of August 22nd. In regard to the Mass, you know that on this subject I did write to you some time ago that a larger fee had been offered to me. Indeed it is not my practice to be greedy just for the sake of obtaining one or two more gulden. My poor health, however, and very many other untoward circumstances compel me to pay attention to such things. The lowest fee which at least four publishers have offered me so far for the Mass is 1000 gulden A.C. at the rate of 20, or fixing the gulden at three Austrian pieces of 20 A.C. However sorry I feel at our having to part company particularly about this composition, yet I know that your integrity would not let me lose over this work which is perhaps the greatest I have ever written. You know that I am no braggart and that I don't like to hand on the letters of other people or even quote extracts from them; but if I chose to do so, I could give you proofs of my statement about this from near and far. Well, I must trust that this question relating to the Mass will be settled as soon as possible, for on its account I have already had to deal with intrigues of all kinds. I should be glad if you would reply as soon as possible and say whether you are prepared to

[1] The letter was written by Karl. The last six words and the signature are in Beethoven's handwriting.

pay me that fee. If you are satisfied, then you need only send
the balance to Brentano, whereupon I will immediately send
you a carefully corrected copy of the score of the Mass, from
which you can engrave it without more ado. I trust that my
dear Simrock, whom I consider at any rate to be the wealthiest
of all publishers, will not let his old friend slip away for the
sake of a few hundred gulden. I will write to you soon about
all the other points. I am staying here until the beginning
of October. No doubt I will receive all the letters you write, just
as I received the last one. But do reply, I beseech you, as soon
as possible. All good wishes for your welfare. Give my
heartfelt greetings to your family. As soon as I am able to
do so, I will write to you myself.

     With cordial remembrances, your old friend

BEETHOVEN

(1099) *To Franz Brentano, Frankfurt am Main*

[*MS not traced*] ¹

SIR !   BADEN, *September* 13, 1822

    From the letter to Simrock you will now have gathered
more or less how things are.² Do please forgive me for de-
laying so long in discharging my debt to you. If Simrock,
to whom I beg you to make the matter quite clear — for in
reality 1000 gulden A.C. at the rate of 20 have been offered
to me for it — objects to paying this sum, then as soon as I
receive his reply to that effect, I will dispatch the Mass to
another quarter where I have been offered 1000 gulden and
where I shall receive the money at once, upon which I will
also discharge my debt to you. Once more I crave your
forgiveness for this. I trust that if my health improves, as it
appears to be improving here at Baden, I shall never again
find myself in the position of making myself a nuisance to anyone. I shall always be grateful to you for your generosity ;

¹ Taken from *ZMW*. II, 428 (no. VII). According to Kinsky this letter
was written by Karl, but the last nine words and the signature were added by
Beethoven.
² This is the preceding Letter 1098, addressed to Simrock, which Brentano was
forwarding for Beethoven.

and I can hardly wait for the moment when I shall no longer have to confess that I am deep in debt to you. I send you my very best wishes. My regard for and my gratitude to you will never cease.

I remain, Sir, your most devoted friend and servant

BEETHOVEN

(1100) *To Carl Friedrich Peters, Leipzig*

[*MS in the Beethovenhaus, Bonn, H. C. Bodmer collection*] [1]

SIR!   BADEN, *September* 13, 1822

No doubt you are just about to include me in the number of those who have let you down. It would certainly be very unpleasant and distressing for me if that were the case. Well, just for today I am letting you know that you will very soon receive all the bagatelles.[2] It is hard for people living in Leipzig to realize that people in and near Vienna can never lead an undisturbed life. I wrote to you some time ago that I intended to move to Baden on August 15th.[3] But the Cardinal came to Vienna, and so I had to stay on there until the end of August. As I was living in the country, that took up a good deal of my time, because I had to go into town to him several times a week. When at last he left Vienna I was able to come here, but that was not until September 1st. And hardly had I arrived here when I met a theatrical manager who is building a theatre in Vienna which he is opening with one of my compositions. So to please him I have had to compose a few new movements.[4]

Now you see that I have been harassed on all sides and have scarcely had any peace or been able to look after my health. I would have sent you these little pieces before now. But among the marches there are a few for which I decided to compose new trios. The same thing applies also to the other works, where here and there something has to be added. But owing to lack of time and on account of my health which I dare not neglect, I could not manage to do this. At all events you will gather from these remarks that I am not a composer

---

[1] Written by Karl and signed by Beethoven with postscripts.
[2] Op. 119.   [3] Cf. Letter 1092, p. 963.
[4] Cf. Letter 1096, p. 966, n. 3.

who writes merely for vile profit. I am very sorry that you sent the money for my works so soon. Nor would I have taken that money, had it not been on account of idle gossip; and of this you may convince yourself with the help of the present enclosure. The writer of it goes to Steiner every day and I presume that he has not held his tongue. You will remember that I implored you to keep everything secret from those people. And why? That I will disclose to you in due course. I hope that God will continue to protect me from all the incessant intrigues of that wicked Steiner. Treat my frankness with charity; and you must never fear that I shall do anything that might disgrace my character or injure another person. And now let me request you not to lend an ear to any idle gossip emanating from Vienna. For those Steiners are exploring every avenue to prevent anybody else from taking an interest in me.

In great haste, with kindest regards, your most devoted

BEETHOVEN [1]

Perhaps you will have more news from me in a few days. Beware of giving heed to *false* reports about me.

(1101) *To Johann van Beethoven, Gneixendorf*

[*MS in the Beethovenhaus, Bonn, H. C. Bodmer collection*] [2]

DEAR BROTHER!   [BADEN, *late September*, 1822]

I have been greatly embarrassed owing to your not having replied. My poor hearing, which cuts me off to a certain extent from human society, led me to believe that you had had a row with Steiner. Moreover I suspected that you would be angry if I omitted to mention that I would repay your debt. So being thus embarrassed and, moreover, anxious about the Mass, I wrote to Simrock (who had also written to me) that I would let him have it for 1000 gulden A.C. Since you say that you want to have the Mass, I fully agree with this arrangement. But I should not like you to suffer any loss in this transaction. The other matters which you raise in your letter we will discuss later. You say that you will soon be coming

---

[1] The last ten words and the two postscripts are in Beethoven's handwriting.
[2] Written by Karl and signed by Beethoven.

to Vienna. If you do, then come to Baden, for I will never go to Döbling again. You will see by the enclosed letter from Steiner that the affair has not yet been quite decided. Meanwhile the Theater in der Josephstadt has given me some work to do here,[1] which is really very difficult to fit in with my water and bath cures, the more so as Staudenheim has now advised me to bathe for an hour and a half. Meanwhile I have already composed a new chorus with dances and solo voice parts.[2] If my health permits, I will compose another new overture.[3] If you would write at once and let me know when you intend to leave Krems for Vienna, I should much prefer this, for I should then know exactly how I stand. My warmest greetings to you and your family. And again I beg you to write soon.

All good wishes.

Your faithful brother
LUDWIG [4]

I too wish with all my heart that you would come to Baden while I am here with my dear uncle. We should certainly have a very good time. My warm greetings to you. I remain your CARL [5]

(1102) *To [Carl Czerny?]*

[Autograph in the Stadtbibliothek, Vienna] [6]

[BADEN, *September*, 1822]

He made out to me at Baden on the 3rd that he had to go to town on account of the C. — but why does the month not begin until October 8th?

If Karl goes to you on Sunday morning, what about the afternoon lesson? — and what about the morning lesson?

I was with him at ten minutes past eight.

---

[1] For performance at the opening of the newly rebuilt theatre on October 3, 1822, under the direction of K. F. Hensler. For this performance Beethoven wrote a new overture in C (Op. 124) and a chorus with soprano solo and orchestral accompaniment (WoO 98) on a text by Karl Meisl. The latter work was not published until 1888 by Breitkopf & Härtel.   [2] WoO 98.

[3] Op. 124.   [4] The last four words are in Beethoven's handwriting.

[5] The whole postscript is in Karl's handwriting.

[6] This pencilled note is neither addressed nor dated nor signed. The last sentence is written on the verso in another hand.

(1103) *To Johann van Beethoven, Vienna*

[*MS in the Deutsche Staatsbibliothek, Berlin*] ¹

MOST EXCELLENT LITTLE BROTHER !   [BADEN, *October* 6, 1822]
Owner of all the islands in the Danube near Krems !
Director of the entire Austrian pharmacy !

In respect of Steiner I am making you the following proposal about the work that was performed in the Josephstadt.
(I saw in yesterday's paper that they have *pompeusement* announced the chorus with march).² Confining ourselves to
the list of prices for the works let us make immediately the
first and last attempt. Apart from the two numbers which they
already possess and one of which they have now announced,
there are still eight numbers which they do not possess : the
overture and seven other numbers. In the list they priced
the overture at 30 ducats and a song with instrumental accompaniment at 20 ducats. So let us keep to that —

An overture at 30 ducats or perhaps 40 ducats, four songs
with instrumental accompaniment, each at 20 ducats, making
80, two pieces of purely instrumental music priced at 10 ducats
apiece : total 140 ducats.³

If they want to have Hungary's first benefactor 'König
Stephan' as well, there are twelve numbers in that work, four
of which are priced at 20 ducats (apiece, of course), each of
the remaining seven at ten ducats, and one at 5 ducats :
summa summarum 155 ducats.⁴

Now please observe that the *top one* is being performed at
the Josephstadt Theatre, but that the other is available only
in score. Should they just take the former, then we will
dispose of the other somewhere else and in that case allow the
party only a short time to make up its mind.

As to the pianoforte arrangement of the march as well as all
other pianoforte arrangements which they are going to publish,
I will correct them at once and return them with all speed.

In regard to the new overture ⁵ you may tell them that

¹ Written by Karl and signed by Beethoven. The letter, now on deposit in
Tübingen University Library, is addressed : c/o Baker Obermayr, Kothgasse 61.
² Op. 114.   ³ Op. 113, with the new overture Op. 124.
⁴ Op. 117.   ⁵ Op. 124.

the old one had to be scrapped,¹ because in Hungary the piece was only performed as an epilogue, but that here the theatre was opened with this composition. Besides, it is not a dead loss so far as they are concerned, for they can still dispose of it everywhere.

The score and everything else can be copied in three days and will not be lost so far as they are concerned, if they announce it in the same way as the march. But they must let us have a definite reply soon.

So that you may have an even clearer picture of this transaction, I am sending you the list. But please keep it carefully and bring it back to me when you visit me with a carriage and horse, as befits you — Some prices are quoted very advantageously.

We send you herewith two snipe and hope that you will thoroughly relish this snipish muck. What you don't need of it you can send to your pharmaceutical factory at Linz.

All good wishes, most excellent little brother!

Read today's epistles of St. Peter and St. Paul! We are hoping to hear now this and now that from you and we are quite amazingly attached to you.

Your faithful brother
Ludwig ²

My greetings to your family.

Please think over very carefully the question of the Mass, because I must reply to Simrock, if you are not to be to some extent the loser. If you are, please do not undertake it. Come to us as soon as possible.

(1104) *To Tobias Haslinger, Vienna*

[Autograph not traced] ³

[BADEN, early October, 1822]

I request the little Ad[jutant] to lend me the score of the overture in E♭.⁴ I will return it immediately after the per-

---

¹ I.e. the overture in Op. 113.

² The preceding four words and the first sentence of the postscript are in Beethoven's handwriting.

³ Taken from Seyfried, *Beethovens Studien*, 1832. *Anhang*, p. 37.

⁴ Probably the overture to 'König Stephan' (Op. 117), which was performed at Baden on October 8, 1822

formance — Please be so kind as to send me also your *Kirnberger* [1] in order to supplement mine. At the moment I am teaching counterpoint to someone and have not yet been able to find my own manuscript on this subject among my untidy piles of papers.

I am your

Mi Contra Fa

(1105) *To Antonio Diabelli*

[Autograph in the Beethovenhaus, Bonn, H. C. Bodmer collection]

DEAR D[IABELLI]! [VIENNA, *November*, 1822]

Patience! I am *not yet* housed as a *human being* should be, *still less* as is suitable and necessary for me [2] — The fee for the variations would be 40 ducats at most, provided they are worked out on as large a scale as suggested.[3] But if this should *not materialize*, then I would quote a *smaller* fee — Now there is still the overture to deal with.[4] As well as this work I would gladly have contributed seven numbers from the *Weihe des Hauses*.[5] For this I have been offered a fee of 80 ducats. In addition I would contribute a Gratulationsmenuett for full orchestra,[6] that is to say, the overture, seven numbers from the Weihe des Hauses and the Gratulationsmenuett, the whole lot for 90 ducats — My housekeeper is going into town today and, what is more, in the morning. Kindly let me have a reply about my offer — I hope to be able to make a start on your variations before the end of next week — All good wishes, my very excellent fellow.

Yours very truly

B[EETHOVE]N

---

[1] Doubtless one of the two volumes of *Die Kunst des reinen Satzes*, by Johann Philipp Kirnberger (1721–1783), published in Berlin in 1771 and 1776.

[2] Early in November, 1822, Beethoven appears to have moved into Kothgasse 60. His brother had rooms in no. 61 in the same street.

[3] Beethoven's thirty-three pianoforte variations on a waltz by Diabelli were published by Cappi & Diabelli in June, 1823.

[4] Op. 124.

[5] I.e. Op. 113, originally 'Die Ruinen von Athen'.

[6] Listed in *KHV*. as WoO 3. The parts of this work were published by Artaria in 1832.

(1106) *To Carl Friedrich Peters, Leipzig*

[Autograph in the Beethovenhaus, Bonn, H. C. Bodmer collection]

SIR !   VIENNA, *November 22*, 1822

I refer to your [communication] [1] of November 9th in which you seemed to me to be reproaching me for my *apparent negligence* — well now, the fee was to have been paid in advance — and — *yet nothing has been received* — However offensive all this may seem to be, yet I know that if we were to meet, you would be reconciled to me in a few minutes — What you are to receive has all been collected already, save for the songs which have *to be selected*; as an *advance instalment* you are receiving one more than we agreed upon — I could send you several more bagatelles than the four we decided on, for there are nine or ten more of them.[2] If you *write to me about this at once*, I could enclose them, or as many as you want, with all the others — My health, I admit, has not been completely restored by the baths which I have been taking, but on the whole it has benefited by the cure. Besides, I have had a rather unpleasant experience here, because somebody else found rooms for me which did not suit me, a matter which it has been difficult to deal with and which has held me up considerably in my work, particularly as it has not yet been settled — In regard to the Mass things are as follows: I had already finished *one* long ago, but I have *not yet* finished another.[3] Well, there will always be *gossip* about people like myself; and you too have been misled by that gossip. *I do not yet* know which of these two Masses you will receive. Harassed on all sides I might almost testify to the contrary of 'the spirit weighs nothing' [4] — I send you my most heartfelt greetings and I trust that the future will ensure the establishment of a relationship which will be advantageous to both of us and which will not be dishonourable for *me*.

Your most devoted

BEETHOVEN

[1] This word has been supplied by the present editor.   [2] Op. 119.
[3] Beethoven probably means that he has finished his 'Missa Solemnis' (Op. 123) and is working at another Mass, one in C sharp minor, a work he planned but never composed.
[4] It has not been possible to trace the source of this quotation.

ANTONIO DIABELLI (1781–1858)
From a lithograph by Joseph Kriehuber (1841)
(*Historisches Museum der Stadt Wien*)

(1107) *To Johann van Beethoven*

[Autograph in the Beethovenhaus, Bonn, H. C. Bodmer collection]

DEAR BROTHER!   [VIENNA, *November*, 1822] [1]

I request you to come to me this morning, for I must have a few words with you — Why this behaviour? Where is it going to lead to? I have *nothing against you.* I don't consider that you are to blame for what happened about the rooms.[2] *Your intention* was good, and indeed it was my own wish that we should be nearer one another. But in this house *the evil* is to be found on all sides. Yet you refuse to hear anything about all this, so what can one say? — What callous behaviour after my being landed in such an embarrassing situation —

Once more I beg you to come to me this morning so that we may discuss all that is necessary — Do not let a bond be broken which cannot but be of advantage to both of us — And why should it be broken? For some idiotic reasons!

With all my heart I embrace you and remain as always your faithful brother

LUDWIG

(1108) *To Joseph Friedlowsky*

[Autograph in the Beethovenhaus, Bonn, H. C. Bodmer collection]

MY DEAR FRIEDLOWSKY!   [VIENNA, *November*, 1822]

I beg you to spare a few minutes, if possible, to come to me, as there is just a small matter that I must discuss with you. Counting on the friendship which you have ever shown me, I rely on your cordial behaviour — I am not allowed to go out so early or I would come myself —

My address is
Kothgasse No. 60
   1st floor

[1] This letter is undated. But the above date has been affixed in pencil in another hand at the top of the first page. And on internal evidence it is probably right.

[2] In November, 1822, Beethoven moved into rooms in Kothgasse 60, where he stayed until May, 1823, when he went to Hetzendorf. His brother had rooms at Kothgasse 61, a house which belonged to his wife's brother.

(1109) *To Ignaz Xaver, Ritter von Seyfried*

[*Autograph not traced*] [1]

[VIENNA, *Autumn*, 1822]

MY DEAR AND BELOVED BROTHER IN APOLLO!

My heartfelt thanks for the trouble you have taken over my *human* work; and I am delighted too that its success has been recognized everywhere.[2] I hope that you will never pass me over if I am in a position to help you with my small powers. At any rate the worthy Civic Commissioners [3] are sufficiently convinced of my goodwill; and in order to prove it to them again, we will have a friendly discussion some time about how we could best serve them — If masters like yourself take an interest in us, then surely our pinions can never droop.

With kindest regards, your friend

BEETHOVEN

(1110) *To Ferdinand Ries, London*

[*Autograph not traced*] [4]

MY DEAR RIES!   VIENNA, *December* 20, 1822

As I have been overwhelmed with work, I can only now reply to your letter of November 15th — I am delighted to accept the offer to write a new symphony for the Philharmonic Society. Even though the fee to be paid by the English cannot be compared with the fees paid by other nations, yet I would compose even without a fee for the leading artists of Europe, were I not still that poor Beethoven. If only I were in London, how many works would I compose for the Philharmonic Society! For, thank God, Beethoven can compose — but, I admit, that is all he is able to do in this world. If God will only restore my health, which has improved at any rate,

[1] Taken from the transcript made by Aloys Fuchs now in the Benedictine Abbey, Göttweig.

[2] At a charity concert given to raise funds for the Bürgerspital Seyfried had conducted Beethoven's new overture, Op. 124, first performed at the opening of the newly rebuilt Josephstadt Theatre on October 3, 1822.

[3] The German term for this body is 'Bürgerschaftskommission'.

[4] Taken from *WRBN*. 182-183.

then I shall be able to comply with all the offers from all the countries of Europe, nay, even of North America;[1] and in that case I might yet make a success of my life.

(1111) *To Carl Friedrich Peters, Leipzig*

[Autograph in a private collection]

SIR!   VIENNA, *December* 20, 1822

As I have a few moments to spare, I am answering your letter this very day — None of the works which belong to you — *are ready* — nothing; but *my time is too precious* for me to set forth to you all the details which have prevented the copying and the dispatch of them. The songs and the marches — are leaving here next week. As to the bagatelles, there are now exactly six of them, and you only want four. I am reluctant to make this division, for indeed I have treated them as belonging together. But if you insist on taking only the four, well then I must make a different arrangement. In any case you know that the fee for each one is 8 ducats; and for the extra two which exceed the number you have asked for, you need not send me a draft for the fee until you have received them — I remember that in my previous letter I offered you several more of them, but I am not pressing you to take them. If you don't want more than four, well so be it; but then I must again make a different selection [2] — Diabelli has not yet received anything from me. Leidesdorf merely asked me to confirm my statement that I would make *him* a gift of the songs in the Modenzeitung, a thing which admittedly I have really only done for a fee.[3] At the same time I find it impossible in all cases to deal in percentages. Indeed I have frequently much difficulty in working them out when I have to — Let me add that my situation is by no means as splendid as you think, for etc., etc., etc.

It is impossible to give immediate consideration to all

---

[1] According to references in the Conversation Books of autumn, 1822, the Boston Music Society had invited Beethoven to compose an oratorio.

[2] Op. 119.

[3] The songs listed in *KHV.* as WoO 145, 148, 149 and 150 had appeared in the *Modenzeitung* at various dates from 1817 to 1820.

these offers. For there are far too many of them. Several
of them can't be rejected. Diabelli is a professional musician,
and what I am giving *him* is far more than my support;
and the same thing applies to Leidesdorf — What people
demand does not always suit the wishes of the composer. If
my income were not entirely *without substance*,[1] I would compose nothing but operas, symphonies, church music, at most
some more quartets — it is precisely about that point that you
want a reply — and at the moment that too has not yet been
decided — but I promise to do what I can —

Of smaller works you could still have : variations for two
oboes and a cor anglais on the theme in Don Giovanni 'Da
ci la mano', which has also been arranged for two violins
and a viola [2] — a Gratulationsmenuett for full orchestra [3] (both
for 40 ducats at most) [4] — I should like to have your opinion
too about the publication of my collected works — In the
most extreme haste, your most devoted

BEETHOVEN

Reply soon. You are not bound in any way — but I am
anxious that *you should receive what you select*.[5]

(1112) *To Artaria & Co.*

[Autograph in the Stadt- und Universitätsbibliothek, Frankfurt am Main]

MOST EXCELLENT GENTLEMEN!   [VIENNA, 1822]
I see that you have been trying to *cajole* me. Well, that
is an honour which is being conferred upon me for the first
time in my life. At the same time by doing this you have
gained honour for yourselves —

Gentlemen !
As to the story about Paris and my brother, I know nothing
whatever about it. I suspect that it has to do with some

---

[1] One of Beethoven's favourite jokes, i.e. 'Gehalt ohne Gehalt'.
[2] WoO 28 was not published until 1914.
[3] WoO 3 was not published until 1832.
[4] The addition in brackets is written at the left side of the last page.
[5] This postscript is written on the top of the first page, practically covering
the introductory 'Euer Wohlgebohrn'.

compositions I gave him.[1] But, since he is not very musical, I should like to be told all the facts of the case, so that no mistake may be made — Hence I request you to be so kind as to give *full information about this* to my friend Herr von Schindler, who is the bearer of this letter.

As always, your friend and servant

BEETHOVEN

(1113) *To the Archduke Rudolph*

[*Autograph in the Gesellschaft der Musikfreunde, Vienna*]

YOUR IMPERIAL HIGHNESS!   [VIENNA, 1822]

I had just arrived home yesterday when I heard that I was not to have the privilege of going to see Y.I.H. Yesterday indeed the weather had a bad effect on me. So unfortunately I am obliged to stay at home today also. But next week I will certainly try to make up for lost time. I only feel sorry for myself at having to be excluded from the privilege of being with Y.I.H. today —

Your Imperial Highness's
loyal and most obedient servant

L. v. BEETHOVEN

(1114) *To the Archduke Rudolph*

[*Autograph in the Gesellschaft der Musikfreunde, Vienna*]

YOUR IMPERIAL HIGHNESS!   [VIENNA, 1822]

To my intense grief I have just heard of Y.I.H.'s indisposition, but I trust that you will soon recover. Why am *I* not a doctor? For I believe that in the end I could find the best means of completely restoring Y.I.H. to health — I will enquire again and hope each time to receive the most reassuring report —

Your Imperial Highness's
most obedient servant

BEETHOVEN

[1] See Beethoven's letter to Antonio Pacini of April 5, 1823 (Letter 1166).

(1115) *To Anton Felix Schindler*

[Autograph in the Deutsche Staatsbibliothek, Berlin]

[VIENNA, 1822]

Most respectfully do I request you to make a clean copy of this invitation on the paper I am sending you. Karl has too much to do. I will have the copy fetched on Wednesday morning.

Please let me have Grillparzer's address.[1] Perhaps I shall call on him in person.

Be patient for a little longer about the 50 gulden, for I can't let you have them. Moreover *you yourself* are partly to blame for this.

Put a cover round the invitation too. I will arrange to have it closed here.

BVN

(1116) *To [Anton Felix Schindler ?]*

[Autograph in the possession of Mrs. I. Henderson] [2]

[VIENNA, 1822]

By the way, be so kind as to keep a constant watch on the *newspapers* to see what the value of the bank share is. That is the safest method. In regard to the affair it would be better if you were to discuss it with someone who is well versed in business matters of that kind . . . a note. . . .

. . . to see you here — if you can't manage it, kindly arrange that we shall have an answer on Sunday morning — because Karl wants to have a *turkey* prepared for you. Such a dish can only be relished in the company of good friends —

[1] See Letter 1169, p. 1028, n. 2.
[2] The autograph is a fragment written on both sides of a torn sheet.

(1117) *To Tobias Haslinger*

[*Autograph in the Stadtbibliothek, Vienna*]

[VIENNA, 1822]

Most excellent fellow, very — very — very splendid, most splendid fellow! First and freshest horse! Please be so good as to let me have the parcel together with your parcel — Most excellent arrangement, send me soon the pianoforte arrangement also [1] — Give some thought to the publication; no fresh copy would be required, since you have the engraved copies and my manuscript as well; — All good wishes, most excellent *little war hero* and *war weapon* of yore. As soon as my *new rank* has been granted, you too will receive no slight reward [2] —

your and thy [3] friend

BEETHOVEN

Probably the best market for the handwritten collected works would be London [4] —

(1118) *To Anton Felix Schindler*

[*Autograph in the Deutsche Staatsbibliothek, Berlin*]

[VIENNA, 1822] [5]

The two sonatas in A$^\flat$ and C minor are to be dedicated to Frau Brentano, née Edle von Birkenstock [6] —

Nothing — to Ries —

[1] In both cases Beethoven uses the word 'Auszug', which can mean 'extract' and 'arrangement' as well as having many other meanings.

[2] Unger, no. 79 n., suggests a reference here to the honorary membership of the Royal Academy of Sweden which had been conferred on Beethoven.

[3] The German original has 'Euer und dein'.

[4] I.e. Haslinger's manuscript collection of Beethoven's compositions.

[5] This pencilled note must have been written early in 1822.

[6] Op. 110 and 111. When first published by Moritz Schlesinger, Paris, only Op. 111 appeared with a dedication, actually to the Archduke Rudolph.

(1119) *To a Fishmonger*

[*Autograph in the possession of Raoul Berger*]

With 5 gulden V.C.   [VIENNA, 1822]
Most politely do I request you to let me have a carp
weighing 3 or 4 lbs. *or, better still,* a pike of at least 3 lbs. If
you have neither of these kinds of fish, then please send me
some other fish of about the same weight. Kindly let me know
the cost.

Your most devoted
BEETHOVEN

(1120) *To a Fishmonger*

[*Autograph not traced*] 1

[VIENNA, 1822]
Most politely do I request you to let me have a carp
weighing three lbs. and a small pike or pike-perch or something
similar.

Yours
BEETHOVEN

1 Taken from Frimmel, *NFP*, December 20, 1903, p. 38. In the Deutsche
Staatsbibliothek, Berlin, there is a single leaf with the words in Beethoven's handwriting: 'Three lbs. of carp or pike or pike-perch'.
In a Conversation Book of Spring, 1819, an interlocutor calls Beethoven an
'ichthyophagite' on account of his predilection for fish. See Schünemann, I, 63.